Ka

Philosophy

Kant & Political Philosophy

The Contemporary Legacy

Edited by Ronald Beiner
and William James Booth

Yale University Press

New Haven & London

Designed by Deborah Dutton.

Set in Times text and Plantin display type by The Composing Room of Michigan, Inc., Grand Rapids, Michigan.

Printed in the United States of America by Edwards Brothers, Ann Arbor, Michigan.

Library of Congress Cataloging-in-Publication Data

Beiner, Ronald, 1953–

   Kant and political philosophy : the contemporary legacy / edited by Ronald Beiner and William James Booth.

      p.   cm.

   Includes bibliographical references and index.

   ISBN 0-300-05687-7 (cloth: alk. paper)

         0-300-06641-4 (pbk.: alk. paper)

   1. Kant, Immanuel, 1724–1804—Contributions in political science.   I. Booth, William James.   II. Title.

JC181.K4B45   1993

320′.01—dc20   93-2945

                                                                              CIP

A catalogue record for this book is available from the British Library.

The paper in this book meets the guidelines for permanence and durability of the Committee on Production Guidelines for Book Longevity of the Council on Library Resources.

10 9 8 7 6 5 4 3 2

To the memory of Judith Nisse Shklar

Contents

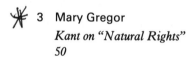

Kant & Political Philosophy

Introduction

The critical philosophy of Kant's mature writings was intended by its author as a single, finely articulated whole composed of theories of knowledge, the will, freedom (moral and political), and history. The fate of most such grand philosophical edifices is that the elaborate articulations binding their various parts are eventually dissolved and those now-detached elements appropriated according to the interests of the times. Kant's works have not been spared this fate, and perhaps they could not and should not have been so exempted. However that may be, one consequence of the dissolution of this grand structure is the mixed reception of Kant's intellectual legacy in the Anglo-American world. On the one hand, his theory of knowledge has long enjoyed a privileged position. If much continental thought seemed to English-language philosophers to be little more than "nonsense on stilts," there was something almost Scottish in Kant's epistemology, which demonstrated a healthy, corrosive skepticism toward metaphysics, an emphasis on what can be given to us in experience, and a project for reining in the dreamy ambitions, the *Träumerei,* of philosophy. That such a project would find a sympathetic resonance among analytic philosophers is scarcely surprising.

The reception of Kant's practical thought in the English-speaking communities has, on the other hand, been rather less warm. His moral philosophy, to be sure, has drawn considerable attention, no doubt because it is such a natural foil to ethical utilitarianism. The philosophy of politics and history, long a subject of interest to European scholars, has until recently received far less notice in Anglo-American studies. The reason for this is quite possibly that the natural terrain of Kant's political thought, contractarian liberalism, has been occupied—or so we thought—almost exclusively by the classic thinkers of the Anglo-American tradition: Hobbes, Locke, Mill, the authors of the Federalist papers, and so forth. Continental liberal thinkers, Kant included, were consigned to the margins of the history of liberal political philosophy. Their nonliberal brethren—for example, Marx and Nietzsche—correspondingly grew in importance. This made it appear as if the great debate of modernity consisted, on the one side, of the continental tradition, hostile to liberalism on collectivist or elitist grounds, and, on the other side, liberalism itself, whose fundamental principles had been set out by its Anglo-American founders.

What was missing from this account of modern political thought was the importance and richness of the continental liberal tradition, whose proponents were engaged in a common enterprise with their English-language counterparts even though they were developing their arguments upon radically different foundations. While this "other liberalism" has yet to be fully explored, names such as Constant, Mme. de Staël, Guizot, and Von Humboldt no longer sound as foreign to the English ear as they once did. The history of relative neglect of Kant as a political philosopher has in large measure also been rectified by the recent surge of Anglo-American interest in Kantian politics. Philosophers and scholars have found his writings a rich source of ideas on the central issues of political thought, ranging from theories of the self to questions of morality and international relations. Scholars interested in liberalism's evolution as well as students of socialist currents of political philosophy have turned to Kant and have not left unrewarded.

The turn to Kant must begin with the luminous core of his political philosophy, that is, with the idea of autonomy. This is to say that standing at the center of Kant's political thought is the notion that persons are free in what he terms the "positive" sense, free because they are or are capable of being the legislators of the maxims of their own conduct. The fact of autonomy is the foundation upon which Kant then erects a theory of politics. Autonomy serves simultaneously as the purpose or ultimate end of the political community, as the basis for an array of hedges restricting the behaviors of both rulers and citizens with respect to their treatment of one another, and as the cornerstone of a theory of relations between states. We might say, then, that the liberal regime, as set out by Kant, has as its purpose the creation of a system of external relations among persons that, to the greatest extent possible, will allow them the space in which to develop their moral autonomy. Here moral and political philosophy, the analysis of the inward autonomy of moral imperatives and the outward freedom of the citizen, converge in the picture of a polity conducive to the cultivation of freedom. The ideal of such a polity, or republican constitution, has both a normative role in Kant's thought—directing persons as it does toward the creation of such a political order—and an imaginative/descriptive side. That latter dimension is to be found in Kant's philosophy of history, the story of the coming-into-being of the republican regime. Thus we see the outline of Kant's subtle blending of the theories of the moral person, the best political form, and the philosophy of history.

The idea of human autonomy also directs Kant's analysis of the rights and duties of citizens and rulers, for it leads to the (negative) argument that the autonomy of the person stands as a barrier against unjustified intrusion by the public authority and by other persons. It is, in short, a theory suspicious of the exercise of power, one in which the exercise of authority must be justified against the prior and irreducible claims of autonomy. The principal justification of the use of coercive power, for Kant, is the preservation of the external freedom of each consistent with the exercise of like freedoms by others. The idea of autonomy does more, however, than establish the foundations of legitimate power, political and private; it also provides a standard and directive that guides the legislator in the making of laws. This guide is not exclusively negative, that is, one which creates only prohibitions against certain types of law, but is also positive inasmuch as it directs the legislator to the proper end or purpose of legislation. And, lastly, this many-sided concept of autonomy, now applied to states considered as "moral persons," leads Kant to a theory of international relations in which most of the central elements of his analysis of domestic regimes are replicated, mutatis mutandis—for example, limits on legitimate interference or domination over another state and the imperative to create a law-governed condition between states.

Kant's political thought thus builds an argument that converges on the classical liberal conclusion of a limited government ensuring the external freedom of its citizens. The construction of that argument, however, rests on a concept of autonomy, of the agency of the self, of the obligations that that quality entails in relations among persons, and of the end or purpose of their association. In sum, liberalism is reconstructed but on a very different foundation. Such an achievement would, by itself, be sufficient to secure for Kant a position at the center of the great liberal thinkers. Yet this finely inflected argument, the spinning out of so many strands of analysis from its core concept, is only one moment in a much larger project. For Kantian political thought is drawn back into the theory of knowledge, aesthetics, and moral life. Kant's epistemology reveals an intimation of freedom in the spontaneity of reason, of the mind as a law-giver to nature. At the same time, it seeks to limit the pretensions of reason, to bind it to what can be given in experience with this consequence, among others, that divine authority no longer can be seen as infusing the world with order and meaning. The theory of knowledge thus provides one part of the background of Kantian politics: freedom against nature, on the one side, and a necessary turn to practical reason as the only source of a possible grounding of concepts of rights, obligations, and legitimacy—a turn made necessary by the limiting of the claims of reason.

What is shown to be possible and necessary by Kant's theory of knowledge, the freedom and limits of reason driving toward the conclusion of the primacy of moral reason, is given a practical and tangible form in his moral philosophy. That is, we are drawn from a notion of the spontaneity of reason as a faculty, of its independence from nature, into an examination of the moral self, of the practical employment of reason in its freedom. What emerges from this analysis is an idea of freedom not as mere unconditioned choice or spontaneity but as the capacity for self-given law. This autonomy is then placed at the center of the Kantian theory of the self as agent: as that sort of being who must be the author of the maxims of his or her own conduct, who is therefore free (and, not being guided unfailingly by instinct, required) to choose and who can therefore elect to make the categorical imperative that maxim, who can, in other words, choose to be autonomous.

The Kantian concept of the moral self and its allied ideas of autonomy and the categorical imperative have been and are still the subject of much forceful criticism, criticism reflected in some essays in this volume. What is nevertheless clear is that Kant was attempting to set the underpinnings not only for a theory of the moral self but also for an analysis of the proper form of community for an association of autonomous beings. The idea of the self leads, then, inexorably to an understanding of the polity in which citizens are at once the authors and subjects of the law, in which (allowing for the important differences between freedom, moral and political) the properties of the self shape the properties of the political community. This latter Kant calls a "respublica noumenon," a "Platonic Ideal," and that picture of the best regime invests virtually the entire Kantian political corpus with its emphasis on self-given law even if, as Kant is frequently at pains to point out, it is, in its most perfect form, unrealizable.

Kant's aesthetic theory, which is at its root a theory of the organization (or formlessness) of nature and of human moral/aesthetic response to it (the beautiful and the sublime), offers yet another way of setting out and approaching questions about politics. Here the issue is nature and politics or, better, whether nature can be understood as organized and thus purposive or whether it must be seen as hostile to man, formless and violent in its exertions. To unpack this question further, we might say with Kant that if nature is purposive and designed then its end must be the advancement of the only thing in creation that is an end-in-itself, the good will (insofar as nature can promote freedom). This leads Kant to a theory of man's moral interest in natural beauty, since the latter by suggesting design in nature (and intimating a wise and benevolent designer) also points to its cooperation with humankind—that man will be rewarded and human culture advanced through the agency of nature and its great Artist. Beauty in nature is thus bound up with a view of historical progress and so with the possibility of, and the hope for, the coming-into-being of a republican regime and world peace. Nature can also be seen, Kant thought, as formless and violent, providing no evidence of purpose or design. Understood in that manner, nature offers humanity not consolation or hope (beauty) but the recognition of human superiority over nature, of the triumph of the will over nature in not yielding to her awful forces—in short, it is the sublime view of nature and man. If the beautiful view of the world leads to the idea of progress in history and to the related notion of a mechanism by which the good regime will be brought about despite man's radical evil, the sublime perspective shifts the emphasis to the free will and its political expression, public law and justice.

The vitality and fecundity of an intellectual tradition is generally visible in the sharpness and intensity of the debates among protagonists of that tradition. This has been no less true of the recent Kant revival. To be sure, this is in no small measure accounted for by the diversity of alternative sources available to those who seek the foundations of a political philosophy in Kant, as we have tried briefly to sketch in this introduction. Thus some contemporary Kantians have looked to the *Groundwork* or second *Critique,* others to the historical writings or the directly political texts; some take their bearings by the *Doctrine of Virtue* or the *Doctrine of Right,* while still others turn to the "Critique of Aesthetic Judgment" or the "Critique of Teleological Judgment." All these highly diverse sources have in recent years yielded rich and comprehensive political philosophies. But perhaps the multiplicity of Kantianisms is rooted more fundamentally in the polarities and tensions in Kant's own thinking. No thinker has ever been more insistent than Kant on the importance of liberating oneself from tutelage; yet it is this same Kant who seems to affirm, in his philosophy of history, nature as a tutelary power serving to educate us to civility. (And what a manipulative and bullying tutor nature is!) Kant declares that the only unconditional good is the good will, which appears to intimate a radically atemporal vision of what truly matters in human life; but at the same time it would seem that history as a philosophical concern is taken more seriously by Kant than by any other thinker prior to Hegel. Kant, in whose thought the concern with happiness is more severely marginalized than anywhere else in our tradition of practical philosophy (of morals and of politics), can still write that pleasure and pain "constitute the absolute, because they are life itself." Kant, "the philosopher of the French Revolution," nonetheless insists upon the absolute immorality of any and all challenges to political authority. Kant, one of the foremost modern philosophers of bourgeois commercialism and cosmopolitan peace, hails the sublimity of war, decries the "low selfishness, cowardice, and effeminacy" of bourgeois commercialism, and warns against the debasing character of cosmopolitan peace. These are, surely, the marks of a thinker of uncommon complexity and subtlety.

Kant's reflection on moral and political relationships between human beings ranges from, at one extreme, exalted contemplation of membership in a "Kingdom of Ends" to, at the other extreme, consideration of the mundane question of constitutional arrangements for a race of intelligent devils. Kant expresses revulsion for the notion that early generations should labor merely to erect an edifice the habitation of which is to be enjoyed only by the last generation, but that does not deter him, so it would appear, from celebrating the destination of the species as a whole. In Hannah Arendt's words, "the very idea of progress," certainly embraced by Kant as the paragon of the Enlightenment that he was, "contradicts Kant's notion of man's dignity." Given these intriguing tensions and aporias, and others of a similar kind, it is perhaps not very surprising that students of Kant have disagreed as radically (and as fruitfully) as they have. Strikingly, the Kant newly discovered by political philosophers is not one Kant but many. Some commentators see Kant as leading directly toward the German idealists; others see him in sharpest antithesis to his idealist successors (and as offering the soundest prophylactic against Hegelian and post-Hegelian delusions). For some, Kant is a "constructivist" à la Rawls; for others, like Patrick Riley in this volume, he is a quasi-Platonist for whom it is possible to attain rational intuition of an objective moral order. There are those who treat the preoccupations of his political writings with utter seriousness; others, by contrast, see in these texts mere playfulness and irony. Some see Kant as anticipating the existentialist affirmation of unbounded human freedom against the bleak background of an indifferent nature, while rival commentators recognize in the objectivity of the moral law a foundation for human dignity that is entirely absent from nineteenth- and twentieth-century doctrines of freedom. Finally, there are those who can see in Kant only a social and political sensibility stunted by Pietist individualism, where others discern a wise appreciation of the unique constraints and possibilities of human sociability. One has reason to hope that these very disagreements will make Kant a continuing object of fascination and intellectual attraction not just for the present generation of theorists, but for generations to come.

Theories of knowledge, of the self and agency, of nature and history—these are but some of the rich veins of Kantian politics. And that list could easily be extended to include, for example, his anthropology and jurisprudential writings. This book reflects this richness and diversity. Some of its chapters explore internal questions in Kant's works; others analyze the legacy of his political thought in relation to liberalism, classical and contemporary. A number of contributions are what Dieter Henrich has termed "argumentative reconstructions" of Kant's texts, forceful efforts to set out and defend Kantian theses. Others are critical of central elements of his legacy, while nevertheless acknowledging their considerable strengths. The concluding section comprises a set of chapters devoted to core current debates in political philosophy, debates directly inspired by Kant or at the very least conducted in his shadow. The book is dedicated to the elaboration, extension, and criticism of the political themes at the heart of Kant's life project, which remain as central to our concerns as they were to his. That Kant was one among our great teachers about political matters has long been known to some; we hope with this volume to help secure that place for him.

Part One

*Kant in the
Tradition of
Political
Philosophy*

Chapter 1

The Elements of Kant's
Practical Philosophy

Patrick Riley

Kant's *Groundwork of the Metaphysic of Morals,* whose two-hundredth anniversary we marked in 1985, is so strikingly original—so truly a thing-in-itself, so phenomenal a noumenon—that one can forget that it has a place *in* the history of moral and political philosophy, even if it altered the course of that history more obviously than it flowed out of it. On an anniversary it is always appropriate to look both backward and forward: in this case, to trace the provenance of some elements in the *Grundlegung,* and to show how those elements are presently treated in important interpretations of Kant by John Rawls ("Kantian Constructivism in Moral Theory," 1980) and Michael Sandel (*Liberalism and the Limits of Justice,* 1982).[1]

On the antiquarian, provenance-tracing side, one should begin by pointing out that the *Groundwork* draws together Platonism, Aristotelianism, and Augustinianism. To reduce it to a formula, one could say that Kant's moral philosophy (to which "true" politics must "pay homage")[2] equals Augustinian good will (*bona voluntas*) as sole "unqualified" good (*De Libero Arbitrio*) plus Plato's notion that moral concepts (for example, ought) are purely rational, nonempirical ideas not derivable from nature or human psychology (*Phaedo* 75d) *plus* Aristotle's idea of a final end (*telos*) that is no mere means to some further end (*Metaphysics* 994b). Looking at the *Grundlegung* historically, one surely finds an Augustinian good will moved by a Platonic moral idea ("ought expresses a kind of necessity . . . found nowhere in nature"), with a view to realizing reason-ordained, Aristotelian "objective ends."[3] To be sure, Kant departs from St. Augustine, Plato, and Aristotle even while clinging to them: for Kant, good will is not Augustinian *delectio,* or delight, in God; rational moral ideas are not just like geometry or "harmony" (*Phaedo* and *Republic*); only moral ends are knowable and Aristotle's broader teleology is "dogmatic."[4] Still, Kantianism is in one sense a quite unique fusing of these antique elements—

This essay appeared previously in *Political Theory* 14 (November 1986), pp. 552–83. Reprinted with permission of Sage Publications, Inc.

against utilitarianism, perfectionism, and theology-grounded natural law, whether Thomistic or Lockean.[5]

As for the contemporary significance of these antiquarian inquiries: if Kant imitates antiquity in a non-Machiavellian way,[6] then Rawls must be treading on disputable ground in calling Kant a quasi-contractarian "constructivist," a "deepened Rousseau," not a quasi-Platonic "rational intuitionist"; and Michael Sandel must be equally contestable in speaking of a Kantian subject prior to and separable from all its ends in a (non-Aristotelian) "universe empty of *telos*."[7] In short: Ernst Cassirer was right when he said that Kant reconciled Plato and Aristotle, Platonic rationalism and Aristotelian teleology—thus going beyond Goethe's insistence in the *Theory of Colors* that the world is divided up into Platonic and Aristotelian camps.[8] And this matters for Kantian politics, since Kant believed that politics and history could slowly achieve a "legal" approximation to certain reason-ordained objective ends, especially eternal peace: "Moral-practical reason within us pronounces the following irresistible veto: there shall be no war."[9]

Is this element tracing a matter of mere antiquarian interest? By no means. The precise relation of the three strands—Augustinian, Platonic, Aristotelian—that fuse to yield Kantianism determines the shape of Kant's republican, peace-loving politics. If everyone had the (more or less) Augustinian good will that he or she ought to have, and therefore could have, the kingdom of ends would be automatically realized; but pathological "self-love" (another Augustinian notion, after all) impedes the coming-into-being of the *Reich der Zwecke*.[10] Since, nonetheless, an eternally peaceful kingdom of ends—a peaceable kingdom—is morally necessary as a reason-ordained objective end that we "ought to have,"[11] the Platonic (rationalist) and Aristotelian (teleological) strands in Kant can be partially realized only if one side of Augustinianism comes to the rescue of the other: if good will is rendered impotent by self-love, if Augustinian morality and Augustinian psychology collide to produce an impasse, then *at best* certain moral ends (for example, peacefulness) can be slowly attained through the self-love of intelligent "devils" who are weak in moral "incentives" (*motiva moralia*).[12] ("Since Kant knew most men to be as Machiavelli pictured them," Judith Shklar writes, "he had to evade his conclusions. . . . Men are always ready for free institutions if the latter do not depend on virtue, if they are fueled by selfish impulses properly balanced.")[13] Eternal peace is a non-natural, reason-given "ought" (Platonism), a final end that is no mere means (Aristotelianism); if men do not choose it from Augustinian good will, perhaps (after a long and devastating "experience") they will choose it from Augustinian self-love, the wish not to be annihilated. Wish replaces will: self-interested citizens of a Kantian republic, operating under the Idea of the "original contract," may dissent from violence, may consent to peace.[14] But if Kantian citizens may finally embrace reason-ordained objective ends from merely legal motives, certain readings of Kant's politics seem to be ruled out: if some ends are indeed reason-given, one should not exaggerate the width of the gap (real as it is) between Kant and Plato; and if reason indeed gives ends, one should not exaggerate the notion that Kantianism is "deontological," antiteleological, and (in effect) anti-Aristotelian.[15]

Thus an apparently historical inquiry into the provenance of some elements of the *Grundlegung* reveals what Kantian politics can be, what counts as a *possible* interpretation. But if it is the relation of (Augustinian) good will, (Platonic) moral rationalism, and (Aristotelian) teleology that draws the outline of Kant's moral (and then political) philosophy, neither is any single element, *an sich,* dispensable: who can imagine full Kantianism without good will, without moral ideas, without objective ends? Kant is and is not an Augustinian, a Platonist, an Aristotelian.

The first important idea that one encounters in the *Groundwork* is that of "good will"—the idea of a "moral causality," itself independent of natural causality, that is the foundation of man's freedom and responsibility.[16] That good will is crucial to Kant's understanding of politics is already clear; public legal justice is necessitated by the partial or total absence of a good will that would yield, if it could, a noncoercive "ethical" commonwealth under laws of virtue.[17] Good will's absence necessitates politics' presence. And the *idea* of an ethical commonwealth generated by good will serves as a kind of utopia that earthly politics can legally approximate through peacefulness, both internal and international.[18] Kant was by no means the first moral philosopher to insist that a good will is the only "unqualifiedly" good thing on earth. On this point he simply echoes St. Augustine's *De Libero Arbitrio,* which argues that a good will "is a will by which we seek to live a good and upright life" and that "when anyone has a good will he really possesses something which ought to be esteemed far above all earthly kingdoms and all delights of the body."[19] (That is remarkably "pre-Kantian"; indeed, one can wonder whether Kant's "kingdom of ends" was not suggested by Augustine's denigration of earthly kingdoms.)

Why should Kant have leaned so heavily on Augustine? Because—as Hannah Arendt has shown in *The Life of the Mind*—the bishop of Hippo was the first philosopher to give absolute primacy to will and good will.[20] (One recalls Aristotle's complaint in the *Ethics* that Plato—at least in *Protagoras*—has no adequate notion of volition; but Aristotle himself is concerned with "willing" mainly in connection with *legal* responsibility.)[21] To be sure, in his late anti-Pelagian works such as *De Correptione et Gratia* Augustine tries to minimize free will and maximize unmerited grace: "The free will will be all the freer when it is subject to the pity and to the grace of God."[22] But Augustine's own early Pelagianism had already had its effect, had already initiated a "voluntarization" of Western thought that made possible Kant's insistence on good will and, much later, Sartre's saying that we are what we "will to be" after our "leap toward existence."[23]

will v. grace in Augustine

In St. Augustine good will and bad will have an enormous range: they are not confined to mere Aristotelian legal accountability but color the whole of the moral life, even giving a new meaning to justice. For St. Augustine insists that "unless something is done by the will, it can be neither a sin nor a good deed," so that "punishments and rewards would be unjust if man did not possess free will"; and that is why he can say, in his late *De Trinitate,* that "one is nearly blessed when one is right in willing whatever one wills."[24] One cannot maintain that St. Augustine is a voluntarist or contractarian in his explicitly political writings, above all *The City of God.* But it is certainly true that Augustine made important voluntaristic moral claims that later grew into political doctrines: in *De Spiritu et Littera,* for example, he insists that "consent is necessarily an act of will."[25] Without that strong Augustine-forged link between consent and will, the social contract tradition—of which Kant is (in part) a part—would be unthinkable, since it defines consent in terms of will, in terms of Lockean "voluntary agreement."[26] And St. Augustine's claim in *De Libero Arbitrio* that "the will, by adhering to the common and un-changeable good, attains the principal and great human goods," that such a will "sins whenever it turns from the unchangeable and common good and turns to its own private good," later made possible Pascal's insistence in the *Pensées* that "one must incline to what is general: and leaning toward oneself is the beginning of all disorder, in war, in policy, in economy, in the particular human body. Thus the will is depraved."[27] That Pascalian Augustinianism is one of the ancestors of Rousseau's insistence that "general" will is good, "particular" will bad; and Kant himself, in his Rousseauian moods, frequently uses the term "general will," particularly in the *Rechtslehre.*[28] The leap from Augustine to Rousseau is, one must confess, great, but Rousseau is not conceivable without Augustine and various seventeenth-century transformations of Augustinianism.[29]

But Kant, given his radical distinction between pathology and morality, could not have accepted Augustine's definition of the content of good will as moral delectation; he could never have said, with Augustine, that the man of good will will "embrace" justice as "the object of his joy and delight."[30] The Augustinian notion of opposing higher delectations to lower ones so that concupiscence is replaced by the love of temperance, prudence, and, ultimately, God—by quasi-Platonic sublimated erotism (as in the *Phaedrus*)—is totally alien to Kant, if not to Pascal, or even Rousseau in some moods.[31] If, then, Kantian good will is not an Augustinian *delectio,* or higher love, what is it? If it is not to be "pathological," it must surely be the capacity to determine oneself to action through what ought to be, so that "ought" is one's complete and sufficient incentive. And if what ought to be is defined as respect for persons as members of the kingdom of ends, then Kantian good will will mean "determining oneself to act from respect for persons."[32] (Respect, for Kant, is not a mere delectio, a merely subjective feeling, because it is inspired by a moral law that "humbles" us, a moral law that provides objective ends—that is, the rational beings who are ends in themselves.)[33] Surely this is a reasonable way to begin; for at the outset one cannot know exactly what good will—originally an Augustinian concept—actually involves.

Kant, then, begins the *Groundwork* with a good will that is not an Augustinian delectio—but neither is it a mere Hobbesian "last appetite" in deliberation.[34] Kantian will is an uncaused causality, a moral cause, an undetermined power of spontaneous self-determination or of "absolute origination" that is not shaped by external nature, internal nature, or divine causality or "concurrence."[35] It is a doctrine of absolute freedom and absolute responsibility, of taking reason-given ends as the motive of one's actions, that might have permitted some of Kant's predecessors to be more coherent. If Hobbes, for example, had been a "transcendental idealist" and not (at least in science and theology) a determinist, one could attach more meaning to his celebrated claim that there is "no obligation of any man"—such as the duty to observe a social contract—that "ariseth not from some act of his own."[36] For Kant the expression "act of his own" is meaningless unless there is a power of absolute origination within the self; from his perspective a Hobbesian falls precisely into "fatalism" by viewing will as an appetite wholly caused by perception of a natural world whose divine first cause reduces everything else to a mere effect.[37] That fatalism is then fatal to Hobbes's own political doctrines: before it can be true that "wills . . . make the essence of all covenants," there must actually *be* a will that is truly efficacious.[38] But for that one needs "absolute origination": persons must be their own causes, hyper-Pelagians, "early" Augustinians.[39]

In the *Groundwork* Kant makes it clear that if one is to conceive a rational being as having a causality that is not caused, one must draw a distinction between "a world of sense and the world of understanding." With respect to the "mere perception and receptivity of sensations" to which a Hobbesian gives fatal weight, one must understand oneself as belonging to the world of sense; but insofar as one is capable of initiating rational "pure activity" through the conception of moral law, one must count oneself as belonging to the intellectual world: "A rational being . . . has two points of view from which he can regard himself, and recognize laws of the exercise of his faculties. . . . First, so far as he belongs to the world of sense, he finds himself subject to laws of nature (heteronomy); secondly, as belonging to the intelligible world, under laws which, being independent of nature, have their foundation not in experience but in reason alone."[40]

If, for Kant, one belonged exclusively to the world of understanding, then all one's actions would conform to the principle of "autonomy of the free will"; if one were entirely a creature of sense, then only a will caused by desire and inclination would be possible. Since, however, human beings (who are "finite rational beings") recognize themselves as "subject to the law of the world of understanding, that is, to reason," this law is an imperative for them.[41] They *ought*, in their own view, to act from principles given by a reason that "has causality"—a causal reason that is "located in its own peculiar sphere, namely, the order of ends."[42]

The notion that reason has causality is an echo—which can only be a deliberate one—of Plato's *Phaedo*;[43] and if good will is not to be pathological "delight," Kant's limited Augustinianism must turn to a limited Platonism. Good will must find its end in reason, not in God (and his purposes for us). One must pass from Christianized Platonism to Plato, from Hippo Regius to Athens.

If Kantian good will is not Augustinian, God-loving, higher delight, but self-determination through reason-ordained ends that we ought to have, it is important to determine just how far Kant thought that reason itself gives or provides or "proposes" objective ends that could be the source of the categorical imperative (and then the "limiting condition" of a rightful politics that "pays homage" to moral ends).[44] One can do this by turning to those passages in *Pure Reason* in which Kant speaks of reason's causality in the practical sphere—passages in which the influence of Plato is especially marked.

Kant starts to discuss reason's practical "causality," using quasi-Platonic language, in the "Transcendental Dialectic" of *Pure Reason*. "I understand by idea a necessary concept of reason to which no corresponding object can be given in sense experience," Kant begins. "Thus the pure concepts of reason . . . are transcendental ideas." Those concepts are "not arbitrarily invented"; they are "imposed by the very nature of reason itself." Kant goes on to urge that "no object adequate to the transcendental idea can ever be found within [sense] experience," and for this reason the transcendental ideas are problematical in our understanding of nature: "the absolute whole of all appearances," for example, is "only an idea"; since we can never represent it in an image, "it remains a problem to which there is no practical solution."[45]

In the moral realm of freedom, by contrast, "the practical idea [for example, 'ought'] is . . . always in the highest degree fruitful, and in its relation to our actual activities is indispensably necessary." Kant argues that this was especially clear to Plato, who realized that "our reason naturally exalts itself to modes of knowledge which so far transcend the bounds of experience that no given empirical object can ever coincide with them, but which must nonetheless be recognized as having their own reality, and which are by no means mere fictions of the brain."[46] Plato, Kant adds, "found the chief instances of his ideas in the field of the practical"—perhaps this refers to Socrates' admission in *Parmenides* that only *moral* "forms" are certainly real[47]—and in that he was right since "it is only by means of this idea that any judgment as to moral worth" is possible. Kant concludes that if we set aside the (vestigial, Pythagorean) "exaggerations" of Platonism, such as the tendency to think of ideas as things that have to be laboriously recalled by reminiscence (in *Phaedo* and *Meno*), then Plato's "spiritual flight" from nature to the "architectonic ordering" of the world according to ideas—principles of morality, legislation, and religion—is "an enterprise which calls for respect and imitation."[48]

Reason in the practical sphere, Kant continues, is "indeed, exercising causality, as actually bringing about that which its concept contains." One is not yet told, to be sure, what reason's "concept" actually does contain, and so as yet there is no source for the categorical imperative; so far there is simply the assertion that the employment of "ideas of reason" in the practical sphere is morally fruitful and "indispensably necessary."[49]

It was, again, no accident that Kant spoke of the "causality" of reason and of ideas: he must have known that in the *Metaphysics* Aristotle attributes to Plato's *Phaedo* the notion that ideas are "causes . . . both of being and of becoming."[50] And in the practical sphere (only), Kant wants to uphold Platonic ideas-as-causes.

In the "Antinomy of Pure Reason" a demi-Platonism reappears, after the resolution of the third antinomy has made a person's self-determination through reason conceivable (by drawing a distinction between phenomenal determination and noumenal self-determination). Kant again takes up reason's causality, saying that reason is something that we distinguish in a quite peculiar and especial way from all empirically conditioned powers. He then offers a passage so important— both positively for his own moral and political philosophy and negatively for his critique of eudaemonism and utilitarianism—that it ought to be fully cited: "That our reason has causality, or that we at least represent it to ourselves as having causality, is evident from the *imperatives* which in all matters of conduct we impose as rules upon our active powers. 'Ought' expresses a kind of necessity . . . which is found nowhere else in the whole of nature. The understanding can know in nature only what is, what has been, or what will be. We cannot say that anything in nature ought to be other than what in all these time-relations it actually is. When we have the course of nature alone in view, 'ought' has no meaning whatsoever."[51]

What is immediately clearest is the negative significance, for both moral and political thought, of this demi-Platonism. If "ought" is a concept "pronounced by reason" whose "necessity" (moral necessity) cannot be found in the whole of nature, then eudaemonism and utilitarianism are automatically wrong in trying to extract moral necessity from natural facts (happiness and the desire for happiness). For Kant a utilitarian has nothing but the course of nature in view; but in that course "ought" has "no meaning whatsoever." For Kant, as for Plato in the *Gorgias,* one cannot derive moral concepts such as "good" from the natural data of psychology (for example, Callicles' "will to power").[52]

Plainly Kant's notion, in the *Groundwork* as much as in *Pure Reason,* that "all moral conceptions have their seat and origin completely *a priori* in the reason"—

Euthyphro question — Justice prior to God?

not in nature or even human nature—owes a large debt to Plato's *Phaedo* 75a–e, in which Socrates urges that "before we began to see and hear and use our other senses we must somehow have acquired the knowledge . . . of all absolute standards. Our present argument applies no more to [absolute mathematical] equality than it does to absolute beauty, goodness, uprightness, holiness and, as I maintain, all those characteristics which we designate in our discussion by the term 'absolute.'"[53]

But the most striking instance of an almost orthodox Platonism in Kant—which in this case may well have arrived via Leibniz—is found in those parts of *Pure Reason* that attack the Cartesian notion that the good and the true are simply products of divine creative will, the effects of God's sheer fiat.[54] It is here that Plato, Leibniz, and Kant stand as one against radical voluntarism.

In the history of pre-Kantian philosophy the notion that the concept of goodness or justice, as an "eternal verity," is not a mere adjunct of power is commonly associated with Plato. Now, although it is not true that Leibniz was a Platonist in any doctrinaire sense, nonetheless he did agree with Plato on many points of fundamental importance. "I have always been quite content, since my youth," he wrote, "with the moral philosophy of Plato, and even in a way with his metaphysics; for these two sciences accompany each other, like mathematics and physics." Leibniz, indeed, was Platonic not only in his concept of justice but even in some of his practical political opinions: he always urged, for example, that "following natural reason, government belongs to the wisest."[55]

With the possible exception of the *Republic,* the Platonic work that Leibniz admired most—at least for use in moral and political philosophy—was the *Euthyphro,* which he paraphrased almost verbatim in his most important work on justice, the *Meditation on the Common Concept of Justice.* In the *Euthyphro,* which deals (in Leibniz's words) with the question whether "the rules of goodness and of justice are anterior to the decrees of God," Plato "makes Socrates uphold the truth on that point."[56] (This question Robert Nozick has styled "*the* Euthyphro question.")[57] And the truth for Leibniz is (as Cassirer puts it) that the good and the just are "not the product, but the objective aim and the motive of [God's] will."[58] That Plato's formulation of this point affected Leibniz is evident in a bare comparison of their words:

> Socrates: Then what are we to say about the holy [or the just], Euthyphro? . . . Is it not loved by all the Gods?
>
> Euthyphro: Yes.
>
> Socrates: Because it is holy, or for some other reason?
>
> Euthyphro: No, it is for that reason.
>
> Socrates: And so it is because it is holy that it is loved; it is not holy because it is loved.
>
> Euthyphro: So it seems.[59]

It is agreed that whatever God wills is good and just. But there remains the question whether it is good and just because God wills it or whether God wills it because it is good and just: in other words, whether justice and goodness are arbitrary, or whether they belong to the necessary and eternal truths about the nature of things, as do numbers and proportions.[60]

But, despite his Platonism on this point, Leibniz did not go as far as Kant was later to go: Kant held not only that God is not the cause of goodness and justice, but that the idea of God is merely deduced, as a "necessary hypothesis," out of the concept of moral perfection. Kant, indeed, became the extreme term in what Plato had begun in the *Euthyphro*, when he argued in *Pure Reason* that the reality of moral laws and their "inner practical necessity" has led philosophers to the postulate of a wise ruler of the world who gives "effect" to those laws; that such laws cannot be regarded as "accidental" and as "derived from the mere will of the ruler"; that (and here the Platonism is clearest) "we shall not look upon actions as obligatory because they are the commands of God, but shall regard them as divine commands because we have an inward obligation to them."[61] This goes beyond what Leibniz could allow, in that it treats God as a postulate whose objective reality is indemonstrable, who is only "practically" necessary. For Leibniz "all reality must be founded on something existent," and even the eternal verities of ethics and mathematics must be coeternal with an actual God who "finds" those verities in his essence.[62] This makes God necessary for, though not the cause of, the truth of the eternal verities; as Leibniz said in his *Notes on Spinoza's Ethics*, "Even if we concede that the essence of things cannot be conceived without God . . . it does not therefore follow that God is the cause of the essence of things; . . . for a circle cannot be conceived without a center, a line without a point, but the center is not the cause of the circle nor the point the cause of the line."[63]

Whatever their differences, Plato, Leibniz, and Kant could roughly agree that (in Leibniz's words), "Non voluntas sed sapienta Dei Justitiae regula ultima est."[64] Still, it is important that Kant refrains from viewing moral "ideas" (justice, good-ness) as in any way analogous to mathematics and geometry; in the *Phaedo* Plato had spoken of "absolute" mathematical equality in the same breath with *moral* "absolute standards," but the Platonic (and Leibnizian) propensity for viewing mathematics as the model of all true knowledge—*Meno*, after all, begins with a priori geometrical knowledge (in an uneducated slave) and moves on to a priori moral knowledge—marks the dividing line between Platonism and Kantianism.[65] And what is especially unacceptable to Kant is any effort to derive the content of morality from a quasi-mathematical "harmony" that fails to make respect-worthy persons central.

To be sure, one cannot simply reduce the whole of Platonism to the love of "harmony"—where harmony itself is mathematics made audible, and mathematics the eternal Pythagorean antidote to Heraclitean flux. But Plato does often say that the harmonious, well-tempered *psyche* is "writ large" in the harmonious *polis* (Wolin's "motionless polity") and then larger in the harmony of the *kosmos,* the singing-in-unison of the spheres (so beautifully recounted by Nettleship in his *Lectures on the* Republic *of Plato).*[66] It is precisely the Platonic (and Leibnizian) tendency to view timeless mathematical verity as the type or model of all true knowledge ("let no one ignorant of geometry enter here")[67] that Kant resists; that is why he calls Leibniz's celebrated "pre-established harmony" the "most whimsical figment philosophy has ever conceived."[68] The wish to "mathematize" ethics, to make it (in effect) "musical"—so that evil is the harmonically dissonant, good the consonant—is as foreign to Kant as it is central to Plato and Leibniz.

For all his quite genuine reverence for Plato, therefore, Kant could never have countenanced the great passage from *Republic* Book IV in which Socrates insists that "Justice . . . means that a man must not suffer the principles in his soul [reason, spirit, appetite] to do each the work of some other, but that . . . having first attained to self-mastery and beautiful order within himself, and having harmonized these three [psychic] principles, the notes or intervals of three terms . . . and having linked and bound all three together and made of himself a unit, one man instead of many, self-controlled and in unison, he should then and only then turn to practice . . . believing and naming the just and honorable action to be that which preserves and helps to produce this condition of soul."[69]

In the *First Critique* Kant had praised those elements of Platonism that he could honestly embrace—the moral rationalism, the notion of the causality of nonempirical practical "ideas"; yet in later works such as "On a Recently Adopted Superior Tone in Philosophy" (1796), which attacks the "new Platonic-mystical language" of those who philosophize "through the influence of higher feeling," Kant distanced himself from that part of Platonism which rests on Pythagorean mathematical mysticism and harmony as the bond of the kosmos.[70] ("Le grand enjeu entre Platon et Kant," as Jacques Derrida says, "c'est évidemment l'interprétation philosophique des mathématiques.")[71] After describing Pythagoras's mathematical theories (including the *Harmonie der Sphären*), Kant comes to the Pythagorean definition of the human soul: "anima numerus se ipsum movens," the soul is a self-moving number. This definition Kant takes to be "understandable" insofar as it stresses self-movement—a will that can become a good will—and the differentiation of thought from "lifeless" matter; but in the very next paragraph he complains that both Pythagoras and (often) Plato philosophized only "about mathematics," hoping in this way to "clear up a mystery, where there is no mystery." Insofar as he is a harmony-obsessed Pythagorean, Kant goes on, Plato is "the father of all *Schwär-*

merei [enthusiasm, fanaticism] in philosophy."[72] Those who love "poetic," "beauti-ful" philosophy, Kant thinks, will love what is most suspect in Platonism; by contrast Aristotle's thought is "work" (*Arbeit*) and something "prosaic." But "at bottom," Kant finally says tartly, "all philosophy is prosaic; and to propose today to return to poetic philosophizing is comparable to suggesting to a businessman that he no longer keep his account-books in prose, but write them in verses."[73] (Kant was surely familiar with Aristotle's complaint in the *Metaphysics* that Plato relies exces-sively on "poetic metaphors.")[74] What is as clear as it is prosaic, for Kant, is "the moral law in us"; to give that up for an "exalted vision" (*schwärmerische Vision*) would mean "the death of all philosophy."[75]

As a generality one might say this: for Kant Plato is right about the *nature* of moral concepts (as reason-provided, non-natural "ideas"); but he is wrong about the *content* of those concepts. Moral content needs objective ends—more precisely, persons as objective ends—not a set of interlocking, ever-expanding Pythagorean harmonies (psyche-polis-kosmos). And when one thinks of ends, or more generally of teleological understanding, one turns from Plato to Aristotle, from the *Phaedo* and *Republic* to the *Metaphysics* and *Ethics*. Since Kant himself makes this very turn, one need only follow him.

Kant, especially in the *Critique of Judgment,* makes heavy use of dedog-matized, "critical" teleology—both generally as a "clamp" holding the whole of Kantianism together and more particularly in the moral-political sphere. This is a limited Aristotelianism, Aristotle transformed from "dogmatism" into "criticism," and then further reshaped by (limited) Platonism and (limited) Augustinianism.

Generally, Kant argues in *Judgment* that nature can be estimated, though never known (*an sich*), through "purposes" and "functions" that mechanical causality fails to explain (since the "generation" and "growth" of a mere blade of grass from mechanical causes is, to us, inconceivable);[76] that persons as free agents have "purposes" they strive to realize and also view themselves as the "final end" of creation;[77] and that art exhibits a "purposiveness without purpose" which makes it not directly moral but the "symbol" or *analogon* of morality.[78] And if telos (some-times confined to a regulative role) can link, or rather be thought of *as* linking, nature, human freedom, and art, it can obviously link (more modestly) two aspects of human freedom: the moral and the legal realms, which share a set of ends (peace and civility).[79]

To be sure, the continuity at this point is not perfect, since Kant says that purposiveness (*Zweckmässigkeit*) is only a "reflective" principle when employed in the "estimation" of nature, while morality by contrast has "objective ends," which are "proposed by reason" and which everyone "ought to have" (*Religion within the Limits of Reason Alone*).[80] A possible continuity is reestablished, however, when

Judgment argues, for once uncautiously, that there must be "a ground of the unity of the supersensible, which lies at the basis of nature, with that which the concept of freedom practically contains."[81] Stated more straightforwardly: a nondiscursive intelligence "other" than ours might see real purposes in nature that are as objective as the moral law. And that could mean that *Judgment,* with its numerous teleological "bridges," helps to establish the architectonic "unity of reason" that is always a central Kantian concern.[82]

But more particularly—in the moral-political sphere—Kant's "critical" teleology suggests that if (depathologized) "good will" means never universalizing a maxim of action that would fail to respect persons as ends in themselves, then morality and politics/law could be connected through that same Kantian teleology.[83] If all persons had a good will, they would respect all others as ends—indeed as members of a "Kingdom of Ends"—since a "rational nature" is "not an end to be effected" but an "independently existing end"; but this does not actually happen, though it *ought* to, thanks to the "pathological" fact that man is "radically evil."[84] Thus Kantian public legal justice is a kind of intersection between the facts of "pathology" and the categorical imperative: if there were a kingdom of ends, the kingdoms of the earth—already denigrated by Augustine—would vanish. If, in sum, good will means respect for persons as ends in themselves, and if public legal justice sees to it that some moral ends (such as the prohibition of murder) get *observed,* if not "respected," then public legal justice in Kant might be viewed as the partial realization of what would happen if all wills were good. And beyond that, of course, Kant frequently suggests that law creates a kind of environment or context for good will, by bracketing out occasions of political sin (such as fear of others' domination) that might tempt (though never determine) people to act wrongly.[85]

The problem with any teleological reading of Kant's practical thought that gives primacy to ends is obvious enough: particularly in the *Grundlegung* he often says that it is best to start moral reasoning with the "formula" of the categorical imperative (asking whether one could will his "maxim" as a universal law), that it is merely "useful" to consider other factors as well (that is, the "matter" or "end" of a maxim and the "complete characterization" of all maxims) in order to bring the moral law "nearer to intuition."[86] Thus there are problems in Kant if one regards even *objective* "ends-in-themselves" as something introduced into the "higher" notion of formal universality merely in order to "gain entrance" for morality, "intuitively" conceived, and if one considers it merely useful (though not essential) to take account of ends as well as formal universality. And Kant himself sometimes seems to invite this. Since, however, he also insists on the notion of an "independently existing end" that one must "never act against," on the "dignity of man as a rational creature,"[87] it is at least possible that the three elements of a moral maxim—

the (universal) form, the matter (or end), and the "complete characterization"—are all *necessary,* and no one of them sufficient (for example, the universal form alone). This interpretation, though far from irresistible, is supported by an important passage from Kant's late and little-read *Tugendlehre:* "Since there are free actions, there must also be ends to which, as objects, those actions are directed. But among those ends there must be some which are at the same time (i.e., by their very concept) duties. For if there were no such ends, and since no action can be without an end, all ends for practical reason would always be valid only as means to other ends, and a categorical imperative would be impossible. Thus the doctrine of morals would be destroyed."[88]

If this is the case—and it is Kant himself who is saying that morality would be *destroyed* if there were no objective ends to serve as the objective of the categorical imperative—then Kant's moral philosophy is only somewhat problematical, not the piece of arid formalism that Hegel said it was.[89] Even though Kant's proof of the validity of an objective end-in-itself is intersubjective rather than (as he hopes) strictly objective—since it rests on everyone's having the same view of himself *as* an ultimate end—the argument is at least persuasive, if not as decisive as Kant may have hoped. Perhaps, in the end, Kant's whole position on this matter, problematical as it is, is best summed up in his *Tugendlehre:* "Man in the system of nature . . . is a being of little significance and, along with the other animals, considered as products of the earth, has an ordinary value. . . . But man as a person, i.e. as the subject of a morally practical reason, is exalted above all price. For as such a one (*homo noumenon*) he is not to be valued merely as a means to the ends of other people, or even to his own ends, but is to be prized as an end in himself."[90]

And in his remarkable late work *The Conflict of the Faculties,* Kant "translated" this very passage—or so it almost seems—into the language of politics: "In the face of omnipotence of nature, or rather its supreme first cause which is inaccessible to us, the human being is, in his turn, but a trifle. But for the sovereigns of his own species also to consider and treat him as such, whether by burdening him as an animal, regarding him as a mere tool of their designs, or exposing him in their conflicts with one another in order to have him massacred—this is no trifle, but a subversion of the ultimate purpose of creation itself."[91]

On this "teleological" view, sovereigns deny the rights of man by treating their subjects as mere means to a "relative" purpose (for instance, territorial aggrandizement); for Kant, war attacks and perverts the legality and civility that (as "qualified" goods) provide a stable context of peace and security within which individuals can safely exercise the sole unqualified good, a good will. So the notion that persons are ends who ought never to be used merely as means to arbitrary purposes provides good will with an objective end that is the source of the categorical imperative, and it sets a limiting condition to what politics can legitimately do. Despite Hegel, then, Kantianism is not merely a "formal" doctrine in which (to quote Hegel's language) "chill duty is the final undigested lump left within the stomach."[92]

Someone could say, of course, that Kant's whole theory of ends is a mere reworking of political, moral, and scientific elements long familiar in Aristotle; the *Critique of Judgment* might be viewed as a gigantic meditation on Aristotle's *Metaphysics:* "The final cause (telos) is an end, and that sort of end which is not for the sake of something else, but for whose sake everything else is; so that if there is to be a last term of this sort, the process will not be infinite; but if there is no such term, there will be no final cause, but those who maintain the infinite series eliminate the Good without knowing it (yet no one would try to do anything if he were not going to come to a limit); nor would there be reason in the world; the reasonable man, at least, always acts for a purpose, and this is a limit; for the end is a limit."[93] One can give a perfectly Kantian sense to this remarkable passage simply by saying that Aristotle's phrase "for whose sake everything else is" refers to Kant's concept of "man considered as a moral agent."[94] But even if Kant could embrace *Metaphysics* 994b, that does not mean that his whole teleology is simply Aristotelian; for Kant the only *knowable* objective ends are moral ones, while nature and art are merely *interpreted* teleologically. In Aristotle, by contrast, one can know that both natural things and works of art have their objective real telos. As he says in the *Physics,* "it is both by nature and for an end that the swallow makes its nest and the spider its web, and plants grow leaves for the sake of the fruit and send their roots down (not up) for the sake of nourishment." And he adds that "art partly completes what nature is unable to elaborate, and partly imitates her. If therefore artificial products are for the sake of an end, so clearly also are natural products."[95] For Kant, Aristotle "says" more than he "knows"; and that is the difference between dogmatism and criticism.[96]

But Kant would not quarrel primarily with Aristotle's understanding of nature; Aristotle's thought as a whole is heavily colored by biology, and it was precisely biology that partly occasioned *Judgment* itself—the problem of accounting (*per impossibile*) for the generation of a mere blade of grass through mechanical causality, without end-oriented growth. What Kant would contest more centrally is Aristotle's occasional effort to assimilate moral ends to natural ones (in the *Politics*) and his usual effort to define the highest human end as contemplation rather than moral action (in the *Nicomachean Ethics,* for example). The occasional assimilation of politics to biology and biological ends is especially marked in Book I of the *Politics:* "because it is the completion of associations existing by nature, every *polis* exists by nature, having itself the same quality as the earlier associations [such as the household] from which it grew. It is the end or consummation to which these associations move, and the nature of things consists in their end or consummation; for what each thing is when its growth is completed we call the nature of that thing, whether it be a man or a horse or a family."[97] From a Kantian perspective, there is simply too much *physis* in this *polis;* one recalls Kant's insistence in *Judgment* that culture and the state are "not nature, nor yet freedom."[98] To be sure, Aristotle insists that while the polis "grows for the sake of mere life, it exists for the sake of a good life"; he is not a primitive advocate of "biopolitics."[99] But it is noteworthy that the will and self-determination that Aristotle stresses in the *Ethics*—though mainly, as was seen, in connection with *legal* accountability—barely appear in the *Politics.*

As for the *Ethics* itself, the telos that it recommends is hardly congruent with Kant's insistence on the overriding importance of practice and good will; Aristotle argues that "the contemplative activity of reason seems . . . to aim at no end beyond itself," to be the sole end in itself, while "the life in accordance with moral virtue is happy in a secondary degree."[100] For Kant the whole doctrine is doubly erroneous; *eudaemonia* (as something "pathological") ought not to be considered as part (or the whole) of morality, and moral virtue cannot be "secondary."

Taking all of Aristotle's teleological notions together, then, Kant could have agreed with the *Metaphysics* that there is indeed something "for whose sake every-thing else is" and that those who neglect final causality "eliminate the Good without knowing it," but that highest good Kant would have called practical, not theoretical—respect for persons, not quasi-divine contemplation. And Aristotle's reading of nature he would have called dogmatic. But if nature cannot be *known* to have objective purposes, then the city cannot be merely the highest and most inclusive "natural" association; it must transcend nature and legally realize some non-natural, objective moral ends (when good will falters). For Kant the natural and the moral realms can be bridged by a teleological "substrate," but bridges, after all, link up things that remain distinct.

Aristotle, then, provides Kant with the notion of a final end that keeps Augustinian good will from slipping into "higher" delight and that keeps Platonic moral "ideas" from modulating into psychic and social "harmony." Kant and Aristotle do not share the same ends, obviously, but they equally want to avoid an infinite regress in which *nothing* is more than a means. The teleological language of ends, final ends, and means is what Kant owes to Aristotle—the Aristotle who, Kant tells us, bears as much as Plato "the seal of antiquity" (*das Siegel des Altertums*) and therefore has "a claim to be read."[101] It was not through inadvertence that Kant spoke, in his final *Critique,* the language of ends and means rather than of good reasons, God's will, or utility: *Judgment* is not just a very long slip of the pen (or of the mind). Kant presumably said what he meant to say: "Since some . . . maintain that the *Critique* is not to be taken literally . . . because Kant's precise words, like Aristotle's, will kill the mind, I therefore declare again that the *Critique* is to be understood by considering exactly what it says."[102]

Despite Kant's limited Platonism—limited in part by Aristotle's teleological criticisms of Plato's vestigial Pythagoreanism ("mathematics has come to be identical with philosophy . . . though they say that it should be studied for the sake of other things")[103]—one must be cautious in discussing the Plato-echoing notion of reason's "causality" in Kant, for in 1980 John Rawls published a remarkable article, "Kantian Constructivism in Moral Theory," which casts grave doubt on the notion that reason can simply "provide" imperatives. Beginning with the notion that Kant is the most important "constructivist" in moral theory—that is, that in Kantian morality there is a "procedure of construction in which rationally autonomous agents subject to reasonable conditions agree to public principles of justice," so that the moral law is the "constructed object" of a correct procedure, not something "found" or "seen"[104]—Rawls goes on to argue that Kantian constructivism can best be understood by contrasting it with (especially Platonic) "rational intuitionism":

> Rational intuitionism may be summed up by two theses: first, the basic moral concepts of the right and the good, and the moral worth of persons, are not analyzable in terms of nonmoral concepts . . . ; and, second, first principles of morals . . . are self-evident propositions about what kinds of considerations are good grounds for applying one of the three basic moral concepts, that is, for asserting that something is (intrinsically) good, or that a certain action is the right thing to do, or that a certain trait of character has moral worth. These two theses imply that the agreement in judgment which is so essential for an effective public conception of justice is founded on the recognition of self-evident truths about good reasons. And what these reasons are is fixed by a moral order that is prior to and independent of our conception of the person and the social role of morality. This order is given by the nature of things and is known, not by sense, but by rational intuition.[105]

In Rawls's view, Kant was no rational intuitionist. It is clear to everyone, Rawls argues, that Kant "would have rejected Hume's psychological naturalism as heteronomous"; but it is "less obvious" that for Kant rational intuitionism is also heteronomous. It is less obvious because Kant is in *agreement* with the rational intuitionists that "the basic moral concepts are conceptually independent of natural objects." But it suffices for heteronomy, Rawls goes on, that moral principles "obtain in virtue of relations among objects the nature of which is not affected or determined by the conception of the person." Kant's idea of autonomy, Rawls insists, requires (as against rational intuitionism) that "there exist no such order of given objects determining the first principles of right and justice among free and equal moral persons. Heteronomy obtains not only when first principles are fixed by the special psychological constitution of human nature, as in Hume, but also when they are fixed by an order of universals or concepts grasped by rational intuition, as in Plato's realm of forms or in Leibniz's hierarchy of perfections."[106] And so, Rawls concludes, while in rational intuitionism there is only a "sparse notion of the person" (as knower of already fixed moral truth), in Kantian constructivism "a relatively complex conception of the person plays a central role." And it is these persons who, as "agents of construction," construct practical principles as their "object."[107] Presumably this refers to Rawls's claim in *A Theory of Justice* that for Kant "moral principles are the object of rational choice," so that "moral philosophy becomes the study of the conception and outcome of a suitably defined rational decision."[108] To be sure, since Rawls's Kantian choosers are "free and equal rational beings," they do not fall into what Rawls calls "radical choice" by "sheer fiat," as in Nietzsche and existentialism: choice is reasonably constrained by the free, equal, and rational "nature" of choosing beings, as well as by those beings' "preference for primary goods" and by "highest-order interest."[109] But none of these constraints is "given" in a rational intuition (though Rawls *does* say that his constraints "seem reasonable"); and so for Rawls it is true to say that "Kant's main aim is to deepen and to justify Rousseau's idea that liberty is acting in accordance with a law that we give to ourselves."[110] Obviously this is an important view: it would, if correct, provide a single provenance for Kant's moral *and* political theory, so that it would be superfluous to trace Platonic, Aristotelian, and Augustinian "strands" in Kantianism. Geneva would displace Athens.

One questions with trepidation the conclusions of one of the most important living students of Kant's practical philosophy. But it is at least *possible* that Kant's undoubted devotion to Rousseau—the "Newton of the moral world"[111]—did not utterly exclude every conceivable "rational intuition." Certainly Rawls is wholly right in saying that Kant would not try to ground morality in "relations among objects the nature of which is not affected or determined by the conception of the person." Kant would not, for example, in the manner of Leibniz, try to relate moral truth to the "other" eternal verities of mathematics and logic. In an important letter from 1696 Leibniz insisted that "eternal truths are the fixed and immutable point on which everything turns. Such is the truth of numbers in arithmetic, and of figures in geometry. . . . That postulated, it is well to consider that order and harmony are also something mathematical and which consist in certain proportions: and that justice being nothing else than the order which is observed with regard to the good and evil of intelligent creatures, it follows that God, who is the sovereign substance, immutably maintains justice and the most perfect order which can be observed."[112]

"Perfect order," then, for Leibniz, is the substrate of justice as much as of mathematics—though Leibniz coupled this quasi-Platonic view with a "Christian" notion that justice is the "charity of the wise."[113] (One says "Christian" because Leibniz synthesizes Pauline antitheses: in 1 Corinthians, chapter 13, charity simply *replaces* the "wisdom" of the Greeks, but Leibniz fuses Jerusalem and Athens in insisting on the charity *of the wise*.) It was Leibniz's conviction that "justice follows certain rules of equality and of proportion which are no less founded in the immutable nature of things, and in the ideas of the divine understanding, than the principles of arithmetic and geometry."[114]

If, however, Kant would plainly not countenance "relations among objects" (for example, mathematical relations) as the source or even *analogon* of ethics—objects that are not "affected or determined by the conception of the person"—what about the conception of the person *itself?* Where does this conception come from? Is it just vestigial Christianity—the "equality of all souls before God," minus God?[115] For Kant, personality (as distinguished from humanity) always means moral personality, the capacity of being moral (or at least willing the moral). And so personality is revealed *through* the moral law: as Kant urges in *Religion within the Limits,* "The predisposition to personality is the capacity for respect for the moral law as *in itself a sufficient incentive* of the will."[116] (Thus there is nothing very "personal" about the persons who stand at the center of Kant's moral philosophy, and who set a "limit" to the politically permissible: they are not richly individuated in terms of particular characteristics or concrete social "roles" (*dramatis personae*) but are simply rational beings capable of respecting other rational beings as "objective ends.")[117] But the moral law, in the language of *Practical Reason,* is a (or rather *the*) "fact of reason"; and that "fact" is (at least arguably) a "rational intuition." "The consciousness of this fundamental law," Kant says, "may be called a fact of reason, since one cannot ferret it out from any antecedent data of reason and since [the law] forces itself upon us as a synthetic proposition *a priori* based on no pure or empirical intuition."[118] (To be sure, Kant argues in the *Groundwork* that we shall never *understand* how pure reason can be practical, but that is another matter.)[119]

Every reading of Kant must "rest" somewhere. Rawls, who denies that consciousness of the moral law (qua fact of reason) is "given" in a rational intuition, rests with "deepened" Rousseau; but a good case (not of course a conclusive one) can be made for resting on the moral law, not as something "constructed" but simply "there." The argument, laid out in schematic form, would be roughly as follows. (1) Criticism (Kant's critical philosophy) "can and must" begin with "pure practical laws" and their "actual existence." The pure practical or moral law is a fact of reason.[120] Or, as Kant puts it in *Pure Reason,* "I assume that there really are pure moral laws which determine completely *a priori* (without regard to empirical motives, that is, to happiness) what is and is not to be done, that is, which determine the employment of the freedom of a rational being in general; and that these laws command in an absolute manner."[121] (2) "*All* moral conceptions have their seat and origin completely *a priori* in the reason," and therefore "the conception of an objective principle, insofar as it is obligatory for a will, is called a command (of reason), and the formula of the command is called an imperative."[122] (3) An imperative is called categorical "if it is conceived as good in itself and consequently as being necessarily the principle of a will which of itself conforms to reason."[123] (4) But categorical imperatives or (applied) moral laws "ought to hold good for every rational creature," and therefore "we must derive them from the general concept of a rational being."[124] (5) But "a rational being," in its turn, "necessarily" regards its own existence as an "end in itself." And what is true of a rational being is true of *every* rational being.[125] (6) Therefore, rational beings, as ends in themselves, furnish the "content" of moral laws, since these must be *derived* from "the general concept of a rational being." So one *begins* with moral law as fact of reason; the content of the moral law is then *derived* from the general concept of a rational being. And this links up with Kant's insistence that "a rational nature exists as an end in itself."[126]

Now if the general concept of a rational being as an end in itself is arguably the content of the moral law as sole fact of reason, then neither the moral law itself nor the public legal justice that realizes some moral ends (even from devilish motives) can be viewed as the "constructed" object of a contractarian procedure. And there is a further problem. Rawls's agents of construction are characterized as "free."[127] But Kant insists always that freedom is known only *through* the moral law, and that would seem to mean that unless there were a moral law we would not think of ourselves as free.[128] That supports *beginning* with the moral law and then finding the law's "content" in "the rational being" as self-conceived end in itself.

Nothing, of course, can detract from Rawls's deserved reputation as the single-handed restorer of Kant's status as a great political theorist, but Kant almost certainly owes more to the extra-Pythagorean Plato than Rawls concedes.[129] Rawls is entirely right to place persons at the heart of Kant's ethics, but that does not necessitate drawing a line *between* persons and "rational intuition." For Kant the moral law (the fact of reason) is built *on* the idea of a rational being, on persons who view themselves as the final ends of creation. One can separate Kant from Plato, to the exact degree required, without locating him too close to Rousseau.

If Rawls gives too little weight to Kant's limited Platonism, Michael Sandel gives equally slight weight to Kant's limited Aristotelianism. In his brilliant study *Liberalism and the Limits of Justice* (1982), Sandel says that "the [Kantian] concept of a subject given prior to and independent of its objects offers a foundation for the moral law that, unlike merely empirical foundations, awaits neither teleology nor psychology. In this way, it powerfully completes the deontological vision. As the right [for Kant] is prior to the good, so the subject is prior to its ends."[130] And near the end of his book Sandel adds that "only in a universe empty of *telos,* such as seventeenth-century science and philosophy affirmed, is it possible to conceive a subject apart from and prior to its purposes and ends."[131] Surely this is trenchant and striking, and made all the more so by the force and grace of Sandel's remarkable writing. Nonetheless, one might complain that Sandel's insistence on a categorical gulf between "deontology" and "teleology" fails to do perfect justice to Kant's moral (and political) thought: after all, Kant always says that we have a "perfect duty"[132] to respect rational beings as objective ends, and that particular fusion of *duty* and *ends* is neither purely deontological nor purely teleological. (But it was not for nothing that Kant, in his late essay entitled "On the Use of Teleological Principles in Philosophy," called moral philosophy "eine reine praktische Teleologie" [a pure practical teleology].)[133] The teleological strand is a crucial part of Kantian morality: Kant says in the *Grundlegung* that we ought to subordinate relative ends or purposes to respect for rational beings as objective ends; he says in the *Tugendlehre* that morality would be destroyed if there were no objective ends for a (more-than-Augustinian) "good will" to will; he insists in *Religion within the Limits* that reason "proposes" objective ends (that is, respect for persons) that we "ought to have."[134] And the whole *Critique of Judgment* is devoted to finding "bridges" between the realms of Kantianism by discovering (or rather reading in) telos everywhere: the third *Critique,* after all, argues that finite human understanding cannot interpret nature without the notions of end, purpose, and function; that art has an intelligent, intelligible structure that makes it purposive without a purpose; that rational beings both have ends and necessarily view themselves as the final ends of creation, not as mere means to alleged divine purposes, in the manner of Locke ("for men being . . . all the servants of one sovereign Master, sent into the world by his order and about his business, they are his property, whose workmanship they are").[135] One simply cannot take seriously Kant's claim that *Judgment* unifies the whole of Kantianism (in a kind of Kantian summa) and maintain that Kant insisted on "a universe empty of *telos*"; to be sure, Kant argued that teleological understanding is only a "reflective" principle usable by "finite" intelligences in the understanding of nature, but he also argued that reason proposes objective moral ends that we ought to have. A rigid Rossian distinction between *deontology* and *teleology* necessarily fails to capture this.

This leads to a further doubt about Sandel's characterization of Kant's moral theory. At one point he says that "for Kant, the moral law is not a discovery of theoretical reason but a deliverance of practical reason, the product of pure will."[136] There is no obvious equivalence, however, between "a deliverance of practical reason" and "the product of pure will": indeed, if one gives central weight to *Religion*'s contention that reason proposes objective ends that we ought to have, then reason's proposal will exclude viewing the moral law as the product of pure will. If reason-ordained objective ends are just there (as facts of reason), moral "production" is out of the question. That is why Sandel is a little misleading when he says that "on the [Kantian] deontological view, what matters above all is not the ends we choose but our capacity to choose them."[137] What matters still more is that persons are "objective ends" who limit our choice of "relative" ends. But both kinds of ends are elements of a "critical" teleology, so that Sandel is nearer the mark when he grants that the Kantian "person is a subject of ends."[138] In contrasting "deontology" with "contingent ends" and "empirical ends," Sandel fails to stress Kant's own notion of one kind of end ("objective") overriding and regulating another kind of end ("relative"). It is not a matter of deontology versus teleology, but of objective ends outweighing relative ones. (It may be that, in stressing "the product of pure will," Sandel has accepted too readily Rawls's notion of a constructivist Kant—ironically enough, since much of *Liberalism and the Limits of Justice* is a sharp critique of Rawls.)

Kant's universe is not exactly empty of telos: it is simply "critical" in its use of teleology. It embraces Aristotle's notion that, to avoid a regressive infinite series of mere means, there must finally be something "for whose sake everything else is"; but it admits that we simply read ends into a nature whose noumenal being (*an sich*) we cannot know. This is clearest, perhaps, in *Judgment* sections 86 and 87: "Now, supposing we follow the teleological order there is a fundamental principle to which even the most ordinary human intelligence is obliged to give immediate assent. It is the principle that if there is to be a final end at all, which reason must assign *a priori,* then it can only be man—or any rational being in the world—subject to moral laws. For—and this is the verdict of everyone—if the world only consisted of lifeless beings, or even consisted partly of living, but yet irrational beings, the existence of such a world would have no worth whatever, because there would exist in it no being with the least conception of what worth is."[139]

Even if, however, the teleological standpoint is only a necessary supposition, that does not empty the Kantian kosmos of telos: it is precisely Kant's point that we unavoidably "read" that kosmos *teleologically,* and that in morality we actually know reason-ordained ends. To speak, therefore, of the moral law as "the product of pure will"—not as the objective end respected by good will—is to convert Kant into an existentialist avant la lettre, to translate him from Königsberg to Paris. But for Kant there was "no exit."

The effort to find the correct meaning of good will, practical reason, and objective ends in Kant's moral and political thought is not merely an effort to find a balance among Augustine, Plato, and Aristotle in the critical philosophy: for Kant arguably preserves what is soundest in those ancient philosophers and cancels what is least defensible. Thus for Kant good will entails (as with early Augustine) responsibility-incurring self-movement, but not "delight" in a God whose real existence is indemonstrable and who therefore cannot be known as "lawgiver."

Practical reason entails (as with Plato) the non-natural distinctiveness of moral "ideas," but not the reduction of ethics to quasi-mathematical "harmony," whether of the psyche, the polis, or the kosmos. Final ends entail something that is no longer a mere means to something higher (as with Aristotle), but not the belief that one can know objective ends in a nature that reaches us only phenomenally, to be "read" teleologically by us. Kant cancels whatever requires "transcendent" knowledge in Augustinianism, Platonism, and Aristotelianism, and he pares those doctrines down to the "limits of reason alone."[140]

And the precise relation of what remains of "criticized" Augustinianism, Platonism, and Aristotelianism matters very much, if one thinks that Kantianism is the least inadequate of moral and political positions—if one thinks that without reason-ordained objective ends (such as eternal peace and republicanism) "public legal justice" would be public and legal but not just—Hobbism at best, the Gestapo at worst; if one thinks, at the same time, that, were public legal justice to provide people with moral motives ("good will"), the attempt would generate an intolerable moral despotism that actually degrades motivation from mere self-interest to terror.[141] (Kantianism is also least inadequate in the sense that, without falling into the ruinous notion that all philosophy is ideology, it can, if tilted slightly leftward, accommodate what is most persuasive in Marxism: for Marx speaks as a left-Kantian when he says that criticism "ends with the doctrine that man is the highest being for man, with the categorical imperative to overthrow all circumstances in which man is humiliated, abandoned, enslaved or despised.")[142]

It is at least arguable that Kant was precisely right to view politics as the legal realization of morally valuable ends; and that is why it is worthwhile to sort out what he did with and to his philosophical inheritance from antiquity. The extraordinary thing about Kant is that he was able to look "radical evil" and historical wretchedness squarely in the face and, without hoping for a miraculous upsurge of good will through "a new creation," was able to predict that the self-love that had hitherto generated war and misery might (by loving itself more wisely) finally embrace republican peace.[143] That is a thought which matters even more now than it did two hundred years ago, when the *Grundlegung* began to make its peace with the world.

Notes

1
John Rawls, "Kantian Constructivism in Moral Theory," *Journal of Philosophy* 77 (September 1980): 515ff.; Michael Sandel, *Liberalism and the Limits of Justice* (Cambridge: Cambridge University Press, 1982).

2
Kant, *Eternal* [Perpetual] *Peace,* in *Kant's Political Writings,* ed. H. Reiss (Cambridge: Cambridge University Press, 1970), p. 125 (translation slightly altered).

3

Kant, *Critique of Pure Reason,* trans. N. K. Smith (London: Macmillan, 1963), pp. 472–73 (A 547/B 575).

4

Kant, *Critique of Judgment,* trans. J. C. Meredith (Oxford: Oxford University Press, 1952), pp. 52–53, 98–100.

5

Kant, *Pure Reason,* p. 644 (A 819/B 847).

6

The "First Appendix" to *Eternal Peace* is the definitive *Anti-Machiavel.*

7

Rawls, "Kantian Constructivism," pp. 554ff.; Sandel, *Liberalism and the Limits of Justice,* pp. 7, 175 (inter alia).

8

Ernst Cassirer, *Kant's Life and Thought,* trans. J. Haden (New Haven: Yale University Press, 1981), pp. 418–19: "Kant felt himself a Platonist specifically in the foundations of his ethics . . . [but he] . . . no less vigorously attached himself to the 'worker' Aristotle."

9

Kant, *Rechtslehre,* in *Kant's Political Writings,* p. 174.

10

See Kant, *Groundwork* [Fundamental Principles] *of the Metaphysics of Morals,* trans. T. K. Abbot (Indianapolis: Library of Liberal Arts, 1949), pp. 52–55, and pp. 20ff., where Kant says that it is *from* self-love that people deviate from moral universality, by making exceptions in their own favor.

11

Kant, *Rechtslehre,* in *Kant's Political Writings,* p. 174: "This task of establishing a universal and lasting peace is not just a part of the theory of right within the limits of pure reason, but its entire ultimate purpose [*Endzweck*]."

12

Kant urges that "when *motiva moralia* are insufficient" one needs a legal-political *potestas executoria* to realize moral ends. See Kant, *Erläuterungen zu A. G. Baumgartens Initia philosophiae practicae primae,* in *Kants Handschriftlicher Nachlass,* vol. 6, ed. Prussian Academy (Berlin: Walter de Gruyter, 1934 [vol. 19 of *Kants gesammelte Schriften*]), no. 6566, p. 82.

13

Judith N. Shklar, *Ordinary Vices* (Cambridge, Mass.: Harvard University Press, 1984), p. 234. Shklar's final chapter, "Bad Characters for Good Liberals," is a remarkable study of Aristotle, Machiavelli, Montesquieu, and Kant.

14

Kant, *Eternal Peace,* in *Kant's Political Writings,* pp. 99–101.

15

See Sandel, *Liberalism and the Limits of Justice,* pp. 175–76.

16

Kant, *Groundwork,* pp. 72–74.

17

Kant, *Religion within the Limits of Reason Alone,* trans. T. M. Greene and Hoyt Hudson (New York: Harper and Row, 1960), p. 86.

18

The idea that the "ethical commonwealth" of *Religion* can serve as Kant's "utopia" was suggested to me by Judith Shklar.

19

St. Augustine, *De Libero Arbitrio* [*The Free Choice of the Will*], trans. R. P. Russell (Washington, D.C.: Catholic University of America Press, 1968), pp. 95–96.

20

Hannah Arendt, *The Life of the Mind: Willing* (New York: Harcourt Brace Jovanovich, 1978), pp. 3ff., and particularly the Augustine chapter.

21

Aristotle, *Nicomachean Ethics*, trans. J. Warrington (London: Everyman, 1963), pp. 107ff. (1135a ff.).

22

The passage quoted, though it epitomizes *De Correptione et Gratia*, is actually from Augustine's *Letter to Hillary of Syracuse* (414 A.D.), in *Oeuvres de Saint Augustin*, vol. 21, ed. G. de Plinval (Paris: Desclée de Brouwer, 1966), pp. 44–45.

23

Sartre, *Existentialism and Humanism*, trans. P. Mairet (London: Methuen, 1948), p. 28.

24

St. Augustine, *De Libero Arbitrio*, pp. 109–10, and *De Trinitate*, in R. Meagher, *An Introduction to Augustine* (New York: New York University Press, 1978), p. 203.

25

St. Augustine, *De Spiritu et Littera*, cited in Neal W. Gilbert, "The Concept of the Will in Early Latin Philosophy," *Journal of the History of Philosophy* 1 (October 1963): 33.

26

Locke, *Two Treatises of Government*, ed. P. Laslett (Cambridge: Cambridge University Press, 1963), pp. 401–02. "Voluntary agreement gives . . . political power to governors for the benefit of their subjects." For a full treatment of Locke's voluntarism and contractarianism, see Patrick Riley, *Will and Political Legitimacy* (Cambridge, Mass.: Harvard University Press, 1982), chap. 3.

27

St. Augustine, *De Libero Arbitrio*, cited in Meagher, *An Introduction to Augustine*, p. 176. Pascal, *Pensées*, in *Oeuvres de Blaise Pascal*, ed. L. Brunschvicg (Paris: Librairie Hachette, 1914), vol. 2, p. 385. For a full treatment see Patrick Riley, "The General Will before Rousseau: The Contributions of Pascal, Malebranche, Bossuet and Bayle," in *Studi Filosofici* (Florence), 1984.

28

Rousseau argues that conforming one's "particular will" (*volonté particulière*) is the essence of virtue; see *Économie Politique*, in *Political Writings*, ed. C. E. Vaughan (Cambridge: Cambridge University Press, 1915), vol. 1, pp. 255ff. Kant, *Rechtslehre*, trans. J. Ladd as *The Metaphysical Elements of Justice* (Indianapolis: Library of Liberal Arts, 1965), p. 78.

29

See Riley, "The General Will before Rousseau."

30

St. Augustine, *De Libero Arbitrio*, p. 97.

31

Plato, *Phaedrus*, trans. R. Hackforth, in *Plato: Collected Dialogues*, ed. E. Hamilton and H. Cairns (New York: Bollingen Foundation, 1961), pp. 409–502 (253b–257b). See A. W. S. Baird, *Studies in Pascal's Ethics* (The Hague: Martinus Nijhoff, 1975), pp. 61–73. See also Pascal's *Ecrits sur la Grace* in *Oeuvres de Blaise Pascal*.

32

Kant, *Groundwork*, pp. 55–56: "The mere dignity of man as a rational creature . . . in other words, respect for a mere idea, should serve as an inflexible precept of the will."

33

Kant, *Critique of Practical Reason*, trans. L. W. Beck (Indianapolis: Library of Liberal Arts, 1956), pp. 76–79: "Respect for the moral law . . . is a feeling produced by an intellectual cause. . . . [It] is therefore produced solely by reason."

34

Hobbes, *Leviathan*, ed. Michael Oakeshott (Oxford: Basil Blackwell, 1957), p. 38.

35

On "absolute origination" see Kant, *Pure Reason*, p. 464 (A533/B561); on the rejection of divine "concurrence" in human actions, see Kant, *Lectures on Philosophical Theology*

(1783–84), trans. A. W. Wood and G. M. Clark (Ithaca: Cornell University, 1978), p. 148.

36
Hobbes, *Leviathan*, p. 111.

37
On this problem in Hobbesianism see the remarkable short essay by Michael Oakeshott, "Logos and Telos," in *Government and Opposition* 9 (Spring 1974), pp. 237–44.

38
Hobbes, *Leviathan*, p. 307.

39
Kant, in *The Philosophy of Kant*, ed. C. J. Friedrich (New York: Modern Library, 1949), p. 367: "The source of evil . . . can lie only in a rule made by the will for the use of its freedom. . . . Determination by natural causes . . . is contradictory to the very notion of freedom."

40
Kant, *Groundwork*, p. 69.

41
Ibid., pp. 70–71.

42
Kant, *Pure Reason*, p. 279 (B425).

43
Plato, *Phaedo*, in *Collected Dialogues*, pp. 81–82 (100c–e). In this passage Socrates tells Cebes that he will "explain causation" through "absolute" moral and aesthetic ideas.

44
Kant, *Eternal Peace*, in *Kant's Political Writings*, p. 125.

45
Kant, *Pure Reason*, pp. 318–19 (A327/B384).

46
Ibid., pp. 310–13 (A314/B371). Cassirer, above all, has brought out the importance of this passage in his *Kants Leben und Lehre*, in *Immanuel Kants Werke*, vol. 11, ed. Ernst Cassirer (Berlin: Bruno Cassirer, 1922), pp. 268–70.

47
Plato, *Parmenides*, in *Collected Dialogues*, p. 924 (130b–d).

48
Kant, *Pure Reason*, pp. 310–13 (A314/B371).

49
Ibid., p. 319 (A328/B385).

50
Aristotle, *Metaphysics*, trans. W. D. Ross, in *The Works of Aristotle*, vol. 8 (Oxford: Clarendon Press, 1928), 991b.

51
Kant, *Pure Reason*, p. 472 (A547/B575).

52
Plato, *Gorgias*, in *Collected Dialogues*, p. 289 (506c–e); for Callicles' "will to power," see A. E. Taylor, *Plato: The Man and His Work*, 7th ed. (London: Methuen, 1966), p. 119: "The ideal of Callicles, like that of Nietzsche, is the successful cultivation of the *Wille zur Macht*." There is some truth in this exaggeration.

53
Kant, *Groundwork*, p. 29. Plato, *Phaedo*, in *Collected Dialogues*, p. 58 (75d).

54
Kant, *Pure Reason*, p. 644 (A819/B847).

55
Leibniz, *Die Philosophischen Schriften*, vol. 3, ed. C. I. Gerhardt (Hildesheim: Olms Verlag, 1965 [reprint of 1887 Berlin edition]), pp. 637, 264.

56
Leibniz, *Theodicy*, trans. A. Farrer (New Haven: Yale University Press, 1952), 2:182.

57
Robert Nozick, *Philosophical Explanations* (Cambridge, Mass.: Harvard University Press, 1981), pp. 552ff.

58
Ernst Cassirer, *Leibniz' System in seinen*

Wissenschaftlichen Grundlagen (Marburg, 1902), pp. 428ff.

59
Plato, *Euthyphro*, 10d–e, in *Collected Dialogues*, p. 141.

60
Leibniz, *Meditation on the Common Concept of Justice*, in *The Political Writings of Leibniz*, ed. Patrick Riley (Cambridge: Cambridge University Press, 1972), p. 45.

61
Kant, *Pure Reason*, p. 644 (A819/B847).

62
Leibniz, *Theodicy*, 2:184.

63
Leibniz, *Notes on Spinoza's Ethics*, in *The Philosophical Works of Leibniz*, 2d ed. trans. G. M. Duncan (New Haven: Yale University Press, 1908), pp. 21–22.

64
Leibniz, "Necessity of Faith," in *Textes Inédits*, vol. 1, ed. Gaston Grua (Paris: Presses Universitaires de France, 1948), p. 252.

65
Plato, *Meno*, in *Collected Dialogues*, pp. 365ff. (82b ff.).

66
Sheldon Wolin, *Politics and Vision* (Boston: Little, Brown, 1960), pp. 212ff. R. L. Nettleship, *Lectures on the Republic of Plato*, ed. Lord Charnwood (London: Macmillan, 1929), pp. 359–63.

67
Taylor, *Plato: The Man and His Work*, pp. 1ff.

68
Kant, "Welches sind die wirklichen Fortschritte, die Metaphysik seit Leibniz' ens und Wolff's Zeiten in Deutschland gemacht hat?" in *Immanuel Kants Werke*, vol. 8, ed. Ernst Cassirer (Berlin: Bruno Cassirer, 1922), p. 265.

69
Plato, *Republic*, in *Collected Dialogues*, p. 686 (443e–444a).

70
Kant, "Von einem neuerdings erhobenen vornehmen Ton in der Philosophie," in *Immanuel Kants Werke*, vol. 6, ed. Ernst Cassirer (Berlin: Bruno Cassirer, 1922), p. 483.

71
Jacques Derrida, *D'un ton apocalyptique adopté naguère en philosophie* (Paris: Éditions Galilée, 1983), p. 40.

72
Kant, "Von einem neuerdings erhobenen vornehmen Ton," pp. 480–87.

73
Ibid., pp. 482, 495n.

74
Aristotle, *Metaphysics*, Book M, 1079b.

75
Kant, "Von einem neuerdings erhobenen vornehmen Ton," pp. 486–87.

76
Kant, *Critique of Judgment*, p. 54.

77
Ibid., p. 109. Cf. 116n: "If there is to be a final end at all, which reason must assign *a priori*, then it can only be man—or any rational being in the world—subject to moral laws."

78
Ibid., p. 59; pp. 223–25: "The beautiful is the symbol of the morally good. . . . [Aesthetic] taste makes, as it were, the transition from the charm of sense to habitual moral interest possible without too violent a leap, for it . . . teaches us to find, even in sensuous objects, a free delight apart from any charm of sense."

79
Kant, *The Metaphysical Elements of Justice*, pp. 20–21.

80
Kant, *Religion within the Limits of Reason*, p. 6n.

81
Kant, *Critique of Judgment*, p. 14.

82
Kant, *Pure Reason*, pp. 653ff. (A832/B860ff.).

83
Kant, *Groundwork*, p. 54: "Rational nature . . . must be conceived, not as an end to be effected, but as an independently existing end."

84
Kant, *Religion within the Limits of Reason*, pp. 15–39.

85
Kant, *Eternal Peace*, in *Kant's Political Writings*, p. 117n.

86
Kant, *Groundwork*, pp. 46–48, 53.

87
Ibid., p. 54.

88
Kant, *Tugendlehre*, trans. J. Ellington as *The Metaphysical Principles of Virtue* (Indianapolis: Library of Liberal Arts, 1964), pp. 42–43.

89
G. W. F. Hegel, *Natural Law*, trans. T. M. Knox (Philadelphia: University of Pennsylvania Press, 1975), pp. 77–79, 132–33.

90
Kant, *Tugendlehre*, pp. 96–97.

91
Kant, *The Conflict of the Faculties*, in *Kant's Political Writings*, p. 185 (translation slightly altered).

92
Hegel, *Lectures on the History of Philosophy*, vol. 3, trans. E. S. Haldane and F. H. Simson (London: Kegan Paul, 1896).

93
Aristotle, *Metaphysics*, 994b.

94
Kant, *Critique of Judgment*, p. 99.

95
Aristotle, *Physics*, in *Aristotle: Selections*, ed. W. D. Ross (New York: Scribners, 1927), pp. 118–19 (199a 15–b28).

96
Kant, *Pure Reason*, p. 428 (A472/B500).

97
Aristotle, *Politics*, trans. Ernest Barker (New York: Oxford University Press, 1962), p. 5 (1252b).

98
Kant, *Critique of Judgment*, p. 224.

99
Aristotle, *Politics*, p. 5.

100
Aristotle, *Nicomachean Ethics*, pp. 229–30 (1177b–1178a).

101
Kant, "Von einem neuerdings erhobenen vornehmen Ton," p. 495n.

102
Kant, *Philosophical Correspondence*, trans. A. Zweig (Chicago: University of Chicago Press, 1967), p. 254.

103
Aristotle, *Metaphysics*, Book A, 992a.

104
Rawls, "Kantian Constructivism," pp. 554, 564.

105
Ibid., p. 557.

106
Ibid., p. 559.

107
Ibid., pp. 518–19, 560.

108
John Rawls, *A Theory of Justice* (Cambridge, Mass.: Harvard University Press, 1971), p. 251.

109
Rawls, "Kantian Constructivism," p. 568.

110
Rawls, *A Theory of Justice*, p. 256.

111
Cited in George A. Kelly's invaluable *Idealism, Politics and History* (Cambridge: Cambridge University Press, 1969), p. 92.

112
Leibniz, letter to the Electress Sophie, in *Textes Inédits*, p. 379.

113
"The treatment of justice and that of charity cannot be separated." Leibniz, *Elementa Iuris Naturalis*, in *Sämtliche Schriften und Briefe* (Berlin: Akademie Verlag, 1923–), Reihe 6, Bank 1, no. 12, p. 481.

114
Leibniz, *Opinion on the Principles of Pufendorf* (1706), in *The Political Writings of Leibniz*, p. 71.

115
As Nietzsche might have argued in *Beyond Good and Evil* or *The Antichrist*.

116
Kant, *Religion within the Limits of Reason*, pp. 22–23.

117
On this point see George Schrader's very helpful essay "The Status of Teleological Judgment in the Critical Philosophy," in *Kant-Studien* 45 (1953–54): 204, 235.

118
Kant, cited in Lewis White Beck, *A Commentary on Kant's Critique of Practical Reason* (Chicago: University of Chicago Press, 1960), p. 166.

119
Kant, *Groundwork*, pp. 78–80.

120
Kant, *Practical Reason*, p. 48.

121
Kant, *Pure Reason*, pp. 636–37 (A807/B835).

122
Kant, *Groundwork*, pp. 29–30.

123
Ibid., p. 32.

124
Ibid., p. 29.

125
Ibid., p. 146.

126
Ibid., pp. 29, 46.

127
Rawls, "Kantian Constructivism," pp. 521, 522, 523, 544, 545.

128
Kant, *Practical Reason*, p. 4: "Had not the moral law already been distinctly thought in our reason, we would never have been justified in assuming anything like freedom."

129
Rawls, to be sure, doesn't simply reproduce or re-present a wholly orthodox Kant: "To develop a viable Kantian conception of justice the force and content of Kant's doctrine must be detached from its background in transcendental idealism and given a procedural interpretation by means of the construction of the original position" ("The Basic Structure as Subject," *American Philosophical Quarterly* 14 [April 1977]: 165). This "must," of course, is contestable.

130
Sandel, *Liberalism and the Limits of Justice*, p. 7.

131
Ibid., p. 175.

132
Kant, *The Metaphysical Elements of Justice*, pp. 19ff.

133
Kant, *Über den Gebrauch Teleologischer Prinzipian in der Philosophie*, in *Immanuel Kants Werke*, vol. 6, p. 514.

134
Kant, *Religion within the Limits of Reason*, p. 6n.

135
Locke, *Two Treatises*, sec. 6.

136
Sandel, *Liberalism and the Limits of Justice*, p. 176.

137
Ibid., p. 6.

138
Ibid.

139
Kant, *Critique of Judgment*, pp. 116–17.

140
This phrase, from Kant's *Religion within the Limits of Reason Alone*, might reasonably be applied to the whole "critical" enterprise.

141
On this point see Shklar, *Ordinary Vices*, pp. 230ff.

142
Marx, "Towards a Critique of Hegel's *Philosophy of Right*," in *Karl Marx: Selected Writings*, ed. D. McLellan (New York: Oxford Press, 1977), p. 69. (By the time of *The German Ideology*, Kantianism was viewed by Marx as an ideology.)

143
Kant, *The Conflict of the Faculties*, in Reiss, *Kant's Political Writings*, pp. 187–88.

Chapter 2

*Kant's Two Conceptions of
the Will in Their Political
Context*

Lewis White Beck

In the *Critique of Practical Reason,* the concept of will is ambiguous. Theories of freedom of the will that seem to have no connection with each other are presented side by side. The reader does not readily see that they are compatible with each other, for Kant does not make it clear that there are two conceptions of the will and that the concept of freedom applied properly to the one is different from the concept of liberty applied to the other. If one does not carefully distinguish the two conceptions, not only the Kantian moral philosophy but also his political theory appears to run into an impasse. If, in order to avoid this impasse, we establish not only a distinction between the two conceptions but go to the other extreme and think that the two conceptions apply to distinctly different and opposed faculties, one of several ethical and political doctrines will be presented as uniquely and genuinely Kantian, and the others will be discarded. The object of this chapter is to make the necessary distinctions and then to establish the connections between them so as to modify three one-sided and extreme views of Kant's social and political teaching.

The *Critique of Practical Reason* inherits, from the two preceding works, two different conceptions of the will, but it does not indicate clearly the difference between the two.[1] Only in reading the *Metaphysics of Morals* does one see Kant, with an appropriate terminology, distinguish between them. The principal writings of Kant had been written without this clarification, and it is somewhat difficult to go back and apply the later distinction to the earlier works in every place where it is necessary for full clarity. It can and ought to be done, though some difficulties will still remain, since the explicit definition of the two concepts in the *Metaphysics of Morals* itself is not without ambiguity.

From the *Critique of Pure Reason* comes the concept of freedom as spontaneity, the faculty of initiating a new causal series in time. The first *Critique* does not profess to demonstrate that this is a "real concept," that is, a concept that really has an object. It shows simply that there is nothing logically impossible in it and that, though it is not necessary to the study of nature by theoretical reason, it is necessary if the structure of theoretical reason is to be perfected. It is nonetheless true that Kant, in 1781, believed that it was a concept applicable to the human will and that it applied to spontaneous and voluntary actions, though the same actions were comprehended, theoretically and empirically, under the causal laws of nature. In the first *Critique* (except for the "Methodology"), Kant was little occupied with problems of moral philosophy. Still, he knew already that a good will is a free will that obeys a moral law, though the formula and the source of this law were not developed in the *Critique of Pure Reason.*

The search for the formula and source of the law for a spontaneous will constitutes the principal task of the *Foundations of the Metaphysics of Morals.* In this little book, however, there appears an entirely new concept of freedom, namely, that of autonomy. Autonomy refers to the creator of law. An autonomous or free will is a will subject to no law except one of which it is itself the author; it is a will independent of any law (like the laws of nature) that has any other source. The faculty that, in this sense, is strictly autonomous is "pure practical reason," and Kant identifies it also with will.

Thus appears the ambiguity of which I have spoken. Kant speaks generally of ① the spontaneous initiation of a causal series as emerging in an act of will; and he ② speaks of the source of the law to which this spontaneity is subject as also a will. But the two conceptions are obviously different, and much later Kant tried to establish the difference between them by introducing a terminological distinction between *Willkür* and *Wille.*[2]

Kant had often previously used these words, sometimes to intimate a tacit distinction that he had not fully developed in his own thought; but more often the words seemed to be interchangeable. And, further, even after he had established the distinction, Kant often did not remain faithful to it; it has been wittily said of Kant that he succeeded in being technical without being precise. Yet I do not believe that he ever used the word *Willkür* when he meant to say *Wille* in a strict sense (though the converse error is common).

The formal definition of *Wille* given in the *Critique of Practical Reason* is "A power to determine the causation [of an act] by the representation of rules."[3] This is the concept already made familiar in the first *Critique*. Since reason is required to derive an act from a rule, law, or maxim,[4] one can say that the will is nothing but practical reason; it is this faculty that makes a rule of reason the efficient cause of an action by means of which an object can be realized, or the means by which one goes

not psych.
desire

from mere idea to the state of affairs envisaged in it. Wille is distinguished from simple desire since it is never determined by the object or even by our concept of the object, but always by a law that can be formulated only by reason, although its application may be to the endeavor for objects of desire.[5] If the motive for an action is found in the lower faculty of desire, it is solely a conception of the object and is always empirical, whether the conception be clear and rational or sensible and confused. The higher faculty of desire is will, which always operates (and not just when it is morally good will) according to a rule presented exclusively by reason (which can be either pure or empirical reason). An impulse and a conception of an object being given as a condition of action, the use of reason, in this case is solely for the purpose of choosing specific rules for achieving the goal of desire. Reason, in this sense, is the art of inference, more specifically here, the art of practical inference. It is here a question of *usus logicus* of practical reason; it is comparable to general logic, which, not concerned with the content of knowledge but only with its form, is the usus logicus of theoretical reason (that is, the art of syllogism).[6]

The faculty thus defined and here named Wille is, much later, identified by Kant with Willkür. It is the faculty of choosing an object that is left incompletely determined by the rule or maxim given, in universal form, by reason. Willkür, therefore, is not exclusively pragmatic in its action; it can be moral. Whether it is pragmatic or moral depends upon the condition of the rule it follows.[7] In each act of volition, there is a material,[8] some object of desire; but it is not necessary to select the rule with respect to our knowledge of the causal conditions under which the object can be realized. If that is a condition for the choice of the rule, the rule is pragmatic or technical. If, on the other hand, it is a rule that specifies the form which every specific technical rule must take—that is, a rule that the maxim of the action ought itself to be universally applicable to rational beings—then the rule is a moral rule. The *logical* use of reason is the same in the moral and in the pragmatic action. But in moral action, there is another use of reason. It is the *usus realis* of reason, and it is this use that defines the function of pure practical reason.

By contrast with Willkür, we have thus a concept of will not as directly determining an action by a rule applied for the satisfaction of an impulse, but a concept of will insofar as it is the legislator of maxims of which we are conscious in the voluntary actions of Willkür.

The rule of reason still leaves undetermined the choice of the object of Willkür, but we are now concerned not with this determination but with the origin of the reason itself. If this rule of reason is derived from our empirical or theoretical knowledge of the causal conditions for achieving an object of desire, there is nothing new in the problem; theoretical or cognitive reason furnishes the knowledge that "A causes B," and practical interest in B converts this into "A is a means of attaining B."

In moral action, the rule cannot have such a material content as its condition, for it would not then be universally valid but valid only on the condition that B was desired. The source of the rule, therefore, cannot be theoretical reason, and the origin of the rule cannot be attributed to the usus logicus of reason, even to the usus logicus of practical reason. Thus reason must have a real use: it should be seen as the faculty of formulating a priori synthetic rules. This corresponds to the use that reason has in transcendental logic (with regard to the formation of theoretical a priori synthetic judgments), and not to the use of reason in general logic, which is solely concerned with the form and implications of the form of judgments. After the *Critique of Pure Reason,* this use of reason is familiar to us in its theoretical function. The second *Critique,* in establishing that there is a *pure* practical reason, establishes in the same way the fact that practical reason has a usus realis and not merely a usus logicus.

The difference between the pure reason of the first and the pure reason of the second *Critique* is not found in the difference between usus realis and usus logicus, but in the kind of a priori synthetic judgments established by reason. If the judgment is practical, that is to say, if it is a rule for Willkür, reason is practical, and pure practical reason is then identified with the moral will.

It thus appears that we now have two concept of will, totally different from each other. The one, which is called Willkür in the *Metaphysics of Morals,* we may refer to as an *executive faculty.* The other, which is pure practical reason, is Wille in the strict sense, and may be called a *legislative faculty.* "From Wille there arise laws; from Willkür, maxims."[9] Willkür is obliged to execute that which pure practical reason in its real use (not its logical use) makes law. Thus, in the final analysis, there are not two distinct wills or two different faculties related only in an external or coercive manner. We find Wille and its laws by means of a regression upon the conditions of Willkür, not by separating them and turning toward some external legislator (God or nature) for Willkür. We are immediately conscious of the moral law every time we conceive of a maxim for our will (though here Kant says, incorrectly, *Wille* when he means *Willkür*).[10] Willkür, the faculty of spontaneity, is wholly spontaneous only when its action is governed by a law of pure practical reason, not when it accepts a rule given by nature for the accomplishment of some desire. Pure reason is effective, that is, practical, only upon the acceptance of its law as a motive (*Triebfeder*) by Willkür. Its law is never a law of action, but a law for the choice of maxims for an action; it leaves specific action undetermined, and Willkür—desire, plus the logical use of reason, plus consciousness of the maxim that expresses the condition of the rule—determines the action itself.

We must now consider the word *freedom* since it is attributed to will in each of the conceptions. Willkür is free to the extent that the conception of *any* law of reason controls its actions, and the degree to which it is in fact free at any moment is an empirical question. We discover (empirically) that man has an *arbitrium liberum,* not an *arbitrium brutum.*[11] This is the freedom Kant calls "comparative." In this comparative sense, freedom is not a question of the will as such, but of a simple desire subjected to some degree of rational control. Thus the arbitrium liberum can in fact be only a part of the mechanism of nature.[12] To show that it is morally free, it is necessary not to question its power to occasion changes in the world but to inquire into the provenance of the law that is included in its maxims. If the latter comes from the apprehension of nature, then comparative freedom is not moral freedom. Willkür is morally free in the measure that its maxims are chosen because they conform to the law of pure practical reason, that is, to the law that the maxims of a rational being are to be universally valid and that the actions of a moral being ought to be based on maxims chosen because they are valid for all rational beings. Though all its actions unfold in the order of nature, and though they can, in principle, be predicted by virtue of our knowledge of the laws of nature, they are nonetheless free actions and we are responsible for them, since they are chosen with respect for a law that is not determined by the state of affairs in nature.

This is the liberty of Willkür. But what is the freedom of pure practical reason of Wille in the narrow sense? It is not free in the sense of being indeterminate, of being free of fetters or in possessing a supernatural spontaneity. It does not possess freedom, Kant once tells us, because it does not act at all.[13] Its freedom is its purity, the nonempirical character of the universal law that it gives. It is freedom in the sense of autonomy. Autonomy is the faculty of making laws by itself and for itself, and the term *autonomy* applies not only to pure practical reason but to pure reason in general.

We can now summarize and bring the two concepts together. Willkür is completely free, that is, spontaneous, only when it adopts as its law an autonomous decree of pure practical reason or Wille. By a kind of hybridization of concepts, we speak of an autonomous Willkür and a spontaneous Wille. Still, it is better to speak of a free and spontaneous Willkür that is not naturally determined as being free in what Kant calls the negative sense, and of an autonomous Wille as being free in what Kant calls the positive sense of freedom.[14]

One of the principal difficulties in moral philosophy before Kant was this: if freedom of choice is granted, how can one subject it to the law and make it moral? The history of the philosophy of the eighteenth century is full of attempts to respond to this question. The most typical one was that there was a motive of the will which was different from the knowledge of the law, and which was added to this knowledge, such as the desire for happiness, or the desire for recompense for certain actions, or the love of God. Since Kant saw clearly that there was a generic difference between morality and prudence, between a truly good will and a will prudent in following its own interests, this kind of answer did not suit him. All explanations of this kind are heteronomous, that is, dependent upon conditions that have to be discovered empirically and that are destructive of the universal necessity that is the mark of the moral obligation. For morality, the consequences of such a heteronomous empiricism are comparable to those of strict empiricism in our knowledge of nature. Both, Kant believed, led to skepticism.

The response Kant made to this question is his most important contribution to moral philosophy. That the will of man both creates and executes obligations is one of the most dramatic theses in Kant's philosophy. It is as dramatic as, and comparable to, the "Copernican revolution" of his theoretical philosophy. As long as the origin of the law, be it natural or be it moral law, was ascribed to the nature of things and as long as it was believed that it could be known only by means of experience, its universality and necessity were illusory. Although one might well be a theoretical skeptic in the manner of Hume, for Kant skepticism in matters of morality seemed to be at once unfounded and ungenuine, and immoral in its effects.

It was known to some of Kant's predecessors that the moral law is rational and is discovered a priori and that it is an obligation of man to render obedience to this law without regard to the reward that followed—at least one believed it followed—the obedience. That morality is the pursuit of a perfection, and that the realization of a perfection is accompanied by pleasure, was recognized by Wolff, for example, who did not fall into the common error of thinking that it was the accompanying pleasure rather than the perfection itself that was the object of choice. But no one seemed to know why one should choose perfections nor how to determine what they were and how to approach them. Their error, Kant thought, was that of trying to establish practical conduct on tautologies. To avoid the tautologies, the disciples of Wolff (e.g., Baumgarten) surreptitiously reintroduced all the hedonistic and eudaemonistic elements that Wolff had, at least officially, suppressed. Kant admitted that that was the only thing they could do; all their material principles, however rationalistically conceived, were only principles of self-love and private happiness.

Now because Kant discovered the law as a product of pure reason and as rendered evident by "the sole fact of pure reason," and because he did not have to try to obtain it from the abstract concept of perfection or the concept of Wolff's "will in general," it was possible for him to see that the will as "creator of the law" was an idealization of the spontaneous Willkür. Granted that, Kant did not have to look for exterior motivation for obedience to that law, nor support it by any appeal to the authority of God or nature. Rational personality as initiator of the laws is a being that is ipso facto an ought for partially rational beings. Or, put another way, the duty of which we are conscious as constraining the actions of our Willkür is a product of law on impulse; the law would be a law that Willkür would obey spontaneously if Willkür did not have an impulsive element and did not to some extent lack rationality. The same faculty, as a pure faculty, initiates the laws and, as sensibly affected, is bound to obey them. "One need only analyze the sentence which men pass upon the lawfulness of the actions to see in every case that their reason, incorruptible and self-constrained, in every action holds up the maxim of the will [*Willens*], to the pure will [*Willen*], i.e., *to itself regarded as a priori practical.*"[15]

Thus Kant can say that the law and the conditions necessary for obedience to it—the spontaneity of Willkür—have one common source, a source which his predecessors did not discover and of which they hardly even felt the need. His predecessors, therefore, were never able to translate their formalistic ontological ethic into a practical doctrine without destroying either the formality of their ontological principle or the purity of the conception of the moral law. All too often, in their ignorance, they did both.

The central point of the Kantian philosophy was anticipated only by Rousseau. It is so essential in the philosophy of Kant that I propose to call it, by analogy to the "Copernican revolution," the "Rousseauistic revolution" in moral philosophy. Rousseau said simply: We are not obligated to obey any law in whose establishment we have not participated. Obligation to any other law is slavery, and obedience to it can be obtained only by a system of reward and punishment in which there is no place for dignity; but obedience to a law one gives oneself is freedom. Others saw in law only a restriction on freedom, a restriction no doubt necessary, but all the same a restriction. Rousseau said: Valid law is an expression of freedom. Kant suggests: "Moral law is nothing else than the self-consciousness of pure practical reason, and is thus equivalent to freedom."[16]

While Rousseau established the essential connection between law and freedom primarily in the political sphere, where his doctrine was adopted with little change by Kant, the doctrine of autonomous government by free citizens of a republic is deepened by Kant into a moral, metaphysical, and even religious conception. Precisely because he developed this doctrine in his theoretical ethics more than Rousseau did, we are in a better position to clarify his political doctrines than we are to clarify those of Rousseau. We can easily see how diverse political views, often imputed to Rousseau and even occasionally to Kant, can be explained, or reconciled, or refuted by turning to the fundamental differences in the two conceptions of will in the principal ethical writings of Kant.

For though it is not hard to find in reading Rousseau an ideology for anarchy or for fascism, it is not so easy to consider Kant under either aspect (though some efforts have been made in these directions). The reply to such efforts is to recall the specific senses of freedom or liberty as related to his two conceptions of will.

The specific question is, Can the human will be at once spontaneous, obedient, and autonomous? These prima facie incompatible attributes can belong to it, if Kant is right. They must belong to it if he is correct, since each involves the others. But if spontaneity and obedience to law are taken in superficial forms, or if obedience and liberty as political concepts are taken in a superficial form, paradoxes can be found in Kant's ethical theory and in his social and political teachings that are exactly parallel to those that have been found, perhaps with more warrant, in Rousseau's. There are three.

1. Kant is individualistic in his ethics and in his political doctrines. But the moral person is only an abstraction for him, a bearer of a formal potential good will, which is supposed to dominate the concrete individual person who, in his specific characteristics, is the locus of moral and political freedom. Hence Kant's individualism is empty; all right and obligation are universal, and all individuals are conceived as so abstractly equal not only in rights but also in obligations that no social system could be made with them.

2. Kant is universalistic in his ethics and in his political doctrines. But the universalism is formal and empty; for the locus of freedom and responsibility lies in the legislation of the individual, and the social and universalistic aspect of morality is left ungrounded, since the latter is necessarily an outward restriction on inward spontaneity and individual freedom.

3. Kant is libertarian and individualistic in his ethical theory, but in order to give form and substance to the social and political dimension of morality, he provides a doctrine of obedience at all costs that is the political opposite of freedom and individualism. The "liberty" he espouses is in actuality that of an army or totalitarian state, not of individuals.

Quite apart from the fact that the objections to Kant expressed in the first two points are incompatible with each other, and that the one cancels the other out—the third being a kind of synthesis of the first two—it is possible to show that none of them is valid. Each arises from a misinterpretation of the conception of will, and associated with this are errors of interpretation of the concepts of autonomy, obedience, and spontaneity.

Each of these criticisms, if fully expanded, would entail the supposition that in Kant's doctrines there are two wills, externally related and necessarily opposed to each other, so that the perfection of one is the ruin of the other. Which paradox is drawn depends upon the critic's belief concerning which conception is the more important to Kant (which happens, of course, to be the one less important to the critic, for such are the ways of philosophical dialectic).

If the Wille of pure practical reason as an abstract epistemic or moral concept is so emphasized that it is made to do the job of execution as well as legislation, being interpreted as fully determining the action to be undertaken, the individual Willkür is restricted and is not free. Thus we have the first paradox. This is perhaps the most common criticism of Kant, and the basis of the charge that there is in his philosophy no place for casuistry and hence no legitimation for a realistic political theory. Recent studies of the casuistic elements in Kant's ethical writings suffice to show that this criticism is not well founded historically.[17]

If, on the other hand, the maxim is thought of as issuing from the individual's private and unique Willkür, it is not possible to see how the maxims decreed will meet the requirements of social uniformity and harmony or how, indeed, they could make any claim to be binding upon others.[18] Hence arises the second paradox, which the romanticists exploited in their use of Kant in their moral and political theory—to whom Kant replied in advance in his *What Is Orientation in Thinking?*

Finally, if the Wille is given an institutionalized form and expression, say in the state, and the Willkür is left with power but no authority, it is something to be thwarted and tamed or eradicated, and there results the tyranny of "Prussianism."[19] This is thought to be realistic, political application of the third paradox, which separates the individual-moral from the social-political elements of the first two.

But the answer to all of them is that there are not two wills. There is one will, with its formal universal condition, which is universally valid practical reason, and with its material condition, which depends upon the specific involvement of the individual in the peculiar circumstances of his world at this time and place. Without the former, there is no law; without the latter, there is no deed. The former is the Kantian equivalent of Rousseau's *volonté générale;* the latter is the ingredient in the *volonté des tous* of Rousseau. But whereas Rousseau taught that the former could be determined in fact only by a vote of the latter, Kant thought it could be approached through a regression upon the conditions of the latter, upon the conditions that give to the latter whatever degree of freedom and spontaneity it can possess.

The alleged paradoxes are not so much paradoxes of an inherent dualism in Kant's ethics as they are manifestations of a paradoxical predicament of human life itself. We find in ourselves individualized manifestations of universal mandates and injunctions. Man is the only being in the world that can get entangled in these paradoxes, with all the horror they bring and all the heroism they demand. For man is the only being in the world who is a citizen of two worlds, subject to both psychological explanation and moral exhortation, and the only being in the world who is torn between the roles of spectator and actor. Man alone can issue, recognize, obey, disobey (and not merely illustrate or fail to illustrate) laws. If he were a beast, he could neither create nor obey laws; were he a god, he could create them without having to obey; were he a slave, he would have to obey but could not create laws. But the human being is, for good or evil, neither beast nor slave nor God.[20]

Had the Kantian teaching avoided either of the first two paradoxes by really separating the will into two faculties, it would have been less responsive and faithful to the fatefully paradoxical aspect of human life itself, for it would have edged man a little nearer to being a slave (paradoxes 1 and 3) or a god (paradox 2).

The greatest error possible in the interpretation of Kant—an error so great that it must seem to be politically or ideologically motivated—is that which leads to the third of the paradoxes. According to this, Kant esteemed obedience so highly that neither moral nor political freedom could exist as more than polite names for obedience to tyranny; and such a doctrine does not stop, any more than the historical impulse it represents, with making people slaves; it regards them as beasts in the mechanism of nature, which may of course include the arbitrary edicts and powers of tyrants.

Fortunately, this greatest error is the easiest to refute. This error not only separates one will into two but locates each in a different person (or institution), each of which is in conflict with the other. The end result is that rights are ascribed to one, and only the duty to obey is ascribed to the other. But if the Kantian answer to the first two criticisms is subtle and must be ferreted out, the answer to the third is clear and forceful in Kant's own words and does not require a reconstruction or reinterpretation of the texts in the light of the distinction between two meanings of the concept of will and freedom. For Kant says: "With regard to the most sublime reason in the world that I can think of with the exception of God—say, the great Aeon—when I do my duty in my post as he does in his, there is no reason under the law of equality why obedience to duty should fall only to me and the right to command only to him."[21] Accordingly, Kant quotes with approval (but with a certain arch cynicism, too) the apothegm of Frederick the Great that he was the servant of his people.[22]

This pretended separation of rights from duties, of obligation-creation from obligation-execution, ignores the fact that all moral discipline is self-discipline, from which it follows that all just government is self-government. By virtue of the same faculty in its legislative and executive functions, its formal and its material conditions, an individual is at the same time the subject and the sovereign both in the realm of ends and in the just political state. Kant's doctrine of man in the state, therefore, does not hold that he can be or ever should become merely an abstract citizen, participating abstractly and uniformly in a volonté générale; nor does it hold that the individual is and must necessarily remain an animal to be tamed only by police machinery working for an alien law. With Rousseau, Kant finds man the citizen as the a priori condition of man as exercising all his spontaneous capacities against the merely natural, that is, the nonpolitical and the nonmoral, mechanism of life.

That this is the proper Kantian order of political and moral concepts is shown clearly in Kant's essays on the philosophy of history and in his conception of the moral commonwealth (the Church invisible) in his book on religion. In each case, the first step of mankind from barbarism to morality is the step into civil society, in which man the animal is tamed into man the citizen, in a state in which virtue can be slowly developed out of its social and political counterfeits. Only along this path does the free Willkür develop out of the arbitrium brutum, and finally the maxim of pure practical reason becomes the determinant of action.

Notes

1
This was pointed out, and its importance emphasized, by Victor Delbos, *La philosophie pratique de Kant,* 2d ed. (Paris: Alcan, 1926), p. 455.

2
"The faculty of desire which operates under concepts, in so far as the principle which determines it to action is in itself and not drawn from objects, is called the faculty of arbitrarily doing or refraining. As related to the consciousness of the power to act to produce the object, it is called *Willkür. . . .* The faculty of desire of which the internal principle of determination resides in the reason of the subject is called *Wille. . . .* [The latter] is practical reason itself" (*Metaphysics of Morals,* Academy ed., 6:213). All references to the Academy edition are to *Kants gesammelte Schriften* (Berlin, 1902–). On the difficulties of translating these words, see my note in *Critique of Practical Reason* trans. Lewis White Beck (Indianapolis: Library of Liberal Arts, 1956), p. 177. (I wish now to call attention to the review of this book by John R. Silber in *Ethics* 73:1979–97, the second part of which is a scholarly study of *Wille* and *Willkür.*) The best effort to clarify the relations and remove the paradoxes involved in the distinction is to be found in H. H. Hudson's "*Wille, Willkür,* and the Imputability of Immoral Actions," *Kant-Studien* 82 (1991): 179–96.

3
Critique of Practical Reason, Academy ed., 5:32; trans. Beck, p. 32.

4
Foundations, Academy ed., 4:412.

5
Critique of Practical Reason, Academy ed., 5:60.

6
Inaugural Dissertation, §§5, 6.

7
On this use of the word *condition,* see my *Commentary on Kant's* Critique of Practical Reason (Chicago: University of Chicago Press, 1960), p. 81.

8
Critique of Practical Reason, Academy ed., 5:34.

9
Metaphysics of Morals, Academy ed., 6:226.

10
Critique of Practical Reason, Academy ed., 5:29.

11
Critique of Pure Reason, Academy ed., A534/B562.

12
Ibid., A803/B831.

13
Metaphysics of Morals, Academy ed., 6:226.

14
Critique of Practical Reason, Academy ed., 5:33; *Metaphysics of Morals,* 6:213–14.

15
Critique of Practical Reason, Academy ed., 5:32; trans. Beck, p. 32; emphasis added. It would have been preferable to have said *Willkür* for *Wille* for pure will.

16

Critique of Practical Reason, Academy ed., 5:29; trans. Beck, p. 29.

17

See, for example, W. I. Matson, "Kant as Casuist," *Journal of Philosophy* 51 (1954): 855–60; H. J. Paton, "Kant on Friendship," *Proceedings of the British Academy* 42 (1956): 45–66; Fr. Marty, "La typique du jugement pratique pur, la morale kantienne et son application aux cas particuliers," *Archives de philosophie* (1935), no. 1, pp. 56–87; my "Apodictic Imperatives," in L. W. Beck, *Studies in the Philosophy of Kant* (Indianapolis: Bobbs-Merrill, 1965), pp. 177–99; and Mary Gregor, *The Laws of Freedom* (Oxford: Blackwell, 1963).

18

This is the criticism in George Santayana's intemperate book, *Egotism in German Philosophy,* 2d ed. (New York: Charles Scribner's Sons, 1940), pp. 50–51.

19

This criticism is stated but not wholly endorsed by John Dewey in *German Philosophy and Politics.* But Dewey did argue that "Prussianism" could arise from Kantianism because "the two worlds of Kant were too far away from each other" and could be connected only through the idealistic theory of history and the state—a theory with totalitarian political consequences.

20

Metaphysics of Morals, Academy ed., 6:241.

21

Perpetual Peace, Academy ed., 8:350n.; trans. L. W. Beck, "Library of Liberal Arts," no. 54 (New York: Liberal Arts Press, 1957), pp. 11–12n. God only is excepted because he is under no law (in the form of an imperative). That is, there is no obligation for God as a holy will. But the same moral law is perfectly manifested in God's holiness and imperfectly manifested in our virtue.

22

Ibid., 8:352; trans. Beck, p. 14.

Chapter 3

Kant on "Natural Rights"

Mary Gregor

kant distinguishes b|w "will and willkür. The obligons has wille; the obligatus willkür.

In "Kant's Two Conceptions of the Will in Their Political Context," Lewis White Beck notes that it is only in the *Metaphysics of Morals* that Kant, with an appropriate terminology, distinguishes between the will as *Willkür,* which I shall call the capacity for choice or simply choice, and as *Wille,* the will.[1] What this distinction provides is a much-needed refinement of the concept of obligation and with it the concept of freedom, which Kant had called "the keystone" of his philosophic system (5:3).[2] As he points out in *The Metaphysics of Morals,* the concept of obligation involves two terms: an obligating subject, constraining someone to comply with a law, and an obligated subject, constrained to comply with that law (6:417). The first is a person regarded as having a will, the second, the same person regarded as having a capacity for free choice. How man's free choice is to be characterized remains to be seen; but this distinction seems admirably suited to the concept of obligation as it is developed, in the *Groundwork of the Metaphysics of Morals,* from the concept of a morally good action, and to the system of distinctively ethical duties presented in Part 2 of *The Metaphysics of Morals, The Doctrine of Virtue.*

Kant distinguishes ... will ...

As Beck observes, however, *The Metaphysics of Morals* is not without its difficulties. Its two parts, *The Doctrine of Right* and *The Doctrine of Virtue,* are distinguished in terms of two kinds of lawgiving, which Kant calls "juridical" or "external" and "ethical" or "internal." What distinguishes them is the incentive that the lawgiver connects with the law in order to constrain someone to comply with it. The concept of ethical obligation need not detain us at present: it is the concept, referred to in the preceding paragraph, of man constraining himself to act through the thought of duty, and it gives rise to a class of duties that Kant calls "duties of virtue." But the sort of constraint involved in juridical legislation is problematic. First, the incentive by which a legislator constrains the subject is drawn from the subject's "inclinations and aversions, and among these, from his aversions" to the disagreeable consequences of breaking the law (6:219). Second, in giving positive laws a legislator constrains the subject to do what he could not know, but for this enactment of law, ought to be done: the legislator is the "author of the law" and binds those subject to it "by his mere choice" (6:224, 227). Duties prescribed by such laws are duties to which there correspond rights on the part of another, ultimately on the part of the legislator, and a right may be defined alternatively as a capacity to put another under obligation or as an authorization to use coercion (6:231). Kant adds, significantly, that a system of positive laws would presuppose a natural law establishing the authority of the legislator to bind others by his mere choice (6:227). *The Doctrine of Right* is an account of this "natural law" by virtue of which a legislator can impose such obligation, thereby making it possible for persons to acquire rights. The account is not without its difficulties. In this chapter I shall consider how Kant's understanding of the relation between the will and the capacity for choice involved in the concept of obligation distinguishes him from his predecessors in the "natural law" and "natural rights" tradition.

Kant's work in political philosophy falls into two categories: his popular "political essays" and his formal and systematic account of the moral principles having to do with rights in *The Doctrine of Right*.[3] The advantage of approaching Kant's political philosophy through *The Doctrine of Right* is that we may expect to find it integrated with the enterprise he began in the *Groundwork* and carried through over a period of some twelve years. At the beginning of his mature work in moral philosophy Kant specified the three main tasks of a moral philosopher as (1) to set forth clearly and to establish the supreme principle of morality, (2) to carry out the full critical examination of practical reason required to secure this principle, and (3) to apply this principle to obtain the whole system of human duties. These tasks correspond roughly to Kant's three major works in moral philosophy, the *Groundwork,* the *Critique of Practical Reason,* and *The Metaphysics of Morals.* In the *Groundwork* Kant's treatment of the subject put under obligation was unsatisfactory, a deficiency he began to remedy in the second *Critique.* In *The Metaphysics of Morals* he was able to give an account of what his political essays simply assumed, that the legislator in a civil society is authorized to give positive laws.

The disadvantage of approaching Kant's political philosophy through *The Doctrine of Right* is that the whole enterprise, as Kant sees it, depends on his distinction between empirical principles and concepts, derived from experience, and "pure" principles and concepts having their source in reason alone. What leads to civil society is the principle that it must be possible for someone to acquire a right, that is, to put oneself in "intelligible" or merely rational possession of an external object of one's choice.

The theme of Kant's preface to the *Groundwork*—repeated at every opportunity in his other two major works—is the absolute necessity of pure moral philosophy in order to account for the moral principles and concepts present obscurely in "the most common human reason" or, as Beck puts it, in "common sense moral knowledge."[4] Among these concepts Kant singles out obligation as one that cannot be accounted for by philosophers who never inquire into the source of moral concepts, whether they are derived from experience of human nature or from reason alone (4:391). Having analyzed the concept of a morally good human action as one done not from any incentive based on the inclinations belonging to human nature, which can be known only empirically, but from the thought of duty, he returns to the theme of the preface in his criticism of attempts on the part of "popular" philosophers to deal with morality. What they present as the basis of moral laws is "now the special determination of human nature . . . , now perfection, now happiness, here moral feeling, there fear of God, a bit of this and also a bit of that in a marvellous mixture"; but they never come to terms with moral concepts because they never think to ask whether the principles of morality are to be sought at all in knowledge of human nature or whether they are to be found "altogether *a priori,* solely in pure rational concepts" (4:410). Subsequently, having arrived by further analysis at the unconditional character of the constraint or necessitation involved in the concept of duty—having, that is, clarified the commonsense concept of obligation—he classifies all "spurious" principles of morality as requiring the will to "go out of itself," to some object already desired, in search of its principle (4:441), whereas obligation involves instead "the relation of a will to itself so far as it determines itself only by reason" (4:427) and so independently of any incentive known only by experience. This "relation of a will to itself" will eventually become the relation of the will to the capacity for choice.

The force of these texts is that analysis of any moral concept discloses its a priori source, and that a philosopher who has not distinguished two radically different kinds of concept is bound to distort the moral concepts that are present in commonsense knowledge of morality because they are inherent in the structure of pure practical reason itself.[5] Such a philosopher will begin, quite properly, with the commonsense knowledge that one ought, for example, to keep one's promises or be helpful to others. These are duties prescribed by moral laws having empirical content. As a philosopher he will attempt to do what common sense does not do, namely, to conceive abstractly the principle underlying such duties. But he will be unable to sort out, in these applied moral laws, what is contributed by experience and what is contributed by reason quite independently of experience. Hence he will look to experience for the basis of the underlying principle itself and thereby "spoil" the sound but unanalyzed concept of obligation present in commonsense moral knowledge.

To approach Kant's political philosophy through *The Doctrine of Right* is therefore to examine it in his own terms. His political thought, with its emphasis on the rights of man, has had a very broad appeal among philosophers who want nothing to do with his theory of knowledge. But a right is, Kant holds, a capacity to put another under obligation, and his theory of rights is dependent upon his analysis of obligation. He was not, of course, the first to attempt a systematic treatment of rights. In the seventeenth century Hugo Grotius and Samuel Pufendorf had tried to work out comprehensive theories of rights based ultimately on the "natural rights" human beings have in accordance with "the law of nature." Though they were not the "popular moral philosophers" Kant had in mind, and though they did not so much "spoil" the commonsense knowledge of obligation as, respectively, evade it or concede defeat, Kant's own theory of rights may be profitably viewed as an attempt to rescue that area of moral philosophy from philosophers who never inquire into the source of our moral concepts.[6]

My assertion that Grotius evaded the concept of obligation was made from a Kantian perspective and should be qualified. *Obligation* can be used to express two closely related concepts: an action that is objectively necessary for an agent who will not necessarily do it, and constraint or necessitation upon the agent to do it. Such an action can be called "obligatory" or "an obligation" (or a duty),[7] and the agent must, in principle, be aware of obligation or motivated to do it (such constraint need not, of course, be effective: in Grotius's phrase, a law can "fail in its outward effect"). From Grotius's Prolegomena to *The Law of War and Peace* and scattered texts within the work it seems possible to put together an account of obligation when the word is used to signify a duty.[8] But as for moral constraint that would yield commonsense knowledge of obligation, Grotius is an exercise in frustration. Perhaps through Hobbes, Pufendorf had become acutely aware of the problem, but his account of constraint to comply with the law of nature, in terms of divine sanctions, proved unsatisfactory even to him. Since all obligation, for both Grotius and Pufendorf, is ultimately derivative from obligation by the law of nature, their accounts of "natural rights" become equally problematic. From a Kantian perspective, the whole endeavor might well be considered a lesson in the futility of trying to account for obligation without distinguishing rational from empirical concepts.

The "law of nature" with which Grotius is concerned is the law arising from human nature, from man's rationality and sociableness (*appetitus societatis*).[9] Man's rationality, by virtue of which he is "capable of law" in the relevant sense of the word, consists in his capacity to know and to apply general principles; his sociability, in his "impelling desire for the social life—not of any and every sort, but peaceful, and organized according to the measure of his intelligence" (p. 11) and in his disposition to do good to others as well as to himself. The general principles that man is capable of knowing and acting upon are based on his sociableness, which, by default of any other conative capacity in his nature, must be assumed to provide his motivation to act in accordance with the law of nature.[10] How we know that sociableness belongs essentially to human nature Grotius does not discuss explicitly, but we can apparently begin with observation of human beings, grasp the tendencies essential to human nature, and then determine what condition would fulfill those tendencies in order to know what sort of thing they ought or ought not to do.[11]

For Grotius, the main division of law is that into (human or divine) volitional law, which has its source in "the will" (p. 44), and the law of nature. Volitional law (*jus voluntarium*) is positive law. Discussing the distinction between the law of nature and divine volitional law, Grotius notes that in the second case an act is right, just, or lawful (*justum*)—that is, due, or required by law (*jure debitum*)—because God has willed that it be done, whereas in the first case God wills that an act be done because it is right (p. 45). The first characteristic of volitional law is, then, the intrinsic contingency of what is prescribed or forbidden; what makes a law volitional is not someone's willing that it be complied with but its proceeding from someone's "free" will. The second—though Grotius is less clear about this—is its being connected with sanctions that the legislator provides in order to secure compliance with it. In both respects the law of nature differs from volitional law; actions in accord with the law of nature are required in themselves, and it is not essential that the law of nature be connected with sanctions. But it is difficult to find texts in which Grotius deals with obligation in the sense of constraint.

Some things, he notes, are such that any deviation from the law of nature is wrong; with regard to other things the law of nature is silent, and such things are called "permissions" (p. 38). Yet the performance or omission of what is permitted by "the first principles of nature" may be "honorable" or "praiseworthy," and one way of doing what is permitted may be better than another. Both divine and human laws tend to require what is praiseworthy, making it due or obligatory (p. 52). Such passages are informative as to what is required by law but not about constraint to comply with it.[12]

In one text, however, it is difficult not to think in terms of the constraint accompanying laws. Having distinguished two senses of the word *jus* he introduces a third, *jus* in its broadest sense, "a rule of moral actions imposing obligation [*obligans*] to what is right." Law in this sense extends to whatever is right, not merely to what is "just" in the strict or proper sense. Immediately after the definition quoted Grotius adds: "we have need of obligation [*obligationem requirimus*]; for counsels and instructions of every sort, which enjoin what is honorable [*honestas*] indeed but do not impose obligation, do not come under the term" law (*legis aut juris*) (p. 38).[13] The distinction between giving counsel and giving law to someone is (at least after Kant) that in the former case one assumes that someone being counseled has an incentive, without the counselor doing anything to produce one, so that the counselor leaves the other at liberty to accept or reject the advice. In giving a law, on the other hand, one provides an incentive to obey the law. Perhaps this is, at least in part, what Grotius has in mind. If so, what is not clear is the source of constraint to comply with law.

The law of nature had long been invoked to support and to set limits upon the use of coercion by civil authorities, that is, to determine how civil laws can be obligatory and when they are not binding in conscience. Grotius extends this appeal to a higher norm into relations among heads of states, as an appeal to the *jus gentium* or customary applications of the law of nature common to most nations in their external affairs. Though both municipal law and the jus gentium are human law, all obligation is ultimately derivative in some way from the law of nature. The question as to how the law of nature brings obligation with it had been discussed by the scholastics. Is it a divine command? If so (and if the question of motivation is raised), how does it constrain us if not by means of divine sanctions? Grotius's contemporary John Selden declared that "the idea of a law carrying obligation irrespective of any punishment annexed to the violation of it . . . is no more comprehensible to the human mind than the idea of a father without a child."[14] Grotius apparently found the idea quite comprehensible. What he found incomprehensible is that the law of nature could be divine volitional law, subject to change.[15] But what precisely Grotius thought God has to do with obligation in accordance with the law of nature is controversial. One interpretation would bring him so close to the problem of constraint that his failure to deal with it would suggest that, despite his distinction between law and counsel, his conceptual framework could not admit commonsense knowledge of obligation.

Grotius readily grants that the law of nature, proceeding as it does from internal principles in man, can be attributed to God as the author of nature and in this sense "may be called divine" (pp. 14, 45). He grants too that God wills that we act in accordance with the law of nature. "The law of nature is a dictate of right reason which points out that an act, according as it is or is not in conformity with rational nature, has in it . . . moral baseness or moral necessity; and that, in consequence, such an act is either forbidden or enjoined by the author of nature, God" (pp. 38–39). Since the acts "in regard to which such a dictate exists are, in themselves, either required [*debiti*] or not permissible," "it is understood that necessarily they are enjoined or forbidden by God" (p. 39). The force of such texts might be only to distinguish the law of nature from divine volitional law. In an often-cited passage, however, Grotius seems to go further. After giving his account of "sociability" as the source of the law of nature properly so called, that is, as having to do with what is right or just in the narrower sense of "leaving to another that which belongs to him, or in fulfilling our obligation to him" (p. 13), he adds that "what we have been saying would have a degree of validity [*locum aliquem*] even if we should concede . . . that there is no God, or that the affairs of men are of no concern to Him" (p. 13).

Debate about this passage has centered on whether Grotius is to be called a rational secularist, that is, whether he intended to account for obligation through the essential traits of human nature apart from any reference to the divine will. In his well-documented exposition of the texts just cited, Charles Edwards suggests that Grotius may expect his readers to be aware of the medieval debate between rationalists and voluntarists and of Suarez's median position, which Grotius himself adopted.[16] In his gloss of Grotius's phrase "a degree of validity," Edwards takes him to be asserting that obligation to comply with the law of nature has a dual character: as indicating what is good or evil the law of nature contains its own principle of obligation, and as grounded in the will of God it also contains an "absolute precept" or command. Demonstration that an action is in accord with human nature would provide only a partial account of obligation; one could know by reason what actions are morally necessary or impossible. A full account would require an action's accord with human nature to be an indication of the divine will. Such an account of the obligatory character of actions by the law of nature is suggestive in two respects. First, it would suggest that Grotius, like Suarez, anticipates Hume's view that reason is impotent. Something other than reason—namely, desire or the will—is necessary to move someone to act in accord with reason's dictates or judgments. In the case of laws, the will of a superior is required to move the will of a subject to comply with the law.[17] Second, it could be taken as expressing an incipient awareness that obligation cannot be got from what Kant would call a "counsel of prudence" or a hypothetical imperative. Something more than the tendencies present in human nature seems to be required, some "absolute command" to fulfill those tendencies. But Grotius does not pursue the implications of such a command and, in effect, gives no account of constraint to do what is objectively necessary by the law of nature.

He recognizes, of course, that human beings may not comply with the law of nature. Since a law without sanctions "fails of its outward effect," God has given volitional laws to instruct those of "feebler reasoning powers" and to control "our more violent impulses" (*impetus*) more effectively (p. 14). In revealing his will he promised rewards to those who keep his laws and threatened to punish those who do not (p. 45). One would think that even an individual whose reason is competent and who is not affected by violent impulses might sometimes have to be constrained to comply with the law of nature. Grotius does note that "in God injustice finds an enemy, justice a protector. He reserves His judgments for the life after this, yet in such a way that He often causes their effects to become manifest even in this life, as history teaches by numerous examples" (p. 17). But this observation occurs in the general context of Grotius's explanation that, while the law of nature "has the reinforcement of expediency" (*utilitas*), obligation to obey it is not based on expediency. He apparently wants to account for obligation without reference to sanctions, but as to the source of such constraint he is uninformative. He may find it obvious that, once reason points out what is required to maintain and augment the social order, man's "impelling desire" for this sort of social life provides all the motivation that is needed. "Even if no advantage [*utilitas*] were to be contemplated from the keeping of the law, it would be a mark of wisdom . . . to be drawn towards that to which we feel that our nature leads" (p. 16).[18] Perhaps this feeling provides constraint upon our impulses and could be effective if they are not too violent.

If the concept of obligation is elusive in Grotius, so too must be that of a right. The difficulty is further compounded if, as Karl Olivecrona argues, "the definition of a right given by Grotius is not adequate."[19] On the one hand *jus* in the sense of a right signifies merely "what is just" (*quod justum est*) and has the negative sense of "what is not unjust" (*quod injustum non est*) or not in conflict with the nature of society of beings endowed with reason (p. 34).[20] Here the notion seems to be that in accordance with the law of nature one has a right to do what does not injure another. In another sense, different from this but derived from it, a right is "a moral quality of a person" by which he is capable (*competens*) of having or doing something justly (*juste*) (p. 35).[21] When this quality is "perfect" it is called a "faculty," and faculties are the concern of "expletive" justice (*justitia expletrix*) or justice strictly and properly so called. When the quality is "imperfect" it is called an "aptitude," a "worthiness" on someone's part to be treated in a certain way (p. 36), and aptitudes are the concern of "attributive [*attributrix*] justice" or justice is a broader sense. Apart from reference to a moral quality or faculty, it is not clear how saying that someone has a right in this derivative sense differs from saying that it would be right for him to have or to do something.

A right in the positive sense of a moral quality, however, functions as a moral power that someone has acquired over the will of another by the other's express or tacit consent. Apart from any such transactions, each has moral power (*potestas*) over "what is his" (*suum*), which includes his life, limbs, and liberty; moreover, the first to take possession of things can extend what is his, since he has a right (in the nonderivative sense) to use them and to consume what he needs (p. 54). Since it would be wrong or unjust for anyone to encroach upon what is his, he can rightly use force to defend it (p. 400). But his right to do so does not involve a moral quality or faculty that he has acquired. For this it is necessary that others transfer to him a part of what is theirs, that is, control over their actions. In this way he extends what is his to include moral power over others' actions and, indirectly, over things. It is then right for him to force others to do what he could not rightly demand that they do had they not transferred to him a part of what was theirs. Because of the power each originally has over his own actions, all rights in this derivative sense must in some way be introduced by concurring acts of will, by which one party transfers to the other some nonderivative right he has (pp. 329, 331).

Rights, in both senses of the word, involve its being right or just for the possessor of the right to use force (pp. 40, 179).[22] Those against whom someone has a right are under obligation by the law of nature, and they may be under obligation to do something apart from any demand actually made by the other (p. 321). Although Grotius has a theory of how rights can be acquired in accordance with the law of nature, he has done little to clarify the concept of obligation through the law of nature. As we have seen, he is unwilling to resort to sanctions connected with it. Pufendorf found it necessary to take that route.

The fact that Hobbes intervened between Grotius and Pufendorf no doubt sharpened the latter's awareness of the difficulties involved in Grotius's account of obligation. Pufendorf takes at its face value Grotius's assertion to the effect that the law of nature would have some place even should no provident God exist (p. 215). Even if Grotius's position were more subtle, requiring a divine command behind the law of nature, sanctions would not enter into his definition of it. Pufendorf's own position is that (1) a law is a "decree," (2) it involves "power" on the part of the lawgiver, to make the subject recognize that he must adapt himself to it (p. 89), and (3) mere power is not enough to account for the obligation a law imposes: "to force [*cogere*] a person, and to obligate [*obligare*] him, are very different things" (p. 96). The former can be done by natural strength alone, but not the latter.

A law in general, according to Pufendorf, may best be defined as a "decree by which a superior obligates a subject to adapt his actions to the former's command" (p. 89). The law of nature is the divine decree, which for us is a command, made known "by the intrinsic suggestion of one's inner light." Given the wisdom and benevolence of the creator, we can see, first, that we are subject to the law of nature; because man's will is free—that is, "not restrained intrinsically to a definite, fixed and invariably mode of acting" (p. 54)—and because an unlimited liberty would be disadvantageous (*inutilem*) to the nature of man, "it is conducive to his welfare" (*salutem*) for him to be constrained by laws (p. 145). To obtain the content of the law of nature we consider what would be advantageous for beings of our nature, who need the help of others to look after their own interest and that of the people whose interest is bound up with their own (pp. 205–08): first to live in society and hence to "cultivate and preserve toward others a sociable attitude," and so not only to refrain from hurting others but to confer benefits on them; to cultivate our mind and body so as to be able better to further their interests; and so forth (pp. 346ff.). These "dictates of reason" are known by consulting "the common nature" of all human beings and considering what its wise and benevolent creator intends man to do (p. 214). But if the dictates of reason are to have the force of laws, "it is necessary to presuppose the existence of God and His providence, whereby all things are governed, and primarily mankind" (p. 215). Since "law necessarily presupposes a superior," Grotius was wrong to say that the law of nature would hold even should no provident God exist.

*Pufendorf → Obligation
↳ Coercion*

But Pufendorf has his own difficulties.[23] The most serious of them, from a Kantian perspective, arises from his attempt to distinguish obligation from mere coercion. Although sanctions are necessary if a dictate of reason is to impose obligation or have the force of law, Pufendorf is quite clear that there is a sharp distinction between mere force and obligation. "An obligation is properly laid on the mind of man by a superior, that is, by one who has both the strength to threaten some evil against those who resist him, and just reasons why he can demand that the liberty of our will be limited at his pleasure" (*ex suo arbitrio*). For then, once he has signified what good awaits those who obey his will and what evil those who resist it, "there must necessarily arise in the faculty of reason a fear mingled with reverence, a fear occasioned by such a person's power, and a reverence arising from a consideration of the causes [or reasons], which should be sufficient, even without the fear, to lead one to receive the command on grounds of good judgment [*per modum consilii*] alone" (p. 95).

Neither "excellence of nature" alone nor power alone is sufficient to impose obligation, "that whereby one is required, under moral necessity to do, or omit, or suffer something" (p. 20). Speaking of both natural obligation and civil obligation, insofar as civil laws are not contrary to the laws of nature, Pufendorf notes that "both obligations agree in this respect, that a man should do, of his own accord and by an intrinsic motive [*motu*], the things which they demand of him. This forms the main difference between obligation and compulsion, since in the latter the mind is forced to do something by mere external violence contrary to its intrinsic inclination, while whatever we do from an obligation is understood to come from an intrinsic impulse [*motu*] of the mind, and with the full approbation of its own judgment" (p. 386). While an obligation "contains a force [*momentum*] sufficient to change the will," and so a threat of evil, it differs from coercion or compulsion in that "the latter only shakes the will with an external force" while an obligation, in addition, forces one to acknowledge that the evil is visited upon him deservedly (p. 91).

Although Pufendorf has given a clear account of the constraint involved in the concept of obligation, he would seem to have taken back with one hand what he gave with the other. For if "the mind" can and should be moved to comply with the law of nature merely by an "intrinsic motive," its recognition of "a just reason,"[24] it would seem that sanctions are—to borrow Grotius's phrase—necessary only to give the law its outward effect, not to constitute obligation itself. But Pufendorf then "spoils" the concept of obligation by reducing this "just reason" to considerations of what would be advantageous to beings with a nature like ours.

As for "a right" (*jus*) in the sense of a moral quality, Pufendorf on the whole elaborates upon and clarifies Grotius's concept. A right is a faculty or power to do something, but not a "natural faculty."[25] A right is rather a faculty by virtue of which some moral effect is brought about in beings of the same nature, the effect being an ion on their part (p. 391). "A right indicates that a thing has been lawfully [acquired] acquired and is lawfully now retained" (p. 19), that is, that in accordance with the law of nature obligation is imposed on others. What Pufendorf suggests is that there are two orders, the physical and the moral, and that in accordance with a "law of nature" that supervenes upon physical nature, the volitions involved in physical actions can produce moral effects, obligations on the part of others. A perfect right (or "power") is "that which can be exercised by force against those who unlawfully endeavor to oppose it" (p. 18); "but the reason why some things are due us perfectly and others imperfectly" is that some of the rules of natural law "conduce to the mere existence [*ad esse*] of society, others to an improved existence [*ad bene esse*]" (p. 118). A perfect right involves its being permissible to use force, but whether or not one may use force to ensure performance of an obligation is, apparently, a matter of the degree of importance of this obligation to the social life that would be advantageous to beings with a human nature.

A thorough study of natural law and natural rights in Grotius and in Pufendorf, and of the relations between them and Kant, is long overdue. Whether Grotius, unlike Pufendorf, was consciously attempting to separate his theory of (perfect) rights from his theory of "the good" or whether he sees respect for rights as obviously part of the organized and peaceful social life toward which human nature tends would have to be decided by a careful study of his amorphous text. For our purposes, however, the question is whether either Grotius or Pufendorf had the conceptual resources to deal with what they were trying to express. If Grotius might have seemed confused about the difference between a descriptive law and a prescriptive law, Pufendorf brought the distinction into relief. Grotius, he noted, should not have presupposed the existence of things noble or base in themselves, before a law, and a law is "imposition," the bidding of a superior (pp. 90, 26). Yet Pufendorf, having accounted for obligation to conform with the law of nature in terms of divine sanctions, suggested that we can and should obey it without regard for them. Since obligation to comply with civil laws and the jus gentium is derived ultimately from obligation to comply with the law of nature, and sanctions are in the end unsatisfactory, the concept of obligation as such is still problematic.

The source of the difficulty, as Kant would see it, is that both Grotius and Pufendorf tried to base "the law of nature" on experience of the tendencies in human nature and hence could get no further than counsels of prudence. Grotius was aware that moral laws are not counsels of prudence in the ordinary sense, but he did ultimately base moral law on a natural tendency, sociability. Pufendorf took a rather different view of human nature and derived the content of the law of nature from it; but he saw that human nature could not yield a law and turned to divine sanctions to provide the binding force of a law. In so doing he used the broader concept of a rational being having a sensible nature and hence an aversion to pain. But a mere "threat of evil" cannot account for obligation. As Pufendorf noted, if such a threat is removed, so too is any motive for obedience. It remains to be seen whether the concept of obligation, apparently familiar to commonsense moral knowledge but recalcitrant to analysis, will yield to Kant's methods.[26]

Experience, Kant maintains, cannot give rise to a law in the sense of a proposition that is strictly universal as distinguished from merely general. Though natural scientists may get along with generalizations based upon experience, it is different with moral laws. "They hold as laws only in so far as they can be seen to have an *a priori* basis and to be necessary" (6:215).[27] Experience, whether of the garden variety or as systematized in anthropology, can inform us about the drives and tendencies present in mankind and how human beings generally have found satisfaction. But such knowledge can be the basis only for counsels of prudence. These may advise us that it would probably not be in the interest of long-term natural desires to satisfy a given inclination, but they must allow for exceptions and leave us at liberty to accept or reject them at our own risk. "But it is different with the teachings of morality. They command for everyone, without taking account of his inclinations, merely because and in so far as he is free and has practical reason" (6:216)—in other words, they bring obligation with them.

Given Kant's distinction between empirical and rational concepts, we may summarize his position in relation to his predecessors. As prescriptive laws concerning not what happens but what ought to happen, moral laws are not "laws of nature" describing how human nature functions but laws having their source in some will. As laws holding for everyone,[28] addressed to an agent who does not necessarily comply with them, they are commands, but commands that neither threaten nor promise anything, since this would again make them conditional. What Pufendorf was groping toward in his distinction between coercion and obligation is that we can be constrained to act or refrain from acting merely by considering whether an action is just or right. But if moral laws are to hold for everyone, this quality of "rightness" cannot consist in what would be fitting or advantageous to "human nature." It must rather consist in its conformity with the principle of rationality as such, that of objective validity or holding for everyone.[29] But this is to say that reason, far from having to rely on man's inclinations for an incentive to determine him to action, itself provides an incentive that may well be opposed to these. And this sort of constraint exercised by his reason upon himself as affected by inclinations is what a person of common sense calls obligation. It is what he means when he says "I ought to keep my promise, and to help others when I can, regardless of whether it is in my short-term or even my long-term interests."

Moral laws have their sources in someone's will; but because moral laws bring obligation with them, they cannot have their source in a will external to the agent, which has to rely on sanctions to constrain him to obey. What analysis of the concept of obligation requires is a new conception of a will that can be the source of moral laws. A noncontroversial definition of a will might be formulated as "the capacity to act according to the conception of laws, i.e., according to principles," which capacity only a rational being has (4:412). But this leaves open the possibility that a will is merely a kind of natural cause determined by psychological events: experience of inclination for an object could determine the will, the function of reason being merely to conceive the desired object and discover the means to produce it.[30] If we are under obligation, the will must still exercise its causality or produce an action in accordance with a law; as Hume had pointed out, unless volition takes place in accordance with a law it would be a matter of chance, for which the agent could not be held responsible.[31] Hence it is not enough merely to say that the will is not determined by preceding events in an agent's mental history: one must specify the law of its activity. This can be done for a will that is under obligation. The law in question is not a law of nature, in accordance with which an external cause produces a change in something else. Instead, reason can determine actions in accordance with its own principle; it can produce actions, in accordance with moral laws, by an incentive arising from reason itself, the thought that the principle of the action could hold for everyone.[32] What is required to account for an agent's being under obligation is "the capacity of pure reason to be of itself practical" (6:214). But this is to say that reason is lawgiving, imposing obligation without having to rely on fear of punishment.

There remains to be considered man as the subject put under obligation. In the *Groundwork* Kant presented his distinction between heteronomous volition and autonomous volition, determined by the thought of the law, with some hesitation. Taken out of context, some of his assertions about "heteronomy of the will," its determination by "alien" causes, might suggest determination by natural causes and raise the question "Is only the good will free?"[33] and, if so, how can we be responsible for our morally bad actions? More generally, the subject put under obligation must be both capable of being constrained to act by the thought of the law and affected by inclinations that would require such constraint. It is not "the will" as lawgiving that fulfills these qualifications. Kant begins his introduction to *The Metaphysics of Morals* by attending to this neglected aspect of willing an action, by virtue of which he can speak of "practical reason putting itself under obligation" (6:440).

The first section of his general introduction to both *The Doctrine of Right* and *The Doctrine of Virtue* considers what mental capacities man must have in order to be subject to moral laws. Having defined, not a will, but a capacity for desire (*Begehrungsvermögen*) as "the capacity of a being to be by means of its representations the cause of the objects of these representations," he adds that if the representations are concepts, the being is said to have a capacity for choice (*Willkür*).[34] He then goes on to discuss the sort of capacity for desire present in man that makes moral laws applicable to him. Within it he distinguishes two functions, that of "the will," which is the source of laws or objective principles of action, and that of the capacity for free choice, which is the source of maxims or subjective principles of action (6:226). The freedom of man's capacity for choice is first characterized negatively as its independence from being determined by incentives arising from his sensible nature; this is a negative concept because it says only that the causal law to which his choice is subject is not a law of nature. The positive concept of freedom is said to be "the capacity of pure reason to be of itself practical," which is possible only by an agent's subjecting a maxim he proposes to adopt to the test of whether it could qualify as a universal law. Kant then indicates that only by this procedure, in which the formal principle of the will acquires empirical content, can pure reason become practical or determine choice: "For as pure reason applied to choice irrespective of objects of choice, it does not have within it the matter of the law; so, as a capacity for principles (here practical principles, hence a lawgiving capacity), there is nothing it can make the supreme law and determining ground of choice except the form, the fitness of maxims of choice to be universal law" (6:214).

Kant sometimes uses *object* in the sense of *end* and at other times in the sense of something, such as a thing, that can be used as a means to achieving an end. The former sense is prominent in *The Doctrine of Virtue,* the latter in *The Doctrine of Right.* Since he has not yet distinguished between these two divisions of a metaphysics of morals, *object* is presumably to be taken in a broad sense that would include both ends and what is used as a means to an end. As "the will," practical reason abstracts from any content supplied by the capacity for choice and gives only the formal principle "so act that your maxim could become a universal law." Through the application of this principle to the capacity for choice we obtain moral laws prescribing what ends are to be adopted and how objects are to be used. We begin, as he has said, with a maxim we propose to adopt and submit it to the test of whether it qualifies for being given as a universal law. Apart from moral laws, all ends would be adopted on the basis of our inclinations; man is a being with needs that give rise to inclinations or habitual desires he wants to satisfy. We then ask, as Kant sometimes puts it, whether the will "contains a law" for a maxim of, for example, never helping others or never exerting oneself to develop one's capacities and talents. If the maxim cannot qualify, the will does contain a law prescribing the duty of including the happiness of others or one's own perfection among one's ends. The formal principle of the will, applied to the capacity of choice *in concreto,* yields moral laws having empirical content. It is still a "pure will" because the incentive it furnishes to the capacity for choice is the thought of this formal principle. Kant's basis for distinguishing the two parts of a metaphysics of morals, however, relegates the sort of duty just exemplified, that of adopting an end, to ethics or *The Doctrine of Virtue.*

 As for this division of a metaphysics of morals, "the act of free choice as such" is, Kant says, the highest concept in such a system of duties (6:218n). What this act is he eventually specifies as the act of setting any end whatever for oneself, which is an act of freedom on the subject's part, not an operation of nature (6:392). Setting an end for oneself, as distinguished from pursuing an end set for one by nature, is what distinguishes a free action from animal behavior, even from the behavior of an animal endowed with a theoretical capacity to conceive this end and discover the causal laws of nature by which to produce it. It may be that the basis on which an agent sets an end for himself is his experience of inclination for the object or condition he envisages; a human being's capacity for free choice "can be affected but not determined" by impulses arising from his sensible nature, and "is therefore of itself (apart from an acquired aptitude of reason [virtue]) not pure but can still be determined to actions by pure will" (6:213). To the extent that the agent adopts his ends merely on the basis of his inclinations, he has not achieved a state of "inner freedom" by complying with what ethical laws require of him. Even so, he sets his ends for himself.

The Doctrine of Right is concerned with man's "outer freedom"; this is freedom in the "external" exercise of his capacity for free choice, external in the sense of manifesting itself in physical actions affecting other people's actions. This must be so if the division of duties is made on the basis of whether moral laws can be given only in internal lawgiving or can also be given externally. External lawgiving, it will be recalled, joins with a law an incentive other than the thought of duty, an incentive drawn from an agent's natural aversions. But, Kant maintains, while I can be constrained by another through natural means to perform an action, I cannot be so constrained to adopt an end: "To have an end that I have not myself made an end is self-contradictory, an act of freedom which is yet not free"; "coercion to ends (to have them) is self-contradictory" (6:381). Kant's essential point would seem to be that it is conceptually possible for someone to be constrained through fear to perform an action, but not to set an end for himself.[35]

The Doctrine of Right is "the sum of laws for which an external lawgiving is possible" (6:229). In it one must, therefore, disregard what ends persons may have set for themselves and consider only their external actions toward those ends. In terms of laws for everyone's external use of his freedom, an action is right if it leaves all others who can be affected by it free to act in pursuit of whatever ends they have set for themselves. Given that a man's capacity for choice is affected by sensible impulses, he may attempt to coerce others to perform actions that are not means to their own ends but only to his, or to refrain from acting even though they are not preventing him from acting toward his end. Such coercion is wrong, an obstacle to a condition or state of outer freedom. Hence coercion that counteracts it is compatible with external laws, or right (6:230–31). Since one is authorized to do what is right, and since it is right to use coercion in keeping with a universal law for the external use of free choice, one has a right or an authorization to use coercion in keeping with such a law (6:232). Although Kant has good reason for not drawing the conclusion at this point, he could easily infer that a condition of outer freedom requires an external lawgiver. It is instructive to consider why he does not.

From what has been said about external lawgiving, it is clear that the body of laws that comprise jus or Right cannot require an agent to adopt any maxim; it is assumed that he has a maxim, and all that is required is that, whatever the maxim, it not issue in actions that would interfere with a condition of outer freedom (6:232, 382). Kant elaborates on this point. "The concept of duty stands in immediate relation to a *law* (even if I abstract from all ends . . .). The formal principle of duty, in the categorical imperative 'so act that the maxim of your action could become a universal *law*,' already indicates this. Ethics adds only that this principle is to be thought as the law of *your* own will and not of will in general, which could also be the will of others" (6:389). The principle expressed in the preceding paragraph as the criterion of right action, the "universal principle of Right," is simply the formal principle of the will within the context of external laws.[36] Hence an agent is aware of obligation, constraint by his own reason, to bring his actions into conformity with this principle. He can make it "not only the rule but also the incentive of his actions" (6:392). Since, within the context of *The Doctrine of Right,* no appeal can be made to an agent's consciousness of obligation, the lawgiver provides another source of constraint. But in terms of this principle alone, there would seem to be no difficulty in reconciling Kant's assertion that "laws proceed from the will" with their being given externally. What is required for obligation is constraint upon an agent's choice to conform with the principle of the will. If his incentive for complying with it is taken into account, such constraint is called "ethical obligation," self-constraint through the thought that his maxim could hold for everyone. If no account is taken of his incentive, the constraint is called simply "obligation." In very broad outline, this is the basis on which Kant can define a right alternatively as an authorization to use coercion or as a capacity to put another under obligation.

From the concept of a right, together with that of "humanity as an end in itself," Kant immediately concludes that human beings, merely by virtue of their humanity, have one and only one innate right (6:237–38).[37] All other rights must be acquired by acts of choice. This one nonacquired right is the right to freedom, which includes the right to equality, to be one's own master (*sui juris*), and so forth. It will be noted that nothing has been said, as yet, about the natural law establishing the authority of a legislator to bind others by his mere choice, that is, to enact positive laws. If Kant were to argue directly from man's innate right to freedom to the need for civil society, it is difficult to see why there would have to be contingent or positive laws, the content of which is chosen by the legislator. Since the innate right to freedom is only a right to freedom of action, an external lawgiver would be needed to provide an incentive deterring people from acts of violence against one another; but that human beings ought not to use violence on one another could be known apart from any enacted law forbidding it.

But the beginning of Kant's Introduction to *The Doctrine of Right* was cited above in a truncated form. Having defined a doctrine of Right as "the sum of laws for which an external lawgiving is possible," he adds that if such laws have actually been given it is a doctrine of positive Right, the concern of jurists. Otherwise it is the doctrine of natural Right, the concern of metaphysicians, which provides the immutable principles for any giving of positive law. The sum of principles having to do with how people can acquire rights by acts of choice, the subject of "Private Right with regard to External Objects," is what establishes the authority of a legislator to bind others by laws that must be promulgated because they cannot otherwise be known. What was lacking in Kant's political essays was an account of how one can acquire rights. There civil society was said to be based on three a priori principles: man's freedom as a human being, his equality as a subject, and his independence as a citizen.[38] The second and third of these are not identical with the rights said, in *The Doctrine of Right*, to be included in his innate right to freedom. There has been a leap from the state of nature to the civil condition that needs to be accounted for, an argument which Kant was perhaps not prepared to give before *The Doctrine of Right*. There his argument to civil society is from the conditions essential for acquiring rights by acts of choice; what is lacking in a state of nature in this respect makes positive laws necessary.

The crucial first part of *The Doctrine of Right*, "Private Right," is unfortunately a very cryptic argument deeply embedded in the context of Kant's critical philosophy. Since I have discussed it elsewhere,[39] I shall attempt only to outline its main steps (6:245–57) and to elaborate on the role played in it by Kant's distinction between the will and the capacity for choice.

In the "universal principle of Right," Kant enunciated the formal principle in accordance with which any external exercise of free choice will be right. But this principle is only a formal criterion of action, the principle of the will "applied to the capacity for choice without regard for objects of choice." In order to derive from the will substantial moral laws, he considers the content of maxims insofar as this is relevant to the external exercise of free choice. The first step might seem to be a very cautious one. Kant notes that someone's maxim of acting for an end he has adopted involves his intention of using objects to achieve his end, and Kant examines the concept of an object of choice as such. This, he suggests, is simply the concept of something that could be used, of that which someone could put to some use. The question then arises whether the will contains a law for the capacity for choice with regard to its objects, that is, whether it is possible, in keeping with the universal criterion for right actions, for someone to make use of what is usable. The will, Kant points out, can give no law absolutely forbidding such use; that would be to suppose that our free choice is limited by its objects rather than merely by its own formal principle. The will must, instead, contain a permissive law, enabling someone to put to use any object of his choice subject to the condition that his maxim is consistent with the criterion of right action. Given this condition, it is right for someone to make use of objects, and he has a right to prevent others from interfering with his use of them. The objective condition of using them is compatibility with the universal principle of Right. The subjective condition of using them is possessing or having them. Hence it must be possible for someone or other to possess any object of choice under the objective condition mentioned.

This argument is on such a high level of abstraction that it may not be clear what has been accomplished. By considering an object of choice as such, apart from any additional features it may have, what Kant claims to have established is that it could be right for someone to exclude others coercively from using an object whether or not he possesses it physically. The concept of an object of choice as such is merely that of "the usable," what someone has the physical capacity to use. Like the ends a human agent adopts, the objects he uses to attain them are in space and time, and his acts of choice are temporal acts performed by someone in a certain region of space. But if an agent possesses an object physically—if, for example, he is holding an apple in his hand—his connection with the object is such that anyone who uses it without his consent violates his innate right to freedom of action. He has, however, the physical capacity to use objects not connected with him in this way: he can, for example, use a field to grow crops regardless of whether he is physically present on it. What Kant has argued is that he could rightly coerce others to refrain from using an object even though their use of it, involving their physical possession of it, would not violate his innate right to freedom. The condition under which he can be in "merely rightful" possession of it, or have a right to it, is that his maxim of excluding them coercively from using it conforms with the principle of the will.

Before considering how this conformity can be brought about, so that someone can acquire any right at all, we may note that objects of choice have features other than their location in space and time that are relevant to their being used conformably with the universal principle of Right. One can make some use of a thing, of another's capacity for choice, and of another person. A thing, something usable that is without the capacity for free choice, may be owned or disposed of as one pleases (provided the use to which one puts it does not violate others' rights); another's capacity for free choice may be put only to a use he has consented to; and while a right to a person has something in common with a right to a thing—namely, that it is a right against everyone rather than against a specific person—the "right of humanity" in that person limits the way in which the object may be used. Consideration of these additional features of an "object of choice" gives rise to the three divisions of "Private Right," the principles of property rights, contractual rights, and domestic rights. How specific Kant's *Doctrine of Right* (the full title of which is *Metaphysical First Principles of the Doctrine of Right*) can become is determined by considerations of what can be known a priori, once these features of objects of choice are specified.[40] Given a maxim of using a certain kind of object of choice, we ask whether the will "contains a law" for such a maxim and in this way develop the system of substantive moral principles to which any giving of positive law is to conform.

To return, however, to the problem of how anyone can acquire a right at all: the difficulty is that he has to bring an object of his choice "under his control" by an act of choice to exclude others coercively from using it. Apart from his act of choice, others would have a right to use it, included in their innate right to freedom of action. He must, therefore, impose on them a "contingent" obligation. His act of choice is a necessary condition for imposing such obligation. But it cannot be a sufficient condition. Laws are objective principles holding for everyone, and obligation is constraint joined with a law. An individual's maxims, the subjective principles on which he acts, come from his sensibly affected capacity for choice and do not of themselves conform with the criterion of Right. It cannot be assumed that someone regards his maxim of taking an object under his control as one on which everyone may act, that in forbidding others to use that object he intends not to use objects they have taken under their control. Yet he can assert a right to an object, or claim to put others under a contingent obligation, only by acknowledging that he is bound to extend to others the capacity to impose obligation that he claims for himself. Having presented the problem—namely, that (a) it must be possible for someone to possess any object of his choice merely by right, while (b) such possession would involve putting others under obligation by a mere act of choice and therefore seems to be impossible—Kant offers his solution. "Now a unilateral will cannot serve as a coercive law for everyone with regard to possession that is external and therefore contingent, since that would infringe upon freedom in accordance with universal laws. So it is only a will putting everyone under obligation, hence only a collective general (common) and powerful will, that can provide everyone this assurance" (6:255–56).[41]

This is to say that people can acquire rights to objects only if they are subject to public laws having to do with how possession is to be acquired and exercised. Their maxims of taking control of objects will then have been brought under laws proceeding from the will of an external lawgiver. But the existence of such a will is what distinguishes the civil condition from a state of nature. Hence it is only within civil society that one can have acquired rights, that is, possess objects merely by right, independently of one's physical possession of them. Thus the command to quit the state of nature and enter civil society is the "natural law"—the law that can be known a priori to be binding—that establishes the authority of an external lawgiver.

According to *The Doctrine of Right,* what makes it morally necessary for people to live in civil society is that only in this way can they acquire the rights that we know a priori they must be able to acquire. The legislator in a civil society must enact laws prescribing what its members have to do in order to acquire definite property, contractual, and domestic rights and securing the rights they have acquired. Two elements are involved in this legislation, as in any giving of law: a law and constraint connected with the law. The second element is perhaps more familiar in accounts of Kant's political philosophy, namely, that in a state of nature there is no one with adequate power to guarantee rights. But rights cannot be guaranteed unless they are determined. As Kant points out, in a state of nature everyone proceeds according to his concepts of rights, and when a dispute arises about what someone has acquired there can be no judge with authority to settle such a dispute, for a judge would have to decide according to his own concepts of rights instead of basing the decision on public laws binding on both parties to the dispute (6:312).[42] There is a gulf to be bridged between metaphysical first principles of Right and laws sufficiently definite to allow disputes about rights to be settled. Hence the "natural law" to live in a civil society involves the authority of a legislator to enact positive laws or bind others by laws the content of which he has chosen. Kant is not particularly concerned with how this gulf is to be bridged: he refers occasionally to custom. His concern is, rather, to specify the high-level principles on which the contingent and chosen enactments of a legislator must be based if people's acts of choice to acquire rights are to conform with the highest-level principle of the will expressed in the universal principle of Right.

What, then, are natural rights for Kant? They are not rights people can acquire in a state of nature, since there are no such rights. Prior to civil society or in abstraction from it, one can be in "provisionally rightful" possession of objects of choice, in accordance with the "Idea" of a will enacting public laws. By this Kant seems to mean that if someone is willing to live in civil society while others are not, he is entitled to coerce them to enter civil society and, in the meantime, to defend by force what he thinks he has acquired. What can be known a priori about such possession and how it is acquired is, Kant holds, contained in his discussion of private Right. The first section of "Public Right" deals essentially with the way in which a state is to be organized so that what can be acquired according to principles of private Right will be determined and secured. Natural Right is the a priori knowable provisions of a constitution, which may not be violated by whatever statutory provisions are added on the basis of experience (6:306). According to principles of natural Right, people have or can acquire rights that may not be infringed upon by laws the content of which is chosen. But there must be such statutory provisions if a civil society is to fulfill its function of enabling people to acquire rights.

Kant's final reflections on the concept of obligation, then, account for it in terms of a will that is pure and a capacity for free choice that, though affected by inclinations, is never determined by them and can be determined by the will. That laws proceed from the will and maxims from the capacity for choice implies that constraint exercised upon choice in accordance with a moral law will be obligation, whether such constraint is exercised only by one's own will, through the thought of the lawfulness of one's maxim, or also by another. Through maxims the principle of the will acquires content, and at some point the empirical content required for external laws is such that a legislator must choose what laws to enact. But what makes them moral laws is not their content but the principle on which they are based. This arises from man's freedom, not from any tendencies observed in human nature. Whether people tend to be sociable or not, whether they are well-disposed or ill-disposed toward one another (6:312), relations of right come into play when the freedom of one can affect the freedom of others. It may well be that human beings want and need to live in society and that this may be advantageous to beings having a human nature. But the relevant consideration is that, whatever human beings may want or need, they cannot avoid interacting with one another. As for what force, coercion, or sanctions can have to do with obligation, Kant argues that such constraint connected with laws derived from the principle of the will is a sufficient condition for bringing everyone's external exercise of free choice under laws, and hence a necessary condition of anyone's acquiring a right.

Notes

1
Although my chapter builds on the distinction as presented by Beck, both in chap. 2 above and in *A Commentary on Kant's* Critique of Practical Reason (Chicago: University of Chicago Press, 1960, pp. 177ff.), he is of course not responsible for the use I have made of it.

2
All references to Kant's works are to the volume and page number of *Kants gesammelte Schriften*, the edition published by the Prussian Academy of the Sciences (Berlin, 1902–). Most translations now give the Academy pagination.

3
On the difference between the continental philosophers' approach to political philosophy through law and the broader approach favored in English-speaking countries, see Ernest Barker's introduction to his translation of Otto Gierke's *Natural Law and the Theory of Society, 1500–1800* (Boston: Beacon, 1957), pp. xvii ff.

4

As Beck points out, *common sense* is not to be taken as a technical term but as signifying "what everyone knows about morality." *Kant: Selections* (New York: Macmillan, 1988), p. 248n.

5

For Kant, analysis of concepts cannot establish their objective reality; it cannot show that there is anything corresponding to them. When the concepts are a priori, a "deduction" is required to justify our use of them. In this chapter I shall not attempt to deal with Kant's deduction, as distinguished from analysis, of the basic moral concepts. In *The Doctrine of Right* he bases his key postulate regarding rights on "a fact of reason," which, he adds parenthetically, is "the categorical imperative" (6:252; see also 232).

6

Although Kant lectured some twelve times on *Naturrecht,* his explicit references to Grotius and Pufendorf are rare; e.g., they are mentioned briefly in *Perpetual Peace* (8:355) and in his "Review of Gottlieb Hüfeland's Investigation of the Basic Principle of Natural Right" (8:125). Two passages on contracts (19:542, *Reflexion* #7874, and 23:264) are said by the editor of vol. 23 to have their source in Pufendorf's *De officio hominis et civis.* For a list of works on *Naturrecht* that would have been available to Kant, see Simone Goyard-Fabré, *Kant et le problème du droit* (Paris: Vrin, 1975).

7

Having drawn the distinction between duty and obligation, Kant himself sometimes speaks of duties as obligations.

8

In the following paragraphs page number references are, for Grotius, to *De Jure Belli ac Pacis Libri Tres,* vol. 2, trans. Francis W. Kelsey (Oxford: Clarendon Press, 1925) and, for Pufendorf, to *De Jure Naturae et Gentium Libri Octo,* vol. 2, trans. C. H. Oldfather and W. A. Oldfather (Oxford: Clarendon Press, 1934). I have occasionally modified the translations. Because of its multiple meanings (a body of laws, right or just or lawful, and a right), the Latin *jus* (or *ius*) presents the same problems of translation as does the German *Recht.* In discussing Kant's position I have adopted the convention of translating *Recht* as *Right* when it is used in the sense of a system of laws. I am indebted to Jerome K. Schneewind's "Pufendorf's Place in the History of Ethics," *Synthese* 72 (1987): 123–55 and to a series of lectures on early modern moral philosophy that he kindly made available.

9

Grotius finds it unprofitable to distinguish between a "law of nature" for nonrational animals and a *jus gentium* in the sense of a law of nature for human beings (p. 41). The jus gentium is, for him, a division of human law (see below).

10

Reason would be "practical" in determining an individual to follow the bent of his human nature toward sociability. If, as Knud Haakonssen maintains ("Hugo Grotius and the History of Political Thought," *Political Theory* 13 [1985]: 242), "the *socialitas* to which we are bound by the law of nature is for Grotius merely respecting another's rights, subjectively conceived," it is difficult to see what account of motivation, and hence of obligation, Grotius could possibly provide.

11

How far Grotius is removed from Kant's position on the source of moral laws may be gathered from his account of how one proves a priori, and hence with absolute assurance, that something is in accordance with the law of nature, namely, by "demonstrating the necessary agreement or disagreement of anything with a rational and social nature" (p. 42). Proof a posteriori consists in consulting what more civilized nations believe to be in accordance with the law of nature.

12

On the whole, the law of nature "has the force of law" in the sphere of what Grotius calls "expletive justice," which consists in not encroaching upon what belongs to others. There are, however, exceptions. "The law of nature, insofar as it has the force of law, holds in view not only the dictates of expletive justice . . . but also actions exemplifying other virtues, such as self-mastery, bravery, and prudence, as under certain circumstances not merely honorable, but even obligatory. And to such actions we are constrained by regard for others" (p. 176).

13

As an example of a law imposing an obligation to do what is honorable Grotius mentions a law imposing a penalty on a man who drinks wine against the orders of a doctor. The example is apparently intended to indicate that "law" in this sense extends beyond "justice." But this would seem to be a volitional law, with regard to which "obligation" as constraint can be easily, if not satisfactorily, accounted for. In *Hugo Grotius: The Miracle of Holland* (Chicago: Nelson-Hall, 1981) Charles S. Edwards comments on the text quoted above: "the sense of obligation was necessary, for only by fulfilling the obligation could a person feel that he was acting justly" (p. 53). His reference may be to Grotius's mention of the peace or "torments and agonies" of conscience, which show that "law, even though without a sanction, is not entirely void of effect" (p. 16). For Kant's view of this refined form of eudaemonism, see 6:377–78.

14

Cited by Richard Tuck, *Natural Rights Theories* (Cambridge: Cambridge University Press, 1979), p. 91.

15

The law of nature is dependent upon God's "free" will only in the sense that he need not have created beings having a rational and social nature; given that he did create them, he could no more change the law of nature than he could make the sum of two and two more or less than four (p. 40).

16

Edwards, *Hugo Grotius*, pp. 47ff. Francisco Suarez, *Selections from Three Works*, 2 vols. (Oxford: Clarendon Press, 1944). Vol. 1 contains the Latin texts and vol. 2 contains trans-

lations of them. Suarez discusses the problem at length in *De Legibus, ac Deo Legislatore,* Book 2, chap. 6, "Is the Natural Law in Truth Preceptive Divine Law?" Promulgation of the law of nature is by the "natural light" of human reason, which knows not only that certain actions conform or do not conform with the law of nature but also that they are pleasing or displeasing to the author of nature (2:207).

17

According to Pufendorf, the most that Grotius might legitimately say is that actions conflict or conform with human nature, not that they are morally base or necessary (see below).

18

Tuck's suggestion is that Grotius "simply assumed that men want to be responsible and social beings even though they may suffer as individuals for those wants in the short term, and that the law of nature obliges them to follow their natural bent." Because one may suffer in the short term for complying with the law of nature, and because its binding force is independent of punishment, Tuck adds that Grotius "was not putting forward a prudential theory of obligation" (*Natural Rights Theories,* p. 68). For Kant, it would make no sense to speak of a "prudential theory of obligation"; if Grotius's position is basically eudaemonistic, he would not have a theory of obligation at all.

19

Karl Olivecrona, *Law as Fact,* 2d ed. (London: Stevens & Sons, 1971), p. 277; when Grotius calls the right of defense a *facultas moralis* (p. 178), Olivecrona says, he "seems to have got his terminology mixed up" (Law as Fact, p. 293). See also Axel Hägerström, *Recht, Pflicht und bindende Kraft des Vertrages nach römischer und naturrechtlicher Anschauung* (Uppsala, 1965).

20

This definition is negative in a twofold sense, as distinguishing "a right" so defined from a "moral quality" or "faculty" and as distinguishing the sphere of "expletive" from that of "attributive" justice, as discussed below.

21

The relation of these two senses of "a right" to Kant's "innate right" and "acquired rights" (*das innere Meine* and *das aüssere Meine*) is obvious. Although Kant's handling of problems is of course distinctive, the problems themselves correspond, often in detail, to those treated by Grotius and Pufendorf.

22

Other distinguishing features are that not violating another's right consists in not harming him, as distinguished from doing good to him, whereas conduct that is fitting involves such virtues as compassion and generosity (p. 37)—it would be just in the strict and proper sense of the word to exact the last penny of a debt owed by a poor man, but it would not be fitting to do so (p. 759); and the virtues with which attributive justice is concerned come under "the rule of love" as distinguished from the law of justice strictly and properly so called (p. 347).

23

The least of them, from a Kantian perspective, is that while the existence of a provident God can be proved by the light of reason (p. 217), the "natural effects" or "sanctions" of the natural law are sometimes evaded in part, while the immortality of the soul, necessary for rewards and punishments in an afterlife, might require revelation. Hence "we cannot avoid having to confess, that for those who follow the mere light of reason this question is still involved in obscurity" (p. 224).

24

As for this "just reason," Pufendorf suggests that it is consideration of favors already received from God, as well as of his benevolence and ability to take better care of our future than we ourselves can (p. 101). This is consistent with Pufendorf's stress on what Grotius would call expediency. But Pufendorf then asks, if God has given us our freedom, why should he not be able to circumscribe a part of it by his own right (*jure suo*)?

25

Speaking of a right to a thing or a real right, Pufendorf notes that someone's natural power

"takes on the nature of a real right, at the moment when this effect is produced in the rest of mankind, that other men may not hinder him, or compete with him against his will" in using the thing (p. 391). On the moral, as distinguished from physical, entities to which Pufendorf devotes book 1, chap. 1 of *On the Law of Nature and Nations,* see the article by Schneewind referred to above. This seems to anticipate, in the very broadest terms, Kant's account of how rights can be acquired, in chap. 2 of "Private Right," "How to Acquire Something External" (6:258ff.).

26

That "obligation" as unconditional constraint, and hence an unconditional (categorical) imperative, is essential to ethics, let alone philosophy of law, has been challenged from so many quarters that I reserve discussion of this issue for another time. What has been said above, however, should give pause to those who would relegate our use of *obligation* in this sense to the heritage of Christianity. It is not to be assumed that "Christianity," without further interpretation, has the conceptual resources to deal with what Kant regards as commonsense knowledge of obligation.

27

This is presumably "seen," though obscurely, by a man of common sense. The conviction that moral laws are universal and necessary would be implicit in the procedure of testing whether one may act on a proposed maxim that Kant attributes to such a man, who, however, would hardly be able to state explicitly that moral laws must therefore have an a priori basis.

28

With regard to specific moral laws, as distinguished from the moral law itself, we must of course add "to everyone in relevantly similar circumstances." How empirical content for the moral law is obtained is discussed below.

29

To put it somewhat differently, the principle of reason in general is that of consistency or noncontradiction—hence Kant's criterion of whether a maxim can without contradiction be willed as universal law and, since consistency is not an empirical concept, his contention that the thought of the conformity of one's maxim with this criterion is a purely rational incentive. Reason in his more technical sense (as distinguished from the understanding) is involved in obligation as unconditional constraint.

30

"Now man as a *natural being* that has reason (*homo phaenomenon*) can be determined by his reason, as a *cause,* to actions in the sensible world, and so far the concept of obligation does not come into consideration" (6:418).

31

David Hume, *A Treatise of Human Nature,* III, i–ii; *An Enquiry Concerning Human Understanding,* VIII. Since for Hume reason is "impotent" and so-called causal laws are merely observed regular sequences of events, volitions are "caused" in the same way that any other event is caused. "Obligation" is located in the passions or sentiments.

32

More precisely, reason produces an act of free choice. For a detailed discussion of the causality involved, see Ralf Meerbote, "Kant on the Nondeterminate Character of Human Actions," in William L. Harper and Ralf Meerbote, eds., *Kant on Causality, Freedom, and Objectivity* (Minneapolis: University of Minnesota Press, 1984), pp. 138–63.

33

The question is put by H. J. Paton in his classical commentary on the *Groundwork, The Categorical Imperative* (London: Hutchinson's University Library, 1947), p. 213. His reply to the question refers to the distinction between *Willkür* and *Wille* in *The Metaphysics of Morals.*

34

Here (6:213), and occasionally elsewhere, Kant mentions *thierische Willkür* or "brute choice," which would presumably be determined by means of nonconceptual representations. What he is here calling "a capacity for choice" and distinguishing from a capacity for free choice, however, seems to be a "will" as traditionally conceived, which is determined by means of concepts.

35

The conceptual impossibility of being *determined* to set an end for oneself is more obvious; but the same conceptual impossibility applies to an action regarded as free. In one text Kant says that "what essentially distinguishes a duty of virtue from a duty of Right is that external constraint to the latter kind of duty is *morally* possible, whereas the former is based only on free self-constraint" (6:383; emphasis added). Perhaps he has in mind that, given the kind of constraint available to an external lawgiver and the status of his subjects as moral agents, the legislator's principle should not be to help them achieve some end, whether it be happiness or virtue, but rather to prevent their interfering with one another's free actions.

36

So, after defining a person as a subject whose actions can be imputed to him, and hence moral personality as the freedom of a rational being under moral laws, Kant adds: "from this it follows that a person is subject to no other laws than those he gives to himself (either alone or at least along with others)" (6:223).

37

The capacity to set an end for oneself is said to be what distinguishes "humanity" from "animality" (6:392), even, I take it, from a "rational animal" as specified in the text cited in note 30. According to the *Groundwork,* the "subject of all ends" is an "objective end," never to be used merely as a means to his own or another's ends (4:431), and hence, in the present context, not to be coerced to perform actions that are means to another's end but not to his own.

38

"Theory and Practice" (8:290); cf. *Perpetual Peace* (6:349–50). These three principles are listed again in *The Doctrine of Right,* at the beginning of "Public Right" (6:314), but there it has been argued that, in what concerns the duties of citizens to one another, public Right adds nothing to the content of private Right but has to do only with the constitutional arrangements by which citizens can enjoy the rights they can acquire.

39

Mary Gregor, "Kant's Theory of Property," *The Review of Metaphysics* 41 (June 1988): 757–87, and "Kant's Approach to Constitutionalism," in Alan S. Rosenbaum, ed., *Constitutionalism: The Philosophical Dimension* (Westport, Conn: Greenwood Press, 1988), pp. 69–87. Since then, Bernd Ludwig's *Kants Rechtslehre* has appeared (Hamburg: Meiner, 1988). In addition to giving a detailed analysis of Kant's argument, Ludwig provides in his footnotes a convenient summary of the extensive work on the *Rechtslehre* now being done in Germany.

40

In *The Doctrine of Virtue* Kant specifies that his discussion of duties will be limited to the duties incumbent upon human rational agents as such (6:468–69). In *The Doctrine of Right*, however, especially in "Domestic Right," features that do not belong to human beings as such—e.g., sex and age—are relevant. Although Kant states (6:205–06) that he has relegated to "notes" (presumably the indented paragraphs in the Academy text) what belongs to "empirical *Rechtspraxis*" as distinguished from "metaphysics," I would be hard put to state the difference between them. Kant says, however, that his *Doctrine of Right is* the sum

of laws or principles that can be known a priori. Beyond it, there is only positive Right.

41

Compare 6:267, regarding original acquisition of land. It should not be surprising that Kant, having drawn his distinction between *Wille* and *Willkür*, disregards it and often uses *Wille* when *Willkür* is called for. But in crucial passages he seems to make some attempt to abide by the distinction of terms. It is worth noting that in the *Vorarbeiten* to the *Rechtslehre* (23), his preliminary notes for the work, he often speaks of an *allgemeine Willkür,* as he does not in the published work.

42

The problem is, perhaps, most acute in Kant's account of the original acquisition of a definite tract of land, by individuals, tribes, and states, which can take place only in a state of nature (6:261–70). As opposed to a labor theory of original acquisition, Kant's theory of acquisition by an act of choice does not involve making observable changes that would mark out boundaries (6:265, 268–69). As to how much someone can acquire, his reply is, in effect, as much as someone can put to some use and can defend against encroachments by others (6:265). This would seem to be involved in his distinction between choosing and wishing (6:213). In view of the fact that states are still in a state of nature, it would seem to follow that in order for a state to be in even provisionally rightful possession of the land it claims it must be willing to enter into a federation of states.

Chapter 4

The Crisis of the End of
Reason in Kant's Philosophy
and the Remarks *of 1764–1765*

Richard L. Velkley

The dominant interpretations of Kant's project of the "criticism of reason" have been epistemological, metaphysical, and moral or practical. According to these interpretations the function of the Kantian criticism of reason is to lay the transcendental basis for objective knowledge, to secure the valid fulfillment of reason's interest in metaphysical "ideas," and to establish the primacy of pure practical reason over theoretical science. Yet none of these approaches sufficiently addresses the place of Kant's thought within a fundamental complex of problems in modern philosophy focusing upon the question of the "end of reason." These problems are apparent in the first foundational attempts of modern philosophy and remain unresolved there until they give rise to a full crisis of reason in the eighteenth century. The question of the end of reason centers on the status of ultimate purposes or goals that determine the function of science and philosophy (that is, of the new scientific philosophy of man and nature in the seventeenth century) and whether scientific reason itself is able to validate and explicate such purposes.

Kant's position within the history of modern philosophy can be indicated by two changes initiated by his thought. His "criticism" is the first of a number of attempts to secure reason against a possible collapse of confidence in its principles, due to an evident gulf between modern scientific concepts of knowledge on the one hand and ordinary experience, moral consciousness, and the metaphysical demands of reason on the other. The latter three concerns can be placed under the rubric of "reason's need for an account of the ends that govern and make sense of its activity as a whole," that is, teleology in some form as an inescapable need of our reason. [1] Kant was not the first thinker to observe that modern scientific concepts dubiously satisfy that need, but he offered a radically new analysis of the problem and a new solution. Like many later "critics" and defenders of reason, Kant tries to resolve the crisis by a demarcation of the grounds and limits of reason. In Kant's case the defense of reason secures a place for rational morality strictly demarcated from the realm of mere "phenomena" subject to description by science. Therewith Kant believes he guarantees the source both of moral obligation and of teleological principles that satisfy the human striving for an ultimate purposive context.

Thus "criticism" tries to demonstrate how moral reason (based on new "transcendental" principles) alone is capable of determining valid ends, but its demonstration forces us to be resigned to recognizing that the grounds of the moral end-determining use of reason (in freedom) are wholly inaccessible to our understanding. While "objective" and rational, the ultimate ends guiding science and reason are not theoretically cognizable. Therewith Kant set the stage for the debate about the rationality of ultimate ends, and about the relation of scientific knowledge to the realm of "value" or ends, that continues to this day. It can be said safely that Kantian "transcendental" defenses of reason as legislating final goods have not yet successfully staved off the challenges of Nietzsche, Weber, and Heidegger concerning the rationality of "values" and the goodness and justification of reason and science. We are still faced with the questions of whether and how reason can ground ethics (as including the account of ultimate purposive contexts) and whether and how, conversely, reason and science can understand themselves as "grounded" in a moral order of some kind.

The other notable change effected by Kant relates directly to the first. Starting with Kant, moral and political thought ceases to take its bearings by human nature in the determination of the good; the theoretical difficulties of starting from human nature persuade Kant and his successors to turn instead to new notions of freedom, history, or culture for this determination. The purely moral and transcendental in practical reflection must be distinguished from the "anthropological." The latter gives us merely the "is" of an empirical theory, whereas moral and practical life requires an "ought," which must therefore be derived from other sources. One can regard the historicist turn in much post-Kantian thought as the adoption of an alternative to Kant's way of grounding the "ought" in self-legislative reason. That is, history rather than universal reason becomes the source of values that cannot be derived from mere nature. Now, one must ask, what is the common ground of the two Kantian innovations? The curbing of the pretensions of theoretical reason in acquiring knowledge of ultimate ends, and the rejecting of human nature as ground of such knowledge—both arise from the modern crisis of ends. The theoretical and practical aspects of the crisis are very much connected, as are the theoretical and practical aspects of Kant's response to it.

This chapter will sketch in a preliminary way how these changes, which are first clearly visible in Kant's critical system of reason, are aspects of a single response to a crisis of reason, and how principally it was Rousseau who made Kant aware of this crisis and who determined basic features of Kant's response. This will disclose that the most familiar way of thinking about the modern crisis of ends (in terms of whether a science of the "is" can establish goods or the "ought") misses much of the richness of the original Kantian way of seeing the problem, which includes profound Rousseauian reflections on the relation of reason and science to the human good, individual and social.

The chief line of argument can, in very compressed fashion, be stated in advance. Modern philosophy aims at an emancipation of the human species from superhuman authorities both for the sake of a superior theoretical science and for the sake of a more salutary practice. This goal requires modern thought to abjure all claims to know ultimate realities, or wholes; these abjured notions include the human highest good or summum bonum. But the rejecting of such notions entails that reason is only instrumental to prerational or extrarational principles (passion or sentiment), which cannot be validated or justified rationally. Modern philosophy— first clearly in Bacon, Hobbes, and Locke, more subtly in Descartes, Spinoza, and Leibniz, and then blatantly again in Hume—elaborates a view that reason is the servant (or even "slave") of the passions. One can say that in all these thinkers reason and perception are enmeshed in a nexus of appetite and striving for power that determines the direction and the employment of rational methods for the finding of certainty and the advancement of knowledge.

The true destiny of this instrumentalist Enlightenment is, as Rousseau shows Kant, a paradoxical decay of the rational advance of mastery over nature and society into a progressive enslavement of man to his own creations. Freedom, self-rule, and the virtues they presuppose are jeopardized by this development, which can be reversed only if reason asserts (on a novel modern basis) its autonomy and rule over the inclinations. But this requires that reason's telos be redefined. In particular it becomes evident to Rousseau that all hitherto proposed notions of "human nature" must fail to provide any satisfactory telos. Rousseau's awakening Kant to this emergency is the sense of the "Rousseauian revolution" in his thought. Among thinkers influencing Kant, Rousseau has most responsibility for the Kantian effort of saving modern rational emancipation from its self-undermining tendencies in a project of redefining Enlightenment and the forms of reason upon which Enlightenment must rest. Rousseau's thought is thus the principal inspiration for Kant's "theodicy of reason."

It may be useful first to characterize the project of modern philosophy in a bit more detail. One can say that this epoch divides into eras corresponding to three different strategies in the effort to emancipate humanity by means of philosophical doctrine. The founding projects of Bacon and Descartes seek to harness inquiry to the increase of human utility, welfare, and power, in order to liberate humanity from the arbitrariness of the revealed divinity, of nature, and of man. The arbitrariness of the last is evident in the wayward and enthusiastic human striving for first causes that is exploitable by theology.[2] These projects culminate in the rational theologies or "theodicies" of Locke, Spinoza, Newton, and Leibniz that serve the ultimate goal of creating an enlightened and self-ruling humanity. If this first modern era can be called a response to "alienation by God and Nature," it already is, in crucial respects, a self-critique by the human mind of natural tendencies that lead it to false deities and thus to self-alienation. A new concept of nature's "laws," programmatically covering the human and the nonhuman worlds, is proposed as the "practical" antidote to destructive metaphysical and theological tendencies, and as the basis of the theoretically true natural philosophy.

The second modern era begins in the eighteenth century, chiefly with Rousseau and Kant, and can be called the response to "alienation by Nature and Reason." Here the emancipatory effort is directed against the apparently inhuman consequences of the modern account of nature (which has achieved victory over the traditional metaphysics and theology) and at the same time against the very idea of an enduring human nature that human effort cannot alter. This era culminates in the historicist or world-view philosophies and ideologies of Fichte, Hegel, Marx, and Dilthey. These replace "human nature" with new ideals of freedom, history, and culture, and they claim that the true foundation of human self-alienation must be located where the earlier Enlightenment did not locate it: not in the human striving for God or first causes, but in the artifices of our secular reason, which were designed to be the beneficent corrective to that striving. Indeed, "Enlightenment" itself is now the target; the new groundings of emancipation in freedom and history (in their "idealist" and "romanticist" versions) have the central intent of reconciling the modern project with a recovery of lost or neglected experiences of things both divine and human. This second era is one of a troubled yet still hopeful self-critique of reason.

The third era is our own. Initiated by Nietzsche and Heidegger, it is the response to "alienation by Reason and Humanity." It is a critique of the "humanism" present in all earlier philosophy, including the earlier modern eras, but especially in the progressivist historicism of the era just previous. Finding overwhelming the evidence for the failure of the preceding modern eras, it takes the modern effort of emancipation forward to a radical terminus by exposing all notions of mind, reason, and humanity in the ill-fated Western tradition as delusions. The sole task remaining to philosophy (or to the thinking that succeeds "philosophy") is the uncovering of how such delusions emerge mysteriously from the ungroundable realms of the unconscious will, of being as tradition, of language and "textuality." "Reason" as the ideal (or obsession) of our civilization occludes these primary contexts or sources. Thus rationality does not clarify and emancipate; it obscures and tyrannizes over being, resulting in a world demonized by technology and forgetful of the divine.

Although we cannot fully examine here the underlying logic of this development, it is nevertheless possible to point to a persisting structural problem in modern philosophy that overtly and covertly contributes to this "dialectic." This is the fact that after rejecting all classical cosmological or moral-teleological contexts for the use of reason, modern philosophy does not supply an adequate new teleological context for the guidance of its methodological and scientific inquiries. Basic to the method of the new sciences of man and nature is the turn to a self-inspecting ("Archimedean") consciousness or "ego" that discovers in itself primary notions of both mind and body for the grounding of secure sciences of these realities. Yet the turn to the "indubitable" primary data of consciousness (clear and distinct ideas, or immediately evident sensations and impressions) must disavow (or relegate wistfully to future discovery) any knowledge of substantial "wholes," including the wholeness of the human being as the unity of mind and body and as the seat of purposive desiring and acting.[3]

According to the modern account of the scientifically intelligible, the prescientific sense of wholeness and of purpose lacks all scientific status. But while having doubtful rationality, this sense (as "nature's teaching" or "wisdom" about pleasure and pain, good and bad) is the necessary starting point for practical reflection and prudence concerning the uses of scientific reason. Such prescientific notions are thus the primary sources of a telos for the conduct of reason and scientific inquiry.[4] More generally, modern scientific "law" abstracts from all specificity of natures and kinds (for example, the species or form of humanness) and thus from the specific purposes connected with kinds as wholes. But if purposiveness cannot be a theme of modern scientific inquiry, the purposes of such inquiry are themselves merely presupposed and cannot be clarified. The project of science cannot be legitimated by its own organon. Science cannot account rationally for its own goodness.[5] Again this insufficiency of reason as regards its telos is inseparable from the instrumentalist conception of reason's status and function. One might say that this instrumentalism is an intended aspect of a general emancipatory conception of philosophy's goal, but that for many modern thinkers (in some cases the same advocates of instrumentalism) it also poses unintended and unwelcome questions about how well that final goal can be defined and justified.

The difficulty of finding a legitimating teleological context for modern emancipatory thought that would relate the modern principles to rationally justifiable ideas of the good (as the noble, sacred, useful, and beautiful) eventually leads to a crisis in the end of reason. One outcome (the most successful) of the crisis is a turn to "history" in various forms as the ultimate context of contexts. Vico, Hume, Rousseau, Kant, and Herder provide the materials from which Hegel and nineteenth-century thought fashion accounts of the progressive fulfillment of reason in a "logic" of self-creative striving toward the complete autonomy promised by modern science.[6] Much twentieth-century thought has preserved the historical character of the ultimate context while rejecting its progressive, rational, and teleological structure.[7] Yet its rejection of telos is paradoxical since implicitly it still turns to history *for the sake of* a more "radical" justification (or perhaps one should say "proposal") of emancipation. The difficulty faced by the entire modern epoch can be summed up in the statement that the epoch is committed to a human project for which it lacks the necessary guiding knowledge of humanness.

With such reflections in mind I turn to Kant's early formative thinking, which led to his new definition of the modern telos. The age of Rousseau and Kant is the age in which the difficulty of the telos first comes into full view to the leading philosophical minds. This age formulated the new principles of freedom and history that replaced nature in a new humanism, a humanism no longer sustained by the radical emancipatory thought of our age. In what follows I limit myself chiefly to indicating in broad brushstrokes the character of Rousseau's contribution to Kant's "revolution" in defining reason's end.

If a chief task of historical reflection is to reexamine the self-evident, thereby showing that what has become self-evident was not always so, then historical reflection on the sources of Kant's philosophy may usefully call into question some prevailing accounts of its intentions. For the moment let us restrict this observation to the moral philosophy. In the view of many, Kant's account of the moral life in terms of the disinterested agency of autonomous individuals is, one could say, the self-evidently true phenomenology of the grounding experiences of moral life. Yet it is fair to say that in his account of morality Kant is not primarily concerned with such phenomenology. His central motivation for taking up the question of the "foundations" of practical reason is different from this, and it is also different from Aristotle's aim of fully articulating common opinions and experiences relating to the human good, ordering and unifying them, tracing them back to first principles when possible, and in the process, correcting them.

Examination of the "precritical" beginnings of Kant's critical philosophy, especially the *Nachlass* of the 1760s, discloses complex relations among metaphysical, moral, and practical considerations that center upon one issue: the end, or the teleology, of human reason.[8] The Kantian moral philosophy assumes some of its definitive features in this period. One can fully understand these features only by considering how they are shaped by the whole context of questions about reason's end. These early sources reveal a Kant profoundly shaken by awareness of a general crisis in his age, relating to the questions of the end, status, and meaning of reason. Certainly Hume's skeptical paradoxes play a significant role in Kant's awareness of this crisis already in the 1760s.[9] But even more decisive is the insight Kant acquired from reading Rousseau's major works in French as they became available to him in the early and middle 1760s: the two *Discourses, Emile,* and the *Social Contract.*

The record of Kant's intense engagement with these writings is found in the collection of reflections known as *Remarks to the Observations on the Feeling of the Beautiful and Sublime,* which now occupies much of the twentieth volume of the Academy edition. This record marks unmistakably a major revolution in Kant's thinking, a fact readily acknowledged by the handful of scholars who have studied it and searched out its implicit argumentation.[10] In the *Remarks* one sees Kant transforming his conception of the relation of metaphysics and of theory in general to practical philosophy and to human rational striving for the good. In short, one sees emerging in embryo a new conception of reason as a whole, involving a supreme practical telos based on "freedom," which conception eventually develops into the critical account of reason's architectonic.

The new foundations are built upon a prior awareness of fundamental weaknesses in earlier conceptions of the relation of reason to practical life. These conceptions one can call the "Enlightenment" doctrines of that relation, formulated originally in the previous centuries by the major philosophical innovators from Bacon to Leibniz but represented in Kant's own time by moral sense philosophy (Shaftesbury and Hutcheson) and the German "rationalist" successors to Leibniz (Wolff and Mendelssohn). At the time of the *Remarks* Kant arrives at the insight that all earlier modern thought has failed to provide a coherent account of reason's teleology. The weakness that Kant discovers in the modern foundations leads him to believe that his age is one of unprecedented dangers to rationality and humanity. The possibility arises of loss of all faith and confidence in the capacity of reason to guide human affairs. But statements about the "current crisis in learning" in Kant's letters of the 1760s are accompanied by declarations that the present age is one of unprecedented opportunities for philosophy to assert its leadership in human affairs and to "establish the lasting welfare of mankind."[11] Thus Kant supposes that Enlightenment in his time is undergoing a critical test from which it should be able to emerge stronger and victorious.

It is fair to say that both Kant's apprehensions of danger and his expressions of hope derive from his reception of Rousseau's analysis of the modern crisis of reason. All the same it is undeniable that, prior to the great impact of Rousseau, Kant had become aware of the failure of reason to attain its most essential and cherished longings, those for metaphysical knowledge; this awareness remains a component of Kant's account of a general crisis in reason. In 1763 he writes a treatise diagnosing the failure of metaphysics to become a science, and he charges recent thinkers with being seduced by the success of mathematical analysis and synthesis to apply the same mathematical "method" in metaphysics. This is the first statement of the profound Kantian thesis that the "discursive" nature of metaphysical concepts renders them unamenable to the sort of "intuitive" evidentiality that modern analysis tries to ascribe to them.[12] What is more, prior to his decisive

Rousseauian turn, Kant lays the basis for the rejection of *any* speculative determinations of reason's end, that is, of any account of the good as grounded in a theoretically knowable order of first causes or substances.[13]

Thus by 1764 Kant has largely accepted what one can call a modern subjectivist and empiricist critique of the possibility of metaphysics. The treatises of 1762–64 show Kant turning radically and irreversibly toward such a subjectivism in the first principles of both theoretical and practical philosophy.[14] The first principles in both areas are immediate certainties, directly available to the subject or ego upon self-inspection, and not providing insight into first grounds. All the same, such subjectivity is understood by Kant as compatible with a certain logical and intentional "objectivity," even in these early writings.[15] In moral questions, this subjectivism is a version of Shaftesbury and Hutcheson: the immediate certainties of moral sense provide universally effective guidance to all humans in their practical affairs.[16]

The moral subjectivism cannot be confused with hedonism or egoism, for it is attempting to provide an adequate foundation for moral life, preserving its distinctive features without "reductionism." Yet its stress on the accessibility of the primary springs of virtuous action to all human beings, without complex education and habituation and thus without reliance upon authoritative customs and ways of life, points to a feature that "moral sense" shares with its more hedonistic competitor (Hobbes and Locke). Like modern "natural right" theory, moral sense theory seeks to create an enlightened and self-ruling humanity with maximal independence of superhuman powers. Both forms of modern moral thought are skeptical of, if not simply hostile to, classical and premodern attempts to define and prescribe a natural or supernatural supreme end, or summum bonum, for human desiring and rational striving.[17] All such attempts are seen as threats to individual self-rule and to social and political peace as well. Theoretically the creators of doctrines of man's final end are only fishing in muddy metaphysical waters, while practically their speculations aid and abet the purveyors of theological intolerance and discord.

Kant is seemingly satisfied with this edifying version of moral and theoretical subjectivism, which one could call "consoling Enlightenment" (derived in large measure from British sources),[18] until all peace is lost when Rousseau's whirlwind of disturbing questions and paradoxes comes along, tearing off the roof and shattering the foundations (which had indeed evinced a certain softness). Rousseau could accomplish this because his penetrating critique of modernism rests upon an acceptance of most tenets of modernism. Rousseau is the "Newton of the moral world," for his discovery of "order where before only chaos prevailed" does not involve a return to any premodern premises about nature and reason, yet it is a devastating critique of modern nature and reason.[19] Rousseau is as skeptical as Kant, the Newtonian, about "hypotheses" or accounts of first causes. Yet Rousseau espies certain dangers lurking in the explicit or implicit teleology in the "enlightened" accounts of the emancipated moral agent. In fact it is in the area of teleological issues that Rousseau is such a great discoverer and innovator, in Kant's view. Thus Kant can declare that Rousseau has uncovered the "hidden law" of human nature that "justifies providence."[20]

Stated briefly, Rousseau's powerful analysis of the modern effort to emancipate humanity through "applied philosophy" exposes the self-destructive course that the growth or progress of reason will follow when guided only by sentimental or passionate ends (even when such sentiments or ends are moral). Kant had been satisfied with a nonpassionate "sentimental" teleology for emancipation; now Rousseau opens his eyes to an unnoticed "teleological problem" in the modern individualist account of reason. The project of freeing the individual from subordination to alien powers, by placing the ground of his action in his own nature, that is, in a reliable subjectivity, has a paradoxical and unwelcome outcome. When Rousseau brings this problematic to light, he calls into question the whole "instrumental" account of reason that had been basic to the modern relation of theory to practice. The crisis of rational instrumentalism that Kant now experiences not only helps to shape his accounts of freedom, morality, and reason as giver of ends, but it is an indispensable element in what we call the Copernican revolution in the Kantian account of reason as a whole.

The main points of Rousseau's analysis are quite familiar—so familiar that one might fail to appreciate how a reader of Kant's age might be shocked by them. What is more, one might fail to grasp how this analysis might compel a thinker of Kant's stature to reshape his whole conception of reason. The crux of Rousseau's argument can be put simply as follows. Rousseau exposes the presence of a tendency within human rationality toward a self-destructive dialectic in which reason, in the guise of imagination, creates new objects for the desires and passions. These invented ideas of happiness hold out to humanity prospects of greater freedom, mastery, and contentment; in reality they enslave humanity to futile quests for satisfaction.[21] The root of this situation is reason's inventive power, which is in large measure independent of natural determination (in a way that is both a bane to well-being and a source of pride). Human reason is neither a mere servant of fixed and reliable instincts with determinate objects of satisfaction, nor anything like a divine reason that never creates objects or goals that exceed its capacity for adequate conception and realization.[22]

Spontaneously, unconsciously, and unwillfully, human reason proposes to the appetites "ideal objects" that tend to exceed human powers of realization and that are furthermore fluctuating and internally incoherent.[23] There is some possibility of limited mastery of this tendency, or of reducing its destructiveness. But there is no chance of removing it altogether from the human constitution. To be rational is to have a dialectical tendency in which ideal goods exceed acquisitive powers, or in which the desires and passions (modifiable by reason) enslave the human agent. The principal chains they forge are those of amour propre, regard for the opinion of others. Chiefly in pursuit of the charms and satisfactions of "opinion," the rational being has an ineluctable tendency to "live outside himself." He is preoccupied with conventional hopes, fears, anxieties, regrets, loves, and hates that opinion generates, and with imaginary goods belonging to an irretrievable past and to an elusive future that a creature of mere instinct never conceives and hence is never troubled to seek. Prerational beings have no concept of time, mortality, selfhood, and comparative worth; all such concepts express a fundamental and inescapable disunity within the human and rational mode of being.[24]

On the basis of this account of reason, Rousseau is able to assert that modern individualist projects of handing over the guidance of reason to the individual's passions and sentiments are misguided and even dangerous. Modern instrumentalism exacerbates an inherently distressing human situation by proposing as a remedy an unadulterated version of the poison. Rousseau is himself very unsure that there is any true remedy or, at least, any universally effective one.[25] That is, he is doubtful that any human institution can rectify altogether the enormous scope of ills introduced by man and by the development of reason. It is necessary, and yet it is impossible or wildly unlikely, for humanity to seize control of the dynamically explosive processes reason has unleashed—processes wherein rationality, enmeshed in the passions, sweeps most human beings away from a life of simplicity, self-sufficiency, and peace of mind.

Rousseau lacks a doctrine of reason's autonomy, in any form, such as might offer some solution; there is no self-legislative reason independent of the passions. There is only passion that legislates over itself in a "rational" or abstractive mode (the general will), thus palliating to some extent its own destructiveness. Rousseau deplores the instrumentality of reason without offering an alternative to it. This is not inconsistency; it means that Rousseau deplores reason itself, and not just an account of it. Given reason's weakness in the role of master and its diabolical power as unwitting author of passionate projects, most human beings, perhaps all, must be slaves to the passions. The response of Rousseau is familiar: the radical distrust of reason, the longing for near-miraculous escape into states of reverie and detachment, the hypothetical and perhaps fictional prerational condition of nature as the sole occasion on which human beings may have experienced some degree of self-sufficiency and contentment. If Kant is bewildered and repelled by these longings and speculations, as the *Remarks* indicates he is, this does not alter the fact that he clearly sees the implications of the dialectic pointed out by Rousseau, both for human misery and for possible emancipation and enlightenment of a new kind.[26] Like Rousseau, Kant is certain that human reason and the human powers as a whole have no determinate end by nature. Neither thinker admits the possibility of a teleological natural order that might act as guide and limit (with appropriate help from conventions) to the destructive longings and projects of this peculiar species that stands midway, as Kant notes, between the cattle and the angels.[27] Furthermore, neither thinker is willing to abandon the basic modern design of enhancing human freedom and independence of superhuman powers and authorities. Yet they both underscore that the modern striving is jeopardizing its goal: autonomy or self-rule is endangered by every form its pursuit has taken in the past. Therefore autonomy of the modern individualist or subjectivist sort must be based upon a new kind of law, on one that humanity or reason freely imposes on itself.

Such a law, not given by God or nature, is needed to limit and govern the dialectical growth of talents, desires, and luxury, to which Kant gives the name "culture." The modern project of achieving an enlightened culture corresponds to the requirements of human dignity, if that project can be protected from its own self-destructive and alienating tendencies. The stakes are high and do not concern solely the fate of certain theories and projects. If reason strives inherently for freedom, but the striving for freedom is dialectical, then the fate of reason itself is in question.[28] Reason must uncover the sources of, and bring under control, its own dialectic; it must rectify itself to preserve itself. At this moment in history, which is like an "absolute moment," reason's dialectical fate has been exposed, and now its inner structure and law can be discovered. The threat of chaos and collapse is veiling the grandeur of the possible providential justification of reason, now emerging. Shortly after he finds the "hidden law" in Rousseau, Kant begins to develop the science of reason's self-knowledge; philosophy is above all the science determining the end, powers, and limits of reason, for the sake of its own soundness and well-being. The language of the "critique of reason" arises in 1765–66, out of the reflection on "crisis."[29]

Not only the nature of the crisis but also the way to its overcoming are suggested by Rousseau, for he pointed out how a new ordering of the soul and its powers might be found (even if he failed, in Kant's view, to grasp fully his own discovery). This ordering will not take its principle from an authoritative external or natural order, but from the will itself. The will that inflicts evil on itself is the only power that can remove the evil. This is the actual meaning of Rousseau's "hidden law."[30] There are two models in Rousseau for such an overcoming: the logic of self-legislative sovereignty in the *Social Contract*, which would preserve the individual will from self-destruction by its total self-alienation to the general will; and the educational plan of *Emile*, which would preserve something like the original freedom and self-sufficiency of the natural state by the careful directing of the growth of the desires and passions toward salutary objects, and away (to the degree it is possible) from the objects of amour propre.

The second proposal is as important as the first for Kant, as the *Remarks* shows and is generally not known. For *Emile* suggests that human autonomy might be grounded in a comprehensive teleological ordering of the faculties and desires, resolving their natural dialectic and bringing them into coherence and harmony— all without subordination to any "dogmatic" authority. Kant believes Rousseau is saying that a new version of the ancient soul-structure can be created on the basis of modern freedom and emancipated individuality. From this Rousseauian suggestion Kant develops his own comprehensive ordering of reason—his architectonic—in which a new summum bonum is based on freedom rather than nature, human or cosmic. This new highest good guides the postulated convergence (necessarily assumed on rational grounds) of the moral ideal of a self-legislative community of rational beings (the kingdom of ends) with the unfolding of human natural powers in "culture." The latter crucially includes the tasks of theoretical inquiry and the investigation of nature as a teleological system furthering human moral ends, as well as the attainment of moral ends through legal means in the areas of political right and "perpetual peace."[31] The new idea of the highest good is, like the speculative metaphysical ideas that tend to be "dialectical," an idea of totality; but it is one that represents the total nondialectical fulfillment of the demands of reason.

Without regulative guidance from such an ordering teleological idea, supreme within the architectonic legislation of the philosopher over all of reason, the human powers must develop in a chaotic and self-conflicting way in all employments.[32] This is the general problem underlying all the critical inquiries into the grounds of the coherent (nondialectical) operation of reason in its theoretical and practical uses. Thus the Rousseauian account of the source of human problems in reason's self-alienation is the primary basis of the "Copernican" conception of the sources of coherence in the self-legislative (nonheteronomous) activity of reason.

More emphatically and profoundly than any other possible source for Kant, Rousseau discloses how "nature" in man is a wholly problematic notion for the guidance of any use of reason in pursuit of the desirable goals of mastery and self-rule. He thus impels Kant toward the "transcendental" grounding of all use of reason that abjures "nature" as a dialectical principle, while not embracing that alternative himself. Nature in the form of allegedly fixed and reliable inclinations does not in fact provide a basis either for universally binding moral legislation or for a perspicuous and coherent unity of rational principles in a "system" of philosophy. With respect to the structural difficulty in modern philosophy described above, it can be said that Kant finds an answer to that difficulty in his Rousseau-inspired view of an autonomous self-ordering rationality. Such rationality can provide the self-legitimating telos for emancipation that had been wanting in the earlier foundations of the modern enterprise.

For the post-Kantian development of modern thought this is a momentous innovation that brings in its wake the most distinctive feature of the philosophy of the past two centuries. This feature is already evident in the 1760s: Rousseau's exposure of the difficulties in modern subjectivist and instrumental reason leads both Rousseau and Kant to a new historical conception of reason. The crucial point is that reason is now seen as wholly uncontainable within a natural order, whether human or cosmic, whether a structure of sentiments and inclinations or an eternal order of laws and decrees. Reason has peculiar self-projecting and self-modifying tendencies that are independent of conscious human purposes and even of the natural constitution of the species. The unfolding of these tendencies in human history brings about unwanted new perplexities, as it brings about advances in faculties and talents.[33] The idea that "Nature is stepmotherly" to the human species is given new meaning by Rousseau and Kant; the insufficiency of nature's gifts to humanity lies not solely in the harshness of the natural state but more saliently in the independence of reason from natural structure.[34] Man's indeterminacy and ability to adopt various stations in creation, celebrated as his "dignity" in the Renaissance, is now portrayed in darker colors as at once a liability and a source of pride. Human weakness is not merely "given" but, disturbingly and mysteriously, it is the unintended outcome of reason's development.

The need to comprehend and direct this human dependence on the dynamism of history is plainly the source of the concentration on history in Fichte, Hegel, Marx, and later thinkers. It is also the source of the gradual erosion of the central place of the natural individual (with his desires and ends) within modern philosophy. The modern individual subject, critically weakened by the arguments of Rousseau and others, becomes the transindividual historical subject in a variety of incarnations—absolute Spirit, the dialectic of capital, the caprices of the will to power, the dispensations of Being and of textual sense and non-sense. The difficulty or impossibility of defining the individual good was built into the foundations of modern thought, and the price that was paid was the eventual abandonment of the true principle or telos of modern emancipation. Before this it was hoped that the modern "ideals" of power, emancipation, and diversity could be achieved by another route. Yet the benevolence of the substitute agency that was offered, the historical "subject," is as doubtful today as it was in the late eighteenth century.[35]

Notes

1

In the *Critique of Pure Reason* philosophy is defined as "the science of the relation of all knowledge to the essential ends of human reason (*teleologia rationis humanae*)" at A839/B867. Hume's ignoring of reason's necessary interest in essential ends is basic to Kant's disagreement with him. Thus see the footnote on Hume in the preface to the *Prolegomena:* this "penetrating man" saw clearly the "negative advantages" that would arise from "moderating the excessive claims of speculative reason" with its "endless disputes that confuse mankind," but he failed to note the "positive damages" that arise "if reason is deprived of its most important prospects according to which alone it can hold out to the will the highest goal of all its strivings." In the years following 1769, when Kant is forming the basic structure of critical philosophy, metaphysics is frequently described as science of "the end and the limits of reason," and the criticism of cognition is seen as a propaedeutic to the determination of the end. For sources see the reference in n. 8 below.

2

The following quotations from two leading historians of science and philosophy of the early modern period help support this view: "The new conception of knowledge, not as divine wisdom in the soul, not as a human wisdom for the conduct of life, but as an effective power over nature through the investigation of the causes of things and the practice of 'natural magic,' we are apt to call 'Baconian.' . . . For both [reformers and humanists], wisdom must be bent to the service of man. When an interest in nature and its possibilities was once aroused, it had likewise to serve man. In its background the Baconian spirit can be best described as a kind of naturalistic Augustinianism, aiming at human salvation and beautitude in this world, through a natural wisdom controlling the forces of nature in the interests of human power. . . . Power and possession, not understanding, above all, not the careful discrimination of the Good Life—such was henceforth to be

the keynote of modern thought. Lost was the old Greek Wisdom, the tragedy of the modern age." J. H. Randall, Jr., *The Career of Philosophy,* vol. 1, *From the Middle Ages to the Enlightenment* (New York: Columbia University Press, 1962), pp. 223, 225, 228. "*Larvatus prodeo.* Descartes was a hard-headed physicist under the mask of a metaphysician. He did not want to 'know' nature since he assumed he knew it already. What he wanted was power over nature. He wanted to know the ways in which man can construct 'his own' nature, which is nothing but machines." G. de Santillana, *Reflections on Men and Ideas* (Cambridge: MIT Press, 1968), p. 212. While these remarks point in a useful direction, they overstate their case and they underestimate the genuinely theoretical interests of Bacon and Descartes.

3

Consider, for example, Locke's *Essay:* "I shall not at present meddle with the physical consideration of the mind; or trouble myself to examine wherein its essence consists; or by what motions of our spirits or alterations of our bodies we come to have any *sensation* by our organs, or any *ideas* in our understandings; and whether those ideas do in their formation, any or all of them, depend on matter or not." These speculations lie outside the design of the essay, whose purpose is "to inquire into the original, certainty, and extent of *human knowledge.*" *An Essay concerning Human Understanding,* vol. 1, ed. A. C. Fraser (Oxford, 1894), pp. 26–27. Kant's doubts about the attainability of metaphysical knowledge of the soul are clearly expressed in a letter to Moses Mendelssohn (April 8, 1766), where in relation to the question "how is the soul *present in the world,*" Kant wonders "whether the necessary *data* for a solution may be lacking. . . . Here we must decide whether there really are not limitations established by the bounds of our reason"; Arnulf Zweig, ed., *Kant: Philosophical Correspondence, 1759–99* (Chicago: University of Chicago Press, 1967), pp. 56–57.

4

See Descartes's *Sixth Meditation* and R. Kennington, "The 'Teaching of Nature' in Descartes' Soul Doctrine," *Review of Metaphysics* 26 (1972): 86–117. See also Hume, *An Enquiry concerning Human Understanding*, section 5, part 2, the concluding two paragraphs on the "wisdom of nature."

5

The difficulty of determining an end for the use of modern rationality seems to me as fundamental to the unfolding self-criticism and "radicalization" of modern thought as modern political "realism" and modern natural right with their inherent difficulties. "Realism" in the sense of doubts about the existence of a beneficent natural order providing a teleological context for reason is common to thinkers as diverse as Bruno, Bacon, Hobbes, Descartes, and Locke—with an attendant call upon mankind to assume a stance of mastery to compensate for nature's niggardliness. On the other hand, there are utopian or "idealist" elements also in this project from the start. The impetus of modern thought to make humanity autonomous or self-sufficient must be related to some unresolved questions in late medieval and Renaissance thinking about the "status of reason in the whole" and the "dignity of man" (especially after Copernicus) and is not derivable only from a Machiavellian critique of classical and Christian utopian politics. Similarly, the difficulties propelling the advance of modern self-criticism surely have much to do with scientific and metaphysical issues about the status of reason and of knowledge of human and nonhuman nature, which are to some extent independent of political doctrine.

6

The "transcendental turn" in Kant's account of reason is closely linked in his thought (and in the idealism that builds on his thought) to the turn to history, in three respects: (1) spontaneous or "creative" notions of reason are central to both "turns"; (2) both transcendentality and history are meant to supply contexts of meaning or justification that the earlier modern scientific empiricism and rationalism

(with their analysis to ultimate "simples") could not, it was thought, supply; and (3) the metaphysical revolution occurring in Kant therefore rests upon and completes the historical achievement of the earlier scientific and cosmological revolution. In Kant's account of theoretical reason, transcendental argument not only provides a context of objective intentionality required but not supplied by the "simple" and "complex" ideas of his predecessors; it also provides a context of legitimation for the metaphysical categories that tend to unfold in a dialectic that earlier thought had not resolved by determining the limits of reason. The latter dialectic tends to destroy all confidence in reason, and hence Kant's criticism of it is instrumental to the overarching aim of determining a nondialectical telos for reason. In the "propaedeutic" (the critique of speculative reason) laying the foundation of this teleological reflection, Kant identifies the context of ordinary experience with the context of metaphysics, through a novel "transcendental logic" that serves to articulate and unite both contexts. This logic is therefore central to a project of reconciling reason's metaphysical strivings, modern scientific canons of knowledge, and ordinary experience or "common reason," which is, above all, moral in character. It would rescue reason from self-destruction that must otherwise result from conflicts between these aspects of reason. The transcendental solution to reason's self-definition presupposes the dialectic that is an expression of its "spontaneity," and as such reason has a "history" in which it gradually arrives (through error) at the "critical" standpoint. So criticism is linked in more than one way to history. See the "History of Pure Reason" that concludes the *Critique of Pure Reason*.

7

This is a common feature of the thought of figures otherwise quite diverse: Heidegger, Gadamer, Foucault, Derrida, T. S. Kuhn, the later Wittgenstein, the "holism" of W. V. O. Quine, and the "fusion of horizons" sought by such writers as Richard Rorty. Some of the principals in the discussion about "foundationalist" epistemology (which discussion is very much a reconsideration of the seventeenth-century foundations) discern the link between the epistemological and teleological questions; see especially the writings of Hilary Putnam and Charles Taylor on this subject.

8

A fuller discussion of this subject is to be found in my book *Freedom and the End of Reason: On the Moral Foundation of Kant's Critical Philosophy* (Chicago: University of Chicago Press, 1989). I provide there the argumentation and documentation for the theses that I can only assert in a short essay—on the centrality of the "end of reason" in Kant's whole endeavor, and on the importance of Rousseau for its formulation.

9

See M. Kuehn, "Kant's Conception of 'Hume's Problem,'" *Journal of the History of Philosophy* 21 (1983): 175–93, and G. Tonelli, "Die Anfänge von Kants Kritik der Kausalbeziehung und ihre Voraussetzungen im 18. Jahrhundert," *Kant-Studien* 57 (1966): 417–56. Kant is aware of Hume's thought by 1766 and holds views on causality similar to Hume's by that time, but not until after 1770 does he take up in earnest "Hume's problem" concerning the legitimation of the metaphysical categories.

10

See the *Bemerkungen zu den Beobachtungen über das Gefühl des Schönen und Erhabenen* (cited hereafter as *Remarks*), vol. 20, pp. 1–192, of the Academy edition of Kant's works, *Kants gesammelte Schriften,* edited by the Prussian Academy of Sciences (Berlin, 1902–). (All subsequent citations to Kant are to the Academy edition.) Mostly it is German scholars who have devoted attention to these reflections, above all Josef Schmucker and Dieter Henrich. On the basis of a study of the whole text (not available until the 1940s), Schmucker argues that they give evidence of a "revolution in Kant" based above all on Kant's reading of *Emile;* he observes that the *Remarks* is a kind of dialogue chiefly with that work but also with other writings of

Rousseau. Schmucker's account of the character and history of the text is very useful; he observes that as notes to an earlier work of Kant (the moral-aesthetic *Observations*) it is neither a completed work nor, probably, preparatory notes for one. See Schmucker's *Die Ursprünge der Ethik Kants in seinen vorkritischen Schriften und Reflexionen* (Meisenheim: Anton Hain, 1961), pp. 173–79. Schmucker further argues that in the *Remarks* a "second phase" of Kant's moral thinking is "not only introduced but decisively determined by Kant's study of the chief works of Rousseau" (ibid., p. 143), a judgment with which Dieter Henrich concurs in "Über Kants Entwicklungsgeschichte," *Philosophische Rundschau* 13 (1965): 252–63.

11

See the letter to Mendelssohn cited in n. 3 above and the letter to J. H. Lambert of December 31, 1765, in Zweig, *Philosophical Correspondence,* pp. 47–49.

12

See *Enquiry concerning the Clarity of the Principles of Natural Theology and Ethics,* trans. D. E. Walford, in *Kant: Selected Pre-Critical Writings,* trans. and intro. by G. B. Kerferd and D. E. Walford (Manchester: Manchester University Press, 1968), pp. 3–35. The discursive character of the categories of metaphysics remains a basic premise of the argument of the *Critique of Pure Reason,* especially the transcendental deduction of the categories.

13

Thus see the reduction of the "good" to immediate certainties of consciousness, without metaphysics, in the "Fourth Reflection" of the *Enquiry,* n. 12 above. Prior to this Kant had criticized Leibniz's theodicy and its manner of grounding the will in a metaphysical order of "sufficient reasons"; see Kant, *Reflexionen* 3703–07, 17:329–39 (ca. 1754). More generally, one can see how Leibniz, in spite of the emphasis on "spontaneity" of monads that is of first importance for Kant, could later fall under a Kantian criticism of "instrumental" views of reason, for Leibniz's effort to salvage some freedom of the will by way of a "middle ground" between "geometric necessity" and perfectly undetermined spontaneity does require that the will be understood on the basis of a natural order that supplies sufficient reason for its choice. One can call this a mild determinism, which rejects a Cartesian-mechanical version of necessitating laws while it endorses a more "dynamical" conception of law according to which nature (including the will) is ordered by "inclining reasons" and "principles of the best." Furthermore, the Leibnizian account of the soul does not draw clear lines between the faculties of perception, appetite, will, and reason. These terms only describe various aspects of a single *conatus* for perfection that constitutes the very substantial being of the monad. See Leibniz, *Monadology,* sections 14, 15, 18, 19, 48–50. Wolff, too, has only a "single-faculty" account of the soul. For Kant's later rejection of Wolff's ethical perfectionism as heteronomous, see *Foundations of the Metaphysics of Morals,* conclusion of the second section.

14

In addition to the *Enquiry,* see the essay *Attempt at an Introduction of Negative Quantities into Philosophy* (1763), 2:165–204, especially the concluding remark.

15

This is evident in the conclusion of the essay *The False Subtlety of the Four Syllogistic Figures* (1762), 2:45–62. Kant maintains this compatibility into the critical period; he is never a Humean "associationist," nor is he ever tempted by any form of solipsism or material idealism (Berkeleyan or otherwise). His "refutation of idealism," while a consequence of his critical arguments, is not the primary object of them. Thus the famous "Refutation" passage in the paralogisms of the *Critique of Pure Reason* presupposes, rather than proves, the general transcendental thesis on the conditions of knowledge that is the outcome of the transcendental deduction.

16

Not only the *Enquiry* but also the Shaftesburyan *Observations on the Feeling of the Beautiful and the Sublime* (1764) and Kant's announcement of his lectures for the winter semester of 1765–66 contain significant references to the moral sense philosophers; see Kant, 2:205–56 and 303–14.

17

See Hobbes, *Leviathan,* chap. 11: "For there is no such *finis ultimis,* utmost aim, nor *summum bonum,* greatest good, as is spoken of in the books of the old moral philosophers." Also Locke, *Essay,* book 2, chap. 21, sections 43 and 44. Compare with these Machiavelli, *Discourses on the Decade of Livy,* book 1, chap. 37 and book 2, Proemium, and Bruno, *Expulsion of the Triumphant Beast,* first dialogue, part 1.

18

See the recent book with this title by A. Altmann, *Die Trostvolle Aufklärung* (Stuttgart: Frommann-Holzboog, 1982).

19

Kant, *Remarks,* 20:58–59.

20

Ibid.; on providence compare pp. 57–58, 68, and 16, in which one finds the Rousseauian idea that only the corrupted human will, tainted by imagination and luxurious tastes, not nature itself, gives rise to human discontent with providence and the order of things. Man alone is responsible for his loss of "naturalness," and he alone is capable of recovering it. But it is not sin or original evil that is behind the loss; the faulty and unwilled unfolding of human rational powers is the culprit (according to the "hidden law"). This "theodicean" insight is connected to the fact that Rousseau also makes evident to Kant that the true "worth of knowledge" lies in its "establishing the rights of mankind" (ibid., p. 44, lines 8–16). In other words, Rousseau indicates the true end to which theoretical efforts (which Kant says he undertakes "by inclination") must be subordinated. Philosophy is properly concerned not with knowledge for its own sake but with the uncovering of the human vocation or man's place in "the world appropriate to him" (ibid., p. 7, lines

8–11). This "place" (which corresponds to what is "right" or just) is defined by the condition of the will in which it attains its proper relation to itself. This requires that human reason renounce speculative striving for unknowable realities, among other things (see n. 22 below). The "hidden law" clarifies how human reason can attain true wholeness, or its justifying end.

It should be noted that for Kant (following Rousseau) "naturalness" is understood in terms of a natural condition that is a construct of reason, and it does not correspond to any theoretical knowledge of human nature such as earlier philosophies sought. It is that construct which renders intelligible, as an "ideal," an accord between rational powers and desire; yet this accord has never been and never can be fully achieved. Thus the language of "loss" of the natural state can be only metaphorical.

21

For this account one should see especially *Discourse on the Origins of Inequality* (1755) and the *Reveries of the Solitary Walker*. The former Kant knew and studied; the latter, published after Rousseau's death, was of course unknown to Kant at the time of the *Remarks*.

22

Here Rousseau points out a feature of rationality, the gulf between imagined goal and practical actualization, that parallels another distinction already noted by Kant—between discursive conception of wholes in metaphysics and their intuitive realization. In both respects, human reason shows itself to be distant from the extremes of subhuman and superhuman "oneness." Yet man's position does not, without extraordinary self-critical efforts on his part, provide equilibrium. Reason can fulfill its true destiny only if it abandons as illusory the search for wholeness as instinctual satisfaction or as total cognition.

23

While such production of ideas in Rousseau is spontaneous in a sense, it is not autonomous of the inclinations and passions. Rousseau's whole account of human evolution rests upon a mutual determination of reason and passion, and certainly his account contains no autonomy of reason of a Kantian sort. Yet the invented ideas have no correspondence to genuine natural need and no foundations in a metaphysical order; while their production is impelled by passion, their actual form is non-teleological and "groundless."

24

Thus Rousseau is the principal source of that tradition of modern thought regarding the phrase "to be rational" as equivalent to the phrases "to be historical" (i.e., always in quest of an elusive goal of rational projection) and "to be alienated." After Kant, the conclusion is drawn for divine reason as well as for human reason that perfect unity and self-accord are not only unattainable but also unthinkable for any rational being; even the divine essence must be historical and alienated. This thought is carried forward by Schelling, Hegel, Marx, Heidegger, and others. It is the heart of post-Kantian "dialectical logic." See, for example, section 5 of the "Attempt at a Self-Criticism" that Nietzsche appended to the 1886 edition of *The Birth of Tragedy*.

25

In several places Rousseau notes that for a corrupt humanity the only cure can be a version of the corruption; the Enlightenment must be reformed by another, more radical, kind of Enlightenment. Hence Rousseau's justification for his literary and philosophical activity; see *Discourse on the Arts and Sciences* (the concluding passage on Bacon, Descartes, and Newton as "preceptors of mankind") and *Preface to Narcisse*.

26

On Kant's bewilderment over some of Rousseau's ideas see 20:43–44.

27

See 15:211, *Reflexion* 488 (from the middle or latter 1760s), where Kant also muses about "whether all human beings are not to a certain extent disturbed" (*gestört*, which might also be rendered "deranged"). See Kant's later essay *Conjectural Beginning of Human History*

(1786), which offers a very Rousseauian exposition of the human discovery of rational powers and freedom of choice, in relation to possibilities disclosed by the imagination. As a result of this discovery man was no longer bound to a single way of life, like the animals, and "stood so to speak at the edge of an abyss," being confronted with an infinity of objects (8:112).

28

See the discussion of the reception of Kant's doctrine as an effort to avert reason's self-destruction by the first generation of Kant's readers (1781–93), in F. Beiser, *The Fate of Reason: German Philosophy from Kant to Fichte* (Cambridge, Mass.: Harvard University Press, 1987).

29

The definition of philosophy as "science of the limits of reason" appears in the *Remarks*, 20:181; see also 2:368 (1766). The term "critique of the understanding" appears in the announcement of lectures for the winter semester of 1765–66; 2:310–11.

30

See n. 20 above.

31

The "Transcendental Doctrine of Method" at the conclusion of the *Critique of Pure Reason*, especially the second chapter (the "Canon of Pure Reason"), presents the outlines of this teleological and systematic ordering of reason as the true fulfillment of critical philosophy; the more elaborated version is the *Critique of Judgment*, above all its teleological sections.

32

For the philosopher as legislator see above all the third chapter of "Doctrine of Method" from the first *Critique* (the "Architectonic of Pure Reason").

33

The "critical" decades of 1781–1800 see a number of Kantian writings on these topics: *Conjectural Beginning, Idea for a Universal History, Perpetual Peace*, significant parts of the *Critique of Judgment, The Strife of the Faculties*, among others. Present in all of them is the adumbration of the ideal of a "moral culture" that will reconcile the disharmonious unfolding of human faculties, so that the rational advance of the species will cease to generate evils that have been the cause for past reproaches against reason, providence, and human nature. Kant's efforts throughout are to prevent universal "misology."

34

For nature as stepmotherly see the first section of *Foundations of the Metaphysics of Morals*.

35

The instrumental account of reason, powerfully criticized by Rousseau and Kant, is closely allied to what is often called the "atomistic" character of early modern liberal morality and politics. Yet it can be said (with special reference to Locke) that earlier modern thinking does not aim (at least in all cases) at social atomizing, nor does it aim at a wholly "detached" individual. Rousseau goes further than anyone in such a direction—surely disclosing thereby what he and others see to be implied in the less radical positions of his predecessors, and thereby laying the basis for the self-destruction of liberalism. But Locke proposes a liberal order of society in which social attachments and sentiments would still play a central role, and the moral sense writers follow him in this. It is fair to say that this liberal tradition does not propose a radically individualist subordination of society to self-preservation, as we so often assume, looking at it through Rousseauian (or Hobbesian) spectacles. And it might be said in defense of that earlier tradition that it rightly argues that human concerns with freedom and self-rule are natural and that such natural concerns are compatible with social attachments and virtues. Yet it cannot be denied that certain flaws in its notions of nature and reason vitiate its achievement. The reforms in the modern foundations sought by Rousseau and Kant are, however, made at the cost of the further weakening of the natural individual.

Part Two

*Kantian
Perspectives on
History
and Politics*

Chapter 5

On the Meaning of Rational Action in the State

Dieter Henrich

Translated by Richard L. Velkley

Kant's essay on the relation of theory to practice comports itself as a piece of philosophical polemic.[1] In parts one and three Kant attacks Garve and Mendelssohn, the most widely read authors in his subject. For the theme of the second part he finds neither a contemporary nor even a thesis to criticize; instead, in rather pro forma fashion he puts the name of Hobbes at the head—pro forma because in reality this essay is not a scholarly disputation. It justifies a form of action that makes an appeal to reason by defending such action against a dictum that would set up an impassible boundary between reason and experience. Kant names this dictum a "common saying"—not a folk proverb, in which moral wisdom dwells. Rather, this saying belongs for Kant in the mouths of "worthy gentlemen" who pursue practical affairs, exercise state power, and reflect on the course of the world with both of these in mind.[2] In Kant's opinion these individuals gain support from an alliance made by the philosophy of the day with human motivations that obstruct the free development of moral consciousness. Kant derived the highest legitimation of his critique from the task of destroying the appearance of truth that this alliance could produce. Thus he already understood his reform of theoretical philosophy as having a "practical intent." More especially, however, his philosophy of right and morals is not to be an analytical science that traces important phenomena back to hidden grounds. Rather, it must bring to clear consciousness and confirm as superior insight what is already implicitly guiding right action. That guiding element is reason, a system of principles that itself is already theory or is in any case the object of a scientific knowledge that deserves the name "theory."[3] The power of theory, of which Kant speaks approvingly, is not a power that he claims for himself and his

---

This is a translation of "Über den Sinn vernünftigen Handelns im Staat," from *Kant. Gentz. Rehberg. Über Theorie und Praxis*. Introduction by Dieter Henrich. © Suhrkamp Verlag Frankfurt am Main, 1967. The translator thanks John Golden for his help.

own discoveries. Nowhere in this essay does Kant speak about his works and doctrines. He speaks for a kind of theory that dwells within the moral consciousness itself and its action. As such this theory has *eo ipso* practical effectiveness. One can obstruct this effectiveness with bad theory or assist it to victory with superior knowledge. Thus Kant's essay has this aim: to render bad theory ineffectual and to make true theory sure of itself.

Theory in the Revolutionary Period

Kant's essay appeared September 1793 in the Berlin *Monatsschrift,* at the time of the decrees for public safety and the revolutionary tribunal. Kant had already been a regular author in this journal for eight years. Its editor, Johann Erich Biester, was previously secretary to the liberal minister von Zedlitz, to whom Kant dedicated the *Critique of Pure Reason*. It was during his tenure as secretary that von Zedlitz began his association with Kant. He was able to win and maintain Kant's trust, and he enticed him to make occasional pronouncements on important controversies of the day. Kant on his part prized any opportunity of addressing the educated public of his Prussian homeland and of creating at the same time an audience in all of Germany. Such opportunities are what the respected journal could afford him. It published treatises on all the themes that were the subject matter of conversations at the tables and in the circles of educated citizens: history, important political events, notable discoveries and observations in the natural sciences, the foundations of right and morality, and translations of classical poetry and some newer poetic compositions. In these surroundings (until the journal's expiration), there appeared from Kant's hand a meteorological and an anthropological treatise and, most important, all his minor works on history, right, and ethics. Furthermore, his major work on religion was planned as a series of essays in the *Monatsschrift;* however, the official censor refused to give the imprimatur to the second installment.

As a substitute for this text Kant wrote the essay on the relation of theory to practice. Thus there were personal implications in the fact that Kant provided unprecedented room for the freedom of the pen in this essay. But one cannot maintain that it was composed in order to find a furtive opportunity for an attack on the censor.

The impetus for the essay came from Garve's critique of Kant's moral philosophy.[4] The critique appeared just as Kant's second essay on religion was refused publication. Kant regarded it as more important than learned refutations from the Wolffian school, which he dealt with only casually and contemptuously, for Garve's critique could result in the public's suspecting that Kant's moral philosophy— which Kant hoped would have broad human impact, not just on the schools—was mere speculation. In the age of sentimentality such a suspicion was lethal for anyone seeking to be an educator and a teacher of wisdom.

Kant's plan grew beyond its original motivation and became in large part a treatise on problems of the state. It was a well-considered move on Kant's part not to limit the discussion of practical philosophy to private morality just when a revolutionary politics was basing itself on a philosophy of political right. Yet his decision to break out of such limits was not due only to this insight. He found himself drawn into a discussion whose direction he had to establish, so as not to be misunderstood by the public and become still more suspect to the government—thus for the sake of prudence as much as the argument itself. Kant had in fact already held a lengthy series of lectures on natural law, but until now he had published only a review in this field, leaving it to his readers to apply his foundations of ethics to right.[5] The latter occurred with a zeal that was increased by the conviction of a connection between Kantian critique and the French Revolution. A number of Kant's followers, among them Abicht and Heydenreich, had already written systems of natural law on Kantian principles.[6] Journalistic controversies over the justice or the perversity of events in France were conducted with manifold references to Kant's doctrine. We can in fact establish that Kant had two of these writings in mind while preparing notes for the *Monatsschrift* essay.[7]

The mathematician Kästner had, in his "Thoughts on the Inability of Writers to Incite Rebellions," written a satire—a rather senile one—about what he took to be the ineffectual zeal of theorizing writers, thereby also throwing a sideways glance at the spokesmen of the Kantian philosophy.[8] Kant had high regard for Kästner and had at one time made some effort to solve publicly a problem posed by him.[9] Now Kant had reason to put Kästner's bilious thesis in its place and to show that political theory cannot provoke a revolution not because it is theory but because it concedes no right to revolution. Nevertheless, as theory it must provide guidance to action. Kant wished also to demonstrate that the dignity of theory does not accrue from its having revolutionary consequences, since ambiguity on just this point was prevalent in the writings of his students. We know that Kant made notes in early 1793 in connection with the work of a student named Schaumann; the work itself was a weak production, yet it might have appeared significant to Kant for the matters at hand.[10]

The idea for the third section of Kant's writing presumably came into being in the same context: a theory that demands respect for right and that at the same time abandons all hope of its actualization would indeed have to be named "mere" theory. Therefore Kant attempted to prove, on the basis of the progress of mankind and insight into human interests, that one can anticipate a condition of the world in which right attains supremacy in the inner life of states. The thought, still very relevant now, that the drive for external freedom is able to check all opposing power was the necessary complement of theory (and of theory-oriented action) that renounced all right of revolution.

This history of the essay's origins allows one to see something characteristic of Kant's philosophical literary activity: that arduously yet steadily the pathos for philosophical enlightenment is developed from a variety of standpoints and impulses, while the connection with more remote problems is unfailingly kept in view. Kant's mode of writing is immune to Kästner's caricature of those who changed with the times and began to write about pedagogy and human rights once these became fashionable topics: "They rolled about their empty barrels, utterly unlike Diogenes who meant satire by it, and believed they were doing something serious."

A New Meaning for Practice

The title of Kant's writing also resulted from the extension of its theme to political right. Garve had objected that Kant's moral doctrine makes a division between the moral law and happiness, which he could very well grasp in his head but could not find in his heart.[11] Kant then "protected his [Garve's] heart against his head."[12] Kant believed that Garve's habit of thinking in the categories of psychology had hindered him from understanding the impulses of his heart, which are based on freedom. Kant's title on theory and practice results from Garve's assertion about the head and the heart, although it cannot be immediately derived from it. First of all Kant had to establish that Garve's objection is actually asserting the same thing as that discourse which wants to make philosophical political right into a mere playing with thoughts, and then Kant could show that it makes sense to criticize both together with one stroke. Both are derivatives of empiricism, to which Kant himself was at one point drawn but which he now regarded as the corruption of all fundamental philosophy. The saying about the productivity of practice and the idleness of theory belongs, however, to the sphere of scientific doctrine and the activity that is guided by that doctrine while it is at the same time distinguished (as a profession) from it. This was the situation in the higher faculties and in the technological sciences that at that time were still to some extent taught in the philosophical faculty. Among them right is the only field in which the "common saying" has a relation to moral principles.

It is rather difficult to determine where such a saying was actually in vogue. It is clear that it presupposes, and at the same time contests, an understanding according to which practice is the application or actualization of a theory. Thus, for example, medical practice is "the other part of medicine in which one seeks, rationally and skillfully, to exercise what one has learned in the initial theoretical part."[13] Doctors and lawyers have a "practice" in this sense. Christian Wolff made the same distinction in his *Philosophia practica universalis*. Practice is for him at once an object itself of science and a doctrine in which one discovers the conditions under which the principles of a theory are rationally applied.[14]

This conception of the relation of theory to practice is in its roots more Roman than Greek. One must indeed distinguish it from the conception underlying the classical controversy on the question of whether the theoretical or the practical life is the more excellent and the source of higher happiness. Pure science, by the Greek conception, is fulfilled in the knowledge of the necessary, which cannot be other than it is and is therefore not amenable to action of any kind. The moral life—in the state or in the limited circle of the wise who have no needs—has its own mode of knowing, one that becomes, however, wholly manifest only in right conduct itself.[15] Here theory and practice do not stand in a relation of principle to application, but of principle to principle.

Now indeed this is notable: Kant proceeds from the first meaning of *practice* when he cites the common saying derived from the model of the applied sciences. But in reality he thereby brings about a revival of a more significant meaning of *practice*. He does so insofar as he brings together under the heading of practice both moral action and political and social life, separating them from the applied sciences and interpreting their principles on the basis of "practical reason"—that is, a reason that in essence relates to action and does not only set forth maxims to be used to profit, as occasion warrants, through action.

Thus Kant brought into being the complex of problems that leaps to mind when we hear the formula "theory and practice." The question is in what sense theory can be the guide to action—not just any theory, but that which has in view the complete interrelation between all essential actions, and not just any practice, but that which brings about or preserves the conditions of an appropriate and rational life. That theory belongs to such action distinguishes this question from that of Aristotle, who regarded only a philosophical theory *about* action as indispensable. That the theory itself is oriented toward practice distinguishes it from science, which is indifferent toward its technical application. Kant introduced both of these distinctions— without intending this—into an already jejune concept of practice, as he made use of the "common saying" in order to unite his empiricist opponents into one chorus and to criticize them as an ensemble. Furthermore, Kant introduced into the concept of practice the connection between reflective action and orientation toward history. Thus, this minor work is the origin of a current problem, regardless of its answers. Its long-range influence is accordingly far more significant than the resonance that it found among Kant's contemporaries.

The Roles of the Critics

Kant's essay was eagerly discussed until after 1800. Among the publications insti-
gated by it is a long series of writings about the most provocative of Kant's theses,
the denial of the right of revolution. In some cases these works grew into hefty
volumes. Among all these texts the works by Friedrich Gentz and August Wilhelm
Rehberg still deserve special attention. In contrast to the other literature belonging
to this milieu, which unfortunately has been forgotten, these writings are still cited
occasionally. This can be explained by the external circumstance that both appeared, like Kant's essay, in the Berlin *Monatsschrift*.[16] Biester brought them to
Kant's attention and bade him to reply; Kant declined.[17] Thus they play a certain,
albeit small, role in Kant's correspondence, but their worth is not determined by
such incidentals. Their importance rests on two grounds: their authors influenced
the development of Germany not only as political publicists but also as politicians;
and although both were students of Kant's philosophy, they turned against Kant in
the theory of the state. Their critique of the events in France led them to formulate a
new and idiosyncratic concept of politics, upon which the shadow of the romantic
theory of the state has fallen; the latter could appeal to this concept while arguing in
a more striking and misguided manner. The contempt expressed by Kant and Fichte
toward this concept seems to exclude according it any substantial weight. Nonetheless, neither the authority of such men nor problematic consequences should stand
in the way of our examining the grounds that the authors brought forth to support
their views. In truth it is not at all easy, amid the play of arguments and counterargu-
ments, to decide between Kant and his two critics.

Friedrich Gentz, jurist, proofreader of the *Critique of Judgment*, and young
man of the world in elegant Berlin, began his literary career in 1791 with an essay in
the Berlin *Monatsschrift*.[18] In it he defended the truth and importance of natural law
against Justus Möser, who criticized the French Revolution on the basis of ancient
right and primeval relations. Gentz's defense was fully in accord with Kant's
teaching as he had imbibed it during his student days in Königsberg. Möser's praise
of the traditional had not led astray the emancipated Kantian who shared in the
enthusiasm for the Revolution. All the same he found persuasive Edmund Burke's
warning about the dangers of a future conjured up by the Revolution. Thus, in
Burke's footsteps Gentz set out on his path as agitator for an alliance against France,
publicist for the Holy Alliance, Austrian privy councillor, and intimate adviser to
the later Metternich. He achieved fame through his brilliant translation of Burke's
magnum opus,[19] which was followed by his critique of Kant's writing on theory and
practice. Very aptly Rudolf Haym has said of the Gentz of this latter text that
"everywhere he is ready to confess himself Burke's student, only he must be
allowed at the same time to regard himself as the perpetual student of Kant."[20]

Kant's teaching and the political experience out of which Burke's thought is drawn prevented Gentz even in later life from promoting, along with the politics of restoration, the nebulous romantic theology that enshrouded it—in contrast to his friend Adam Müller. In Gentz's view Metternich signified the defense against the danger of the Terror and of the Napoleonic centralized state, but not the foundation of a holy world on principles that deny human rights. But it must be added nonetheless that in the actual battle of opinions Gentz distanced himself so much from this position that one could no longer recognize it. The insufficiency of his conviction can be identified by pondering the motivation and fairness of his critique of Kant.

August Wilhelm Rehberg, a Hanoverian of strict probity, often chided for dryness, and an autodidact in philosophy, was still a young man when he won the second prize from the Prussian Academy—as previously Kant himself had—for the solution of one of its questions.[21] But through his reading he became early on a Kantian of a skeptical variety peculiar to himself. He published several fundamental investigations of Kantian themes and entered an important book into the controversy about Jacobi's views on Lessing.[22] Kant's prize pupil Jachmann visited him during a journey through Germany's chief centers of learning and characterized him to Kant as "the finest mind among all your students with whom I have thus far made acquaintance."[23] Of an enterprising sort, he first was secretary to the episcopal regent of Osnabrück and soon thereafter a ministry official in Hannover. Through these offices he was brought into personal contact with Justus Möser and English political life, in which Burke was playing a prominent role. He discussed all literature dealing with the French Revolution for the Jena *Allgemeine Literaturzeitung,* and through this activity, which brought him notoriety, he developed from philosopher into political writer. In his official capacity he labored for a reform of the representative constitution. Yet his modest reform program ran aground on the feudal system of the agrarian state of Hannover, which furthermore had become the object of great-power politics among Napoleonic, English, and Prussian forces. Thus retiring from political life, he witnessed the Restoration as a critic of current events and the political literature. Like Gentz, Rehberg turned the theoretical principles of the Kantian philosophy against its political consequences and set forth the thesis that the laws of the moral world cannot be made immediately effective and dominant in political action.

The Clash of Arguments

A century of Kant scholarship has helped us to acquire an interest in Kant's minor works and to develop a discriminating understanding of them. This is also true of the essay on theory and practice. It contains many passages that are excellently suited for interpreting theses from the chief works in moral philosophy; it has other passages that can be properly construed only with the help of the chief works. One would never be able to support a judgment about Kant's doctrine on the basis of this essay alone. Also, this essay holds a special position within the historical development of the critical philosophy, above all as the first text on the theory of right, coming half a decade before the *Metaphysics of Morals.*

Yet all of these aspects must be set aside if one wants to investigate the discussion between Kant and his two critical students. They did not need to delve into the problems of the foundations of ethics since especially in this area as in many other respects they followed Kant. Furthermore such problems do not actually belong to the aim which Kant set for himself in this essay and on which any criticism preeminently had to focus. Two things—this aim and the time in which the essay appeared—justify the fact that Gentz and Rehberg concentrate their discussions on two of Kant's points: the relation of political right to politics, and the meaning of the right of resistance.

The Relation of Right to Politics

Gentz and Rehberg are in agreement that one cannot derive sufficient guidance for political action from rational political right alone. Kant would have agreed with this proposition. For him *theory* means in matters of right only the rational science of principles. One may not escape its requirements through an appeal to experience. But on the other hand, prudence, which gets its acumen from experience, is needed to know "how theory can be better and more universally put to work."[24]

Gentz appears to be satisfied with this point but objects that the knowledge involved in such prudence deserves the name of theory—a theory which Kant indeed did not reject but which he did not properly estimate.[25] Gentz ascribes tasks to this theory that Kant wants to accomplish through pure political right: for Kant the legitimacy of the republican constitution follows directly from the idea of the state. Every state that is not in accord with this constitution should seek to approximate it and in any case should be governed in a republican spirit. Gentz adopts Kant's theory of the political contract—oriented toward Rousseau—but contests the consequence that Kant drew from it. For Gentz the question about the right constitution is only to be decided by having regard for how the *security* of the original contract is best guaranteed. Thereby he echoes Hobbes—presumably without intending it— but does not follow Hobbes all the way to the opinion that security applies only to life and that this can be attained only through the absolute power of the state. A "theory grounded in experience," studying human beings and "social relations," must solve the problem of the right constitution, and this solution must comply with the special conditions of existence for particular states.[26] Rehberg took over the formula "theory grounded in experience"; this formula signifies a politico-sociological science of the state with a pragmatic intent.[27]

Thus Kant's two critics gave the status of program to a new undertaking with a future. It is Humean empiricism applied to political science and pursued with a pragmatic intent; it is as different from politics in the classical canon of the sciences as it is from modern natural law arising from the *esprit de geometrie*.[28]

Gentz arrived at this program by reducing the claims that he wished to concede to natural law; constitutional doctrine became for him an empirical problem. Rehberg went even further in this direction; making a rigorous use of Kant's distinction between intelligible and sensible worlds, he truncated the rational science of politics to the requirement of respect for moral freedom. For this reason it also became impossible for him to maintain along with Gentz that rational political right already itself determines the final end of politics and that "theory grounded in experience" only provides the means to guarantee its actualization. This theory now moves into the service of "the salutary," by which Rehberg evidently intended everything that secures and furthers the preservation of life, culture, and a stable, reliable social order.[29]

On this foundation one cannot see how it is possible to criticize given relations in state and society on grounds of justice. Along with the Kantian relation of theory to practice, Gentz and Rehberg seem to have sacrificed the critical potential of Kantian natural law. When one adds that both authors were apologists for the feudal state and the privileges of the nobility, the suspicion arises that their argument against Kant only serves the aim of exculpating a corrupt system and of making it seem indispensable. Contemporary polemics already reproached them for being hirelings of the nobility who perverted Kant's doctrine of freedom into its opposite. This reproach could gain substance from the practical circumstances of Gentz's life, in particular. Yet this reproach does not resolve the problem that the program of a "theory grounded in experience" lays hold of and brings to consciousness. And it underestimates another type of critique that stands at the disposal of this theory: if the conditions of life, which at one time a given political order encompassed, have so changed that now the same order impedes them, then reform is unavoidable. Rehberg made a cogent use, although an excessively cautious one, of this critique. How this critique relates to one based on consciousness of human rights is a question that has not been given a satisfying answer by Rehberg, Gentz, Kant, or anyone up to the present day.

The Right of Resistance

Kant had expounded in his essay the view that every attempt at violent change of a constitution is illegal. Thus to the astonishment of his opponents no less than of his followers, the great revolutionary of speculative thought declared himself the severest enemy of every political revolution. In the meantime the rumor had spread that Kant was filled with enthusiasm for the French Republic and eagerly awaited all reports about a favorable course of events for it in France and Europe. These two facts are hard to reconcile. Gentz and Rehberg, both of whom in the wake of Burke judge more skeptically the transformation of France and her politics, nonetheless would not accept Kant's lapidary denial of the right of revolution.

Gentz confirmed in Kant's doctrine the "remarkable contrast between the very promising and hopeful basic principles and the devastating conclusion, immediately following after them." He spoke of the "disconsolateness" of a doctrine that enlivens the consciousness of freedom and right in the citizen only to imprison him forever, on grounds of right, within a system affording few rights or even worse.[30] From this contrast he extracted a further argument for the necessity of taking guidance in politics from a "theory grounded on experience": the state at its founding must be so established that the need for revolution cannot at all arise within it.

One easily observes that this argument is a dead end. For it offers no principle of right whatsoever to those who, finding themselves in a bad political order, seek to create a new condition in accordance with the insights about domestic peace granted by a theory grounded on experience. The bare reminder that the use of force incites revolt is addressed to the powers that be. It establishes no right of rebellion—only the need for caution on the part of the ruling power. The latter's bad conscience could always assuage itself with the philosopher's argument that resistance is an even worse injustice. Thus the knowledge of the injustice of revolution is, for those who live under a good constitution, further reason for being contented with their condition, for its not compelling them to resort to this means. But Gentz can give no help to all those for whom Kant's doctrine is truly relevant and whose situation Gentz considered hopeless.

Rehberg proceeded more consequentially. He disrupted Kant's thesis and substituted for it the corresponding one of Burke. Rebellion applied for Burke in the case of "necessity," that is, in the situation of extreme distress when the people have no alternative way of securing their existence and humanity.[31] In accord with him Rehberg perceived the fundamental error of modern political philosophy to lie not in the recognition of this right but in the attempt to define the concept of the state through reference to it. A right that will be asserted "only when the oppressed can nowhere find right" should not become the object of prolix debates. For thereby it loses its essential meaning and becomes the programmatic formula of a politics only seemingly strengthening, while in truth destroying, the foundations of political society. Rehberg amplified this Burkean thought with an acute observation: it is impossible to oppose entirely the right of resistance, for every sovereign is defenseless without the consent of citizens to his regime. It belongs to the essence of consent that it can be withheld and withdrawn.[32] This observation, too, belongs to the context of a thinking akin to Burke's, according to which the state must be conceived as a community based on trust. Now surely it is true, and long ago seen by Aristotle as well as Montesquieu, that any interpretation of the state on the model of a private contract is defective. Yet it is another point that is valid here, and indeed precisely for a "theory grounded on experience": groups bound together by mutual trust and interest might protect a tyrannical sovereign against the majority of citizens, who had long since withdrawn their confidence from him. In such a case mute action is no longer able to throw a lonely tyrant from his throne. The open conflict penetrates into every area of life and will, so far as possible, have to be carried on publicly. Thus a public agreement concerning the right of resistance is at core quite different from a legalistic attack on the substance of political life or a rumbling of empty barrels, rolled about by orators in obedience to fashion. Certainly there was a multitude of such men at the time of the Revolution, and they darkened its light like gnats. This explains in good measure the rapid decline of the pathos for freedom into jargon, avoided by the genuine thinkers.

Kant on Revolution

Kant's stance toward the right of revolution and the French Revolution still needs interpretation.[33] For the reader of his essay on "Theory and Practice" the question is at the same time urgent and unanswerable: how the revolutionary clarion call of fundamental rights and the admonition on behalf of the integrity of all authority could come from the same mouth.

It is relatively easy to survey and extract from Kant's text the argument he employs to arrive at the exclusion of the right of revolution: the essence of the state consists in the establishment of the general will. In it are united the freedom of every individual with that of all others under laws of right, so that they form one will possessing the power to execute the full force of law against every particular will.[34] Only in this way can the idea of right be actualized, for it presupposes security and unrestricted jurisdiction. Thus it is impossible to combine the concept of the state with a legal reservation setting forth the conditions for the state's annulment by groups of citizens. For the constituted force of the general will entails the restriction of every particular will. Were one to define a higher tribunal that could oppose or supersede this force, then either the idea of the state would be annulled or this higher tribunal would itself be the sovereign. Both cases are opposed to the presupposition of a publicly acknowledged right to alter the state through force.[35]

This last twist in Kant's thinking implies a peculiarity of his theory. It not only rejects every illegal use of force against the state but it goes beyond this in asserting that the idea of right is incompatible with a constitution that provides for institutions controlling the force of the state and having at their disposal executive power against the head of state. "There cannot in the constitution itself be any article making it possible for some force in the state to oppose the highest executive power, in the event of a transgression of the constitutional laws by him."[36] Thereby Kant declares the illegality of a supreme court with constitutional jurisdiction and of the parliamentary right of reservation in constitutional monarchies.

Until now no one has observed that Kant did not at all times think this way. In notes from the prerevolutionary period Kant rejected only coup d'etat and insurrection; he distinguished both, however, from legal acts of limiting the power of the state through a parliament and supreme court. In both cases "there is . . . no insurrection, because the resistance is legal." "A court of justice can exist which . . . judges and regulates . . . actions and commands of the sovereign." "Who shall give rulings, i.e., judge with the force of law, so that obedience [to the sovereign] is countermanded? In England the parliament can do this because it already has authority, but no one among the people *per turbas*."[37] Accordingly Kant at this time regarded representation of citizens as indeed an essential element of a just constitution, for through this device popular resistance can become legal. "The people must have complete representation and as such have not only the right of resistance but also the force of authority, so that it can restore its freedom without insurrection and refuse its obedience to the sovereign."[38] Whoever argues in this way assumes a right of resistance that is inalienable and that must have implications for constitutional natural right.

Not much later Kant left these thoughts behind. Surely there is ambiguity in the fact that this occurred precisely at the time of the French Revolution. Even so, no cause exists for accusing Kant of accommodating his theory to political authority. One can and must proceed on the assumption that there were theoretical grounds occasioning Kant's revision. On closer examination of the matter, perhaps while he prepared to write "Theory and Practice," it occurred to him that the power of the state must be indivisible. The relation of parliament to government permits a renouncing of obedience only when parliament itself is the sovereign. That is a strong argument for the republican constitution, which Kant moreover derived from the idea of the original contract. But where that is lacking, no limitation on princely authority is allowed to make up for the deficiency.

Now Kant elevated the French constitution far above the English, which previously he had extolled. He regarded the widely hailed freedom of the English as discredited by the English attempt to overthrow the French regime. "While at one time England could count on the sympathy of the better human beings in the world due to its courageous upholding of its frequently challenged (merely apparent) freedom, now it has forfeited all of it, since it has been of a mind to overthrow the proposed (much more fundamentally free) constitution in France, because of the danger of the overthrow of its own constitution."[39] When we hear Kant speak in this way, a more probable accommodation emerges: that the change in his theory was promoted by his wrath at England, the archenemy of revolutionary France. The English constitution now appeared to him to be a contradictory hybrid. Instead of rational political unity it knows only the antagonism of two sovereigns.

Yet the praise of the French Revolution is not praise of its revolutionary origin. For the absolute primacy of republican government Kant paid a high price: the impossibility of altering the state on grounds of right. If one power in the state could oppose another one, then this power would be able to change the constitution. A suspended power is excluded from the condition of political life and hands over to the remaining sovereign the possibility of either restoring it or ascending to being sole sovereign. But if such a right is lacking, so also is every right of changing the basic elements of a constitution. For Kant could not concede to the sovereign the right of annulling the entire constitution. If the sovereign is established through the general contract in every possible volition, then the sovereign may not suspend this contract and recreate the natural condition. Therefore, the illegality is the same whether a monarch abdicates and summons a republic or whether a parliament subdues a tyrant.

Thus Kant had developed his theory of right to its ultimate conclusion of total immobility, and he legitimated quite literally for eternity the constitution of any sort of state. He had narrowed the space in which he could expect results from his appeal to freedom. He placed his hopes for reform not in the constitution but in the system of governing and administration. Even in a monarchical state that has no representation the manner of governing can be republican. It can be conducted in a spirit fully imbued with consciousness of the dignity of all citizens. Kant calls such a government "patriotic."[40] Prussia had come closer to this through Frederick; Kant looked forward to a time when all states would be patriotic.

Nevertheless, it is not very satisfying to be forced to imagine the emergence of a world of patriotic states that as a whole have monarchical or aristocratic constitutions and that remain thus because principles of right obstruct their transformation into modern republics. But indeed there is no alternative for Kant's theory of the state. And right, the apple of God's eye, must be regarded as holy.[41] Even so Kant's thought in its entirety does offer other grounds for hope—grounds provided by the actual course of history: one can demonstrate that humanity's longing for freedom and its ability to exercise it will grow in the course of ages.[42] Human nature will not always be confinable within the limits of the law. Thus revolutions arise and republics in their train. Once they have made their appearance, they then enjoy the same right of defense against overthrow that all constitutions enjoy.[43] Only this time that right is directed against attempts at monarchical restoration. That which is ruled out from the standpoint of the intelligible idea of right can nonetheless be predicted according to the laws of the sensible world. It remains lamentable, all the same, that one has to anticipate progress through actions that must be regarded as supremely unjust from the standpoint of the idea, toward which the unfolding of progress is oriented.

And revolution is supremely unjust because it is an attack on the foundations for all actuality of right—the fundamental contract.[44] In this connection one has to understand that Kant does not just renounce revolution with regret but emphatically condemns it.[45] Revolution is in the realm of right what Kant calls "devilish" in morality: a will that opposes the principle itself, not merely evading it in one or another instance.[46] Here we see theoretical consistency governing the judgment of a thinker and, what is more, even the passion with which he expresses it.

Kant believed that his verdict against revolution could not, at least, be employed to demand unconditional obedience from citizens. The attempt to overthrow the authority of the state is wholly different from the refusal of obedience and public protest against illegal or immoral commands. He regarded such resistance as positively obligatory. Yet even for Kant it was possible to conceive conditions like those which have become reality for us, circumstances in which the person who places his hopes in passive resistance alone must be ready to encourage millions to face martyrdom. On at least one occasion Kant penned some sentences describing circumstances where force against the sovereign is justified. He names such instances "as would indeed not arise in a civil order (*in unionem civilem*), e.g., religious compulsion, compulsion to perform unnatural evils: assassination, etc."[47] In such cases a people is authorized to take preventive action and to hinder the government from proceeding with such deeds. But if one concedes this much, then one also has left room for an active right of resistance. It might seem that resistance against the government is not equivalent to an attack on the sovereign, but Kant expressly pronounced this distinction to be irrelevant.[48] And the context of the early reflection shows that Kant actually weighed a right of using force to alter the state—in the case of crimes of the state against humanity in its citizens. Yet Kant held even these considerations insufficiently strong to bar the conclusion that he later saw forced upon him.

Kant would not acknowledge revolution even on the basis of *moral* motives, which in drastic situations must look beyond all principles of right. In his ethics he had unmasked the popular conception that one could unburden oneself of duties of right when it is a matter of performing "the good." The heart of this critique is the correct thought that one may not do injury to right merely for the sake of well-being—even should it be the good of others who require selfless assistance. Kant was so dominated by this thought that without reflection he used it to answer a completely different question, that is, whether it could be imperative to defend the human rights of others through resistance to a violation of right, even if one thereby moves, in an extreme situation, outside the limits of political right. If such an act should not be advocated as a right, it can nevertheless fulfill a moral requirement and have moral greatness.[49] No theory will be satisfying that does not at least concede this much. Kant's theory is not wholly incapable of this.

Yet Kant himself thought differently. For him there was simply no ground on which a revolution as such could be defended. Then how should one understand his enthusiasm for the events in France? Kant worked out an elegant solution for his own problem of "uniting his head with his heart": the French Revolution is improperly named—it is actually no revolution at all. When the king summoned together the Estates General and delegated to them the task of reforming France, they thereby acquired full authority for giving their fatherland, according to their own judgment, a new constitution. Reforms are after all matters for the sovereign. Thus the king abdicated and simultaneously returned the Estates to the state of nature. "They were the representatives of all the people, once the king granted them unlimited authority to make decrees."[50] The conclusion is surprising: since in Kant's view it is the sovereign who overthrows the constitution by abdicating without an heir, Louis XVI is actually the only revolutionary of 1789. Of course, there were further transformations of the state as the Revolution progressed. Louis, who ascended the scaffold, had also been king in the new constitution. Thus he was manifestly not executed for being the revolutionary of the old order. It is well known that Kant raged against his execution as a perversion of the law of the state.[51]

In this way Kant reached casuistically his judgments, from the point of view of political right, about events having truly revolutionary character. He could therefore also welcome the Irish revolution against England without being untrue to his principles.[52] He never tried to work for a republic in Prussia. He approved of the fact that this weak state was monarchically organized to oppose the threat of Russian and Austrian power; a patriotic monarchy seemed to him to be the best guarantee of its citizens' freedom.[53] Often he thought that one indeed could interest this kingdom in the French Revolution, for he expected a readiness for a general peace in Europe to spread along with the Revolution. And in this way Prussia, and with it Königsberg, could live more securely.

Thus in the final analysis Kant's enthusiasm for the French Revolution was quite reconcilable in his mind with his duties as his monarch's subject and professor. This enthusiasm was appropriate for the attempt to secure the rights of humanity and to actualize fully the idea of the state, under favorable conditions. Even more, it was appropriate for the moral disposition that undertook such projects and that aroused similar dispositions throughout Europe. The recent example of this will "never be forgotten . . . so that it shall begin again in other ways, until it succeeds, and from that point onward cannot cease."[54]

The Unsolved Problem

"It will not cease." Gentz and Rehberg mistrusted this abjuring of a consummation. They wished to know the conditions under which reaching and preserving the goals of humanity "has success." They believed that enthusiasm renders the masses blind to the dangers inherent in all politics and inclined them to risk frivolously what was painstakingly acquired by generations—not the Holy Empire, but the system of the enlightened regime and its culture that respected particulars and cautiously developed the existing order. They opposed their concept of practice to Kant's, which claimed to be adequate for all practice—although indeed not for the revolutionary sort.

It was an error of both writers to suppose that one could ascertain the conditions of the good political order without taking into account the consciousness of the citizens who are integral to this order. Constitutions and complex ways of life never exist only as facts and cannot be, like organisms, merely the object of salutary guidance and intervention. Politics must exhibit their meaning and communicate it to citizens. Politics has genuine success only when it corresponds to a primary stratum of consciousness and is able to justify or to form a constitution with reference to it. The principle that politics must start from given conditions is an insufficient basis for any actual politics. While this principle has played a valuable role through its criticism of politics *more geometrico,* standing by itself it is abstract and leads to misjudging the particular character of circumstances. Changes can occur in the latter that call forth a new consciousness; conversely, a new consciousness can emerge that makes other changes inevitable. Even a liberal form of politics, if it cannot find a footing in such processes, necessarily ends up wanting to retard them or discovers itself again in league with a Holy Alliance. The empiricism of the allegedly real does not understand what is occurring when history advances. Metternich was the master of such empiricism.

Kant reproached this kind of practice for having intellectual arrogance and "mole-like vision."[55] The reproach is made polemically in the interest of rational right. Yet Kant's kind of practice also has its blind spot. It commences as desire for right and as moral imperative. But when the time comes for action, it becomes entangled in real factors that it does not perceive, because it looks too far beyond them. Gentz and Rehberg knew the mischief that this can cause. Thus, it is for persuasive reasons that they postulate a science of politics and society. And hence the question at issue between Kant's essay and the criticism of his two students is a momentous one about fundamentals.

We are familiar with two efforts of mediation wanting to perform justice to both points of view and nonetheless taking a stand in only one of the two principles—in the autonomy of theory or that of practice. Hegel sought to grasp conceptually all existence out of ideality, which actualizes itself in what exists. And Marx placed his system of mediation on the side of reality, as its basis, admitting only variations in the infrastructure. For the one, experience is conceived through theory; thus practice is determined by theory, without abandoning the standpoint of theory. For the other, all theory is derivative from practice in the universal system of self-production by the empirical human species.

Much can be said for regarding both attempts as failures. Success will not come to the effort to derive completely the categories of right from the process of labor and to make the self-interpretation of mankind a mere function of factual reproduction. And the effort equally miscarries of emancipating a dimension of ideality from all relation to existence, in order then to have historical worlds materialize out of this ideality as quintessence. In the dynamic of economic development consciousness is everywhere implicit, as product as much as condition. It can no more be derived from its various relations than these can be from it. Whoever contradicts this loses the basis for the definition of the concept of right. All the same, the concept of right by itself offers no guidance to action; it must be connected with an interpretation of the condition of the world, and only in this way can it become a program of political action. It is evident from the nature of interpretations and programs that they presuppose real conditions which they must investigate and to which they must seek to correspond. This does not signify that their purpose is only to justify such relations and that no means exist of consciously transcending the limits of the given. Yet every action, including the action of criticism, moves within a context of meaning that is concrete and motivated by a given set of conditions, and on whose basis alone one can attain something surpassing them.

An interdependence exists between reality and interpretation, and this interdependence forms the genuine dimension of conscious action. It remains the unsolved problem of philosophical theory to grasp this dimension conceptually and therewith to further a consciousness that can hold fast to this dimension and orient itself within it. The neglect of this task shatters the delicate balance between rational practice and humanity.

Notes

1
[Trans.: Immanuel Kant, *Über den Gemeinspruch: Das mag in der Theorie richtig sein, taugt aber nicht für die Praxis* (*On the Common Saying: That May Be True in Theory, But It Does Not Hold for Practice*, 1793). The page numbers for this and other works of Kant will be taken from the Prussian Academy edition of Kant's works, with the designation *AA* for *Akademieausgabe*. The present "Theory and Practice" essay is at *AA* 8:273–314. An edition of this essay is also provided in Henrich's *Über Theorie und Praxis.*]

2
Über den Gemeinspruch, AA 8:277.

3

Ibid., *AA* 8:275.

4

Christian Garve, *Versuche über verschiedene Gegenstände aus der Moral, Literatur und dem gesellschaftlichen Leben* (Breslau, 1792). [Trans.: A passage from this work (pp. 111–16 of the original) appears together with two later lectures of Garve examining the views of Kant on revolution and Rehberg on theory and practice in Henrich's *Über Theorie und Praxis*, pp. 131–59.]

5

See the review (1786) of Gottlieb Hufeland, *Versuch über den Grundsatz des Naturrechts,* in *AA* 8:125–30.

6

J. H. Abicht, *Neues System eines aus der Menschheit entwickelten Naturrechts* (Bayreuth, 1792); A. L. Ch. Heydenreich, *Entwurf der Grundsätze des absoluten Naturrechts* in *Originalideen über die interessantesten Gegenstände der Philosophie,* vol. 1 (1793), pp. 77ff.

7

The attempt by Paul Wittichen ("Kant und Burke," *Historische Zeitschrift* 93 (1904): 253ff.) to prove from a Latin citation Burke's significance for the first draft of Kant's essay is unconvincing. Kant always had at his disposal suitable citations from the extensive passages of Roman literature that he knew by heart. He could have found the opposition between theory and political experience equally as well in Justus Möser: "Thus have nations acted that are guided by experience and not mere theory." This passage is found in Möser's essay *Wann mag eine Nation ihre Konstitution verändern?* in the same Berlin *Monatsschrift,* vol. 2 (1791), pp. 400–01.

8

See A. G. Kästner in *Gesammelte poetische und prosaische schönwissenschaftliche Werke,* vol. 3 (Berlin, 1841), pp. 171ff.

9

See sec. 14 of Kant's *Dissertation* of 1770.

10

J. Ch. G. Schaumann, *Versuch über Aufklärung, Freiheit und Gleichheit, . . .* (Halle, 1793). One finds the evidence for Kant's referring to Kästner and Schaumann as he prepared to write on theory and practice in Rudolf Reicke, *Löse Blätter aus Kants Nachlass,* vol. 1 (Königsberg, 1889), pp. 148–49 and 179. The preliminary studies for this writing are collected in vol. 23 of the Academy edition, pp. 125ff.; however, they are taken out of the original context in which they stand in the *Löse Blätter,* thus rendering comprehension more difficult in some cases.

11

See Garve, *Versuche über verschiedene Gegenstände aus der Moral, Literatur und dem gesellschaftlichen Leben.*

12

Über den Gemeinspruch, AA 8:285.

13

Zedler's *Universal Lexikon,* vol. 29 (1741), the pertinent article.

14

Christian Wolff, *Philosophia practica universalis,* Pars II, Praefatio.

15

Aristotle, *Ethica Nicomachea,* 1140b.

16

F. Gentz, *Nachtrag zu dem Räsonnement des Herrn Professor Kant über das Verhältnis zwischen Theorie und Praxis* (December 1793); A. W. Rehberg, *Über das Verhältnis der Theorie zur Praxis* (February 1794). [Trans.: These are reprinted in Henrich, *Über Theorie und Praxis,* pp. 89–111 and 113–30, respectively.]

17

See the letter from Biester of 17 March 1794 and Kant's reply of 10 April 1794.

18

F. Gentz, *Über den Ursprung und die obersten Prinzipien des Rechts,* in the April 1791 volume, pp. 370ff. For Gentz one can compare the interesting interpretation by Golo

Mann, *Friedrich von Gentz* (Zürich, 1947), and the outstanding study by Paul R. Sweet, *Friedrich von Gentz* (Madison, Wis., 1941).

19

See the edition of E. Burke, *Betrachtungen über die französische Revolution,* translated by F. von Gentz with introduction by D. Henrich (Frankfurt am Main: Theorie-Suhrkamp, 1967).

20

Haym's presentation of Gentz, which is also revealing about Haym himself, is in the corresponding article of Ersch-Gruber. [Trans.: See Johann Samuel Ersch and J. O. Gruber, *Allgemeine Encyclopädie der Wissenschaften und Künste* (Leipzig, 1818–50).]

21

A useful study of Rehberg remains to be written.

22

A. W. Rehberg, *Über das Verhältnis der Metaphysik zu der Religion* (Berlin, 1787). E. Adickes says of this work, "An excellent book, which does credit to its motto" (*German Kantian Bibliography,* No. 392). The motto reads: "Drink deep or taste not."

23

The letter of 14 October 1790, in *AA* 11:225.

24

Über den Gemeinspruch, AA 8:288–89.

25

Gentz, *Nachtrag,* in Henrich, *Über Theorie und Praxis,* p. 103.

26

Ibid., p. 103.

27

Rehberg, *Über das Verhältnis,* in Henrich, *Über Theorie und Praxis,* p. 127.

28

G. Hufeland formulates a comparable program in his *Versuch über den Grundsatz des Naturrechts* (Leipzig, 1785), pp. 288ff., with respect to "a new necessary science."

29

Rehberg, *Über das Verhältnis,* p. 127.

30

Gentz, *Nachtrag,* pp. 105, 107.

31

See the Gentz translation of Burke, *Betrachtungen über die französische Revolution,* p. 61.

32

Rehberg, *Über das Verhältnis,* pp. 125ff.

33

My arguments in this section have been criticized by Werner Busch, *Die Entstehung der kritischen Rechtsphilosophie Kants* (Berlin, 1979), and Claudia Langer, *Reform nach Prinzipien* (Stuttgart, 1986).

34

According to Kant every human being in the natural condition has the *right* to compel every other to enter the political association. Through this thought Kant attempts, still in the spirit of natural right, to mediate the factual origination of the state through domination and the idea of the original contract. Compare *Metaphysik der Sitten, AA* 6:312, and above all the lectures on the metaphysics of morals in the transcript of Vigilantius, *AA* 27:515ff.

35

See Karl Vorländer, "Kants Stellung zur Französischen Revolution," in *Philosophische Abhandlungen, Hermann Cohen zum 70. Geburtstag* (Berlin, 1912); Werner Haensel, "Kants Lehre vom Widerstandsrecht," in *Kantstudien Ergänzungsheft* 60 (Berlin, 1926); Kurt Borries, "Kant als Politiker" (Leipzig, 1928), pp. 169ff.; Julius Ebbinghaus, "Staatsgewalt und Einzelverantwortung," in *Zu Deutschlands Schicksalswende,"* 2d ed. (Frankfurt, 1947), pp. 58ff.; Hans Reiss, "Kant and the Right of Rebellion," *Journal of the History of Ideas* 17:179ff.

36

Metaphysik der Sitten, AA 6:319.

37

Reflexion 8043, 8051, 8044 (*AA* 19:591).
Turba is the term by which political philoso-
phy designated revolution (as insurrection).
For the concept of revolution see Karl
Griewank, *Der neuzeitliche Revolutionsbegriff*
(Weimar, 1955).

38

Reflexion 8046 (*AA* 19).

39

Reflexion 8077 (*AA* 19:605).

40

Über den Gemeinspruch, AA 8:290–91.

41

Zum ewigen Frieden, AA 8:352–53 (second
note to the First Definitive Article).

42

Compare *Streit der Fakultäten* (part 2), *AA*
7:79–94, and *Zum ewigen Frieden* (1st supplement), *AA* 8:360–68.

43

Metaphysik der Sitten, AA 6:323.

44

Über den Gemeinspruch, AA 8:299.

45

Metaphysik der Sitten, AA 6:320ff.

46

*Religion innerhalb der Grenzen der blossen
Vernunft, AA* 6:35.

47

Reflexion 8051 (*AA* 19:594).

48

Metaphysik der Sitten, AA 6:319.

49

See J. B. Erhard, *Über das Recht des Volkes
zu einer Revolution* (Jena and Leipzig, 1795),
p. 69.

50

Reflexion 8055 (*AA* 19:595).

51

Metaphysik der Sitten, AA 6:320n.

52

Compare the diary of Abegg, still un-
published but cited by Karl Vorländer, *Immanuel Kant: Der Mann und sein Werk,* vol.
2 (Leipzig, 1924), p. 310.

53

Streit der Fakultäten, AA 7:86n.

54

Reflexion 8077 (*AA* 19:609); compare *Streit
der Fakultäten, AA* 7:87–89 (second part,
sec. 7).

55

Über den Gemeinspruch, AA 8:277.

Chapter 6

Commerce and Community
in Kant's Early Thought

Susan Shell

This chapter is concerned with certain anticipations of Kant's later political thought—specifically, with his protracted efforts in the 1750s to comprehend the universe (both physically and metaphysically) as a "community" of reciprocal, dynamically related elements. When Rousseau in the early 1760s "turned [Kant] around" by teaching him the supreme importance of the rights of man, he not only chastened Kant's metaphysical ambitions but also turned them in a new direction. Kant's earlier struggles with the idea of community made him particularly suscepti-ble to Rousseau's radical suggestions concerning the potential wholeness of the moral and political—that is to say, human—world, and with it the true nature of human dignity.[1]

In his introduction to the *Rechtslehre* (1797) Kant draws a peculiar and striking analogy between the juridical community of wills related through the laws of freedom and the natural community of matter(s) related through the laws of physics.[2] In each case, individuality and unity are reconciled in community, that is, in a whole formed through the reciprocal connection of independent elements.

Community so understood has the peculiar virtue of rendering wholeness intelligible without appealing, in the manner of ancient and scholastic science, to an "essential form," in other words, a ruling part by virtue of which the whole is governed or informed. Ancient and scholastic thought tended to think of wholeness as a function of "ruling and being ruled"—of a hierarchical ordering of hetero-geneous parts according to nature. As Aristotle puts it at the beginning of the *Politics:* "In all cases where there is a compound, constituted of more than one part but forming one common entity . . . a ruling element and a ruled can always be traced. This characteristic is present in animate beings by virtue of the whole constitution of nature, inanimate as well as animate; for even in things which are inanimate there is a sort of ruling principle, such as is to be found, for example, in a musical harmony" (1245a). So conceived, compound wholes owe their unity to a ruling part that informs the whole. All of nature is "in a way" governed by a principle of ruling and being ruled. Kant's understanding of unity, by contrast, makes form not a ruling part superior by nature to other parts, but a principle of interconnection among coequal parts. Its mode is not dominion but "reciprocity."

The conception of totality as a reciprocal community of coequal parts already appears in Kant's earliest works, in which he attempts to reconcile Leibnizian perfectionism with Newtonian mechanism. In such works as his *Nova dilucidatio* and *Universal Natural History and Theory of the Heavens,* Kant advances a notion of nature or the world-whole as a universal mechanical system that is at the same time the object of God's plan.[3] But these works also reveal the problematic character of totality-cum-community as Kant initially conceives it. The effort to think of the whole as a reciprocal community of self-subsistent elements founders on the question of the relation between that community and God who "grounds" it, that is, on Kant's characterization of the whole both as infinite (as befits the power of God) and as systematically bounded (as befits the capacities of human intelligence to grasp it).

Kant's idea of metaphysical totality is thus from the beginning affected by a peculiarly modern political analogy. The ancient conception of the hierarchically ordered regime (which permeated scholastic metaphysics) is largely replaced in Kant's thought by a model of reciprocal equality whose closest political analogue is market society.[4]

Largely but not entirely. In the first place, the informing laws of reciprocal (ex)change (*Wechsel*) that unite the elements of the world are themselves conceived by Kant as purposively implanted by a transcendent God. (To be sure, God governs not as a ruling participant—as direct intervention in the course of nature would imply—but only as an original source or "ground.") In the second place, the "rational spirits" (such as man) who do participate in nature's course constitute among themselves a hierarchy (or "ladder of perfection") based on their respective capacities to comprehend the whole, a hierarchy that progressively approaches divine perfection without ever being able to reach it.[5] As will appear below, Kant does not so much abandon teleology as appeal to it in a new way.

From the beginning, Kant's notion of community trades on a distinction between internal substance and external form, a distinction that arises from his effort to combine an essentially Leibnizian definition of beings as monadic (or internal) unities with an insistence on the reality of physical interaction (*Wechselwerkung* or *commercio*) as described by Newton's laws. The conflict between Newton and Leibniz arose in part from Leibniz's qualified "monadic" reprisal of the scholastic notion of substantial form. Leibniz's monads (unlike Newton's atoms) are simple and indivisible by virtue of an inward identity (on the model of human consciousness) rather than by arbitrary fiat (for how else impose a limit on the infinite divisibility of matter understood purely as extension). Unlike atoms, monads are true wholes containing the inward principle of their own unity. At the same time they are also parts of the world-whole, not through a problematic interplay with other atoms (which would call into question each monad's radical simplicity) but rather through their "inward" (re)presentation of that greater whole. Each monad is unique by virtue of the unique degree of clarity and distinctness that characterizes its representation of the universe. For its part, physical interaction is merely a *phenomenon bene fundatum,* based on the change in inward state that each monad interprets as an event in the external world.

Leibniz is able to conceive parts of nature as simple unities and the whole of nature as a complete totality without giving up the validity of mathematical physics, which assumes the homogeneity of matter and boundlessness of space. But to do so he must sacrifice (from Kant's point of view) the reality of the physical interaction governed by those mathematical laws.[6]

Like Leibniz, Kant attempts to understand nature both physically and metaphysically, both as the object of mathematical laws and as a complete totality composed of simple elements. The difference between them begins with their differing views of man himself. As early as 1755, Kant is convinced that consciousness is the product of real interaction between body and soul. The simple identity of Leibniz's monad is shattered rather than supported by man's own internal experience. Unlike the monad, whose simple unity bespeaks its immortality, the conscious self is a divided entity, defined by a community of body and soul that is at once a given fact and an "unexplored problem." The relatively crude epistemologies of these early works will later give way to more complicated formulations; but what never changes is Kant's concern with the problem posed by this inner mystery of a self that is at once of nature and against it. For this reason, perhaps, several of Kant's early writings are haunted by the horror of death as a succumbing to natural flux, and by a not always convincing insistence on human immortality.[7]

The problem of community emerges with particular force in the *Nova dilucidatio* (1755). The basic issue that Kant confronts is one of accounting for (our knowledge of) the world as a complex unity.

What is noteworthy, from the perspective of the later development of his thought, is Kant's early association of the unity of the world-whole with "community," that is, with formal or "external" reciprocity among elements that are substantially or "internally" independent. The difficulty to be resolved for Kant is how substances can be conceived in these two necessary but seemingly incompatible ways: on the one hand, substances, as simplest elements of matter, cannot themselves undergo change (that is left to their accidents). But on the other hand, the physical laws of reciprocal action seem to entail the action of one substance upon (and hence a change in the essential nature of) another. How, then, are such universal principles of reciprocal interaction as the law of conservation (and with it the idea of the world as a physical totality) to be reconciled with the notion of simple and unchanging substances? Rejecting Leibniz's appeal to the principle of "pre-established harmony" for its reduction of physical interaction to the status of a mere "phenomenon," Kant appeals instead to an initial "grounding" act of God: God somehow contrives that substances, in their very "internal" existence, are so related to one another as to be mutually interactive: "Finite substances stand, through their mere existence (*Dasein*) in no relation to one another and therefore have no community, except insofar as they are maintained in reciprocal relation through the common ground of their existence, namely the divine understanding" (1:413; 100). Apart from such a common ground "the universal relatedness of things [*allgemeine Verknüpfung*] would be inconceivable" (1:414; 103).

Relatedness must be thought of in this way because our knowledge of determinate substances (things determined in a particular way) must ultimately refer their cause to a ground beyond themselves, a ground Kant here associates with the will of God. Leibnizian monadism had turned on the claim that substances internally or analytically "contain" the successive determinations of their own inner states. The changes that a substance appears to undergo in the "external" world are in reality a function of the dynamics of its own inner state, derivable in principle from an analysis of the essential nature of the substance itself. Contingent and analytic truths are thus in principle identical, however much we may distinguish them in practice. Scientific knowledge finds its ultimate "necessity" in the analytic entailment of what is conceptually contained in the predicate (or determination) by what is conceptually contained in the subject (or substance).

Kant, on the other hand, begins by defining impossibility (or the incompatibility of a subject and a predicate) in such a way that every subject has a range of possible predicates, none of which can be singled out as determinate through analysis alone. Every subject has a range of predicates with which it is compatible but none of which it necessarily entails to the exclusion of the rest. The actual determination of a substance thus requires a ground (*Ratio, Grund*) independent of and antecedent to the substance itself. No substance contains the ground of its own necessity. And since to know a thing for Kant means to know its reason (*Ratio*) or cause, knowledge of contingent truths about substances, that is, their determination in one among many possible ways, must look finally beyond substances to the arbitrary choice of God, who has called a substance into existence in a particular way.

What follows from this is that the knowable connection between subject and predicate must be preceded by "existence," or the actual instantiation of a substance in a particular way among the many that are analytically possible. Knowledge requires the prior determinate existence of the substance known. But the question that remains is how this knowledge is communicated to us. If analysis of our concepts cannot by itself yield knowledge about what exists, such knowledge must somehow be communicated by our "contact" with these existents themselves. And yet, as John Reuscher points out, it is difficult to see how this is possible. The intellectual connection between subject and predicate in the mind of God, a connection that ultimately explains what it is that makes our knowledge of something, our own conjunction of subject and predicate, "true," seems to be in principle inaccessible to us. At the same time, mere "contact" with the thing does not seem to yield the knowledge of cause required for knowledge as such, since no thing contains the ground of its own necessity. [8]

As a result, the beginnings of a deep concern with the problematic relation between thought and matter begin to surface. Kant's efforts to discover the conditions of knowledge as such point to the need to cast a more refined light upon this relation.

At the same time, Kant's more explicit concern is with the implications for worldhood of this common referral of all knowledge of determinate substances to the will of God. For it means that all substances are intrinsically united by virtue of the very cause that renders them individually determinate. Thus the problem of reconciling individual substances with the reciprocal community implied by the laws of physics is resolved by an appeal to their "communal" (*gemeinschaftliche*) ground. Where self-subsistent, monadic substances can only coexist, Kant's existents are immediately provided with a basis for community.

Kant's objection to Leibniz turns not on a rejection of the scholastic identification of substance and permanence but rather on its more absolute assertion. The rich internal dynamic of Leibniz's "windowless" monad is impossible for the same reason that a substance cannot change itself. A "simple substance cut off from every external connection and left by itself in isolation" is "obviously *per se* immutable." Consequently, "in a world devoid of all motion (as a matter of fact, motion is the phenomenon of change in the connection of things) not the least trace of succession is to be found even in the internal condition of substances" (1:410; 96).

Kant is not willing to leave succession to the "arbitrary" ground that would make knowledge, for us at least, impossible. Succession is governed by a necessity accessible to us, as evidenced by our knowledge of the physical laws of motion. The change in inner state that must ultimately be referred to the will of God is penultimately referred to a "real relation" between substances, a relation without which "time and succession [would] take their leave." Kant thus rejects the Leibnizian claim that substances change by virtue of "an internal principle of activity," and with it the claim that change is a function, not of the "real" interaction of substances, but of their "preestablished" internal harmony. Inner change can only occur because substances are united by real relations governed by the law of action and reaction.

Anticipating his later critical thought, Kant steers a middle course between "idealism" and "realism": knowledge involves a mental representation of the whole (as Leibniz recognized); but such representation, to the extent that it involves an awareness of change, requires real interaction. Finite human intelligence is by definition subject to external opposition. The successive character of our knowledge goes together with an awareness of time that implicates us in turn in the real world of material exchange. To think as a finite being is to think successively and therewith to be linked to a body subject to destruction. To escape mutability and its hazards would be to ascend to the timelessness of the divine mind, and thus to obliterate consciousness as we know it. Leibniz's immediate—and sanguine— identification of substance, consciousness, and immortality is thus thrown radically into question.

At the same time, Kant's reprisal of real interaction stops short of what he calls "true physical influx." Interaction (*commercio*) does not imply a flow from one substance to another, as "influx" literally implies. Substances have the power to determine other substances, not by virtue of their own "inner characteristics" but only by virtue of the connection in which such substances are held in the idea or "schema" of "an infinite being" (1:415; 104).

Thus substances are mutually dependent without ever breaching one another's internal integrity. Whatever determinations and changes occur always pertain merely to their "external aspect." Kant locates the superiority of his account to the absolute idealism of Leibniz on the one hand and to crude materialism on the other, in its disclosure of the very origin and ground of "the mutual connection of things," an origin not to be found in substances considered in isolation. As individuals we are sustained not by internal principles unique to each consciousness but by an immediate and at the same time common (or communal) relation to the grounding intelligence of God.

The soul is thus spared the ravages of crude or true flux, the homogeneous flow of force that Kant replaces with a reciprocally interactive or "commercial" reality. By replacing Leibnizian "force" with "reality" as that which the physical universe "conserves," and by at the same time identifying reality with the infinite potency of divine creation, Kant lays down his own schema for nature as a totality at once boundless and contained.

Leibniz had understood the total quantity of reality of the universe as a maximum limited by the condition of "compossibility"—the incompatibility of some intrinsically possible substances with others. God, according to Leibniz, creates the best (most real) world possible, and not every substance intrinsically possible in the sense of being thinkable without contradiction. But for Kant God's power succumbs to no such limitation. God's will is not determined by an independent standard of compossibility. Rather, God precedes possibility. The total quantity of reality that the universe "conserves" is not a "maximum" conditioned by the possible but a direct expression of God's infinite plenitude.

Kant's treatment of perfection as a conjunction of unity and infinite diversity is linked directly to this claim. God's decision to create an endless diversity of existents does not await a prior calculation of their mutual possibility. If Leibniz's God is a prudent maximizer, subjecting his expenditure of power to the rule of a prior cost-benefit analysis, the infinite potency of Kant's God suffers no such maximizing limitation; reality is both infinite (by virtue of God's power) and unified (by virtue of his harmony of purpose). If Leibniz's God is the prototypical entrepreneur, bound in his choice of this world as the "best possible" by the cosmic equivalent of the profit motive, Kant's is a kind of cosmic invisible hand, harmonizing through common laws and "behind the scene" a whole whose elements appear to go their separate ways.[9]

Kant's attempt to set forth the foundations of metaphysical knowledge culminates in two "new principles" concerning, respectively, succession and coexistence. The first asserts change or succession (in a substance's inner state) to be a function of reciprocal dependence, that is, real interaction or commerce (*commercio*) among substances (1:410; 96). The second asserts that substances "by their mere existence" are unrelated and enter into "commerce" only insofar as they are so maintained by God, the "common ground" of their existence (1:413; 100). To be comprehended, worldhood requires both a principle of succession (without which elements would merely coexist as ontological isolates) and a principle of ultimate grounding in a schema whose immediate comprehension of the whole transcends succession. We need to assume the divine schema as ground of the whole. But we cannot understand the schema itself. To this extent, we cannot fully grasp the whole, or make its possibility fully intelligible to ourselves.

One implicit argument of the *Nova dilucidatio,* then, runs something like this: things belong to a common world not through coexistence alone but through their thoroughgoing mutual relatedness. At the same time, Leibniz's effort to internalize this mutual relatedness, that is, to deny the reality of physical interaction, is nullified for Kant by what he calls the principle of "determining reason." Every substance "contains" all the predicates with which it can possibly be united, which it does not logically contradict. Thus its factual union with a given predicate to the exclusion of all other possible predicates (with which it may in the past or future be united) cannot be determined by a principle internal to the substance itself but requires some external agency. Our own experience of the phenomenon of motion (in which one inner determination succeeds another) therefore precludes our monadic isolation. To be conscious of change and succession is to be subject to external determination. But this subjection does not constitute a threat to our substantival integrity as knowers. Both the permanence of substance and the worldhood constituted by the laws of motion find reconciliation in their referral to a common ground, that is, to God's interlocking purposes, which determine things both in their individual existence and their mutual "commercial" relatedness. Indeed, assurance of our own substantive integrity seems to depend on our ability to render the whole intelligible in these terms. But our very need to represent this ground in terms of a schema suggests the difficulty. A "schema" is literally a diagrammatic or spatial plan for what is (for us at least) a temporal process.[10] Kant can make the whole intelligible only by referring it to a ground in which the unity that we experience successively (and which remains to this extent disunity) arises out of an immediate purposive harmony. The principle of succession that links us to the world and plays itself out in time is just what must be overcome if the world is to be grasped in its entirety.

The tension between limitless succession and immediate totality is a central theme of Kant's other major work of the same year, the *Universal Natural History and Theory of the Heavens*. Where *Nova dilucidatio* lays down the metaphysical principles underlying our knowledge of the world-whole, the *Universal Natural History* spells out their implications for a physical account of nature. This work is an inquiry into the "constitution and mechanical origin of the world-whole constructed according to Newtonian principles," that is, an extension of mechanical principles beyond the static planetary boundaries (to which Newton confined them) to the natural order "in its entirety."

In drawing out the universal implications of Newton's laws Kant believes he can meet the objections, both philosophic and religious, raised by his predecessors.

Newton had rejected a mechanical history of the solar system, on the grounds that the emptiness of space precludes the sort of material community needed to explain in strictly mechanical terms the mutual influence of the planets. Instead, he insisted that the system could only have come about through the immediate action of God (1:262; 113). Kant counters by turning to history itself for the requisite material foundation. While vast stretches of space are now empty, he argues, this need not always have been the case. The physical community of influence that seems lacking when attention is directed merely to the present can be uncovered successively by tracing the evolution of the heavenly system from an original "state of nature" in which matter was evenly dispersed throughout space.

But in extending Newton's principles beyond the present heavenly order to an explanation of its genesis Kant runs the grave risk of suggesting the Epicurean all-sufficiency of nature and with it the redundancy of God: "If the structure of the world with all its order and beauty . . . is only an effect of matter left to its own universal laws of motion, and if the blind mechanics of the natural forces can evolve so masterfully out of chaos . . . then the proof of the divine author that is drawn from the spectacle of the beauty of the universe wholly loses its force. Nature is thus sufficient for itself; the divine government is unnecessary; Epicurus lives again in the midst of Christiandom" (1:222; 82).

Kant must thus rebut the charge of atheism; he must show that a complete mechanical cosmogony supports faith rather than undermines it. The key to doing so, according to Kant, lies in the principles of Newtonian science itself, which replace the Epicurean appeal to chance with an insistence on the lawlike necessity of nature's course. Like Epicurus, Kant will explain the evolution of the universe in its present state out of a primitive chaos in which the elements of matter are evenly dispersed. But unlike Epicurus he will attribute this evolution, not to chance, as if the present arrangement of the planets "might just as easily have turned out otherwise," but to a necessity intrinsic to the constitution of matter itself. Where Epicurean matter is "free" in the sense of acting "without a cause," Kantian matter "is bound to certain necessary laws" (1:228; 86).

Kant's distinction between the cosmos as described by Epicurus and the actual universe repeats the distinction that he elsewhere draws between a mere aggregate of coexistents and a genuine whole or "world." Where the constituents of an aggregate lack a principle of mutual connection, those of a whole are linked by necessary laws of interaction. Against Epicurean anarchy or freedom without cause, Kant poses his own model of freedom consistent with the rule of law. Matter remains free in that it acts according to its own nature, while at the same time it remains bound to certain laws. The principle of connectedness by which the elements of the universe are joined is thus one of "reciprocal or mutual determination," in which the independence of the elements is reconciled with their mutual relatedness.

Epicurus's "deepest error"—his "absurd" appeal to chance or "freedom without cause"—led Epicurus to derive "reason from unreason." The necessity that underlies the laws of motion is incompatible, according to Kant, with atheism. Nature (as he argued in *Nova dilucidatio*) cannot ground its own necessity. To uphold the principle of universal mechanism is thus to reject Epicurean materialism, or the homogeneity of thought and matter. Universal mechanism cannot be comprehended without appealing to a higher principle of (divine) reason. Nature conceived as a self-contained, reciprocal totality, a perfect machine, points necessarily beyond nature to an original grounding source, a source from which nature itself is radically distinct (1:228; 86).

In Kant's version of Epicurean chaos, order arises neither from chance nor from the direct intervention of God, but from a matter "that essentially contains the principles of its own motion." Each element of primitive matter is, on the one hand, irreducible and self-subsistent, and yet at the same time related to all other elements through an "original community" in the creative intellect of God. The material community that obtains at the beginning of creation would not suffice without the prior act of creation itself, that is, without the community that derives from the relation of nature to something beyond itself.

Rather than "planting Epicurus in the midst of Christiandom," Kant's efforts aim to reveal the intrinsic harmony between mechanistic science and a rational teleology: the essential character of each element of nature is at the same time a reflection of God's purpose in creating it. Nature for Kant is a kind of self-winding watch, a *perpetuum mobile* that reveals the hand of God not through the inadequacy but rather the perfection of its interactive mechanism.

Kant's idea of perfection thus takes its bearings not from the Aristotelian and scholastic notion of a virtue or qualitative excellence of a specific kind (as in the "virtue" of a horse) but from that of reciprocal harmony as such. Kant portrays the universe as analogous to a machine whose perfection lies in its own infinite articulateness. Both here and in his later critical treatment of living beings as "organic" or "infinitely well-wrought" machines, Kant collapses the Aristotelian distinction between animals, who have a principle of motion in themselves, and tools, whose end is always beyond themselves. The teleological impetus of the *Universal Natural History* thus anticipates Kant's (and Hegel's) later distinction between intrinsic or "organic" and extrinsic purposiveness. [11] It is not merely the machine as a product of human making that inspires Kant's conception of the whole, for machines in the ordinary sense are means and tools rather than intrinsic unities. As Hegel suggests, Kant's conception of the organic machine—a machine as an intrinsic whole or unity—seems to borrow at least partially from a peculiarly modern conception of political community. Kant's whole is informed not by a ruling part (as in the Aristotelian regime) but by a principle of reciprocal equality that he himself later likens to a republican form of government. [12]

In Kant's version of Epicurean chaos, order arises neither from chance nor from the continual intervention of God, but from a matter "that essentially contains the principles of its own motion." Accordingly, Kant's point of historical departure is that first moment in which matter was infinitely and equally distributed throughout space, that is, that "state of nature" in which "nothing has yet developed" and which is "the very simplest that can follow upon nothing" (1:263; 114). But what does it mean to be the simplest that can follow upon nothing, or as he also puts it, to be as "unformed as possible"? Matter has an elemental form, an "internally dictated character," which though apparently "struck out" at random, gives matter in its simplest and apparently formless state a tendency to develop itself into a "more perfect constitution." We are compelled to regard matter as internally receptive (of the "character" impressed upon it by the divine understanding) and at the same time externally active. The contradiction between these two opposing ways of regarding matter—as passive and active, intrinsically formless and intrinsically informed—is overcome in the idea of form as telos, that is, as a divinely dictated principle of temporal development. Passive with respect to God, matter is active with respect to its own historical evolution. A rational conception of matter thus involves an appeal to teleology as the original ground of the self-organizing tendency of nature. At the same time, Kant sidesteps the question of the relation between the characters of the various elements in their infinite diversity and the comprehension of this diversity by universal laws of motion. Kant appeals, not to the classical telos of heterogeneous kinds, but to one realized in and by nature as a whole. His standard of perfection is thus intrinsically unitary or homogeneous. At the same time, he attributes the initial disruption of the primal repose to the diversity of the elements, to the "difference in kinds," without which universal equilibrium (*Gleichheit*) among the dispersed elements would prevail in perpetuity. Reconciliation of the infinite diversity of the elements with their intrinsic unity, their capacity to order themselves into a common system, is achieved through its quantitative translation, that is, through the expression of qualitative diversity in terms of variable degrees of specific density. Thus Kant is able to insist both on the qualitative diversity of the elements (or "matters") and on the quantitative commensurability of matter in general.[13] The heterogeneity of intrinsic diversity of the elements is no bar to their formal homogeneity or commensurability (1:263–64; 114).

The common characteristic by which all matter is united is its susceptibility to the forces of attraction and repulsion. Repulsion (*Zurückstossungskraft*), Kant's own addition to the Newtonian system, is that force without which dispersed matter would simply collapse toward the points of greater attraction (*Anziehungskraft*), creating isolated clumps of matter that would coexist forever in static equilibrium. The dynamic interaction of matter requires this additional force, which Kant associates especially with the volatility of gasses of "strongly smelling bodies," that is, with the tendency of matter to disperse itself through a kind of self (or mutual) aversion.

Accordingly, the primal repose of the initial chaos "could last only an instant," as the denser matters would begin immediately to exercise their forces of attraction against those less dense. Where a merely homogeneous universe would remain forever at rest, a universe combining commensurability with infinite variety, the homogeneous with the heterogeneous, gives rise to an orderly or law-governed dynamic (1:264; 114).

Like Epicurus, Kant begins with falling bodies, but ones whose straight course is deflected not by an inexplicable "swerving" but by the lawful forces of repulsion, as particles attracted toward a central body "resist" each other's motion. Kant attributes the "free circular motion" of the planets in their orbits to the force of attraction in combination with this latter force, whereby movements "in conflict with each other . . . tend to bring one another to a uniformity [*Gleichheit*], that is, into a state in which one movement is as little obstructive to the other as possible" (1:266; 116). Kant's notion seems to be that particles will be drawn into elliptical vortices in which the sinking force [*Senkungskraft*] exercised by the center of attraction is countered by centrifugal force [*Schwungskraft*] caused by mutual repulsion, vortices that the same force of repulsion will gradually tend to regularize, so that particles come to orbit the center at a distance proportional to their density.

One is struck by the political—indeed Hobbesian—resonance of this model, in which the chaos of an original "state [*Zustand*] of nature" gives rise, through a combination of mutual conflict and mutual attraction to a common center, to free yet ordered motion, and in which bodies bring one another into a state of least reciprocal action (*Wechselwirkung*) or minimum mutual obstruction. Indeed, Kant's derivation of the "constitution" (*Verfassung*) of the planetary system seems to anticipate to a remarkable degree Kant's later definition of a just "constitution" as one allowing "the greatest possible human freedom in accordance with laws by which the freedom of each is made to be consistent with that of all others."[14] The resulting planetary system, in which planets orbit the sun in order of increasing density as they approach the center, suggests to Kant a model for accounting for the origin of the larger stellar systems. The principles that explain the formation of the solar system can by analogy be extended to the galaxies or fixed stars. This extension provides not merely for a quantitative expansion of the reach of mechanical cosmology, but for its true comprehensiveness: the principles that enable Kant to generate the solar system will allow him to "grasp together in a single doctrine the infinity of the entire creation" (1:265; 115).[15]

Kant is driven by the very boundlessness of the universe to extend the principles of systematic constitution to nature in its entirety. What is true of the parts ad infinitum must be true of the whole. Further, if nature were not united into a single system by the connecting power of attraction and centrifugal force, its structures would be unstable, and the order of its secondary systems sustainable only by a continuing miracle.

But several obstacles stand in the way of conceiving nature as system. In the first place, the infinity of space does not seem to support system's requirement of a central point.[16] Kant counters (inadequately) that although space as such has no center, some area of space must contain the densest matter, and that this area will constitute a de facto center of greatest attraction, a kind of "pivot" of nature into which the rest would collapse if the forces of attraction were not countered by the laws of repulsion and resistance (1:312; 153).[17]

In the second place, there is the related difficulty of conceiving nature as an interactive or reciprocal totality that is at the same time inclusive of infinity. Kant answers by supposing that while matter is infinitely dispersed from the moment of creation, organized nature must become so: the development of organized nature begins at the center of attraction, gradually extending outward so as "to fill up infinite space in the progress of eternity" (1:312; 153). The notion of nature as an unbounded totality (or infinite system) is thus represented by the image of a circle extending progressively outward from a central point: "however far the development of nature may extend, it will make only one single system in the infinite sphere of creation." We can conceive of nature as a systematic whole, a totality composed of an infinite number of elements, by representing their interconnection temporally, as a history with a beginning but no end. Only the divine intelligence can grasp eternity and so take in infinite totality at a single glance. For man it is necessary to conceive the systematic order of the whole as nature's endless organizing task (1:314; 155).[18]

Creation is at once God's immediate product and an ongoing, infinite process, in which the closure implicit in reciprocal unity is reconciled with boundlessness.

In this process, the decay of regions previously organized is more than offset by the ordering of the new:

> One can reckon the inevitable tendency, which each world-edifice [which has already been] brought to perfection has [in a] gradually [increasing degree] toward its destruction, among the reasons which can assure that the universe in other regions becomes conversely fruitful in [producing new] worlds to offset the lack which it has suffered at one [specific] place. The entire piece of nature that we know . . . confirms this fruitfulness of a nature that is without limits, because it is nothing else but the exercise of divine omnipotence itself. Uncounted animals and plants are destroyed daily and are a sacrifice to transitoriness; but nature, through an inexhaustible capability of generation, brings forth no fewer [animals and plants] in other places and fills out the emptiness. Considerable pieces of the earth's surface, which we inhabit, become again buried in the sea, from which a favorable period had brought them forth; but in other places nature completes the defect and brings forth other regions . . . in order to spread over these new riches of her fruitfulness. In such a way worlds and world-systems . . . are devoured by the abyss of eternity; however, creation is always busy in setting up new formations in other celestial regions and in repairing loss with gain. (1:316–17; 156–57)

Nature is thus at once finite and infinite, the metaphorical invocation of fecundity suggesting the analogy of life, in which the transitory character of the individual is offset by the eternity of the species. But precisely this analogy points up the difficulty: the classical doctrine of eternal species contradicts the biblical doctrine of creation. Kant's attempt to reconcile the finitude of nature qua creation with its infinity qua expression of the infinite power of the creator depends on a fundamental equivocation concerning the relation between nature and God. Kant's representation of nature as an infinite whole thus requires him to be both a theist and a pantheist, just as it forces him to conflate—or confuse—the relation between parts and wholes with the relation between finite numbers and infinity.

This fundamental equivocation finds further expression in Kant's representation of nature as a kind of cosmic economy. To this "economy of nature"[19] the destruction of a world is "no true loss" (*Verlust*): "Nature demonstrates her richness in a kind of squandering [*Verschwendung*] which, while some parts pay tribute to transitoriness, maintains itself undamaged through innumerable new products in the entire extent of her perfection. What an uncountable amount of flowers and insects perishes every cold day; but how little does one miss them, regardless [of the fact that] they are the splendid artifacts of nature and pieces of evidence of divine omnipotence; in another place this loss will be offset by overflow."

Nor is man, who seems to be the masterpiece of creation, exempted from this law.

> Nature demonstrates that she is just as rich, just as inexhaustible in bringing forth the most excellent among creatures, and that their decay is a necessary nuance in the manifoldness of her suns because their production costs her nothing. The harmful effects of polluted air, the earthquakes, the floods wipe out entire nations from the surface of the earth, but it does not appear that nature thereby suffers any loss. In a similar way entire worlds and systems leave the stage after they have played their role. The infinity of creation is great enough to view in relation to itself a world or a Milky Way of worlds [in the same way] in which man looks upon a flower or an insect in comparison with the earth. Thus, while nature decks out eternity with changing shows, God remains busy in an unceasing creation to shape the means for the formation of still greater worlds. (1:318; 157–58)

Indifferent to degrees of excellence, Nature's economy conflates value and existence, as it both binds together and dissolves organized bodies through a common system of exchange. Thus man's regard for himself as the "masterwork" and most excellent part of creation must defer to that point of view according to which every part is equally significant (or insignificant) because equally necessary to the whole.

Man is thus beset by a problem to which death and dishonor equally adhere, and in which pride is linked inextricably with fear. The material vulnerability that subjects man to the economy of nature poses a threat not only to his body but also to his self-esteem. In the face of this dismaying prospect, Kant urges that we "accustom our eye to nature's terrible convulsions," and thereby come to give it "a kind of approval." What is taken from man as a participant in nature's "play" is in a sense restored to him as a spectator and observer. For what man learns as observer is that death is the price of participation in the whole from whose play all value ultimately derives. In the "theater of the ongoing changes of the universe" everything must "play the role that taxes each finite being, namely that each should bring its levy to transitoriness" (1:319; 158).[20] By identifying with the whole, man finds a kind of satisfaction to offset his own material fungibility within it.

This satisfaction is increased by imagining nature not merely as an economy of equivalence, in which vitality balances decay, but one of boundless increase: so long as one may imagine, "as is likely," that organized nature will persist in its developed state for a longer time than it took for its formation, then "regardless of all the devastations that transitoriness incessantly serves up," the extent of the [organized] universe will increase" (1:319–20; 159). So construed, nature as a closed economy of equivalence (in which nature merely breaks even, so to speak) gives way to nature as an open economy of limitless abundance, in which production costs her nothing.

But the highest degree of satisfaction and approval Kant reserves to an image of nature that transcends mere linear progress, replacing it with one of perpetual alteration (*Veränderung*). The infinite potency of nature supports the supposition that the decayed portions of the universe will regain their former order, subject as they are to the same forces that led to their original organization out of chaos. Thus nature's progressive development is at the same time an eternal recurrence, a repeating wave of creation and destruction. Kant attempts to combine the image of boundless advance, or linear progress, with one of phoenixlike oscillation: "If then we follow this phoenix of nature, which burns itself out only to revive from its ashes . . . across all infinity of times and spaces . . . then one's spirit, which reflects on all this, plunges into a deep astonishment" (1:321; 160).

We are left wondering whether nature as a whole is to be conceived as a closed or open system. The image of the universe as an infinitely expanding circle coexists uneasily with one of eternal recurrence, of pulsating expansion and contraction in which nothing finally is gained or lost. Boundless potency seems to contradict the law of conservation. This basic tension between closure and expansion (a tension that cuts to the heart of the German idealist notion of dynamic totality) will later be made much of by Marx, who treats it as symptomatic of the fundamental contradiction inherent in the capitalist system between the circulation of value and its reproduction. However this may be, Kant here seems unable to settle upon a stable image for the structure of the universe, one that does justice both to the principle of infinite force or potency and to the principle of conservation.[21]

It seems at first as though this reconciliation is figuratively achieved by the image of an oscillating universe, whose cycles of organization and decay repeat forever. But this image rests on an equation of the original and later conditions of chaos that is at odds with the systematic interconnectedness (or material "community") of nature. The process of organized creation can repeat exactly only if the conditions are exactly the same. But this is precisely what Kant's argument calls into question: if everything in nature is interdependent, the primal state of chaos that extends throughout the universe originally must differ essentially from subsequent states of chaos that coexist with organized regions elsewhere in space. Infinite chaos and finite chaos cannot be the same. To this extent, Kant's argument for a recurrence to order seems to deny the existence of a unique or primal disorder, and with it creation itself. The image of phoenixlike repetition (which presupposes the similarity of each state of chaos) is at odds with the idea of divine creation (which implies an original chaos essentially different from those that follow, given the systematic interdependence of nature on which Kant insists).

The argument for nature's infinity as a necessary consequence of God's boundless potency ends by attributing to nature a boundless potency that calls into question divine creation. To put the difficulty another way, Kant's effort to make infinity imaginable by projecting the act of creation over time ("creation is not the act of a moment") leads to a fundamental equivocation as to whether nature is the product of creation, or itself its ongoing process.

This equivocation is reflected in Kant's suggestions that nature, which qua process fills out time to eternity, must qua product come finally to an end. To be sure, these suggestions are themselves equivocal. There is, says Kant, "a certain transitoriness even in the great [context and syntax would lead us to expect *greatest*] of the works of God." But he adds that "all that is finite, whatever has a beginning and origin, has the mark of its limited nature in itself; it must perish and come to an end." The inevitable exhaustion that overtakes every organized natural structure both does and does not, it seems, apply to nature as a whole. If some passages suggest a process of outwardly expanding renewal, in which stellar systems collapse into their center and are reborn, others suggest a pulsating cycle that encompasses nature in its entirety. Here it is not just the revolving movements of stars or planets, but those of the universe as such that "arrive at a state of final exhaustion" (1:318; 157).[22] By this account it is not merely the finite stellar systems but the universe itself that is subject to an eternal pattern of contraction and expansion.

In the end, Kant's image of the universe as an expanding yet eternally repeating order fails to congeal. His combination of the arrow and the phoenix "astonishes" the spirit; but the "transitoriness" of its "immense object" fails to satisfy the soul (1:321; 160). Projected over time into infinity, the structure of the heavens refuses to stand still.

Kant has postulated a principle of systematic, universal connection that can contain infinity and, in particular, that infinitely potent flux by which formed bodies (including our own) are created and destroyed. The proliferating and fecund heterogeneity of nature that awed imagination is brought to order by principles that understanding can grasp. So ordered, imagination's "abyss" becomes reason's system and whole. But the discrepancy remains between what the mind can take in and subdue at a glance and what refuses to stand still. The spirit that reflects upon all of this plunges into "sunken astonishment," while the transitoriness of nature (or our image of it) fails to satisfy the soul. As the *Nova dilucidatio* suggested, the principle of succession that informs both the world and our knowledge of it aborts our effort to grasp nature as a whole. The soul seeks (but cannot rationally find) knowledge beyond the chain of flux that binds it to the world. What is permanent in nature is not a stable order of eternal kinds but laws of motion or change. The soul must therefore look beyond reason for assurance of its own permanence.

At this point Kant discards the expanding circle/phoenix image and recurs to divine understanding as the ultimate (yet, to our reason, inaccessible) ground of creation. In its "community" with this source the human spirit is elevated above the height of its own perishableness. The eternal life and happiness that revelation promises places the soul in a position from which it can see the "tumult of the elements and ruins [*Trümmern*] of nature" whose "havoc," caused by the frailty (*Hinfälligkeit*) of things of the world, roars by beneath its feet. The soul observes the world without engaging it. From such a height the regularity or certainty of the whole and our own security, the well-ordered character of the whole and our own well-being, no longer divide themselves. Kant's very characterization of happiness in terms of a nature that shows transparent *Sicherheit,* suggesting as it does both regularity (in itself) and security (for us), or rather an assimilation for both viewed and viewer of certain knowledge and security, points to the limits of his rational systematization of the universe. For the elements that retain their essential living force in perpetuity are quite distinct from the all too alterable living bodies on which human spirits depend (at least so far as reason can tell).

Accordingly, the spirit seeks knowledge of God, source of the light spread over nature, "as from a midpoint." The system of nature can adequately be grasped only from a point that is both within the system and beyond it. "When the chains which keep us bound to the futility/vanity [*Eitelkeit*] of the creatures, have fallen away at the moment which has been determined for the transformation of our being, then will the immortal spirit, freed from dependence on finite things, *find in community with the infinite being the enjoyment of true happiness. . . . Nature, seen from this center,* will show on all sides complete security, complete adaptation. The changeful scenes of nature will not be able to disturb the restful happiness of a spirit which has once been raised to such a height" (1:322; 161; emphasis added).

Nature thus revolves around a double center: the one within "perhaps reserved for future times to discover," the one beyond apparently accessible only through revelation. And yet after denouncing the arbitrary fancies of the British astronomer Thomas Wright for their "fanatical inspiration" (*Begeisterung*) in placing God at the material center of creation, Kant suggests another route of access to its spiritual center.

Where Wright confounded the physical and spiritual centers of the universe, Kant insists on their emphatic distinction: "Divinity is everywhere equally present in the infinity of the entire cosmic space; everywhere, where there are natures capable of swinging themselves upward [*emporschwingen*] above dependence of the creatures to community with the highest being, he is found to be equally near. The whole of creation is penetrated by his force; but he who is able to liberate himself from the creature, and who is noble enough to see that the highest reach of happiness can alone be sought in the enjoyment of this primary source of perfection,—he alone is able to find himself nearer to this true attracting-point of all excellence than anything else in the whole of nature" (1:329–30; 167).[23]

To seek the higher community of God is already, at least in part, to find it. One removes oneself from the economy of nature and its vanities by devalorizing it—by "nobly" recognizing that the highest rung of happiness must be sought beyond it. To this extent our very dissatisfaction with the "commercial" community of nature is a sign and foretaste (*kosten*) of our removal from it.

The possibility of such a standpoint, which would hoist man beyond the exchange-based, or mediate, community of nature into "immediate community with the infinite being," suggests an alternate and securer basis for human self-respect. The true human remedy lies not merely in acceptance of death as the natural wage of existence, but also in the "sweet hope" of a spiritual existence without death. Although reason cannot guarantee this hope, it must not contradict it. The problem of grasping the world as an intelligible whole and the problem of human dignity/happiness are thus inextricably linked: to establish the possibility of the whole conceived as a community of independent elements is to establish the possibility of human immortality.

At the same time, Kant insists that all rational life insofar as we are capable of knowing it discursively depends upon matter both for its physical existence and as a medium of cognition. The independent equality of the noble contrasts with the common, hierarchically graded, dependence of all rational creatures insofar as they cognize the (physical) world or act within it.

Kant locates the most perfect class of rational beings further rather than closer to the physical center; for the perfection of rational creatures "turns very much on the fineness of the matter which influences and determines them to their perception of the world and their reaction upon it," the "inertia and resistance of matter" limiting "the freedom of the spiritual being for action and the distinctness of its sense of external things." These observations suggest a "law according to which the dwelling-places of the rational creatures are distributed according to their relation to the common center." The resulting ladder of perfections would have a beginning, corresponding to the material center of the universe, in which the rational would "come in contact with [*zusammenstossen*] the irrational," but no end, "since there is no limit to the progress beyond which [reason] can be carried," for rational creatures can infinitely approach "the supreme excellence of the Deity, without . . . ever being able to reach it" (1:330–31; 166–68).

Where the noble exhibit a mutual equality in their immediate community with God, rational beings, to the extent that they are linked with matter, constitute a hierarchically ordered "spiritworld" whose members asymptotically approach the excellence of God without ever being able to reach it.

Kant's account of spiritual unity involves a twofold commensuration of the infinitely diverse: on the level accessible to ordinary reason, diversity is correlated with variation in the specific density of matter. At this level, in other words, all variety is relational; what makes each element what it is and different from every other element is its place on an intensive scale that relates it to every other element. On the level promised or promoted by our spiritual elevation, on the other hand, all elements are immediately united through their common origin as products of divine creation. Here each element is essentially determined and stands on its own without bearing or dependency on any other element. Here the connection of each element to the rest and hence the unity of the whole lies not in any interrelatedness per se, but in their common source—the creative intellect of God, which immediately intuits each in its essential independence. God appears both as primal ground, in which homo- and heterogeneity find their immediate source, and as final end, a "differential limit" that the strivings of rational beings infinitely approach but never achieve.[24]

Against the dynamic vision of the spiritual whole, in which God plays the part of a differential limit, a whole whose parts are related progressively along a scale that has a beginning (in zero, or the *Zusammenstoss* with matter) but no end, Kant contrasts an image of spiritual totality that is not merely approached asymptotically but immediately grasped. So construed, totality is a community whose parts or members are not defined through their (external) interrelatedness (as when a point is defined by its relation to all other points) but through their respective (internal) essences, essences whose common ground is the creative act of divine intellection by which each is what it is and at the same time immediately related to the whole.

The switch point between these two images of totality, that is, as asymptotical limit and as immediately self-particularizing whole, is man, who feels torn between that quantitative presentation of the whole to which his reason gives access (one in which his own position, as we shall see, is a middling one), and his desire for and/or foretaste of an immediate qualitative merger with the divine "that reason cannot be bold enough even to aspire to," a merger that hoists man beyond all that the most advantageous natural situation can provide.[25]

Kant's spirited discussion of extraterrestrial life so embarrassed his Victorian translator Hastie that he omitted it entirely from his otherwise reverential treatment of the *Universal Natural History and Theory of the Heavens.*[26] Nevertheless, however foreign to our usual notions of a mechanical system, this discussion constitutes an essential element of Kant's defense of universal cosmology according to mechanical principles.

In contrast to Wright, Kant places the lowest class of intelligent beings at the center of the universe, where they are "sunk into a stiff and immovable matter." Spiritually considered, the physical point of greatest attraction is a kind of sinkhole (*Senkungspunkt*), bringing rational beings to the deepest level of abasement, which culminates in a total lack of deliberation and thinking, that is, in a collision (*zusammenstossen*) with unreason.[27] Kant's reversal of Wright is thus crucial to the double center of attraction that sustains his image of the natural whole, and with it the distinction between reason and unreason.[28]

Kant's insistence on this distinction in turn sets his cosmology apart from its Epicurean and interventionist counterparts, each of which in its own way blurs or denies this distinction: where Epicurus refuses to recognize the intelligent ground of nature's lawful coherence, those who appeal to the direct intervention of God in the world place God "in the machine," as if God lacked the power to render creation self-sustaining. Kant's double center of attraction allows him to avoid a twofold "abyss"—the one to which Lucretius is led by his materialist denial of the existence of God (1:227; 85), and the one to which well-meaning believers are led by their conflation of God and nature.

The double center of attraction thesis informs the structure of Kant's "proof" as well. The proof of Kant's theory makes a double appeal to teleology: first to the purposiveness associated with internal coherence, and second to the purposiveness associated with an external end. Where the first part of Kant's proof—the refutation of materialism—derives the necessity of a divine maker from the lawful coherence of nature, the second part of his proof—the denial of God's miraculous intervention—appeals to a standard of natural perfection commensurate with the purpose of a divine maker.[29]

Whether the evolution of the universe is "uncompelled" or forced upon a "recalcitrant" matter by a "foreign hand" (1:332; 168) turns finally on the question of what sort of nature befits the power and purpose of a divine creator.[30] Mechanical cosmology cannot exclude the possibility of miracles and thus establish its own universality without appealing to a teleological ideal. The physical community of matter must be reconciled with the metaphysical community of the "eternal natures" united in God's plan.

At the same time, the harmonization of mechanism and teleology must not itself violate mechanism's claim to universality. Kant's teleology involves a recourse to theodicy, but not the crude version that "explains" natural phenomena (e.g., the cooling breezes of Jamaica) in terms of their "usefulness to man" (1:333; 169). Even if the appeal to nature's anthropocentric adaptation were plausible on its face, which Kant denies, such divine interference on man's behalf would bring God "into the machine," thereby abolishing nature as an intrinsic unity. The perfection of the whole lies not in its adaptation to the special (and external) ends of man but rather in its intrinsic harmony, that is, its reconciliation of universal law with a diversity so infinite as to embrace "all possible varieties" (*Abwechselungen*) including "even defects and deviations." The same unlimited natural fruitfulness brings forth the inhabited planets and the comets, the useful mountains and the harmful crags, the virtues and the vices (1:347; 181).

To counteract the illusion (*Wahn*) that sees "the immediate application of divine wisdom" in nature's utility and harmony, Kant urges that we direct our gaze not to our own planet only but also upon the whole. The "dialectical illusion" of Kant's later critique is anticipated here.[31] In both cases, what must be guarded against is the naive belief that nature is ordered so as to be in harmony with human desire, so that what man wants he can have. But Kant is here not yet ready, as he will later be, to renounce entirely the possibility of a theoretical theodicy. If naive theodicy loses sight of the whole by focusing on the merely human part, Kant's higher version will allow man to see both whole and part at once, that is, to take in the cosmos as a whole without giving up the standpoint of his own place within it.

Kant's appendix "On the inhabitants of the stars" is intended to provide such a truly universal (one is tempted to say cosmopolitan) perspective, by means of a "comparison, based on the analogies of nature, between the inhabitants of the various planets" (1:358; 182). Mechanism is to be reconciled with teleology (and man's telos in particular), not by the sort of special pleading that violates nature's interconnectedness, but rather by the systematic integration of the natural and spiritual communities. The key to this integration lies in making intelligible the community of reason and matter—in other words, by placing their relationship "under a certain rule" according to which rational natures become more excellent in proportion to the distance of their habitants to the sun (1:358–59; 189). According to this rule, the end or "perfection" of natural bodies can be understood to lie in their capacity to sustain varying degrees of intelligent life. But the rule rests, in turn, on the "essential" dependence of reason upon its material abode.

In the face of a universe adapted to the needs of universal cosmic life, man should regard his own pretensions as he receives the witty tale about the lice who regard the beggar's head on which they live as the center of the universe and themselves as the masterpiece of creation, until a little Fontenelle of their species, who has observed other lice on the head of a nobleman, sets them right. The figurative point of the joke—that man excuses in himself pretensions he would find laughably absurd in others—is supplemented by its literal meaning: on the scale of life man (or the common run of men: Kant exhibits here no sublime respect for mankind as such) is not far from the level of the bloodsucking insects, creatures who have more reason to think us made for them than we have to think them made for us. Life gives rise, in the case of man, to a special problem. The louse imagines nature to be infinitely well adapted to its existence, and it has no regard for the remainder of creation except insofar as it refers to its species as the center (*Mittelpunkt*) of its aim. Man in his complacency makes the same vain assumption; yet in his case it is infinitely less well supported (1:354; 185). Man seems to be of all creatures the one "least able to achieve his end" (1:356; 187). Man is the creature for whose end nature seems least well adapted.

There is another respect in which men and lice differ. Neither the necessitating laws of motion, nor the principle of plenitude that gives each species its unique importance, can sustain the individual's sense of his own worth (1:354; 185).[32] Nature's very inexhaustibility leaves her indifferent to the individual, whose preservation and decay she leaves to universal laws. The louse takes this in stride, identifying its own end with that of its species. But man, as is illustrated by the example of Alexander the Conqueror, turns his pretension not only innocuously against the rest of nature, but also evilly against his own kind.

When we examine the relations among rational beings as a function of their physical relations, man, who is of all rational beings the one we know best, must serve as a "ground and general reference point" despite that fact that his inner constitution remains "an unexplored problem" (1:355; 186). Man is a mystery to himself, a mystery that Kant partly unlocks by deducing what man must be, given the cosmic relations he has already laid out. Thus he will consider how the limitations to human thought and mobility would change if the distance of his body from the sun were altered; for however infinite the distance between the ability to think and the motion of matter, "it is certain that man—who obtains all his concepts and representations from the impressions that the universe by means of bodies bestirs in his soul, both with respect to their meaning and to the capacity to connect and compare them which one calls the capacity to think—is fully dependent on the properties of the matter to which the Creator has connected him" (1:355; 187). The capacity to "connect and compare" by which thinking is defined is thus to be applied to thought itself.

Man's body, like that of all other rational creatures, is indispensable to his thought, which achieves perfection only when the fibers of his (bodily) tool achieve the strength and endurance that is the completion of their development. Bodily and mental development thus go together. Yet in most men this development is arrested prematurely at the level necessary to satisfy the needs to which one is subject through one's "dependence on external things." One "absorbs," "grows," "propagates," and "dies." Of all creatures man least achieves the end of his existence, because he throws away his excellent capacities upon ends that other creatures achieve more surely and decently with far less. The tool that should serve a higher end than mere propagation remains in most men "sluggish" and "inflexible." Only a few individuals develop, late in life, the capacity to "unite abstract concepts" and to "rule the inclinations of the passions through a free application of understanding" (*Einsichten*) that constitutes the proper excellence of human nature. For most people, the higher forces, which ought to be master of the lower ones, remain their servant. Man's crime is thus a sort of profligacy of spirit, which "overspends" its forces, and to the wrong effect, a failure that would make man the most contemptible of creatures in the eyes of true wisdom, if hope of the future did not "lift him up" and if he could not look forward to a complete development of the powers shut up in him.[33]

Kant locates the "obstacle" that keeps human nature in such "deep degradation" in the specific characteristics of man's bodily constitution:

[in the] grossness of the matter in which his spiritual part is sunk [*versenket ist*], the inflexibility of the fibers, and the languor and immobility of the vital juices that should obey its stirrings. The nerves and fluids of his brain provide him only with crude and indistinct concepts; and because he cannot resist with representations sufficiently powerful to compensate for the excitations of sensible experience in the interiority of his faculty of thought, so is he carried away by his passions, stunned and destroyed by the tumult of the elements that maintain his [bodily] machine. The efforts of reason on such account to lift itself above this, and to remove itself from this confusion through the light of judgment, is like sunshine when thick clouds continually interrupt and darken its clarity. (1:356; 187)

Man's spiritual powers are easily exhausted, because he is always fighting for a clarity greater than that provided by his crude organs of sensation, and because the powers of inner representation necessary to such an effort are insufficient to resist the excitations of sensible experience. Man's higher vocation is predicated on a power to join together abstract concepts, a power that is continually opposed by the "tumult of the elements" that sustain his physical machine. The needs of his body and the ends of his nature do not quite seem to mesh.

The result is exhaustion and powerlessness: "the activity of meditation [*Nachdenkens*], and of representation clarified by reason, is a toilsome state, in which the soul cannot place itself without opposition, and from which, through a natural tendency of the bodily machine, it soon falls back into the passive [*leidenen*] state, in which sensible excitations determine and govern all his actions" (1:357; 187–88). Against the prejudice or prejudgment (*Vorurteil*) that makes the man the center of creation, Kant opposes the ideal of judgment (*Urteil*) as the true sun that flashes through the cloud of "confused concepts" (ibid.). Prejudice is accordingly the source of sin as well as error. Judgment involves separating out universal knowledge, obtained from the comparison of ideas, from mere sensible impressions; but the resistance of matter makes this a laborious task, and man consequently prone to "overhasty" conclusions, and unwilling to see things "from another side."[34]

The difficulty, moreover, is an intrinsic one—man depends, both physically and mentally, on the very natural forces that obstruct his clarity. Paradoxically, man's specific quality appears to lie in a unique inability to achieve his own perfection. To this Kant has two responses, one looking to the orderly arrangement of nature as a whole, the other hoisting man altogether beyond it.

On the one hand, Kant argues that man's anguished state is a function of his cosmic position midway between the inner and outermost planets, and thus it represents not a failure of nature but a necessary shading in the arrangement of the whole. According to the rule we have already encountered, mental agility, like the fineness of the matter to which it is bound, varies in inverse proportion to its distance from the sun. The excellence of thinking natures "stands under a certain rule" according to which it varies in the same inverse proportion. The finer the matter, the less solar heat required for its vital force, the more elastic and enduring will be the fibers of its tool, the clearer will be its impressions, and the quicker will be its connecting and comparing thoughts (1:359; 189). Physical "elasticity"—the combination of flexibility and steadfastness that Kant associates with mental strength—is also connected with livelier effect—that is, more consequence from less "actuality"—and hence with a prolongation of the experience of time itself. The greater agility and flexibility of the higher beings enable them not only to extract and compare concepts more quickly and with less effort, and thus approach the immediate (and timeless) apprehension of the whole reserved for the divinity, but also to live longer or, what amounts to the same thing, accomplish more.

The near balance in man between material and spiritual forces that makes the achieving of man's proper end so difficult is thus to be understood as a function of the requirements of his "animal economy" as they reflect his cosmic position midway between the innermost and outermost planets. The material obstacles that impede the human soul are also the conduits of its life-giving energy. The inhabitants of the various planets could not exchange places without bringing about their mutual physical destruction, by dissipation in the case of the more volatile natures, by freezing in the case of the more sluggish (1:358; 188).

The result of these "comparisons" is a "relation" that brings together mechanical calculation with the motivations of final purpose, and whose degree of credibility, Kant insists, approaches certainty. This relation "opens up a field for agreeable speculation."

The inhabitants of the outer reaches lead a kind of charmed life, in which the insights of the intellect have far greater force than sensual allurements and so easily overcome them. Such natures would "quietly receive and reflect God's image, as an ocean undisturbed by the storms of passions" (1:360; 190). (This passage suggests that for man, as well, mastery of the passions may yield immediate access to God.) Kant is also willing to propose a teleological explanation for the rings of Saturn and the moons of the various planets (whereas he earlier ridiculed a teleological explanation for Jamaica's breezes); what he had earlier opposed was not teleology per se but its anthropocentric undermining of the universality of mechanical cause. But Kant's discovery of a "lawful" relation linking the physical and spirit worlds makes it possible to reconcile universal mechanism and teleotheodicy.[35]

That God has disposed the natural world for the benefit of the rational beings that inhabit it and that this disposition should lie in the intrinsic constitution of matter is no less likely than Kant's previous claim as to matter's intrinsic propensity to mechanical orderliness: "If one rightly considers, how can one justify the sort of judgment in which one regards nature as a loathsome [widerwärtiges] subject, which only through a sort of compulsion that sets limits to its free motion, can be held in the track of order and in communal [gemeinschaftlichen] harmony?"[36]

The more man learns of nature, the more he realizes that the universal constitutions of things are not "foreign to one another." One comes to recognize rather their essential affinity,[37] in which the "reciprocal action [Wechselwirkung] of the elements" makes for the beauty of the material world and the profit (Vorteil) of the spirit world. In this manner, "the individual natures of things" constitute a "system, so to speak" in which each "is related to the other" and which stems from their ultimate "community of origin" as objects of creation (1:364; 193–94).

But Kant, who has held his own speculative freedom "in track" by cleaving to the analogy of physical relations, permits himself a final liberty to address the particular concerns of men by seeking out the cause of human unhappiness. Man's wretched proneness to sin and misery, Kant suggests, is caused by his "middle station" (Mittelstand) in the cosmos.[38] Both "error and vice" arise from a peculiar (dis)proportion between the forces of the body and the soul, which make man's reason capable of overcoming the seductions of sensation (unlike beings below him) but only through laborious exertion (unlike beings above him). Among the possible proportions of force between body and soul whose community defines all rational creation, man is that switch point at which a preponderance of passivity and a preponderance of activity meet. Man is uniquely susceptible to error and sin because his nature is uniquely indeterminate. If his rational forces were greater his determination would be effortlessly active; if they were less it would be inescapably passive. The excellence automatic in the former would be impossible in the latter. Man's apparent flaw arises from the near equality of his rational and material forces. In the reciprocal community of his inner nature neither tendency nor telos is authoritative.[39]

Man's degradation and teleological inversion is thus not a failure on nature's part (which would threaten the harmony of the whole) but a necessary shading within it. If Kant's "relation" holds, and spiritual excellence is proportional to distance from the physical center, there must be some being in whom these variables cross. Man thus stands at an alternate midpoint of creation, the fulcrum of neither the physical nor the spiritual worlds but of their systematic community. Man can realize his (higher) end (and so is not at a standstill) but only through a struggle to free himself, or, more accurately, a willingness to engage in the struggle.

Man's middle position between "wisdom and unreason" places him in the "dangerous middle road," the "dangerous intermediary point" (*Zwischenpunkt*) between weakness and capacity. Man is both physically and morally midway between the two "endpoints" (*Endpunkten*) of creation. He is the key to our understanding of the relation between reason and matter, the spirit and the natural worlds, not only because of all rational creatures he is best known to us, but also because of his centrality to the whole. If the material and rational worlds can constitute a "system, so to speak," the center of that system is in a real sense man himself. The fate that allows him to sink "infinitely beneath the lower classes," the fate that allows him to be "tempted by seductions," may also provide him a privileged access to the whole (1:366; 195).

Thus Kant responds to the apparent defectiveness of the human condition not only with consolation (it's a dirty planet, but someone has to live on it), but also with mitigation. In its peculiar combination of freedom and constraint, Kant's conjectural cosmology (or imaginative speculation held on track by the analogy of physical relations) opens an "agreeable" path to something like the universal knowledge he earlier described as so laborious and painful for man.

And yet Kant immediately adds that "we do not rightly know what man actually is, however much consciousness and sense may instruct us on the matter." Still less do we know "what man may yet become." The soul's desire for knowledge snatches desirously after distant objects, seeking light, and wondering if it will "remain forever tied to this point of space, to our earth," or whether it may not some day come to inhabit distant planets, so that the moons of Jupiter may come to shine on us (1:366–67; 195–96).

Such "uncertain pictures of the imagination" are permissible and pleasing but inadequate as a basis of hope for the future. In his fundamental mysteriousness to himself, man returns to the problem of death: "After vanity [*Eitelkeit*] has exacted its due [*Antheil*] from human nature, the immortal spirit will with a quick impetus [*einem schnellen Schwunge*] swing itself upward [*empor schwingen*] above all that is finite, and set its existence in a new relation toward the whole of nature, a relation that derives from closer connection with the highest being. Henceforth, this elevated nature, which has the source of happiness in itself, will no longer dissipate itself among external objects in search of repose in them" (1:367; 196). But this too proves to be only an agreeable speculation, whose true import is the pleasurable tranquility it induces in the human soul:

> In fact [*in der That*] when one has filled one's breast with such considerations and the preceding ones, the sight of the starry heavens on a clear night gives a kind of pleasure that only noble souls can feel. In the universal stillness of nature and repose of the senses, the hidden knowledge capacity of the immortal spirit speaks an ineffable language and yields undeveloped concepts that can be felt but not described. If there are among the thinking creatures of this planet debased beings who unaware of the excitements [*Reizungen*] that so great an object can entice in them, are in the position of fastening themselves to the servitude of vanity, how unhappy is our planet! . . . But how fortunate is the same planet, in that among all most desirable conditions a way is open to them to arrive at a happiness and elevation infinitely beyond the excellence/advantages [*Vorzüge*] that the in all ways most profitable [*allervortheilhafteste*] equipment of nature can achieve in all the world bodies.[40]

Kant's ultimate response to the human predicament is thus twofold. On the one hand he holds up the prospect of infinite spiritual progress (individual or generic) within the universe, whereby rational creation as a whole may achieve its ultimate purpose and perfection.[41] Our ignorance of what man actually is suggests the possibility that the immortal soul in the infinity of its future may one day find itself in a more advantageous cosmic location.

But however "agreeable" such conjectures, they remain fantastic and uncertain (owing, perhaps, to their very "unhinderedness," their freedom from the necessitating laws to which mechanical science proper remains bound). However diverting, such unsure images cannot adequately ground our hope. For that, it seems, the immortal spirit must "swing itself up with a quick swing" over all that is finite and so enter into a "new relation with all of nature," setting forth its existence out of a closer connection with the highest being. In addition to what Kant will later call the beautiful ideal of nature as a freely ordered harmony, Kant furnishes a "sublime" ideal of supernatural transcendence, in which "full satisfaction" is an accomplished fact, not merely the goal of interminable striving. In its immediate connection with the highest being, in its avoidance of the external relations by which merely natural community is defined, such a being would enjoy a kind of invulnerable life and motion.

But the near-redundancy that undercuts Kant's description of this deed—a "swing" by means of a "quick swing"—suggests its problematic character.[42]

The "open way" to such elevation remains perhaps purposely ambiguous. Where Kant earlier spoke of revelation, he now suggests that cosmology itself offers a path to self-sustaining pleasure. This path seems to take the following route. On the one hand, the great object of cosmology, for those mindful of it, provokes excitements sufficient to outweigh all baser attractions. On the other hand, the mind's efforts to comprehend this object "fill" the spirit and, in the face of the starry heavens on a still night, lend it repose. The effort to grasp the whole simultaneously moves the spirit and sets it to rest. The pleasure deriving from this conjunction of excitement and repose is akin to the self-sufficient pleasure that Kant had earlier (prudently) associated with the hereafter. The felt "content" of experience ordinarily associated with the flux of nature and the senses here arises out of and against their "stillness." Our noble capacity to experience this independent pleasure is thus itself the surest sign of our connection to divinity. The fantasy of perpetual progress gives way to the noble assurance of immediate transcendence.

At the same time, one is struck by a certain sleight of hand that undermines Kant's construct. In the final analysis, Kant's vision—simultaneously tranquilizing and exciting—is threatened by a central fissure. Our grasp of the physical and spirit worlds as a "system, so to speak" indicates that we do not yet grasp it as a system. The "open way" Kant charts takes man outside of—and to this extent subverts—the totality of the system.

Through a speculative—or imaginative—extension of the Newtonian system to the whole of creation Kant works to reconcile the unity of the whole with the self-subsistence of its elements. To the original community that all beings share as creations of a common God is joined a harmony of ends projected temporally into eternity. But the image remains an unstable one. It is unclear whether man's (or spirit's) excellence lies in perpetual progress or in immediate transcendence, in worldly participation or unworldly withdrawal.[43] The task of comprehension that Kant sets for himself cannot be accomplished without knowing what Kant admits he doesn't know—what man actually is and may become.

In the end Kant's effort to represent the world as a totality founders on the continuing tension between the independence of its elements and their unity. Kant's reconciliation of this tension takes the form of a double community: that which adheres in the reciprocal relation of substances one to the other, and that which obtains from each substance's immediate relation to God.

To the extent that the two midpoints of Kant's system fail to mesh, the unity Kant seeks is no true unity. Immediate unity (in God) is at once the ground of nature's reciprocal community and its infinitely distant goal. Kant's effort to think the whole as a unity of substances thus both requires the infinity of creation (as the "point," so to speak, where the parallel lines of absolute unity and infinite diversity meet) and is done in by it. In the *Universal Natural History* this tension pervades the image or series of images by which Kant seeks to represent the universe—as both oscillating and expanding, progressing and eternally recurring.

At the same time, Kant's appraisal of the human situation suggests a third locus of community at a midpoint of creation that is neither wholly within nature (as is its physical center) nor wholly beyond nature (as is its spiritual center). Like all created spirits, man himself enacts the mysterious community of matter and spirit in which the unity of creation ultimately resides. What makes man unique (and uniquely wretched) in comparison with other spiritual/material beings is the peculiarly balanced reciprocity of matter and spirit within him. Man alone is undetermined, perched on a razor's edge between the predominance of spirit to which his higher nature draws him and the predominance of matter to which his lower nature drags him. Unable to escape the problem of his own double nature, and the degradation it entails, man also enjoys a kind of privileged affinity with the whole that otherwise eludes him. (Like the whole of creation man himself is an example of what Kant will later call "dynamic equilibrium.")

Thus Kant's unepicurean devotion—in a work that otherwise pays much homage to Epicurus—to the idea of immortality. The whole, according to Kant, is to be thought of as a community of reciprocal exchange or "commerce" among self-subsistent elements. The problem of the human soul, which is susceptible to external flux and yet aware, however dimly, of its own permanence, is thus the prototype of the connection between permanence and flux by which the whole as such is constituted.[44]

But the community of matter and spirit that defines the human soul remains a problem. If the structure of the human soul reflects that of the whole, it does so precisely through its "noble" capacity "to swing itself, by means of a quick swing" above all that is finite. The redundancy of Kant's language suggests the unfounded character of what it describes. The ground of man's noble elevation is the attraction exercised by his vision of the world as a totality. But the vision remains fundamentally defective, and to this extent "repulsive." Kant's project, which calls upon man to be the part whose contemplation of the whole completes the whole, thus falls prey to circularity. The whole cannot be grasped as whole until it is completed; but it cannot be completed until man grasps the whole. Hence the two paths between which Kant oscillates—the quick *Schwung* of liberating attraction and the infinitely long struggle toward absolute comprehension. But comprehension perpetually pursued is comprehension infinitely postponed. The infinity that poses the difficulty also permits Kant to evade the difficulty.

In the end, Kant's "Universal History" seems to value contemplation of the whole less than the "noble independence" that is evinced by one's desire for it, a preference that gives his account a peculiarly moral—one is tempted to say "Kantian"—flavor. If so, Kant's later self-confessed "turn," under Rousseau's tutelage, from the pursuit of mankind's honor achieved through speculative knowledge to the defense of human rights takes on new meaning.

Theory and practice are together for Kant from the beginning. Rousseau did not so much moralize Kant as redirect his moral concern from cosmic to human community and its more adequate economy of intrinsic worth or dignity. In such community Kant would later discover the true "intelligible world"—or the only one truly available to us—and with it compelling support at last for man's individual integrity within a larger whole. The physical economy of nature, alternately infinite and finite, gives way to the kingdom of ends and its moral economy of absolute worth. The dual points of attraction—both ground and abyss—that center Kant's early cosmology give way to the moral will as itself the final ground of human purposiveness and perfection.

But the notion of infinite totality, which Kant's early cosmology was meant to regulate, never ceased to exercise its compelling charm. Suppressed as a theoretical delusion in Kant's critique of pure reason, it reemerged as a "regulative idea" in his doctrines of teleological and aesthetic judgment, politics, and history. If Kant's early idea of metaphysical community partially models itself on civil or market society, his later idea of cosmo-political community as the infinitely receding goal of history reflects, in turn, the displaced appeal of this ever-beckoning point of attraction.[45]

The reciprocal community that informs the world as we are capable of knowing it ultimately rests for Kant on a primal experience of the simultaneous identity of, and difference between, attraction and repulsion (whose dynamic relation prefigures what Hegel will later call the "identity of identity and difference").[46] A teleological impetus is thus implicit in reciprocity itself. Without this dynamic impetus, Kant's commercial community—whose simultaneous equilibrium and expansion Marx would later adopt as his model for the demonic machinery of capitalism— would not be intelligible. If we abstract from God (knowledge of whom Kant cannot unproblematically sustain) we are left with the ambiguity, or doubleness, of attraction itself to accomplish the merger of identity and difference. Attraction is itself repulsive. The metaphysics of community in Kant's early thought is grounded or done in by the dynamics of its own ambiguous erotics.

Notes

1

See Kant's *Gesammelte Schriften* (Academy ed.), 20:44. In the same confessional remarks Kant pays tribute to Rousseau for discovering the "concealed law" hidden under the "manifoldness of the available shapes of mankind" (20:55).

2

Metaphysische Anfangsgründe der Rechtslehre (Academy ed.), 6:233; *The Metaphysical Elements of Justice*, trans. John Ladd (Indianapolis: Bobbs-Merrill, 1965), pp. 37–38.

3

Principiorum primorum cognitionis metaphysicae nova dilucidatio; citations below to *Nova dilucidatio* refer to the Academy edition, followed by references to the English translation by John A. Reuscher in *Kant's Latin Writings, Translations, Commentaries and Notes*, ed. Lewis White Beck (New York: Peter Lang, 1986). Citations below to the *Universal Natural History and Theory of the Heavens* refer to the Academy edition, followed by references to the English translation by Stanley L. Jaki (Edinburgh: Scottish Academy Press, 1981). Jaki's singularly unsympathetic translation has the virtue of being complete (unlike the better known and in some ways more faithful Hastie translation).

4

Compare, for example, John Locke's description of the state of nature as one of equality "wherein all the power and jurisdiction is reciprocal." *Second Treatise of Government*, para. 4.

5

On the "ladder" or "great chain of being" in the eighteenth century, see Arthur O. Lovejoy's classic study *The Great Chain of Being* (Cambridge, Mass.: Harvard University Press, 1936).

6

Nor is this the only objection Kant has to raise. Leibniz's theodicy had justified the evil in the world by appealing to a logical necessity beyond the will of God. This is not the best world simply, but the best world possible, given God's good will and the constraints that make some good things mutually exclusive or "incompossible." As we shall see, however, Kant's early theodicy is of a different sort; Kant will argue for the goodness of the world based on its conformity to a model of perfection understood as the reconciliation of manifoldness and unity. God's justification lies not in his maximizing of "reality," subject to the constraints of what is mutually possible, but rather in the absolute plenitude and completeness of his work. If any necessity constrains God's will it is the necessity to utilize his capacities to their fullest and thus to create a world as infinite as God himself. On the implications of this difference, see Dieter Henrich's discussion of Kant's early remarks on optimism (1754) in "Über Kants früheste Ethik," *Kant-Studien* 54 (1963): 404–11.

7

See especially his three essays on the Lisbon earthquake of 1755 (Academy ed., 1:417ff.) and his letter of condolence to Frau von Trunk, mother of a former student (Academy ed., 2:37ff.). As in his later treatment of sublime terror, Kant tends to associate the horror of death with images of the cataclysmic and abysmal—e.g., earthquakes and oceanic whirlpools in which one is swallowed up. On the theme of earthquakes see Peter Fenves, *A Peculiar Fate: Kant and the Problem of World History* (Ithaca: Cornell University Press, 1990).

Kant's early denial of the Leibnizian "identity of indiscernables" means that for Kant the soul has no immediate internal assurance of its own uniqueness (as distinguished from its identity) and hence of its larger necessity, given the principle of plenitude, or of a world "without essential gaps." For Kant, unlike Leibniz, it is in principle possible for numerically distinguishable entities to have the same "inner determination" or essence. Thus if the soul (or any other substance) is to be part of the (a) world, the principle of connection cannot lie merely with its "inner determination" (as would be the case, given the principle of plenitude, if every substance were essentially unique). If one looks to its inner determination alone, a substance could exist in no world or in a world of its own, separate from (our) world.

8

See Reuscher's helpful "A Clarification and Critique of Kant's Principiorum Primorum Cognitionis Metaphysicae Nova Dilucidatio," *Kant-Studien* 63 (1977): 18–32.

9

On Leibniz and the profit motive see Martin Heidegger, *The Metaphysical Foundations of Logic,* trans. Michael Heim (Bloomington: Indiana University Press, 1984), p. 115; and Jon Elster, *Leibniz et la formation de l'esprit capitaliste* (Paris: Aubier, 1975). Kant's approach to the question of theodicy thus develops along lines substantially different from that of Leibniz. For Kant God's justification lies not in having created a world with the most good possible given the limits of compossibility but rather in the intrinsic harmony of the whole. What seems evil to us, i.e., out of step with our desires, stems from our inability to assume the perspective of the creator of the whole, to grasp it as a totality in which unity and boundless diversity, conservation and infinity, are reconciled.

10

Compare Kant's later critical treatment of schemata as bridges, via "the transcendental determination of time," between transcendental concepts and appearances (*Critique of Pure Reason,* A138ff./B177ff.).

11

See the *Critique of Judgment,* 5:372–77.

12

See the *Critique of Judgment,* 5:372; and Hegel, *Lesser Logic,* section 198.

13

Kant thus skirts the difficulty entailed by his conception of matter both as a single *Grundstoff* and as consisting of an infinite diversity of elements. See his letter to J. F. Gensichen (April 19, 1791), in which he reaffirms his support for the basic mechanical position taken in the *Universal Natural History:* "the theory is that prime matter, dispersed throughout the universe in vaporous form, contained the materials for an innumerable variety of substances" (Academy ed., 11:252–53; trans. Arnold Zweig, *Kant's Philosophical Correspondence* [Chicago: University of Chicago Press, 1967], pp. 171–72).

14

See *Critique of Pure Reason,* A316/B373). The principle of "least reciprocal action" is generally attributed to Maupertuis.

15

So extended, Kant's project has a dual significance that anticipates his later critical discussion of the sublime: on the one hand, there is that "immeasurable greatness and the infinite manifoldness and beauty of the universe" that "puts us in quiet astonishment" and "moves the imagination." On the other hand, there is the "rapture that seizes the understanding" when "from another point of view it considers how so much greatness flows from a single rule" (1:306; 142). Imagination's awe in the face of nature's prodigality is countered by reason's grasp of the ordered submission of this plenitude to one law. Given Kant's association of perfection in these early works with the reconciliation of infinite diversity and thoroughgoing unity, it is interesting to see a division of labor already arising for him between imagination and reason.

16

Cf. 1:246; 100 and Francis Bacon: The "first question concerning the Celestial Bodies is *whether there be a system,* that is, whether the world or universe compose altogether one globe, with a centre; or whether the particular globes of earth and stars be scattered dispersedly, each on its own roots, without any system of common centre" (Bacon, *Descriptio globi intellectualis,* quoted in Lovejoy, *Great Chain of Being,* p. 109).

17

Kant's argument modifies his earlier derivation of the force of repulsion from the fact that without it dispersed bodies of matter would establish themselves in static equilibrium. In fact, what the force of repulsion counters is the universal sinking force that would bring all matter in the universe collapsing toward a common center or *Abgrund*. On the importance of this modification, see note 27 below.

18

Compare Kant's later, critical characterization of science as a progressive task whose organizing telos gives unity to the limitless field of the empirically given.

19

For the phrase "economy of nature" (*Ökonomie der Naturreiche*) see 1:458.

20

Portions of organized creation cease to be worthy of existence when they have played out the full variety of their possibilities; the telos of organized subsystems of creation is maximum systematic complexity, i.e., maximum diversity consistent with universal law. On the implications of this formal definition of perfection see note 6 above.

21

Cf. Kant's later excitement over the concept of negative quantity and "real"—as opposed to merely "logical"—opposition. The idea of real opposition (e.g., between positive and negative vector forces) makes it possible to reconcile infinite expansion of the magnitude of force with the balanced equality implicit in the law of conservation. Each vector force may be as great in magnitude as one pleases; so long as they are equal, the result is zero. Infinite expansion of the total quantity of (positive and negative) force is thus made consistent with the law of conservation. See Kant, "Attempt to Introduce Negative Quantities into Philosophy" (1763). (The distinction between real and logical opposition is one that Kant in all probability learned from Hume.)

22

In context this phrase refers to world systems rather than to nature as a whole.

23

The wisdom that "frees one from dependence on the creature" is the "noble perception" that the greatest happiness is to be sought beyond it. Those who achieve such noble wisdom "swing themselves" into a community beyond that of physical matter, a community to whose center all are equally near; *schwingen*, which can be translated as "to oscillate," should be compared to *Schwung*, the technical term for "momentum." See, for example, 1:230; 88, and 1:266, where Kant attributes the stability of the planetary system to the "hovering" (*schweben*) that arises from equality between the force of attraction (*Senkungskraft*) and that of orbital momentum (*Schwungskraft*). A primal source of Kant's later concept of dynamic equilibrium would seem to lie here, in the notion of the *schweben* that arises from "equality" between the forces of "oscillating or swinging" and of "sinking." See also his later critical discussion of the feeling of the sublime as arising from a "tremor" (*Erschütterung*) induced—in the face of a single object—by a rapid alteration between repulsion and attraction (*Critique of Judgment*, 5:258). On the importance of the concept of *schweben* to Fichte's interpretation of Kant see his *Science of Knowledge* ([1794] Berlin: Walter de Gruyer, 1971), 1:224, 243.

24

Cf. 1:309–10n.; 151n: "The notion of an infinite extension of the world finds opponents among metaphysicians and has only recently found one in Mr. M. Weitenkampf. If, because of the supposed impossibility of a quantity without [definite] number and limits, these gentlemen cannot accommodate themselves to this idea, then I would wish to ask in passing: whether the future course of eternity will not comprise in itself a true infinity of variety and changes and whether this infinite series is not already at once fully present to the divine mind? If God can make actual in a series following upon one another the concept of infinity which is at once present to his mind, why can't the divine mind represent the notion of another infinity in a conjoined connection relating to space and thereby make the extent of the world limitless? . . . I will avail myself of the opportunity which presents itself to remove the difficulty in question through an explanation drawn from the nature of numbers . . . : whether that which has been *brought forth* through a power directed by the Highest Wisdom to reveal itself may not relate as a differential magnitude to that which it *could have brought forth*."

25
The "whole" of creation is thus presented according to three models of unity: immediate, progressive, and reciprocal. Whereas the material realm expresses itself in terms of all three models, the spiritual realm is here limited to the first two. Only with Kant's late elevation—under Rousseau's influence—of moral equality to the status of a reciprocal "law" governing the moral/intelligible world is this asymmetry between the two realms corrected.

26
On extraterrestrial life as a common theme among eighteenth-century thinkers as diverse as Locke, Berkeley, Leibniz, and Wolff see Michael J. Crowe, *The Extraterrestrial Life Debate, 1750–1900: The Idea of a Plurality of Worlds from Kant to Lowell* (Cambridge: Cambridge University Press, 1986), pp. 3ff. Quotations from Alexander Pope's "pluralist" *Essay on Man* appear throughout the *Universal Natural History and Theory of the Heavens,* though Kant avoids Pope's association of God with the physical center of the universe. Kant's preference for the theodicy of Pope over that of Leibniz is the theme of his early remarks on "Optimism." See note 6 above.

27
It is perhaps useful to keep in mind Kant's lifelong concern with earthquakes and abysses [*Abgründen*]. On Kant's personal susceptibility to vertigo, to which he attributed his notorious inability to travel, see *Anthropology from a Pragmatic Point of View,* Academy ed., 7:169n; trans. Mary J. Gregor (The

Hague: Martinus Nijhoff, 1974), p. 46. The vertiginous physical center of attraction (which requires the counterforce of repulsion to prevent individual bodies from merging with the central core) is to be contrasted with the divine center of attraction, which— "equidistant" from all points—preserves rather than threatens the integrity of individual units. The contrast between the threatening attraction that governs the physical universe (and calls forth, in us at least, its physical opposite—repulsion) and a nonpolar, individually substantiating attraction directly associated with (divine) reason, constitutes the core of Kant's later analysis of the sublime. See *Critique of Judgment,* 5:258: "In presenting the sublime in nature the mind feels agitated, while in an aesthetic judgment about the beautiful in nature it is in restful contemplation. This agitation . . . can be compared with a vibration, i.e., with a rapid alternation of repulsion from, and attraction to, one and the same object. If a [thing] is excessive for the imagination (and the imagination is driven to [such excess] as it apprehends [the thing] in intuition), then [the thing] is, as it were, an abyss in which the imagination is afraid to lose itself. Yet, at the same time, for reason's idea of the supersensible [this same thing] is not excessive but conforms to reason's law to give rise to such striving by the imagination. Hence [the thing] is now attractive to the same degree to which [formerly] it was repulsive to mere sensibility." Note that while Kant refers to the effect of the object in question upon imagination as initially repulsive, the cause of that repulsiveness—imagination's fear of losing itself—presupposes a prior state of attraction, one which (appears to) put imagination in jeopardy. There are thus, contrary to Kant's explicit statement, not one but two forces of attraction operative in Kant's model of the sublime—one appealing to imagination, the other to reason. As in the *Universal Natural History,* the abyss (*Abgrund*) of physical attraction that threatens to swallow up the individual is offset by the ground (*Grund*) of rational/moral attraction that substantiates and upholds him.

28

Kant's association of spiritual attraction with originating sustenance and of physical attraction with material obliteration may suggest a connection in Kant's mind with filio-material/sexual love. Kant's generally negative remarks about women (as cowardly, incapable of genuine principles, and manipulatively seductive) are to be contrasted with his praise for his own mother, who died when Kant was thirteen. "I shall never forget my mother," Kant is reported to have said late in life, "for she implanted and nurtured the first seed of the good in me; she opened my heart to the influence of nature; she awakened and broadened my ideas, and her teachings have had an enduring, beneficent effect on my life." Kant's mother also seems to have been instrumental in the fostering of Kant's intellectual gifts, recognizing them early and steering him toward academic study. Kant's comment is remarkable for its conflation of the male and female generative roles in the person of his mother, who "planted" and "nurtured" the seed of the good in him. As Ernst Cassirer notes, Kant's mother's image seems to have left a stronger impression upon him than that of his father; see Cassirer, *Kant's Life and Thought,* trans. James Haden (New Haven: Yale University Press, 1981), p. 13. That Kant was a sickly child may have added to the care devoted to him by his mother, who had already lost four children; see Arsenij Gulyga, *Immanuel Kant,* trans. from Russian by Sigrun Bielfeldt (Frankfurt am Main: Suhrkamp, 1985), p. 21. The role of Anna Regina Kant in awakening Kant both to the beauty of nature and to moral goodness is reminiscent of the role played by the Savoyard Vicar in Rousseau's *Emile,* a work that had enormous impact on Kant when he read it in midlife. It is almost as if Rousseauian moral doctrines associated with the speech of the Savoyard Vicar find a hold in Kant precisely because they echo/replace moral affinities Kant previously associated with maternal influence. As Kant's "Remarks" on the *Observations concerning the Sublime and the Beautiful* reveal, Rousseau provides Kant with a rational, and explicitly

masculine, model for such affinities. See my "Kant's Political Cosmology," in Howard Williams, ed., *Essays on Kant's Political Philosophy* (Chicago: University of Chicago Press, 1992). For a somewhat different treatment of Kant's relation to his mother, see Hartmut and Gernot Böhme, *Das Andere der Vernunft* (Frankfurt am Main: Suhrkamp, 1985), pp. 483ff.

29

Kant's later critical distinction between "internal" and "external" purposiveness is prefigured here: the reciprocal harmony implicit in a self-sustaining mechanical system is only thinkable by virtue of an appeal—later reduced to the status of a "subjective principle of judgment"—to the artful arrangement of a (hidden) God. At the same time, such arrangement is only intelligible, on the analogy of human *techne,* through an appeal to some extrinsic end, be it only the contemplation of our work ("And God saw that it was good"). We humans ordinarily make machines for the sake of some extrinsic end, unless the internal harmony of the machine (as Kant will later argue is the case with art) is itself the end. In the *Universal Natural History* both internal and external purposiveness are mediated by the concept of beauty, whereby rational creation is empowered, through its contemplation of the whole, to experience the artful arrangement (that on the analogy of ordinary human techne is a mere means) as an end in itself, an activity that Kant identifies with the "end of creation." Kant's argument thus equivocates between identifying the end of creation with the harmony of the whole and identifying it with the contemplation of that harmony (an equivocation later echoed in Hegel's distinction between logic and history). In any case, it becomes essential to Kant's purpose to demonstrate that man himself, whose contemplation of the harmony of the whole constitutes (part of) the end of creation, does not himself constitute, by virtue of his wretchedness, a breach in that harmony. Nature cannot be beautiful unless it harmonizes with the needs of humankind.

30

"If one considers that nature and the eternal laws that are prescribed to substances for their commerce are not a principle that is necessary self-substantially and without God, that precisely because nature displays in them so much agreement and order . . . it must be recognized that the essences of all things have their communal origin in a grounding essence. . . . If, I say, . . . one ponders this then nature will appear more worthy than she is commonly regarded" (1:332; 169). Kant again reverts to a political metaphor: nature conforms to God's law not under restraint—like a recalcitrant subject submitting to foreign authority—but in free conformity to the plan of nature's constitution. God is a political architect whose subjects freely follow the dictates of his plan. One is again reminded of the hidden but effective guidance explicitly politicized in Smith's later image of the "invisible hand."

31

See *Critique of Pure Reason* A62f./B86f.

32

As noted above, Kant's denial of the Leibnizian "identity of indiscernables" makes the Kantian individual dispensable in a way that Leibniz's monad was not: as interpreted by Kant, the principle of plenitude gives assurance only to the species—not to the individual—of its necessity.

33

Kant's moral/intellectual critique of humankind thus rests upon a double ranking: on the one hand there is the graded ranking of excellences of perfections in which some creatures stand above and others below us. On the other, there is the matter of achieving the excellence appropriate to one's nature, an all-or-nothing standard that threatens to depress man to the rank of most contemptible. Excellence and honor cleave to separate scales, or threaten to without the "uplifting" hope of a future life to rectify the discrepancy. Leibniz's notion of "maximum reality" suffers from a similar confusion between rankings, as Lovejoy points out: If human beings possess more

reality than, say, crocodiles (as Leibniz maintains), it would seem that the best of all possible worlds should contain more humans and no crocodiles (though this, of course, Leibniz denies).

34

The centrality of judgment and comparison to Kant's understanding of human thought is brought out even more forcefully in his essay "On the False Subtlety of the Four Syllogistic Figures" (1760). On error and evil as consequences of egoism, or the attitude of "being occupied with oneself as the whole world," see Kant, *Anthropology from a Pragmatic Point of View,* Academy ed., 7:130; trans. Mary J. Gregor (The Hague: Martinus Nijhoff, 1974), p. 12. (Subsequent references to *Anthropology* are to these editions.) The opposite of egoism—metaphysical, aesthetic, and practical—is pluralism, or the attitude of regarding and conducting oneself as a "citizen of the world."

35

This position is for Kant enhanced by (apparent) empirical evidence that the density of the planets is consistent through and through, a fact that supports the thesis of their mechanical origin. If God had directly intervened in accommodating the planets to the needs of rational beings, he would only have needed to concern himself with their surfaces. See Kant's reference to Buffon at 1:345; 179.

36

On the "repellent" character of nature bereft of intrinsic lawfulness, see also Kant's remark that our notice of comets would be "repulsive" (*anstössig*), could we not provide ourselves with a mechanical explanation for their seemingly purposeless course (1:338; 173).

37

Verwandtschaften; the elements of creation coalesce through a kind of free (or elective) affinity.

38

A condition, Kant allows, we may share with the Martians.

39

So represented, man's inner nature appears as the classical, teleologically determinate soul on the verge of becoming the modern, teleologically indeterminate self. For the importance of this transformation, both for Kant and for modern thought generally, see Richard Velkley, *Freedom and the End of Reason: On the Moral Basis of Kant's Critical Philosophy* (Chicago: University of Chicago Press, 1989), chap. 2.

40

These sentiments are echoed in the famous passage that closes the *Critique of Practical Reason:* "Two things fill the mind with ever new and increasing admiration and awe, the oftener and more steadily we reflect on them: the starry heavens above me and the moral law within me" (Academy ed., 5:162; trans. Lewis White Beck (Indianapolis: Bobbs-Merrill, 1956), p. 166.

41

Cf. Kant's later contention that "in man (as the only rational creature on earth) those natural capacities which are directed to the use of his reason are to be fully developed only in the race, not in the individual" ("Idea for a Universal History," second thesis; Academy ed., 8:18–19).

42

Man, it seems, is the only rational being who must and can emancipate himself. It is not man's intellectual force (which is "mediocre") but his capacity to overcome his natural languor that raises him to (and perhaps beyond) the level of the beings whom nature has most happily endowed.

43

See Kant's later discussion of sublime horror in his *Considerations of the Beautiful and the Sublime* (1762), of which the dream of one Carazon (a parsimonious merchant) that he is doomed to an eternal life of absolute isolation provides the terrifying example. Kant's presentation of the dream underscores both his emerging critique of contemplative withdrawal and his emerging readiness to see in

moral community (the rejection of which brings on Carazon's punishment) an answer to the human predicament. Cf. John Sallis, *Spacings: Of Reason and Imagination in the Texts of Kant, Fichte, and Hegel* (Chicago: University of Chicago Press, 1987), pp. 82–83.

44

In its insistence here on immortality (or its hope) as a necessary constituent of human happiness, Kant's thought differs from both the original and later (modern) versions of Epicureanism. See Leo Strauss, *Spinoza's Critique of Religion* (New York: Schocken Books, 1956), p. 29. One root of this difference would seem to lie in Kant's association of immortality with the impossibility of pain (where Uriel da Costa, for example, fears immortality because it entails the possibility of eternal pain; see Strauss, p. 63). Thus happiness for Kant arises not from the remembrance in tranquility of past pleasures (as with Epicurus) but from mastery of the natural sources of discomfort (a view typical of the modern Epicureans). What distinguishes Kant from these moderns and brings him at least superficially closer to Epicurus is his choice of internal control (or the renunciation of physical desire) rather than external control as the preferred means of achieving this mastery. This choice is abetted by Kant's subsumption of physical pleasures and pains under the common rubric of external "excitements" (*Reizungen*) inimical to happiness (i.e., in his conflation of sensitivity and irritability), in contradistinction to the higher excitements elicited by rational desire for a (future) existence devoid of bodily attachment. Happiness consists in the foretaste of invulnerable pleasure. Noteworthy in this regard is Kant's allusion in his later *Anthropology* to the crying infant of Lucretius: where Lucretius's infant cries in anticipation of evils to come, Kant's infant cries in response to present evils. One lesson to be drawn from the original version of the passage (namely, that indifference to the future is desirable) is absent from Kant's adaptation (7:268; 136).

45

The spiritual point of attraction here identified with God is replaced in Kant's later thought by the "idea," conceived as a rational projection. Rousseau's suggestions concerning the autoerotic or projective character of human thought (and imagination in particular) is thus decisive for Kant. What Yirmiahu Yovel describes as an "erotic" component in reason (as Kant critically conceives it) is in fact autoerotic. Indeed, the break between Kant's precritical and critical thought can be located in the latter's identification of reason's vocation not with the theoretical pursuit of the unconditioned "ground" but rather with the practical effort to realize an "idea" projected by reason itself. Critical philosophy renounces the "abyss" of metaphysics, Kant's "first love," in favor of reason's own free projection. From the standpoint of the critical philosophy, Kant's earlier distinction between the rational and physical points of attraction—between ground and abyss—becomes blurred or insignificant. What sustains the distinction between reason and matter is no longer the (forced) differentiation of rational and physical objects of desire, but rather the freedom of reason itself. Reason's erotic reach is no longer elicited or "attracted" by some external object (as in classical/scholastic models of desire) but emanates instead from its own self-grounded or spontaneous activity. So conceived, desire sustains rather than threatens the integrity of the self. See Yirmiahu Yovel, *Kant and the Philosophy of History* (Princeton: Princeton University Press, 1980), pp. 15ff. Kant's eagerness to regard as "ideas of reason" what for Rousseau remain projective illusions of imagination has something to do with the fact that those projections supplement and support a metaphysical scaffolding Kant had previously erected.

46

This dynamic theory of matter stays with Kant throughout his life. See, for example, his *Metaphysical Foundations of Natural Science,* as well as the *Opus postumum* (in which he makes several attempts at an a priori derivation). For a "sociological" approach to the dynamics of attraction and repulsion, see Böhme and Böhme, *Das Andere der Vernunft,* pp. 83ff.

Chapter 7

The Politics of Kant's Philosophy

Joseph M. Knippenberg

Since its inception, political philosophy has had at least two aspects, one consisting in inquiry into "normative" questions, like the character of the best regime and the principles of political right, and the other considering the relation between the philosopher and the political order. While the former line of inquiry is evident in almost every great work in the tradition of political philosophy, systematic treatments of the latter theme are few and far between. Indeed, most such works are written by classical political philosophers and are inspired by the life and death of Socrates. Modern treatments of this theme are, needless to say, much less particular and personal, appearing generally under the rubric of "theory and practice." It would not be much of an exaggeration to say that the presence and prominence of this question for the ancients, as opposed to the relative silence of the moderns, constitutes one of the characteristic differences between the two.

It might be fairly easy to explain the difference. Perhaps there has been progress: Socrates succeeded in persuading the Athenians and their successors that philosophizing was a respectable enterprise; what was once a problem is one no longer.[1] But this explanation overlooks the fact that the enforcement of religious orthodoxy persisted for more than two millennia after Socrates' execution. His successors might have found ways of dealing with it. For some living in Christian times the appearance, at least, of patriotism, as opposed to piety, could be presented as an admirable vice, if not an actual virtue.[2] What remains distinctive about the philosopher in these circumstances is that he is an adviser or writer, not an actor or practitioner. He can at least appear subservient to the interests of another. If he has interests of his own, it behooves him in his apparent weakness not to call attention to them, not to offer a thematic treatment of the self-consciousness of the philosopher.[3]

If this was Machiavelli's strategy, others, like Hobbes, chose a different route, trying to appeal to virtually everyone's self-interest and taking it more or less for granted that they would all rather pursue it in an enlightened fashion than not. All the philosopher has to do is offer advice about self-interest properly understood and, sooner or later, almost everyone will be able to accept it. Stated somewhat more precisely, the philosopher can try to make common cause with almost everyone against the designs of the vainglorious and ever-contentious few.[4]

It may not, however, always be possible to draw the lines quite so conveniently. There may be times when a philosopher cannot so readily define and appeal to a generally acceptable common good; he may, in other words, be or feel forced to take sides in a dispute between significant and apparently irreconcilably opposed interests. He is on the spot. In such a situation, the philosopher must decide, first of all, where his allegiance lies and, second, how best he can, by his writing and other activity, promote his interests and principles. He must figure out the relation between his political theory and his political practice. Perhaps more important, he cannot simply obscure and obfuscate his own unique role. If, then, we wish to compare and contrast the "ancients" and the "moderns" on the issue of the political situation and role of the philosopher, there may well be no clearer and more readily accessible case than when the philosopher is thus on the spot.

In this regard, the life and works of Immanuel Kant are particularly interesting. In his famous statement of Rousseau's influence on himself, Kant acknowledges both the "private" pleasures and "public" or political responsibility of the philosopher. While Kant was "by inclination a researcher," who felt "the complete thirst for knowledge" as well as both the "greedy disquiet" leading him to go further and the "contentment with each step forward," Rousseau's example led him to conclude that he "would find [himself] more useless than an ordinary worker if [he] did not believe that this consideration—restoring the rights of mankind—could give all the others a worth."[5] However the writings and actions of his predecessors might be interpreted, Kant unequivocally denies that philosophers as such can have a political "class consciousness" separate from those of their fellow human beings. Their political engagements cannot thus be merely prudential and self-serving accommodations to the existing order, but may be dictated by principle.[6]

Kant pursued this political task in circumstances that were, for a time, less than completely propitious, for he was living during a great political upheaval under a regime that was in some respects quite reactionary. While he was greatly interested in and to some degree favored the republican goals of the French Revolution, he could not readily say so during the reign of Prussia's King Friedrich Wilhelm II, whose government exercised censorship over statements on this and other matters.[7] Kant was thus compelled to consider how he and other philosophers could promote republicanism and other such concerns while living under a regime hostile to them.

The Task of the Philosophic Writer

In essays published both before and after the reign of Friedrich Wilhelm II, Kant insists that writers, scholars, and intellectuals have an important role to play in promoting the public good. If enlightenment, the "original destiny" of human nature, is to proceed, it must be promoted by the efforts of those few who, "by cultivating their own minds, have succeeded in freeing themselves." Teaching in the universities and, especially, writing in the journals, they can "as scholars freely and publicly submit to the judgement of the world their verdicts and opinions, even if they deviate here and there from orthodox doctrine." They can, moreover, "put before the public their thoughts on better ways of drawing up laws, even if this entails forthright criticism of the current legislation."[8] So far as political education depends upon the discovery of the truth rather than upon an assertion of the positive authority of the state, "free teachers of right [*freie Rechtslehrer*], that is, the philosophers" are crucial figures, for they are "the natural heralds and expositors . . . among the people" of "natural rights and rights arising out of common human understanding."[9]

Kant acknowledges not only that such activities "are objectionable to the state, which always desires to rule alone," but also that in some instances such objections are justified: "There must always be statutory precepts of the government regarding teachings to be set forth in public, since unlimited freedom to proclaim any sort of opinion publicly is bound to be dangerous both to the government and to the public itself." "Religion," as he puts it in another place, "is a most important political need," serving "the civil good of the commonwealth in general."[10] If he is not to be simply a subversive or revolutionary—something of which he insists "the class of philosophers is by nature incapable"—Kant must have some way of accommodating himself to these political requirements.[11] We are left, then, with a series of questions. What sorts of philosophical and ethical teachings are salutary? What sorts can or must the government tolerate or permit? And how can the philosophic writer effectively promote the public good in the face of governmental resistance?

Some indication of Kant's understanding of his role as a philosophic writer can be gleaned from his treatment of the relation between science and morality in the first *Critique*. The problem, as he sees it, is that the modern scientific account of natural necessity undermines man's naive and prescientific belief that he is obliged to govern himself in accordance with the moral law.[12] One role of critical philosophy is to limit the pretenses of the former point of view, showing how it is possible to think of man as both free and determined, albeit in different respects. Thus critical philosophy yields "the inestimable benefit, that all objections to morality and religion will for ever be silenced, and this in Socratic fashion, namely by the clearest proof of the ignorance of the objectors."[13]

That the task of critical philosophy with respect to these concerns is merely defensive is clear from yet another consideration. Kant admits that the "hope of a *future* life," "the consciousness of *freedom*," and "the belief in a wise and great *Author of the World*"—all demanded by morality—do not, strictly speaking, derive from the teachings of either science or critical philosophy. As he puts it in his lectures on moral philosophy, "In theology, so far as it is necessary for natural religion, the ordinary man is as far advanced as the speculators [*speculative Köpfe*]."[14] The critical limitation of science does not establish these beliefs but merely leaves them intact, defending them against all human pretenses to theoretical knowledge. In this way, people can be guarded against the excesses of pseudorationalism, on the one side, and those of fanatical obscurantism, on the other.[15] The progress of critical philosophy will, Kant expects, vindicate ordinary human understanding in the decisive respect: in the moral matters of greatest concern to them, individuals need heed no authority but their own reason. As he says, "there is no need of science or philosophy for knowing what man has to do in order to be honest and good, and indeed to be wise and virtuous."[16]

There remains, nonetheless, a problem in this account. Kant admits or asserts repeatedly that many people will be unable to comprehend his writings and arguments, for "the common human understanding" is unfit "for such subtle speculation." Furthermore, most ordinary people will have no real interest in the questions he addresses.[17] How, then, will critical philosophy have its salutary effect? Kant's first response is that the "esoteric" sciences, once they are well-rounded, may admit of a certain popularization: arguments may be stated more elegantly and clearly, illustrations and examples may be supplied, and different approaches to exposition may be taken. But since he lacks a "talent for lucid exposition," he is willing to leave the task of popularizing critical philosophy to "men of impartiality, insight, and true popularity." His primary audience must then be those whom he variously calls "the learned public," "future teachers," or "all thinking men."[18] Of course, to the extent that there is a limit—insurmountable by even the most capable popularizer—to the general public's interest in and capacity for critical philosophy, the most that Kant may reasonably expect is that people be reassured, on good authority, as it were, that metaphysicians' speculations cannot seriously threaten their faith or their moral beliefs.[19]

As has been indicated, matters should be a little different in the application of moral doctrine, as opposed to its critical and metaphysical grounding. Ordinary men often display great subtlety in their reasoning about moral questions.[20] It should then be possible to write profoundly *and* popularly about this subject. Kant believes that this can indeed be done: moral philosophy can provide both "didactic" and "polemical" assistance to the common man. In the first place, it can "set forth the system of morals more fully and intelligibly and . . . present its rules in a form more convenient for use."[21] Thus, for example, Kant sketches an appropriate "moral catechism" in his *Doctrine of Virtue*. And he stresses over and over again the importance of an emphasis on human dignity in moral education and writing.[22]

The second service provided by moral philosophy is similar to the role of criticism in metaphysics, for there are competing claims in the former just as there are in the latter. In and of itself, ordinary moral insight is quite sufficient, but once disputes arise, as inevitably they must, it stands in need of assistance. Because human beings are almost always divided between duty and inclination, any doctrine that vindicates the latter by presenting it in the guise of morality is likely to win more than a few adherents. As Kant puts it, "the people naturally adhere most to doctrines . . . which can best accommodate their duties to their inclinations." Once such teachings arrive on the scene, moral philosophy is required to preserve the purity of the moral doctrine, to counter the human tendency to use eclectic teachings to rationalize transgressions. The moral doctrine thus articulated is perfectly comprehensible and, indeed, most attractive to people, even if they, in the confusion of their sentiments, are unable to arrive at it on their own.[23]

In sum, it is possible to argue that many, if not all, of Kant's apparently unpolitical writings have a public purpose, that of furthering the true moral ends of ordinary human beings. Kant does not write merely for philosophers, and he does not think merely to satisfy his love of wisdom.

Then there are Kant's more explicitly political writings, by means of which he can directly or indirectly address statesmen, their advisers, and, for that matter, "the entire *reading public*."[24] As he puts it in *Reflexionen zur Anthropologie,* "Everything seems to depend upon beginning with that which has general influence, that is, with the government. Hence one must encourage philosophers, historians, poets, and especially clerics to keep this idea [of general moral reform] in mind."[25]

For this reason, the "secret" article of his perpetual peace proposal requires that "the maxims of the philosophers on the conditions under which public peace is possible shall be consulted by states which are armed for war."[26] So as not to impugn the authority of the state, such consultations can be conducted "secretly" by allowing philosophers the freedom publicly to speak and, more important, to write about issues of war and peace. Those in power can, Kant insists, rest assured that such writings will not endanger their position, for "the people [will] take scarcely any or no notice at all . . . of [them]." Freedom of speech allows men of action to conceal their dependence upon men of ideas.[27]

One may of course wonder whether politicians will actually follow the advice they receive from this source, especially if it seems either impractical or contrary to their interests. The fact that Kant on more than one occasion gives advice suggests that he does not believe that it is given in vain; without some "hope for better times to come," no one—not even Kant—would wish "to do something useful for the common good."[28] He must believe that there is some way of appealing to statesmen without presupposing that they are favorably disposed.

Whatever its significance in other respects, Kant's "philosophy of history" may well be the ground of such an appeal. Beginning from the recognition that individuals motivated by the desire for glory must believe that their actions can win them fame in the future and that the key to glory is success,[29] Kant constructs an account of history that seems at least in part to be intended to persuade these glory-seekers that the determination of events on a cosmic scale is out of their hands. He claims that history is tending inevitably in a cosmopolitan direction and that the people of the future "will value the history of the oldest times . . . only from the point of view of what interests *them*, i.e., the positive and negative achievements of nations and governments in relation to the cosmopolitan goal."[30] Statesmen can hope to be remembered well only if they contribute to this purpose. Any "anti-cosmopolitan" advantage they seize—regardless of its magnitude in the short run—will work to their long-term disadvantage: the "trace" a politician leaves will be a "hated remnant" if he has acted in such a way as to hold up the world's "progress toward a system."[31] To the extent that this argument succeeds in enlisting those who would otherwise scorn the cosmopolitan cause, it is salutary, even if it cannot be justified theoretically.[32]

The Political Strategy of Kant's Philosophy of History

Let us then examine Kant's treatment of history in greater detail. His historical researches are indeed quite clearly subordinate to his moral and political concerns. Thus, for example, the most striking feature of his approach to historical study is its orientation toward the future rather than the past. He is more concerned with tentatively predicting and prophesying how nature will work itself out over time than with reconstructing the antecedent causes of any given event. He "hopes," he says, to find in history "a regular movement [*Gang*] among freely willed actions," revealing overall "a steadily advancing but slow development of man's original capacities."[33] If such a pattern cannot be found, "we are faced not with a law-governed nature, but with an aimless, random process, and the dismal reign of chance replaces the guiding principle of reason." As he puts it in *The Conflict of the Faculties*, "the whole traffic of our species with itself on this globe would have to be considered as a mere farcical comedy."[34] Were nature as a whole, including human nature, to seem so unreceptive to moral intentions, the psychological ground for both political and moral action—if not necessarily the obligation to engage in it—would be undermined.

It is relatively easy to see how such hope is absolutely essential to the encouragement of any morally grounded political action. Unless there is a "hope for better times to come," "an earnest desire to do something useful for the common good would [never inspire] the human heart."[35] A moral person who acts politically almost always has a project that cannot be completed instantaneously but instead requires a coherent succession of actions over a period of time. He cannot simply regard each moment as a discrete occasion to which a moral maxim can be applied, for he is trying to create something that exists and persists in this world, thereby exercising a kind of "causality in respect of nature as a whole."[36] His success depends not on constantly following some moral maxim—reflecting a "timeless" good will—but on actually attaining his goal.

Furthermore, every political project quite clearly requires the manipulation of people and things; although "the art of utilising nature for the government of men" may not be "the whole of practical wisdom," it may yet be some *part* of it.[37] Every political project must to some extent aim at the manipulation or transformation of nature. If nature and human nature simply resisted such attempts at control or transformation, if no political good attained could long be maintained, then it would be difficult for anyone but a fool to sustain an interest in politics.[38] Without some hope that one's deeds will have an enduring impact on the world, no one would engage in political activity except for very narrowly and immediately selfish ends. Thus Kant's account of the progressive transformation of nature—the "empirical" assurance of its susceptibility to human control—seems necessary at least to sustain and encourage the political efforts of well-intentioned people.

Yet a cursory glance at Kant's account of the historical process that culminates in perpetual peace seems to *rule out* the efficacy of any decent political action. While Kant asserts that "no less an authority than the great artist *Nature* herself" guarantees the attainment of perpetual peace, he indicates that nature does so without regard to human intentions. It seems that perpetual peace can and will result almost automatically, without any necessary action on its behalf by human beings: "The mechanical process of nature visibly exhibits the purposive plan of producing concord among men, even against their will and indeed by means of their very discord."[39]

Of course, the process that leads to this result is not very pretty. This observation should not be surprising, given the fact that nowhere in the process should we expect to see the manifestation of a good will. Its mainspring seems to be what Kant calls the "unsocial sociability of men," the competitive urge that leads people to cultivate themselves in all respects, using their reason to develop the arts and sciences.[40] Since all these things are developed not only in the course of but for the sake of competition, they cannot avoid being used for this purpose; as they all serve to increase human powers, they necessarily make the competition more destructive. Nations will stop fighting with one another only when they have reached the point of "complete inner exhaustion of their powers."[41]

But, Kant insists, this competition is "essentially healthy," for without it "human talents would remain hidden for ever in a dormant state, and men, as good-natured as the sheep they tended, would scarcely render their existence more valuable than that of their animals." War and conflict are part and parcel of what makes us human.[42]

For Kant, cultivation and conflict are thus two sides of the same coin. In the long run, the former seems to make possible the overcoming of the latter, so that the gains achieved in cultivation are not necessarily destroyed in the end. Human beings can hope for a time when they can exercise their capacities fully *and* live peacefully. How this condition is supposed to come into being is, however, not entirely clear. It seems conceivable but hardly inevitable that, when people have fought themselves to a standstill, there will be someone who can lead them out of the quandary they have created for themselves. If they have made themselves miserable enough, they should certainly be a receptive audience, sufficiently concerned with defending what little they have to restrain their ambition. Furthermore, the federal arrangement that is to bring perpetual peace into being is not so complicated and foreign to human experience as to be incapable of being discovered and of winning the informed consent of those who are to be involved.[43] There is, in other words, some ground for hoping that human beings can develop from sheep into something other than dead wolves.

As noted above, the problem with this account of how perpetual peace comes into being is that it does not seem to leave any room for conscious human action on its behalf. Juridical perpetual peace is produced by nature against man's conscious (but immoral) will. When human beings want peace, nature wills war so that the development of their innate capacities will be spurred. Later, when under the influence of its contrivance men want war, nature leads them to peace so that they can partake of the fruits of their progress. There is neither need nor, apparently, room for effective moral action in this process. If he cannot and need not be effective, how can the moral man be encouraged by this account to be politically active? Why should he not just wait for events to play themselves out?[44]

Kant's response to this query is twofold. In the first place, nothing in this account positively rules out the possibility that any given moral intention may, "accidentally," be fulfilled in this world. As long as moral success is possible, moral action remains obligatory.[45] Second, from the account given above, it is not clear that "history" does anything more than provide for the *possibility* of the attainment of perpetual peace. The necessary conditions may be in place, but without someone to take the initiative in establishing the federation, nothing would happen. Human agency may be required at the crucial moment. And even if there were a guarantee that *someone* would take the initiative, no one would thereby be absolved of any responsibility. After all, the claim that nature has its own intentions does not mean that they can never coincide with man's moral intentions. Every moral person ought to regard himself as potentially a self-conscious "instrument" for fulfilling the natural destiny of mankind.

To understand how this human agency might work requires a still closer examination of Kant's explanation of how nature "guarantees" perpetual peace. The argument falls into two parts: an account of "the situation in which nature has placed the actors in her great spectacle, for it is this situation which ultimately demands the guarantee" and an account of how the guarantee itself is provided.[46] First, Kant explains how the natural process leads human beings to spread over the entire earth, a condition made *possible* by the availability of some means of livelihood everywhere and made *necessary* by war.[47] Then he proceeds to explain how nature uses war to compel humans "to enter into more or less legal relationships." This part of the account has a curious status, however. At first, Kant promises it as part of his explanation of nature's arrangements for man, implying that this part of man's history follows a course similar to that of those which preceded: as nature dispersed human beings all over the globe, so it eventually forces them to live under conditions of political right. Yet, before Kant explains specifically how nature accomplishes this goal, he introduces a new distinction—between "what nature does to further *her own end* with respect to the human race as an animal species" and what it does "in relation to the end which man's own reason prescribes to him as a duty, . . . his *moral purpose.*"[48] Nature exhausts its contribution to man's "animal" ends by populating the entire globe. Nature seems to do this entirely on its own, without requiring an active human response other than that capable of being given by any "instrumentally" rational animal.[49] In regard to the latter end, however, nature is no longer a sovereign, but only an aid to man in completing his own rational projects. Although Kant still speaks of "nature's compulsion" and of what "nature *irresistibly* wills," he also speaks of "how the mechanism of nature . . . can be used by reason" and of how it "can be applied to man."[50] Needless to say, *some* self-conscious being has to possess that reason and apply that mechanism to attain that moral end. Nature seems to require the participation at least of human understanding to "guarantee" that man will accomplish his moral purpose.

This point is confirmed by an examination of Kant's account of how nature guarantees the attainment of political right, first through the formation of a civil state and then through the founding of a republic. By dispersing human beings all over the globe, nature forces "peoples" to impinge upon one another. In order to secure itself against its neighbors, each people must "form itself internally into a state."[51] This result nature seems to accomplish by itself. The real problem lies in establishing a government that secures the rights of man. Here nature's contribution seems to be limited to providing the forces that people can manipulate so as to establish such a constitution. They can channel their selfishness and their suspicion—provided, as it were, by nature—in such a way as to secure the rights of all. Nature itself does not bring into being the institutions that accomplish this end; rather, human beings must themselves discover and found them, understanding and making use of natural impulses. The founding of a republic seems to depend less on simple natural coercion and more on human dispositions and understanding. Someone has to wish to set up a constitution that secures the rights of man and also has to know how to do it.[52] While nature clearly provides the forces that can be known and manipulated, it does not so clearly provide the knowledge or the will to do so. Kant himself never says that by nature human beings are so defensively oriented that they are all only worried about securing their rights.[53] Hence nature, in his view, cannot "cause" men to wish to establish a constitution that will secure all their rights. Without such natural necessity, the situation may be ever so ripe— nature having taken care of everything else—but the final step may never be taken. The defensively oriented, for example, may not prevail against the offensively minded. As a result, the natural forces of history could well be stuck for a long time before the gates of the republic.

Still, even after this discussion Kant persists in speaking of the "irresistible will" of nature. Certainly he can no longer simply mean that human beings have no option but to acquiesce in or respond in a particular or predetermined way to natural necessity. Nature does not compel them to form republics in the same way that it compels them to disperse themselves all over the world. Nevertheless, it remains true that all the events and actions leading to the founding of a republic can be regarded as part of the natural order. After all, everything that takes place in the world must be explicable fully in terms of natural causality. Because every act is thus explicable, Kant can truthfully say that the irresistible will of nature leads to this result; at least in retrospect, every act can and must be said to follow necessarily from a particular natural cause. Of course, there may well be *several* possible responses to every given natural event, each of which (if it had occurred and, as such, were an object of experience) could be said after the fact to follow "neces-sarily" from the event. Under such circumstances, the retrospective account of natural necessity cannot be used to predict what will happen at a given moment. If every response can equally be said to be necessary, then the occurrence of one rather than another is an accident. What from one point of view is nature's irresistible will is from another an accident.[54] From these considerations, we can begin to see why Kant claims, as he does in the *Idea for a Universal History,* that the "fulfilment [of his 'chiliastic' expectations] can be hastened, if only indirectly, by a knowledge of the idea they are based on," by an appreciation, in other words, of his "prophetic" account of history.[55] He expects his historical writings to have political conse-quences, asserting in his *Reflexionen* that "the writers of history have all the responsibility" and that "history itself must contain the plan for the betterment of the world."[56]

His prophecy can contribute to its own fulfillment—indeed, it "must be regarded . . . even as capable of furthering the purpose of nature itself"—if the persons who are shown this manner of conceiving the movement of history can be inspired in critical instances to "push" it in the proper direction.[57] The help he expects them to give to nature is not, as we have seen, a matter of immediately fostering the conditions under which perpetual peace might be possible. Kant does not expect statesmen to contribute self-consciously to this sort of progress. While his writing might produce a popular and intellectual enthusiasm for and agitation on behalf of this goal, he does not believe that politicians in general will take either the people or the intellectuals seriously, unless, as he says, "the circumstances are sufficiently pressing."[58] Then they might be compelled to respond to informed public opinion. In the second place, he neither expects nor recommends that anyone, even a moral statesman, force matters before the time is ripe. While it is always in principle possible to act in accordance with the moral law, it is also true that the more complicated the moral task is—the more individuals on whom its completion depends—the less likely anyone will be successful in carrying it out. Thus, keeping a promise (assuming that it requires only an act of will) is a good deal less dependent upon fortune and circumstances than arranging a perpetual peace treaty among states. Diplomatic success in such an instance demands that states cannot help but assent to the agreement, a conjunction of interests an individual statesman is unlikely to be able to arrange on his own. Thus Kant counsels that the principles of moral politics be applied prudently, actually *blaming* "despotic moralists" who recommend "premature measures." Prudence, for Kant, entails remembering that the end dictated by morality—that is, perpetual peace—"cannot be realised by violent and precipitate means, but must be steadily approached as favourable opportunities present themselves."[59] Statesmen should wait until the time is right, until things have naturally proceeded to the point where their measures might succeed; before then, they are most likely to fail, thereby discrediting morality and perhaps unintentionally causing a great deal of suffering. In other words, just as Kant's account of history leaves room for moral action, his account of moral politics leaves room for a prudent sensitivity to historical conditions. His writing appears, in this respect, to be most statesmanlike.

As should be clear, however, Kant does not permit statesmen *at any time* to disregard the formal rules of respect for individual dignity: "A true system of politics cannot . . . take a single step without paying tribute to morality." Consent, or at least the *possibility* of consent, must be every "moral politician's" touchstone.[60] Nevertheless, as we have seen, he is not thereby prevented from making use of natural mechanisms, for example, in establishing a constitution that deserves the consent of those who live under it. Indeed, Kant at one point speaks of a *duty* to make use of a natural mechanism. Individuals may be treated as means if they are at the same time treated as ends in themselves.[61]

Kant's Own Situation

A prudent sensitivity to historical conditions would seem to raise questions about Kant's own activity as a writer. He is, after all, making moral and political recommendations long before the time is ripe for their adoption. While he is certainly not in a position to act on his own recommendations, could he not so inflame public opinion as to make it difficult for statesmen to act prudently and responsibly? Could he not be charged with preparing the way for the very "despotic moralists" he blames?

Kant can defend himself against this charge. In his *Idea for a Universal History,* he stresses the importance of "the present case," because "we might by our own rational projects accelerate the coming of this period which will be so welcome to our descendants." What uniquely characterizes this age is that it is "the age of enlightenment, the century of *Frederick.*" By saying, "*Argue* as much as you like and about whatever you like, *but* obey," the "enlightened despot" Friedrich makes it possible for men freely to pursue and exchange knowledge without posing a threat to the current political order. Under his regime, knowledge can spread and projects can be developed without immediately initiating potentially harmful political change. As Kant indicates, he regards himself as fortunate to live in a situation in which "a lesser degree of civil freedom gives intellectual freedom enough room to expand to its fullest extent." In this particular circumstance, Kant can be confident that the political and moral seeds he sows will not sprout too soon. The "age of *enlightenment*" merely prepares the way for the enlightened age.[62]

That Kant is capable of responding differently in another circumstance is clear from the following considerations. After the death of Friedrich, the intellectual climate in Prussia changed substantially. The government of his nephew, Friedrich Wilhelm II, a Rosicrucian, exercised its power of censorship much more vigorously, intending, so it seemed, to "stamp out the enlightenment."[63] Where once it had been rather easy for scholars publicly to say almost anything they wished, they were now called to account for their writings, especially in matters of religion. While the actions of Friedrich Wilhelm's government fell far short of those of the Spanish Inquisition, Kant *was* threatened with "unpleasant measures" if he did not cease "misusing" his philosophy "to distort and disparage man of the cardinal and basic teachings of the Holy Scripture and of Christianity."[64] The age of enlightenment seemed to have come to an end. The government would no longer ignore the potential political consequences of scholarly activity. As a result of this experience,

Kant trod more lightly, acknowledging that "religion is a most important political need" for "the civil good of the commonwealth in general" and that "the *whole* truth" need not be stated in public.[65]

In this context, his elaborate insistence at the beginning of *Perpetual Peace* that his proposals be treated as irrelevant makes sense: if political threats are taken seriously, then he must pretend not to be a threat. Now, in the course of stating his *clausula salvatoria* Kant carefully avoids explicitly agreeing with the position he attributes to "the worldly-wise statesmen." Even if he himself does not believe that "abstract ideas" cannot *ultimately* have consequences, he is certainly willing to take advantage of the "faith" others have in this "truth." By appealing to the cynicism of statesmen, Kant hopes to secure the freedom of speech that had once been a matter of course.[66]

Thus as a writer Kant is acutely sensitive to the political conditions under which he operates, altering his approach, if not his goals, as the times change. Indeed, in his situation—in an enlightening, as opposed to enlightened, society—the best means of engaging in politics for moral purposes may well be by writing so as to lay the groundwork for future action, rather than by acting directly in the present. Whatever may be the case when the situation is finally ripe, in less propitious circumstances the epitome of the moral and prudent political actor is, in Kant's view, the intellectual, who writes for an audience of readers much like himself. In this respect, then, the philosophic writer is "merely" another kind of politician. Were complete enlightenment possible, there would indeed be no difference between philosophers and statesmen. But inasmuch as "the possession of power inevitably corrupts the free judgement of reason," such writers can best serve the common good by remaining on the sidelines.[67] It remains for us to ask whether this recommendation has in the long run produced better political advice than that of those writers who address themselves more directly to political leaders.

To return, then, to the question with which we began: the Kantian philosopher is a distinctive character, albeit not in the same way as his Socratic counterpart. For the latter, there is an insuperable disproportion between philosophy and politics; for the former, there is merely a distance that is perpetually being diminished by reform. *At the moment,* the Kantian differs from the ordinary politician in the ground of his action: after all, moral principle differs from self-interest, whether individual or collective. But the long-term promise of the political action of Kantian intellectuals is the eclipse of "politics as usual"; the goal is the *moral* manipulation of nature, with all those concerned giving their consent. In the end, there is no reason why the philosopher should differ at all from the statesman. That "end" may be a long way—perhaps infinitely far—off. In the meantime, we can hope, Kant says, that the paths of the two are converging.

Notes

1

Plato, *Apology of Socrates,* 18b and 38c.

2

See Niccolo Machiavelli, *The Prince,* trans. Harvey C. Mansfield, Jr. (Chicago: University of Chicago Press, 1985), pp. 101–05, 14–15; and Leo Strauss, *Thoughts on Machiavelli* (Chicago: University of Chicago Press, 1978), pp. 79–80.

3

Machiavelli, *The Prince,* pp. 3–4, 92–95.

4

See, e.g., Thomas Hobbes, *Leviathan,* ed. C. B. Macpherson (Harmondsworth, Eng.: Penguin, 1968), pp. 727–29; and Alexis de Tocqueville, *Democracy in America,* vol. 2, trans. George Lawrence (Garden City, N.Y.: Doubleday, 1969), pp. 525–28).

5

Immanuel Kant, *Bemerkungen zu den Beobachtungen über das Gefühl des Schönen und Erhabenen,* in *Kants gesammelte Schriften,* vol. 20 (Berlin: Walter de Gruyter, 1942), p. 44, my translation. See also Susan Meld Shell, *The Rights of Reason* (Toronto: University of Toronto Press, 1980), pp. 20–32.

6

Cf. Hannah Arendt, *Lectures on Kant's Political Philosophy,* ed. Ronald Beiner (Chicago: University of Chicago Press, 1982), p. 29; Ronald Beiner, "Hannah Arendt and Leo Strauss: The Uncommenced Dialogue," *Political Theory* 18 (May 1990): 247–48; Immanuel Kant, *Critique of Pure Reason,* trans. Norman Kemp Smith (New York: St. Martin's, 1965), A831/B859; and Leo Strauss, *Persecution and the Art of Writing* (Westport, Conn.: Greenwood Press, 1948), pp. 7–8, 33–34.

7

See Immanuel Kant, *The Conflict of the Faculties,* trans. Mary J. Gregor (New York: Abaris Books, 1979), pp. 153, 155; and Peter Burg, *Kant und die Französische Revolu-*

tion (Berlin: Duncker und Humblot, 1974), pp. 38–41, on the French Revolution; and cf. Kant's preface to *The Conflict of the Faculties* (pp. 9–21) for a discussion of his encounter with censorship under Friedrich Wilhelm II.

8

Immanuel Kant, *What is Enlightenment?* in Hans Reiss, ed., *Kant's Political Writings,* trans. H. B. Nisbet (Cambridge: Cambridge University Press, 1970), pp. 55, 57, 59.

9

Kant, *Conflict of the Faculties,* p. 161 (changes in the translation are mine); see also pp. 27, 43.

10

Kant, *Conflict of the Faculties,* pp. 21, 55, 161; changes in the translation are mine.

11

Immanuel Kant, *Perpetual Peace,* in *Kant's Political Writings,* p. 115.

12

See, e.g., Immanuel Kant, *Critique of Pure Reason,* Bxxvii; and Stanley Rosen, "Man's Hope," *Social Research* 48 (Autumn 1981): 623, 628.

13

Kant, *Critique of Pure Reason,* Bxxxi.

14

Kant, *Critique of Pure Reason,* Bxxxii–xxxiii; *Moralphilosophie Collins,* in *Kants gesammelte Schriften,* vol. 27 (Berlin: Walter de Gruyter, 1974), p. 307, my translation; and Rosen, "Man's Hope," p. 622.

15

Kant, *Critique of Pure Reason,* Bxxxiv, A744–57/B772–85, A819/B847; *Verkündigung eines nahen Abschlusses eines Tractats zum ewigen Frieden in der Philosophie,* in *Kants Werke,* vol. 8 (Berlin: Walter de Gruyter, 1968), pp. 411–22, esp. pp. 419–22; letter to Heinrich Jung-Stilling (after 1 March 1789), in *Philosophical Correspondence, 1759–99,* ed. and trans. Arnulf Zweig (Chicago: University of Chicago Press, 1967), p. 131; *Idea for a Universal History,* in *Kant's Political Writings,* pp. 42–43, 52–53); and Hans Saner, *Kant's Political Thought,* trans. E. B. Ashton (Chicago: University of Chicago Press, 1973), pp. 230–34.

16
Immanuel Kant, *Groundwork of the Metaphysic of Morals,* trans. H. J. Paton (New York: Harper and Row, 1964), pp. 59, 64, 72.

17
See, e.g., Kant, *Critique of Pure Reason,* Axviii, Bxxxi, xxxiv; *Prolegomena to Any Future Metaphysics,* ed. Lewis White Beck (Indianapolis: Bobbs-Merrill, 1950), p. 11; and *Conflict of the Faculties,* pp. 15, 35–37.

18
Cf. Kant, *Critique of Pure Reason,* Axviii, Bxxxvii-xliv; *Prolegomena,* pp. 3, 9, 11, 129, 131; *Critique of Practical Reason,* trans. Lewis White Beck (Indianapolis: Bobbs-Merrill, 1956), p. 168; and Hannah Arendt, *Lectures on Kant's Political Philosophy,* pp. 38–39.

19
Kant, *Critique of Pure Reason,* Bxxxii–xxxiv.

20
See Kant, *Critique of Pure Reason,* Bxxxiii; *Groundwork,* p. 72; and *Critique of Practical Reason,* p. 157.

21
Kant, *Groundwork,* p. 72.

22
Cf. Kant, *The Doctrine of Virtue,* trans. Mary J. Gregor (Philadelphia: University of Pennsylvania Press, 1964), pp. 151–58); and, e.g., *Moralphilosophie Collins,* 27:278, 344. For an extended discussion of the didactic importance of an appeal to "proper pride" and dignity, see Joseph Knippenberg, "Moving beyond Fear: Rousseau and Kant on Cosmopolitan Education," *Journal of Politics* 51 (November 1989): 809–27.

23
Kant, *Conflict of the Faculties,* p. 51. Cf.

Kant, *Groundwork,* pp. 72–73, 76–79; and Wolfgang Kersting, "Kann die Kritik der praktischen Vernunft populär sein?," *Studia Leibnitiana* 15 (1983): 82–93.

24
Kant, *What is Enlightenment?* p. 55.

25
Kant's concern here is that, lacking confidence that others will reciprocate, a man who would be good will not take the risk. Hence individual reform and general reform are inextricably linked. Kant, *Reflexionen zur Anthropologie,* in *Kants gesammelte Schriften,* vol. 15 (Berlin: Georg Reimer, 1913), p. 613, my translation; cf. p. 606.

26
Kant, *Perpetual Peace,* p. 115.

27
Kant, *Conflict of the Faculties,* p. 161. Cf. Machiavelli, *Prince,* p. 94.

28
Kant, *On the Common Saying: "This May Be True in Theory, but It Does Not Apply in Practice"* (hereafter cited as *Theory and Practice*), in *Kant's Political Writings,* p. 89; and *Prolegomena,* p. 130.

29
Cf. Machiavelli, *Prince,* p. 71.

30
Kant, *Idea for a Universal History,* p. 53.

31
Kant, *Reflexionen zur Anthropologie,* 15:629. In this and related notes, Kant suggests that a "cosmopolitan" method of publicity can "raise the spirit of the regent" and "turn his desire for honor to the world as a whole and to the regard of the human race."

32
Cf. Marvin Zetterbaum's account of the edificatory purpose of Tocqueville's claim that the attainment of equality of conditions is inevitable; Zetterbaum, *Tocqueville and the Problem of Democracy* (Palo Alto, Calif.: Stanford University Press, 1967), pp. 1–21.

33

Kant, *Idea for a Universal History*, p. 41; change in the translation is mine. See also Arendt, *Lectures*, p. 8. Although William Galston briefly discusses the political purpose of Kant's philosophy of history, he does not treat this particular point; see Galston, *Kant and the Problem of History* (Chicago: University of Chicago Press, 1975), pp. 203–04.

34

Kant, *Idea for a Universal History*, p. 42; *Conflict of the Faculties*, p. 147; and *Reflexionen zur Anthropologie*, 15:644.

35

Kant, *Theory and Practice*, p. 89. Kant does speak specifically about the duties of those who have political power. See, e.g., Kant, *Perpetual Peace*, pp. 118, 123.

36

Kant, *Critique of Pure Reason*, A807/B835.

37

Kant, *Perpetual Peace*, p. 117; see also pp. 112–13. Thus humanity may "never *simply*" be treated "as a means, but always *at the same time* as an end." Also, "A person can serve as a means for others, for example, through his work, but only insofar as he does not cease to be a person and an end" (Kant, *Groundwork*, p. 96; emphasis added); and *Moralphilosophie Collins*, 27:343.

38

Kant, *Theory and Practice*, p. 88.

39

Kant's *Perpetual Peace*, p. 108; cf. *Idea for a Universal History*, p. 48.

40

Kant, *Idea for a Universal History*, p. 44.

41

Kant, *Idea for a Universal History*, p. 47; cf. *Theory and Practice*, p. 90. For a brief rehearsal of Kant's account, see Thomas L. Pangle and Clifford Orwin, "The Philosophical Foundation of Human Rights," in Marc F. Plattner, ed., *Human Rights in Our Time*

(Boulder, Colo.: Westview Press, 1984), pp. 8–10.

42

Kant, *Idea for a Universal History*, pp. 45, 47; cf. also *Conjectural Beginnings of Human History*, trans. Emil Fackenheim, in *On History*, ed. Lewis White Beck (Indianapolis: Bobbs-Merrill, 1963), pp. 66–67; and *Critique of Judgment*, trans. J. H. Bernard (New York: Hafner, 1951), p. 102.

43

Consider the report of F. H. Hinsley: "The following comments were made by my son, Hugh Hinsley, aged eleven years. . . . He asked me to tell him about the Second World War. When I had finished he said, 'Why don't all countries agree to an everlasting peace treaty?' I explained that this had been tried but that it was difficult to keep the promise. 'Then why don't they have a governor of the world? If I were governor of the world, I'd make them keep their promises.' I explained that world government presented some difficulties, that it was not easy to have a single government, for, say, England and Italy. 'I can see Italy and England are too far away [from each other]. But if I were governor of the world I'd live in the middle. I'd live in the middle of the countries like Italy, France, Germany, and England—in what's that country in the middle—in Switzerland.' I asked what would happen if, say, Germany still disobeyed his government. 'I'd get all the others to set about her.' I said he would then have a war on his hands. 'Oh, yes, it wouldn't be any good; but wouldn't they all want to keep together if the world was attacked by Martians?' I recorded this talk, I believe completely faithfully, at once. I had never previously discussed this kind of subject with him. Probably most modern children think in the same way." F. H. Hinsley, *Power and the Pursuit of Peace* (Cambridge: Cambridge University Press, 1967), p. 13n.

44

Kant considers a similar problem with regard to the quiescence of the religious, who do nothing in the hope that God will take care of everything. Cf. *Moralphilosophie Collins,* 27:321.

45

See, e.g., Kant, *Theory and Practice,* pp. 62, 89; and *Perpetual Peace,* p. 116. Perhaps it would be better to say "as long as moral success is *not impossible,* moral action is obligatory," for Kant insists that the fact of duty is much more certain than any prospect of its success or failure. To hear the call of duty, then, is to commit oneself to the attempt to carry it out; one cannot hear this call and subsequently believe that it cannot be fulfilled. Cf., e.g., Kant, *Critique of Practical Reason,* p. 148; and Allen Wood's discussion of the *absurdum practicum* argument in *Kant's Moral Religion* (Ithaca: Cornell University Press, 1970), pp. 25–34.

46

Kant, *Perpetual Peace,* p. 109.

47

In the *Critique of Judgment,* Kant offers a somewhat different account of these facts (pp. 215–16).

48

Kant, *Perpetual Peace,* pp. 110, 112.

49

Ibid., p. 111n. Human beings can interfere with what seems to be a wholly impersonal natural process—the floating of driftwood to places where there are no trees, making it possible for humans to survive there—by more efficiently utilizing the wood native to their region, thereby reducing the amount of driftwood. To save his account of nature's inexorable purposefulness, Kant must assimilate this kind of human volition to nature. He does so by making peaceful commerce—supplying what has apparently become a defect in nature's purposefulness—the result of another more powerful natural compulsion. Man is nothing here but an instrumentally rational animal. For another example of how human activity contributes to nature's purposefulness, cf. Kant, *Critique of Judgment,* p. 213.

50

Cf. Kant, *Perpetual Peace,* pp. 112, 113; and *Collegentwürfe aus den 80er Jahren,* in *Kants gesammelte Schriften,* vol. 15 (Berlin: Georg Reimer, 1913), p. 801.

51

Kant, *Perpetual Peace,* p. 112.

52

Cf. Kant, *Critique of Judgment,* p. 282, and his *Idea for a Universal History,* p. 47, for a similar argument with regard to the cosmopolitan constitution.

53

On the contrary, he frequently makes precisely the opposite claim. See, e.g., Kant, *Theory and Practice,* p. 91; and *Perpetual Peace,* pp. 111–12.

54

What is said at one point to be the working of nature—the creation of a republic—is said at another point to be the result of "good fortune" (*Glück*). Cf. Kant, *Perpetual Peace,* p. 112, with *Perpetual Peace,* p. 104.

55

Kant, *Idea for a Universal History,* p. 50. For a different assessment of Kant's discussion of prophecy, see William James Booth, *Interpreting the World* (Toronto: University of Toronto Press, 1986), pp. 108–12. In general, Booth suggests that Kant's "beautiful" account of history is aimed more at comforting mere observers than at encouraging moral action. The moral man, he insists, sublimely faces up to the inhospitable character of nature. Kant, however, distinguishes between "observers" and "citizens of the world" (*Weltbeschauer* and *Weltbürger*) and, of course, writes his *Idea for a Universal History* "from a cosmopolitan [*weltbürgerlich*] point of view." Cf. Kant, *Reflexionen zur Anthropologie,* 15:518.

56

Kant, *Reflexionen zur Anthropologie,* 15:628.

57

Kant, *Idea for a Universal History,* p. 51.

58

Kant, *Theory and Practice,* p. 91; see also *Perpetual Peace,* pp. 93, 100.

59

Kant, *Perpetual Peace,* pp. 119–22; cf. his discussion of *leges latae* on p. 97 and also *Conflict of the Faculties,* p. 167n. See also Dick Howard, "Kant's System and (Its) Politics," *Man and World* 18 (1985): 79–98.

60

Kant, *Perpetual Peace,* p. 125; cf. *Conflict of the Faculties,* p. 165, and *Theory and Practice,* p. 79.

61

See Kant, *Perpetual Peace,* p. 109, and *Groundwork,* p. 96. Consider also his account of juridical punishment, the object of which is to "warn," to "correct," or to "set an example." As he puts it, "Rulers do not punish because [the law] has been broken, but so that it will not be broken." Those who are punished are used as means to prevent future crimes. They are, however, also treated as ends insofar as the deterrent (*poena pragmatica*) can be no harsher than the morally fitting punishment (*poena vindictiva*). Executing shoplifters may effectively deter shoplifting, but it is unjust. Cf. Kant, *Praktische Philosophie Powalski,* in *Kants gesammelte Schriften,* 27:150; and *Moralphilosophie Collins,* 27:286.

62

Kant, *Idea for a Universal History,* p. 50; and *What is Enlightenment?* pp. 55, 58, 193n.

63

Mary J. Gregor, "Translator's Introduction," in Kant, *Conflict of the Faculties,* p. ix. For accounts of the situation in Prussia, see Johannes Müller, *Kantisches Stattsdenken und der preussische Staat* (Kitzingen/Main, Federal Republic of Germany: Holzner-Verlag, 1954), pp. 43–47; and Klaus Epstein, *The Genesis of German Conservatism* (Princeton: Princeton University Press, 1966), pp. 104–11, 142–53, 341–69.

64

Kant, *Conflict of the Faculties,* p. 11.

65

Ibid., pp. 21, 53.

66

Kant, *Perpetual Peace,* pp. 93, 104; *Idea for a Universal History,* pp. 47–48, and Leo Strauss, *Persecution and the Art of Writing,* p. 33n. Kant uses a similar device in *Conflict of the Faculties,* where he excuses Prussia from the duty of adopting a republican constitution because monarchy is "the only [form of government] by which that nation can defend itself against powerful neighbours." At the same time, he defends as loyal monarchists those who favor republicanism abroad "because the nation is the more assured against any danger the more other nations pursue a republican policy." Of course, "the more assured against any danger" Prussia is, the less justification there is for adhering to monarchy. Although Kant opposes any immediate innovation, his rationale implies that Prussia cannot forever remain exempt from its duty. He is sufficiently careful neither to call for immediate change nor to state outright that it will eventually be justified. See *Conflict of the Faculties,* p. 155n.

67

Kant, *Perpetual Peace,* p. 115.

Chapter 8

Liberalism and
International Relations

Michael W. Doyle

Liberal principles and institutions have had three striking effects on the foreign affairs of liberal states. They have created incentives for a separate peace among liberal states, for aggression against nonliberals, and for complaisance in vital matters of security and economic cooperation. In the first part of this chapter, I illustrate the extent of these effects in the history of liberal foreign relations. In the second part, I argue that these effects cannot be fully accounted for either by balance of power theory or by Marxist theories of capitalist foreign policy. In the third part, I show how a Kantian theory of liberal internationalism can account for these effects and how, despite liberal aggression and complaisance, the peace among liberals has been expanding for almost two centuries.

Liberalism has been identified with an essential principle—the importance of the freedom of the individual. Above all, this is a belief in the importance of moral freedom, of the right to be treated and a duty to treat others as ethical subjects, and not as objects or means only. A commitment to this principle has generated rights and institutions.

A threefold set of rights forms the foundation of liberalism. Liberalism calls for freedom from arbitrary authority, often called "negative freedom," which includes freedom of conscience, a free press and free speech, equality under the law, and the right to hold and therefore to exchange property without fear of arbitrary seizure. Liberalism also calls for those rights necessary to protect and promote the capacity and opportunity for freedom, the "positive freedoms." Such social and economic rights as equality of opportunity in education and rights to health care and employment, necessary for effective self-expression and participation, are thus among liberal rights. A third liberal right, democratic participation or representation, is necessary to guarantee the other two. To ensure that morally autonomous individuals remain free in those areas of social action where public authority is needed, public legislation has to express the will of the citizens making laws for their own community.

Liberalism is thus marked by a shared commitment to four essential institutions. First, citizens possess juridical equality and other fundamental civic rights such as freedom of religion and the press. Second, the effective sovereigns of the state are representative legislatures deriving their authority from the consent of the electorate and exercising their authority free from all restraint apart from the requirement that basic civic rights be preserved. Most pertinently for the impact of liberalism on foreign affairs, the state is subject to neither the external authority of other states nor to the internal authority of special prerogatives held, for example, by monarchs or military bureaucracies over foreign policy. Third, the economy rests on a recognition of the rights of private property, including the ownership of means of production. Property is justified by individual acquisition (for example, by labor) or by social agreement or social utility. This excludes state socialism or state capitalism, but it need not exclude market socialism or various forms of the mixed economy. Fourth, economic decisions are predominantly shaped by the forces of supply and demand, domestically and internationally, and they are free from strict control by bureaucracies.

These principles and institutions have shaped two high roads to liberal governance.[1] In order to protect the opportunity of the citizen to exercise freedom, laissez-faire liberalism has leaned toward a highly constrained role for the state and a much wider role for private property and the market. In order to promote the opportunity of the citizen to exercise freedom, welfare liberalism has expanded the role of the state and constricted the role of the market. Both, nevertheless, accept the four institutional requirements and contrast markedly with the colonies, monarchical regimes, military dictatorships, and communist party dictatorships with which they have shared the political governance of the modern world. (For a list of liberal regimes see table 1 in the appendix to this chapter.)

The International Relations of Liberal States

The first effect of liberalism on the foreign relations of liberal states is the establishment of a peace among liberal states.[2] During the nineteenth century, the United States and Great Britain engaged in nearly continual strife. But after the Reform Act of 1832 defined actual representation as the formal source of the sovereignty of the British parliament, Britain and the United States negotiated their disputes despite, for example, British grievances against the Union blockade of the South, with which Britain had close economic ties. Despite severe Anglo-French colonial rivalry, liberal Britain and liberal France formed an entente against illiberal Germany before World War I. And in 1914–15, Italy, the liberal member of the Triple Alliance with Germany and Austria, chose not to fulfill its treaty obligations under the Triple Alliance to support its allies; instead, Italy joined in an alliance with

Britain and France that had the result of preventing it from having to fight other liberal states, and then it declared war on Germany and Austria. And despite generations of Anglo-American tension and Britain's wartime restrictions on American trade with Germany, the United States leaned toward Britain and France from 1914 to 1917, before entering World War I on their side. Nowhere was this special peace among liberal states more clearly proclaimed than in President Woodrow Wilson's "War Message" of 2 April 1917: "Our object now, as then, is to vindicate the principles of peace and justice in the life of the world as against selfish and autocratic power and to set up amongst the really free and self-governed people of the world such a concert of purpose and of action as well as henceforth ensure the observance of those principles."[3] Beginning in the eighteenth century and slowly growing since then, a zone of peace, which Kant called the "pacific federation" or "pacific union," began to be established among liberal societies. (More than forty liberal states currently make up the union. Most are in Europe and North America, but they can be found on every continent, as table 1 indicates.)

Of course, the outbreak of war, in any given year, between any two states, is a low probability event. But the occurrence of a war between any two adjacent states, considered over a long period of time, would be more probable. The apparent absence of war between liberal states, whether adjacent or not, for almost two hundred years thus may have significance. More significant, perhaps, is that when states are forced to decide on which side of an impending world war they will fight, liberal states wind up all on the same side, despite the complexity of the paths that take them there. And we should recall that medieval and early modern Europe were the warring cockpits of states, wherein France and England and the Low Countries engaged in nearly constant strife, until in the late eighteenth century there began to emerge liberal regimes. At first hesitant and confused, but later clear and confident as liberal regimes gained deeper domestic foundations and longer international experience, a pacific union of these liberal states became established. These trends do not prove that the peace among liberals is statistically significant, nor that liberalism is the peace's sole valid explanation.[4] Yet they do suggest that we consider the possibility that liberals have indeed established a separate peace—but only among themselves.

This is a feature, moreover, that appears to be special to liberal societies. Neither specific regional attributes nor historic alliances or friendships describe the wide reach of the liberal peace. The peace extends as far as, and no further than, the relations among liberal states, not including nonliberal states in an otherwise liberal region (such as the North Atlantic in the 1930s) nor excluding liberal states in a nonliberal region (such as Central America or Africa).

And relations among other groups of states with similar structures or with compatible values are not similarly peaceful.[5] Feudal warfare was frequent and very much a sport of the monarchs and nobility. There have not been enough truly totalitarian, fascist powers (nor have they lasted long enough) to test fairly their pacific compatibility, but fascist powers in the wider sense of nationalist, capitalist, military dictatorships fought each other in the 1930s. Communist powers have engaged in wars more recently in East Asia. We have not had enough socialist societies to consider the relevance of socialist pacification. The more abstract category of pluralism does not suffice. Certainly Germany was pluralist when it engaged in war with liberal states in 1914, as was Japan in 1941. But they were not liberal. Peace among liberals thus appears to be a special characteristic.

Liberalism is also said to carry with it a second effect—what Hume called "imprudent vehemence," or aggression against nonliberals.[6] Peaceful restraint only seems to work in the liberals' relations with other liberals. Liberal states have fought numerous wars with nonliberal states. (For a list of international wars since 1816 see table 2 in the appendix to this chapter.) Both liberal France and Britain fought expansionist colonial wars throughout the nineteenth century. The United States fought a similar war with Mexico in 1846–48, waged a war of annihilation against Native Americans, and intervened militarily against sovereign states many times before and after World War II.

Nonetheless, establishing the statistical significance of Hume's assertion appears remarkably difficult. The best statistical evidence, presented by Steve Chan and Erich Weede, indicates that "libertarian" or "democratic" (slightly different measures), indeed, are more war-prone than nonlibertarian or nondemocratic states.[7] But *war-proneness* is not a measure of *imprudent aggression*. Many wars are defensive, and thus prudent by necessity. Liberal states have been attacked and threatened by nonliberal states that do not exercise any special restraint in their dealings with liberal states. Authoritarian rulers both stimulate and respond to an international political environment in which conflicts of prestige, interest, and pure fear of what other states might do all lead states toward war. War and conquest have thus characterized the careers of many authoritarian rulers and ruling parties, from Louis XIV and Napoleon to Mussolini's Fascisti, Hitler's Nazis, and Stalin's communists.

But neither can we simply blame warfare on the authoritarians or totalitarians, as many of our more enthusiastic politicians would have us do.[8] Liberal states ("libertarian") acted as initiators in 24 out of the 56 interstate wars in which they participated between 1816 and 1980. Nonliberals were on the initiating side in 91 out of the 187 times in which they participated in interstate wars.[9] Although nonliberal states initiated a higher percentage of interstate wars, liberal metropoles were the overwhelming systemic participants in extrasystemic wars, colonial wars, which we can assume to have been by and large initiated by the metropole (see below). Furthermore, according to Walter Clemens, the United States intervened in the Third World more than twice as often in the period 1946–76 as the Soviet Union did in 1946–79.[10] Relatedly, Barry Posen and Stephen VanEvera found that the United States devoted one quarter and the Soviet Union one tenth of their defense budgets to forces designed for Third World interventions (where responding to perceived threats would presumably have a less than purely defensive character).[11]

Although liberal initiation of wars suggests some basis for Hume's assertion, it does not resolve the claim he made. Initiation or response may reflect either aggressive or defensive policy, in that an aggressive policy may provoke a rival to initiate a war and a defensive policy may require preemption. Hume appears to be suggesting that liberal policy has a tendency to be unnecessarily aggressive. In order to assess his assertion, we need to take into account the specific circumstances—the threats with which the state is faced, its resources, and its goals—and doing this requires a historical understanding of time and place. If liberals were always aggressive or always nonaggressive in relations with nonliberals, we could reasonably argue that they were or were not unnecessarily aggressive. But even though studies have demonstrated the existence of something special in foreign relations among liberals, relations between liberals and nonliberals appear more complicated. Unless we can normalize not just the number but the situations of liberal relations with nonliberals and nonliberal relations with nonliberals, the best we may be able to do is illustrate imprudent vehemence.

Most wars seem to arise out of calculations and miscalculations of interest, misunderstandings, and mutual suspicions, such as those that characterized the origins of World War I. But we can find expressions of aggressive intent and apparently unnecessary vehemence by the liberal state characterizing a large number of wars.[12]

In relations with powerful nonliberal states, liberal states have missed opportunities to pursue the negotiation of arms reduction and arms control when it has been in the mutual strategic interest, and they have failed to construct the wider schemes of accommodation that are needed to supplement arms control. Prior to the outbreak of World War I, Lord Sanderson leveled this charge against Sir Eyre Crowe in his response to Crowe's famous memorandum on the state of British relations with Germany.[13] Sanderson pointed out that Crowe interpreted German demands to participate in the settlement of international disputes and to have a "place in the sun" (the colonies) like that enjoyed by the other great powers as evidence of a fundamental aggressiveness driving toward world domination. Crowe may well have perceived an essential feature of Wilhelmine Germany, and Sanderson may have been naive in his attempt to place Germany in the context of other rising powers (bumptious but not aggressively pursuing world domination). But the interesting thing to note is less the conclusions reached than Crowe's chain of argument and evidence. He rejects continued accommodation (appeasement) with Germany not because he shows that Germany was more bumptious than France and not because he shows that Germany had greater potential as a world hegemon than the United States, which he does not even consider in this connection. Instead he is (legitimately) perplexed by the real uncertainty of German foreign policy and by its "erratic, domineering, and often frankly aggressive spirit," which accords with the well-known personal characteristics of "the present Ruler of Germany."

Similar evidence of irrefutable suspicion appears to characterize U.S. diplomacy toward the Soviet Union. In a fascinating memorandum to President Wilson written in 1919, Herbert Hoover (then one of Wilson's advisers) recommended that the president speak out against the danger of "world domination" by the "Bolsheviki"—a "tyranny that is the negation of democracy." Rejecting military intervention as excessively costly and likely to "make us a party in reestablishing the reactionary classes in their economic domination over the lower classes," Hoover proposed a "relief program" designed to undercut some of the popular support the Bolsheviks were garnering both in the Soviet Union and abroad. Although he acknowledged that the evidence was not yet clear, he concluded: "If the militant features of Bolshevism were drawn in colors with their true parallel with Prussianism as an attempt at world domination that we do not stand for, it would check the fears that today haunt all men's minds." (The actual U.S. intervention in the Soviet Union was limited to supporting anti-Bolshevik Czechoslovak soldiers in Siberia and to protecting military supplies in Murmansk from German seizure.)[14]

In the postwar period, and particularly following the outbreak of the Korean War, U.S. diplomacy equated the "international Communist movement" (all communist states and parties) with "Communist imperialism" and with a domestic tyranny in the Soviet Union that required a cold war and international subversion as a means of legitimizing its own police state. John Foster Dulles most clearly expressed this conviction, together with his own commitment to a strategy of "liberation," when he declared: "we shall never have a secure peace or a happy world so long as Soviet communism dominates one third of all the peoples that there are, and is in the process of trying at least to extend its rule to many others."[15]

Opportunities for splitting the Communist bloc along cleavages of strategic national interest were delayed. Burdened with the war in Vietnam, the United States took ten years to appreciate and exploit the strategic opportunity of the Sino-Soviet split. Even the signal strategic, "offensive" success of the early cold war, the defection of Yugoslavia from the Soviet bloc, did not receive the wholehearted welcome that a strategic assessment of its importance would have warranted.[16] U.S. relations with both China and Yugoslavia were subject to alternating ideological moods: visions of exceptionalness (they were "less ruthless," more organic to the indigenous, traditional culture) sparred with bouts of liberal soul-searching ("we cannot associate ourselves with a totalitarian state").

Imprudent vehemence is also associated with liberal foreign policy toward weak, nonliberal states; no greater spirit of accommodation or tolerance informs liberal policy toward the many weak, nonliberal states in the Third World. This problem affects both conservative liberals and welfare liberals, but the two can be distinguished by differing styles of interventions.[17]

Protecting "native rights" from "native" oppressors, and protecting universal rights of property and settlement from local transgressions, introduced liberal motives for imperial aggression. Ending the slave trade destabilized nineteenth-century West African oligarchies, yet encouraging "legitimate trade" required protecting the property of European merchants; declaring the illegitimacy of suttee or of domestic slavery also attacked local cultural traditions that had sustained indigenous political authority. Europeans settling in sparsely populated areas destroyed the livelihood of tribes that relied on hunting. The tribes, quite defensively, retaliated in force; the settlers called for imperial protection.[18] The protection of cosmopolitan liberal rights thus bred a demand for imperial rule that violated the liberty of Native Americans, Africans, and Asians. In practice, once the exigencies of ruling an empire came into play, liberal imperialism resulted in the oppression of "native" liberals seeking self-determination: movements for self-rule were suppressed to avoid local chaos and the intervention of another imperial power attempting to take advantage of local disaffection.

Thus, nineteenth-century liberals such as Gladstone pondered whether Egypt's protonationalist Arabi rebellion (1881–82) was truly liberal nationalist (they discovered it was not) before intervening to protect strategic lifelines to India, commerce, and investment.[19] These dilemmas of liberal imperialism are also reflected in U.S. imperialism in the Caribbean where, for example, following the Spanish-American War of 1898, Article III of the Platt Amendment gave the United States the "right to intervene for the preservation of Cuban independence, the maintenance of a government adequate for the protection of life, property, and individual liberty."[20]

The record of liberalism in the nonliberal world is not solely a catalog of oppression or imprudence. The North American West and the settlement colonies of Australia and New Zealand represent a successful transplant of liberal institutions—albeit at the cost of Native American and Aboriginal rights—in a temperate, underpopulated environment. Similarly, the twentieth-century expansion of liberalism into less powerful nonliberal areas has also had some striking successes. The forcible liberalization of Germany and Japan following World War II and the long covert financing of liberal parties in Italy are the more significant instances of successful transplant. Covert financing of liberalism in Chile and occasional diplomatic demarches to nudge aside military threats to noncommunist democratic parties (as in Peru in 1962, South Korea in 1963, and the Dominican

Republic in 1965 and again in 1978) illustrate policies which, though less success-ful, were directed toward liberal goals. These particular postwar liberal successes also are the product of special circumstances: the existence of a potential liberal majority, temporarily suppressed, which could be readily reestablished by outside aid or unusually weak oligarchic, military, or communist opponents.[21]

Elsewhere in the postwar period, when the United States sought to protect liberals in the Third World from the "communist threat," the consequences of liberal foreign policy on the nonliberal society often became far removed from the promo-tion of individual rights or of national security. In Vietnam and elsewhere, interven-ing against "armed minorities" and "enemies of free enterprise" meant intervening for other armed minorities, some sustaining and sustained by oligarchies, others resting on little more than U.S. foreign aid and troops. Indigenous liberals simply had too narrow a base of domestic support. These interventions did not advance liberal rights, and to the extent that they were driven by ideological motives they were not necessary for national security.

To the conservative liberals, the alternatives are starkly cast: Third-World authoritarians with allegiance to the liberal, capitalist West or "Communists" sub-ject to the totalitarian East (or leftist nationalists who, even if elected, are but a slippery stepping-stone to totalitarianism).[22] Conservative liberals are prepared to support the allied authoritarians. The communists attack property in addition to liberty, thereby provoking conservative liberals to covert or overt intervention, or "dollar-diplomacy" imperialism. The interventions against Mossadegh in Iran, Ar-benz in Guatemala, Allende in Chile, and the Sandinistas in Nicaragua appear to fall into this pattern.[23]

To the social welfare liberals, the choice is never so clear. Aware of the need for state action to democratize the distribution of social power and resources, they tend to have more sympathy for social reform. On the part of "radical" welfare liberals this sympathy can produce a more tolerant policy toward the attempts by reforming autocracies to redress inegalitarian distributions of property in the Third World. This more complicated welfare-liberal assessment can itself be a recipe for more extensive intervention. The many conservative oligarchs or military bureaucracies with whom the conservative liberal is well at home are not so congenial to the social welfare liberal; yet the communists are still seen as enemies of liberty. They justify more extensive intervention first to discover, then to sustain, Third-World social democracy in a political environment that is either barely participatory or highly polarized. Thus Arthur Schlesinger recalls President Kennedy musing shortly after the assassination of Trujillo (former dictator of the Dominican Republic), "There are three possibilities in descending order of preference, a decent democratic re-gime, a continuation of the Trujillo regime [by his followers] or a Castro regime. We ought to aim at the first, but we can't really renounce the second until we are sure we can avoid the third."[24] Another instance of this approach was President Carter's support for the land reforms in El Salvador, which was explained by one U.S. official in the following analogy: "There is no one more conservative than a small farmer. We're going to be breeding capitalists like rabbits."[25]

The third effect apparent in the international relations of liberal states is what Hume called "supine complaisance," which takes two forms: a failure to support allies or a failure to oppose enemies.

Liberal internationalism has been shortsighted in preserving its basic preconditions under changing international circumstances, and particularly in supporting the liberal character of its constituent states. The liberal community of nations has failed on occasion, as it did in regard to Germany in the 1920s, to provide international economic support for liberal regimes whose market foundations were in crisis. It failed in the 1930s to provide military aid or political mediation to Spain, which was challenged by an armed minority, or to Czechoslovakia, which was caught in a dilemma of preserving national security or acknowledging the claims (fostered by Hitler's Germany) of the Sudeten minority to self-determination. Farsighted and constitutive measures seem to have only been provided by the liberal international order when one liberal state stood preeminent among the rest, prepared and able to take measures, as did the United States following World War II, to sustain economically and politically the foundations of liberal society beyond its borders. Then measures such as the British Loan, the Marshall Plan, the North Atlantic Treaty Organization (NATO), the General Agreement on Tariffs and Trade (GATT), the International Monetary Fund (IMF), and the liberalization of Germany and Japan helped construct buttresses for the international liberal order.[26]

Ideologically based policies can also lead to a failure to support current or potential allies. Oligarchic or authoritarian allies in the Third World do not find consistent support in a liberal policy that stresses human rights. Contemporary conservative critics claim that the security needs of these states are neglected, that they fail to obtain military aid or more direct support when they need it (the Shah's Iran, Humberto Romero's El Salvador, Somoza's Nicaragua, and South Africa). Equally disturbing from this point of view, communist regimes are shunned even when a detente with them could further U.S. strategic interests (Cuba, Angola). Welfare liberals particularly shun the first group, while laissez-faire liberals balk at close dealings with the second. In both cases our economic or strategic interests are often slighted.[27]

Another manifestation of complaisance lies in a reaction to the excesses of interventionism. A mood of frustrated withdrawal affects policy toward strategically and economically important countries. Just as interventionism seems to be the typical failing of the liberal great power, complaisance characterizes declined or not quite risen liberal states.[28] Especially following the exhaustion of wars, representative legislatures may become reluctant to undertake international commitments or to fund the military establishment needed to play a geopolitical role. Purely domestic concerns seem to take priority, as they did in the United States in the 1920s. Rational incentives for "free riding" on the extended defense commitments of the leader of the liberal alliance also induce this form of complaisance. During much of the nineteenth century the United States informally relied upon the British fleet for many of its security needs. Today, the Europeans and the Japanese, according to some American strategic analysts, fail to bear their "fair" share of alliance burdens.

Liberalism, if we take into account both Kant and Hume, thus carries with it three legacies—peace among liberals, imprudent vehemence toward nonliberals, and complaisance toward the future. The first appears to be a special feature associated with liberalism and it can be demonstrated statistically. The latter two cannot be shown to be special to liberalism, though their effects can be illustrated historically in liberal foreign policy. The survival and the increasing number of liberal states suggest that imprudent vehemence and complaisance have not overwhelmed liberalism's efficacy as a form of governance. Democratic liberal states appear to have the capacity to correct the worst foreign policy disasters, as the U.S. did in the disengagement from Vietnam. But even if these three effects are significant features of the foreign relations of liberal states, are liberal principles and institutions the true source of these effects?

Incomplete Explanations

Neither realist (statist) theories of the balance of power nor Marxist theories of capitalist foreign policy account well for these legacies. Each can explain certain effects; neither accounts for them considered together.

Realists hold that the effects of differing domestic regimes (whether liberal or not) are overridden by the international anarchy under which all states live. Hobbes does not bother to distinguish between "some council or one man" when he discusses the sovereign. The type of domestic regime does affect the quantity of resources available to the state and the quality of its morale. But for the realist the ends that shape policy are determined by the fundamental quest for power that shapes all politics or the competitive structure of the international system.[29]

At the level of the strategic decision-maker, realists could argue that a liberal peace could be merely the outcome of prudent diplomacy. Some, including Hobbes, have argued that sovereigns have a natural duty not to act against "the reasons of peace." Individuals established (that is, should establish) a sovereign to escape from the brutalities of the state of nature, the war of all against all, that follows from competition for scarce goods, scrambles for prestige, and fear of another's attack when there is no sovereign to provide for lawful acquisition or regularized social conduct or personal security. "Dominions were constituted for peace's sake, and peace was sought for safety's sake"; the natural duty of the sovereign is therefore the safety of the people.[30] Yet prudent policy cannot be an enforceable right of citizens because Hobbesian sovereigns, who remain in the state of nature with respect to their subjects and other sovereigns, cannot themselves be subjects.

The international condition for Hobbes remains, moreover, a state of war. Safety enjoins a prudent policy of forewarning (spying) and of forearming oneself to increase security against other sovereigns who, lacking any assurance that you are not taking these measures, also take them. Safety also requires (morally) taking actions "whatsoever shall seem to conduce to the lessening of the power of foreigners whom they [the sovereign] suspect, whether by slight or force."[31] If preventive wars are prudent, the realists' prudence obviously cannot account for more than a century and a half of peace among independent liberal states, many of which have crowded one another in the center of Europe.

At the level of the international system, three "games" explain the fear that Hobbes saw as a root of conflict in the state of war. First, even when states share an interest in a common good that could be attained by cooperation, the absence of a source of global law and order means that no one state can count upon the cooperative behavior of the others. Each state therefore has a rational incentive to defect from the cooperative enterprise even if only to pursue a good whose value is less than the share that would have been obtained from the successful accomplishment of the cooperative enterprise (this is Rousseau's "stag dilemma"). Second, even though each state knows that security is relative to the armaments level of potential adversaries and even though each state seeks to minimize its arms expenditure, it also knows that, having no global guarantee of security, being caught unarmed by a surprise attack is worse than bearing the costs of armament. Each therefore arms; all are worse off (this is the "security dilemma," a variant of the "prisoner's dilemma"). Third, heavily armed states rely upon their prestige, their credibility, to deter states from testing the true quality of their arms in battle, and credibility is measured by a record of successes. Once a posture of confrontation is assumed, backing down, although rational for both together, is not rational (first best) for either individually if they have an expectation that the other will back down first (the game of "chicken").

Recent additions to game theory specify some of the circumstances under which prudence could lead to peace. Experience, geography, expectations of cooperation and belief patterns, and the differing payoffs to cooperation (peace) or conflict associated with various types of military technology all appear to influence the calculus. Differing military technologies can alter the payoffs of the security dilemma: making the costs of noncooperation high, reducing the costs of being unprepared or surprised, reducing the benefits of surprise attack, or increasing the gains from cooperation. In particular, Robert Jervis has examined the differing effects of situations in which the offense or the defense has the advantage and in which offensive weapons are or are not distinguishable from defensive weapons. When the offense has the advantage and weapons are indistinguishable, the level of insecurity is high, and incentives for preemptive attack correspondingly are strong.[32] When offensive weapons do not have an advantage and they are distinguishable from defensive weapons, the incentives for preemptive attack are low, as are the incentives for arms races. Capable of signaling with clarity a nonaggressive intent and of guaranteeing that other states pose no immediate strategic threat, statesmen should be able to adopt peaceable policies and negotiate disputes. But this cannot be the explanation for the liberal peace. Military technologies changed from offensive to defensive and from distinguishable to indistinguishable, yet the pacific union persisted and persisted only among liberal states. Moreover, even the "clearest" technical messages appear subject to garbling. The pre-1914 period, which objectively represented a triumph of the distinguishable defense (machine guns, barbed wire, trench warfare) over the offensive, was subjectively, as Jervis notes, a period in which military leaders appeared to place exceptional premiums on the offensive and thus on preemptive war.[33]

Raymond Aron has identified three other types of prudential interstate peace consequent upon the structure of the international system: empire, hegemony, and equilibrium.[34] An empire generally succeeds in creating an internal peace, but this is not an explanation of peace among independent liberal states. Hegemony can create peace by overawing potential rivals. Although far from perfect and certainly precarious, U.S. hegemony, as Aron notes, might account for the interstate peace in South America in the postwar period during the height of the cold war conflict. The liberal peace cannot be attributed, however, merely to effective international policing by a hegemon—Britain in the nineteenth century, the United States in the postwar period—even though a hegemon might well have an interest in enforcing a peace for the sake of commerce or investments or as a means of enhancing its prestige or security. Hegemons such as seventeenth-century France were not peace-enforcing, and the liberal peace persisted in the 1920s and 1930s despite the fact that international society lacked a hegemonic power. This explanation also overestimates both British and American hegemonic control. Neither England nor the United States was able to prevent direct challenges to its interests (colonial competition in the nineteenth century, Middle East diplomacy and conflicts over trading with the enemy in the postwar period). Where then was the capacity to prevent all armed conflicts between liberal regimes, many of which were remote and others strategically or economically insignificant? Liberal hegemony and leadership are important, but they are not sufficient to explain a liberal peace.

Peace through equilibrium (the multipolar classical balance of power or the bipolar "cold war") also draws upon prudential sources of peace. An awareness of the likelihood that aggressive attempts at hegemony will generate international opposition should, it is argued, deter these aggressive wars. But bipolar stability discourages polar or superpower wars, not proxy or small power wars. And multipolar balancing of power also encourages warfare to seize, for example, territory for strategic depth against a rival expanding its power from internal growth. Neither readily accounts for general peace or for the liberal peace.

Realism does, however, provide a plausible account of imprudent vehemence and supine complaisance, the other two effects associated with the foreign relations of liberal states. Realism does not guarantee that states will be prudent. It only holds that imprudent states will not be successful. The international state of war offers many opportunities for aggression, and a concern with enhancing the balance of power can account for an interest in imperial expansion and for many of the cold war interventions. The rational pursuit of narrow state interests can also explain incentives toward appeasement, particularly in multipolar systems, such as that of the 1930s, when liberal and other states might reasonably doubt the willingness of other status quo states to come to the aid of a state willing to challenge the imperial ambitions of revisionist states.

Marxism, another major theory of international relations, also cannot fully account for all three effects associated with liberal foreign relations. Focusing on class warfare domestically and internationally, Marxist "ultraimperialism" as developed by Karl Kautsky has a theory that can lead to expectations of a form of peaceful rivalry among capitalists.[35] But only liberal capitalists maintain peace. Pre–World War I Germany and pre–World War II Japan were both capitalists, and they fought against liberal capitalist states. Leninists, on the other hand, do expect liberal capitalists to be aggressive toward nonliberal states, and this is a plausible alternative explanation of liberal imperialism and interventionism. But they also (and especially) expect them to be aggressively imperialistic toward fellow liberal capitalists.

Thus realist and Marxist theories can account for aspects of certain periods of international stability. And they each can account for incentives toward imprudent aggression and complaisance. But neither the logic of the balance of power nor of international hegemony nor of ultraimperialist cooperation explains the separate peace maintained for more than 150 years among states sharing one particular form of governance—liberal principles and institutions.

A Kantian Theory of Liberal Internationalism

Most liberal theorists also have offered inadequate guidance in understanding the exceptional nature of liberal pacification. Some have argued that democratic states would be inherently peaceful simply and solely because in these states citizens rule the polity and bear the costs of wars. Unlike monarchs, citizens are not able to indulge their aggressive passions and have the consequences suffered by someone else. Other liberals have argued that laissez-faire capitalism contains an inherent tendency toward rationalism, and that, since war is irrational, liberal capitalist states will be pacifistic. Others still, such as Montesquieu, claim that "commerce is the cure for the most destructive prejudices" and that "peace is the natural effect of trade."[36] While these developments can help account for aspects of the liberal peace, they do not explain the fact that liberal states are peaceful only in relations with other liberal states.

Kant's theory of liberal internationalism helps us understand these three features of liberal foreign relations. The importance of Immanuel Kant as a theorist of international ethics has been well appreciated.[37] But Kant also has an important analytical theory of international politics. "Perpetual Peace," written in 1795, helps us understand the interactive nature of international relations. Methodologically, Kant tries to teach us that we cannot study either the systemic relations of states or the varieties of state behavior in isolation from each other. Substantively, he anticipates for us the ever-widening pacification of a liberal pacific union, explains that pacification, and at the same time suggests why liberal states are not pacific in their relations with nonliberal states. Kant argues that perpetual peace will be guaranteed by the widening acceptance of three "definitive articles" of peace. When all nations have accepted the definitive articles in a metaphorical "treaty" of perpetual peace he asks them to sign, perpetual peace will have been established.

The First Definitive Article requires that the civil constitution of the state be republican. By *republican* Kant means a political society that has solved the problem of combining moral autonomy, individualism, and social order. A private-property and market-oriented economy partially addressed that dilemma in the private sphere. The public, or political, sphere was more troubling. His answer was a republic that preserved juridical freedom—the legal equality of citizens as subjects—on the basis of a representative government with a separation of powers. Juridical freedom is preserved because the morally autonomous individual is by means of representation a self-legislator making laws that apply to all citizens equally, including himself. And tyranny is avoided because the individual is subject to laws he does not also administer.[38]

Liberal republics will progressively establish peace among themselves by means of the pacific federation or union (*foedus pacificum*) described in Kant's

Second Definitive Article. The pacific union will establish peace within a federation of free states and securely maintain the rights of each state. The world will not have achieved the "perpetual peace" that provides the ultimate guarantor of republican freedom until "a late stage and after many unsuccessful attempts" (*Universal History*, p. 47). Then good will, right conceptions of the appropriate constitution, and great and sad experience will have taught all nations the lessons of peace. Not until then will individuals enjoy perfect republican rights or the full guarantee of a global and just peace. But in the meantime the "pacific federation" of liberal republics— "an enduring and gradually expanding federation likely to prevent war"—brings within it more and more republics (despite republican collapses, backsliding, and disastrous wars), creating an expanding separate peace (*Perpetual Peace*, p. 105).[39] And Kant emphasizes: "It can be shown that this idea of federalism, extending gradually to encompass all states and thus leading to perpetual peace, is practicable and has objective reality. For if by good fortune one powerful and enlightened nation can form a republic (which is by nature inclined to seek peace), this will provide a focal point for federal association among other states. These will join up with the first one, thus securing the freedom of each state in accordance with the idea of international right, and the whole will gradually spread further and further by a series of alliances of this kind" (ibid., p. 104).

The pacific union is not a single peace treaty ending one war nor a world state nor a state of nations. He finds the first insufficient. The second and third are impossible or potentially tyrannical. National sovereignty precludes reliable subservience to a state of nations; a world state destroys the civic freedom on which the development of human capacities rests (*Universal History*, p. 50). Although Kant obliquely refers to various classical interstate confederations and modern diplomatic congresses, he develops no systematic organizational embodiment of this treaty, and presumably he does not find institutionalization necessary.[40] He appears to have in mind a mutual nonaggression pact, perhaps a collective security agreement, and the cosmopolitan law set forth in the Third Definitive Article.[41]

The Third Definitive Article establishes a cosmopolitan law to operate in conjunction with the pacific union. The cosmopolitan law "shall be limited to conditions of universal hospitality." In this he calls for the recognition of the "right of a foreigner not to be treated with hostility when he arrives on someone else's territory." This "does not extend beyond those conditions which make it possible for them to attempt to enter into relations [commerce] with the native inhabitants" (*Perpetual Peace*, p. 106). Hospitality does not require extending to foreigners either the right to citizenship or the right to settlement, unless the foreign visitors would perish if they were expelled. Foreign conquest and plunder also find no justification under this right. Hospitality does appear to include the right of access and the obligation of maintaining the opportunity for citizens to exchange goods and ideas, without imposing the obligation to trade (a voluntary act in all cases under liberal constitutions).

Perpetual peace, for Kant, is an epistemology, a condition for ethical action, and, most important, an explanation of how the "mechanical process of nature visibly exhibits the purposive plan of producing concord among men, even against their will and indeed by means of their very discord" (*Perpetual Peace,* p. 108; see also *Universal History,* pp. 44–45). Understanding history requires an epistemological foundation, for without a teleology, such as the promise of perpetual peace, the complexity of history would overwhelm human understanding (*Universal History,* pp. 51–53). But perpetual peace is not merely a heuristic device with which to interpret history. It is guaranteed, Kant explains in the "First Addition" to *Perpetual Peace* ("On the Guarantee of Perpetual Peace"), to result from individuals fulfilling their ethical duty or, failing that, from a hidden plan.[42] Peace is an ethical duty because it is only under conditions of peace that all persons can treat each other as ends (*Universal History,* p. 50). In order for this duty to be practical, Kant needs, of course, to show that peace is in fact possible. The widespread sentiment of approbation that he saw aroused by the early success of the French revolutionaries showed him that we can indeed be moved by ethical sentiments with a cosmopolitan reach (*Contest of Faculties*), pp. 181–82).[43] This does not mean, however, that perpetual peace is certain ("prophesyable"). Even the scientifically regular course of the planets could be changed by a wayward comet striking them out of orbit. Human freedom requires that we allow for much greater reversals in the course of history. We must, in fact, anticipate the possibility of backsliding and destructive wars; these will serve to educate nations to the importance of peace (*Universal History,* pp. 47–48).

But in the end our guarantee of perpetual peace does not rest on ethical conduct, as Kant emphasizes: "We now come to the essential question regarding the prospect of perpetual peace. What does nature do in relation to the end which man's own reason prescribes to him as a duty, i.e., how does nature help to promote his moral purpose? And how does nature guarantee that what man ought to do by the laws of his freedom (but does not do) will in fact be done through nature's compulsion, without prejudice to the free agency of man? . . . This does not mean that nature imposes on us a duty to do it, for duties can only be imposed by practical reason. On the contrary, nature does it herself, whether we are willing or not: *facta volentem ducunt, nolentem tradunt.*" The guarantee thus rests, Kant argues, on the probable behavior not of moral angels but of "devils, so long as they possess understanding" (*Perpetual Peace,* p. 112).

In explaining the sources of each of the three definitive articles of the perpetual peace, Kant then tells us how we (as free and intelligent devils) could be motivated by fear, force, and calculated advantage to undertake a course of actions whose outcome we can reasonably anticipate to be perpetual peace. But, while it is possible to conceive of the Kantian road to peace in these terms, Kant himself recognizes and argues that social evolution also makes the conditions of moral behavior less onerous, and hence more likely (*Contest of Faculties,* pp. 187–89).[44] In tracing the effects of both political and moral development, he builds an account of why liberal states do maintain peace among themselves and of how it will (by implication, has) come about that the pacific union will expand. He also explains how these republics would engage in wars with nonrepublics and therefore suffer the "sad experience" of wars that an ethical policy might have avoided.

The first source of a liberal peace derives from a political evolution, from a constitutional law. Nature (providence) has seen to it that human beings can live in all the regions where they have been driven to settle by wars. (Kant, who once taught geography, reports on the Lapps, the Samoyeds, and the Pescheras.) "Asocial sociability" draws humans together to fulfill needs for security and material welfare as it drives them into conflicts over the distribution and control of social products (*Universal History,* pp. 44–45; *Perpetual Peace,* pp. 110–11). This violent natural evolution tends toward the liberal peace because asocial sociability inevitably leads toward republican governments and republican governments are a source of the liberal peace.

Republican representation and separation of powers are produced because they are the means by which the state is "organized well" to prepare for and meet foreign threats (by unity) and to tame the ambitions of selfish and aggressive individuals (by authority derived from representation, by general laws, and by nondespotic administration; *Perpetual Peace,* pp. 112–13). States that are not organized in this fashion fail. Monarchs thus encourage commerce and private property in order to increase national wealth. They cede rights of representation to their subjects in order to strengthen their political support or to obtain willing grants of tax revenue.[45]

Kant shows how republics, once established, tend toward peaceful international relations. He argues that once the aggressive interests of absolutist monarchies are tamed and once the habit of respect for individual rights is ingrained by republican government, wars will be recognized as disastrous to the people's welfare.

> If, as is inevitably the case under this constitution, the consent of the citizens is required to decide whether or not war should be declared, it is very natural that they will have a great hesitation in embarking on so dangerous an enterprise. For this would mean calling down on themselves all the miseries of war, such as doing the fighting themselves, supplying the costs of the war from their own resources, painfully making good the ensuing devastation, and, as the crowning evil, having to take upon themselves a burden

of debts which will embitter peace itself and which can never be paid off on account of the constant threat of new wars. But under a constitution where the subject is not a citizen, and which is therefore not republican, it is the simplest thing in the world to go to war. For the head of state is not a fellow citizen, but the owner of the state, and war will not force him to make the slightest sacrifice so far as his banquets, hunts, pleasure palaces and court festivals are concerned. He can thus decide on war, without any significant reason, as a kind of amusement, and unconcernedly leave it to the diplomatic corps (who are always ready for such purposes) to justify the war for the sake of propriety. (*Perpetual Peace*, p. 100)

These domestic republican restraints introduce republican caution, Kant's "hesitation," in place of monarchical caprice. And republican caution seems to save republics from the failings Hume saw as characteristic of "enormous monarchies," which are prone to "strategic overextension," bureaucratic and ministerial decay into court intrigue, and praetorian rebellion.[46] Representative government allows for a rotation of elites, others have argued, and this encourages a reversal of disastrous policies as electorates punish the party in power with electoral defeat. Legislatures and public opinion further restrain executives from policies that clearly violate the obvious and fundamental interests of the public, as the public perceives those interests.[47]

Yet republican caution does not guarantee prudence. Liberal publics can become disaffected from international commitments and choose isolationism or appeasement, as Britain and the United States did in the 1920s and 1930s. And republican caution does not end war or ensure that wars are fought only when necessary for national security. If it did, liberal states would not be warlike or given to imprudent vehemence, as they have often been. It does ensure that wars are only fought for popular, liberal purposes. The liberal legacy is laden with popular wars fought to promote freedom, protect private property, or support liberal allies against nonliberal enemies. Kant's own position is ambiguous. He regards most of these wars as unjust and warns liberals of their susceptibility to them (*Perpetual Peace*, p. 106). At the same time, Kant argues that each nation "can and ought to" demand that its neighboring nations enter into the pacific union of liberal states (p. 102). Thus, to see how the pacific union removes the occasion of wars among liberal states and not wars between liberal and nonliberal states, we need to shift our attention from constitutional law to international law, Kant's second source of the liberal peace.

Complementing the constitutional guarantee of caution, international law adds a second source—a guarantee of respect. The separation of nations that asocial sociability encourages is reinforced by the development of separate languages and religions. These further guarantee a world of separate states—an essential condition needed to avoid a "global, soul-less despotism." Yet, at the same time, they also morally integrate liberal states: "as culture grows and men gradually move towards greater agreement over their principles, they lead to mutual understanding and peace" (*Perpetual Peace,* p. 114). As republics emerge (the first source) and as culture progresses, an understanding of the legitimate rights of all citizens and of all republics comes into play; and this, now that caution characterizes policy, sets up the moral foundations for the liberal peace. Correspondingly, international law highlights the importance of Kantian publicity. Domestically, publicity helps ensure that the officials of republics act according to the principles they profess to hold just and according to the interests of the electors they claim to represent. Internationally, free speech and the effective communication of accurate conceptions of the political life of foreign peoples is essential to establish and preserve the understanding on which the guarantee of respect depends. Domestically just republics, which rest on consent, then presume foreign republics to be also consensual, just, and therefore deserving of accommodation. The experience of cooperation helps engender further cooperative behavior when the consequences of state policy are unclear but (potentially) mutually beneficial. At the same time, liberal states assume that nonliberal states, which do not rest on free consent, are not just. Because nonliberal governments are perceived to be in a state of aggression with their own people, their foreign relations become for liberal governments deeply suspect. In short, fellow liberals benefit from a presumption of amity; nonliberals suffer from a presumption of enmity. Both presumptions may be accurate. Each, however, may also be self-confirming.

Finally, cosmopolitan law adds material incentives to moral commitments. The cosmopolitan right to hospitality permits the "spirit of commerce" sooner or later to take hold of every nation, thus impelling states to promote peace and to try to avert war. Liberal economic theory holds that these cosmopolitan ties derive from a cooperative international division of labor and free trade according to comparative advantage. Each economy is said to be better off than it would have been under autarky; each thus acquires an incentive to avoid policies that would lead the other to break these economic ties. Since keeping open markets rests upon the assumption that the next set of transactions will also be determined by prices rather than coercion, a sense of mutual security is vital to avoid security-motivated searches for economic autarky. Thus, avoiding a challenge to another liberal state's security or even enhancing each other's security by means of alliance naturally follows economic interdependence.

A further cosmopolitan source of liberal peace is that the international market removes difficult decisions of production and distribution from the direct sphere of state policy. A foreign state thus does not appear directly responsible for these outcomes; states can stand aside from, and to some degree above, these contentious market rivalries and be ready to step in to resolve crises. The interdependence of commerce and the international contacts of state officials help create crosscutting transnational ties that serve as lobbies for mutual accommodation. According to modern liberal scholars, international financiers and transnational and transgovernmental organizations create interests in favor of accommodation. Moreover, their variety has ensured no single conflict sours an entire relationship by setting off a spiral of reciprocated retaliation.[48] Conversely, a sense of suspicion, such as that characterizing relations between liberal and nonliberal governments, can lead to restrictions on the range of contacts between societies. And this can increase the prospect that a single conflict will determine an entire relationship.

No single constitutional, international, or cosmopolitan source is alone sufficient, but together (and only together) they plausibly connect the characteristics of liberal polities and economies with sustained liberal peace. Alliances founded on mutual strategic interest among liberal and nonliberal states have been broken, economic ties between liberal and nonliberal states have proven fragile, but the political bonds of liberal rights and interests have proven a remarkably firm foundation for mutual nonaggression. A separate peace exists among liberal states.

But in their relations with nonliberal states, liberal states have not escaped from the insecurity caused by anarchy in the world political system considered as a whole. Moreover, the very constitutional restraint, international respect for individual rights, and shared commercial interests that establish grounds for peace among liberal states establish grounds for additional conflict in relations between liberal and nonliberal societies, irrespective of actual threats to national security.

And in their relations with all states, liberal states have not solved the problems of international cooperation and competition. Liberal publics can become absorbed in domestic issues, neglecting international security. And international liberal respect does not preclude trade rivalries or guarantee farsighted collective action to promote international security and welfare.

Preserving the legacy of the liberal peace without succumbing to the legacies of liberal imprudence is both a moral and a strategic challenge. The bipolar structure of the international system and the near certainty of mutual devastation resulting from a nuclear war between the superpowers created a "crystal ball effect," which helped to constrain the tendency toward miscalculation that was present at the outbreak of so many wars in the past.[49] But this "nuclear peace" appeared to be limited to the superpowers. It did not curb military interventions in the Third World. Moreover, it was subject to a desperate technological race designed to overcome its constraints. Recently, in Panama and the Persian Gulf, we experienced crises that pushed the great powers over the brink of war. We must still reckon with the imprudent vehemence and moods of complaisant appeasement that have almost alternately swept liberal democracies.

Yet restraining liberal imprudence, whether aggressive or passive, may not be possible without threatening liberal pacification. Improving the strategic acumen of our foreign policy calls for introducing steadier strategic calculations of the long-term national interest and more flexible responses to changes in the international political environment. Constraining the indiscriminate meddling of our foreign interventions calls for a deeper appreciation of the "particularism of history, culture, and membership."[50] But to the extent past foreign policy failures have reflected liberal vehemence and complaisance, both the improvement in strategy and the constraint on intervention will require an executive freed from the restraints of a representative legislature in the management of foreign policy and a political culture indifferent to the universal rights of individuals. And these, in their turn, could break the chain of constitutional guarantees, the respect for representative government, and the web of transnational contact that have sustained the pacific union of liberal states.

Appendix

Table 1
The Liberal Community
(By date "liberal")

Period

Period		
1700s	Swiss Cantons[a] French Republic 1790–95 United States[a] 1776– *total number–3*	Chile 1891– *total number–13*
1800– 1850	Swiss Confederation, United States France 1830–49 Belgium 1830– Great Britain 1832– Netherlands 1848– Piedmont 1848– Denmark 1849– *total number–8*	1900– 1945
1850– 1900	Switzerland, United States, Belgium, 　　Great Britain, Netherlands Piedmont –1861/Italy 1861– Denmark –1866 Sweden 1864– Greece 1864– Canada[b] 1867– France 1871– Argentina 1880–	Switzerland, United States, Great 　Britain, Sweden, Canada Greece –1911, 1928–36 Italy –1922 Belgium –1940 Netherlands –1940 Argentina 1943 France –1940 Chile –1924, 1932 Australia 1901 Norway 1905–40 New Zealand 1907– Colombia 1910–49 Denmark 1914–40 Poland 1917–35 Latvia 1922–34 Germany 1918–32 Austria 1918–34 Estonia 1919–34

The Liberal Community, cont.

Period

Finland 1919–	Sri Lanka 1948–61, 1963–71,
Uruguay 1919–	1978–83
Costa Rica 1919–	Ecuador 1948–63, 1979–
Czechoslovakia 1920–39	Israel 1949–
Ireland 1920–	West Germany 1949–
Mexico 1928–	Greece 1950–67, 1975–
Lebanon 1944–	Peru 1950–62, 1963–68, 1980–
Iceland 1944–	El Salvador 1950–61
total number–30	Turkey 1950–60, 1966–71, 1984–
	Japan 1951–
1945ᶜ– Switzerland, United States, Great	Bolivia 1956–69, 1982–
Britain, Sweden, Canada,	Colombia 1958–
Australia, New Zealand, Finland,	Venezuela 1959–
Ireland, Mexico, Iceland	Nigeria 1961–64, 1979–84
Uruguay –1973, 1985–	Jamaica 1962–
Chile –1973	Trinidad and Tobago 1962–
Lebanon –1975	Senegal 1963–
Costa Rica –1948, 1953–	Malaysia 1963–
France 1945–	Botswana 1966–
Denmark 1945–	Singapore 1965–
Norway 1945–	Portugal 1976–
Austria 1945–	Spain 1978–
Brazil 1945–54, 1955–64, 1985–	Dominican Republic 1978–
Belgium 1946–	Honduras 1981–
Luxemburg 1946–	Papua New Guinea 1982–
Netherlands 1946–	Argentina 1983–
Italy 1946–	South Korea 1988–
Philippines 1946–72, 1987–	Taiwan 1988–
India 1947–75, 1977–	*total number–53*

Note: I have drawn up this approximate list of "liberal regimes" according to the four Kantian institutions described as essential: market and private property economies; polities that are internally and externally sovereign; citizens who possess juridical rights; and "republican" (whether republican or parliamentary monarchy), representative government. This latter includes the requirement that the legislative branch have an effective role in public policy and be formally and competitively (either inter- or intraparty) elected. Furthermore, I have taken into account whether male suffrage is wide (that is, 30 percent) or, as Kant would have had it, open to "achievement" by inhabitants (for example, to poll tax payers or householders) of the national or metropolitan territory. This list of liberal regimes is thus more inclusive than a list of democratic regimes, or polyarchies. Female suffrage is granted within a generation of its being demanded by an extensive female suffrage movement, and representative government is internally sovereign (including, especially, sovereignty over military and foreign affairs) as well as stable (in existence for at least three years). (Banks and Overstreet, 1983; U.K. Foreign and Commonwealth Office, 1980; *The Europe Yearbook, 1985;* Langer, 1968; U.S. Department of State, 1981; Gastil, 1985; Freedom House, 1991.)

ᵃThere are domestic variations within these liberal regimes. For example, Switzerland was liberal only in certain cantons; the United States was liberal only north of the Mason-Dixon line until 1865, when it became liberal throughout. These lists also exclude ancient "republics," since none appears to fit Kant's criteria (Holmes, 1979).

ᵇCanada, as a commonwealth within the British empire, did not have formal control of its foreign policy during this period.

ᶜThis is a selected list, excluding liberal regimes with populations less than one million. These include all states categorized as "Free" by Freedom House and those "Partly Free" (45 or more free) states with a more pronounced capitalist orientation.

Table 2
International Wars Listed
Chronologically

British-Maharattan (1817–18)

Greek (1821–28)

Franco-Spanish (1823)
First Anglo-Burmese (1823–26)

Javanese (1825–30)
Russo-Persian (1826–28)
Russo-Turkish (1828–29)

First Polish (1831)

First Syrian (1831–32)
Texan (1835–36)

First British-Afghan (1838–42)
Second Syrian (1839–40)

Franco-Algerian (1839–47)
Peruvian-Bolivian (1841)
First British-Sikh (1845–46)

Mexican-American (1846–48)
Austro-Sardinian (1848–49)
First Schleswig-Holstein (1848–49)
Hungarian (1848–49)
Second British-Sikh (1948–49)
Roman Republic (1849)

La Plata (1851–52)
First Turco-Montenegran (1852–53)

Crimean (1853–56)

Anglo-Persian (1856–57)
Sepoy (1857–59)
Second Turco-Montenegran (1858–59)

Italian Unification (1859)
Spanish-Moroccan (1859–60)
Italo-Roman (1860)
Italo-Sicilian (1860–61)

Franco-Mexican (1862–67)
Ecuadorian-Colombian (1863)

Spanish-Santo Dominican (1863–65)

Second Schleswig-Holstein (1864)
Lopez (1864–70)
Spanish-Chilean (1865–66)

Seven Weeks (1866)
Ten Years (1868–78)
Franco-Prussian (1870–71)

Dutch-Achinese (1873–78)

Balkan (1875–77)
Russo-Turkish (1877–78)

Bosnian (1878)
Second British-Afghan (1878–80)

Pacific (1879–80)
British-Zulu (1879)
Franco-Indochinese (1882–84)

Mahdist (1882–85)
Sino-French (1884–85)
Central American (1885)
Serbo-Bulgarian (1885)
Sino-Japanese (1894–95)
Franco-Madagascan (1894–95)

Cuban (1895–98)
Italo-Ethiopian (1895–96)

First Philippine (1896–98)

Greco-Turkish (1897)
Spanish-American (1898)
Second Philippine (1899–1902)

Boer (1899–1902)
Boxer Rebellion (1900)
Ilinden (1903)
Russo-Japanese (1904–1905)

Central American (1906)
Spanish-Moroccan (1909–10)

Italo-Turkish (1911–12)
First Balkan (1912–13)
Second Balkan (1913)
World War I (1914–18)

Russian Nationalities (1917–21)
Russo-Polish (1919–20)
Hungarian-Allies (1919)
Greco-Turkish (1919–22)
Riffian (1921–26)

International Wars Listed Chronologically, cont.

Druze (1925–27)
Sino-Soviet (1929)
Manchurian (1931–33)

Chaco (1932–35)
Italo-Ethiopian (1935–36)
Sino-Japanese (1937–41)
Changkufeng (1938)
Nomohan (1939)
World War II (1939–45)

Russo-Finnish (1939–40)

Franco-Thai (1940–41)
Indonesian (1945–46)
Indochinese (1945–54)
Madagascan (1947–48)

First Kashmir (1947–49)
Palestine (1948–49)
Hyderabad (1948)
Korean (1950–53)
Algerian (1954–62)

Russo-Hungarian (1956)
Sinai (1956)

Tibetan (1956–59)
Sino-Indian (1962)
Vietnamese (1965–75)
Second Kashmir (1965)
Six Day (1967)
Israeli-Egyptian (1969–70)

Football (1969)
Bangladesh (1971)
Philippine-MNLF (1972–)
Yom Kippur (1973)
Turco-Cypriot (1974)
Ethiopian-Eritrean (1974–)

Vietnamese-Cambodian (1975–)

Timor (1975–)
Saharan (1975–)
Ogaden (1976–)
Ugandan-Tanzanian (1978–79)

Sino-Vietnamese (1979)
Russo-Afghan (1979–)
Iran-Iraqi (1980–)

Source: Reprinted, by permission of Sage Publications, Inc., from Melvin Small and J. David Singer, *Resort to Arms* (Beverly Hills, Calif.: Sage, 1982), pp. 79–80. Note: This is a partial list of international wars fought between 1816 and 1980. In appendices A and B Small and Singer identify a total of 575 wars in this period, but approximately 159 of them appear to be largely domestic, or civil wars.

This definition of war excludes covert interventions, a few of which have been directed by liberal regimes against other liberal regimes. One example is the United States' effort to destabilize the Chilean election and Allende's government. Nonetheless, it is significant that such interventions are not pursued publicly as acknowledged policy. The covert destabilization campaign against Chile is recounted by the U.S.

Congress, Senate Select Committee to Study Government Operations with Respect to Intelligence Activities, *Covert Action in Chile, 1963–73*, 94th Cong., 1st sess. (Washington, D.C.: Government Printing Office, 1975).

The argument of this article (and this list) also excludes civil wars. Civil wars differ from international wars not in the ferocity of combat but in the issues that engender them. Two nations that could abide one another as independent neighbors separated by a border might well be the fiercest of enemies if forced to live together in one state, jointly deciding how to raise and spend taxes, choose leaders, and legislate fundamental questions of value. Notwithstanding these differences, no civil wars that I recall upset the argument of liberal pacification.

Notes

1
The sources of classic, laissez-faire liberalism can be found in Locke, the *Federalist Papers*, Kant, and Robert Nozick, *Anarchy, State and Utopia* (New York: Basic Books, 1974). Expositions of welfare liberalism are in the work of the Fabians and John Rawls, *A Theory of Justice* (Cambridge, Mass.: Harvard University Press, 1971). Amy Gutmann discusses

variants of liberal thought in *Liberal Equality* (Cambridge: Cambridge University Press, 1980). Uncomfortably paralleling each of the high roads are "low roads" that, while achieving certain liberal values, fail to reconcile freedom and order. An overwhelming terror of anarchy and a speculation on preserving property can drive laissez-faire liberals to support a law-and-order authoritarian rule that sacrifices democracy. Authoritarianism to preserve order is the argument of Hobbes's *Leviathan*. It also shapes the argument of right-wing liberals who seek to draw a distinction between authoritarian and totalitarian dictatorships. The justification sometimes advanced by liberals for the former is that they can be temporary and educate the population into an acceptance of property, individual rights, and, eventually, representative government. See Jeane Kirkpatrick, "Dictatorships and Double Standards," *Commentary* 68 (November 1979): 34–45. Complementarily, when social inequalities are judged to be extreme, the welfare liberal can argue that establishing (or reestablishing) the foundations of liberal society requires a nonliberal method of reform, a second low road of redistributing authoritarianism. Aristide Zolberg reports a "liberal left" sensibility among U.S. scholars of African politics that was sympathetic to progressive autocracies; see *One-Party Government in the Ivory Coast* (Princeton: Princeton University Press, 1969), p. vii.

2

Clarence Streit seems to have been the first to point out (in contemporary foreign relations) the empirical tendency of democracies to maintain peace among themselves, and he made this the foundation of his proposal for a (non-Kantian) federal union of the fifteen leading democracies of the 1930s; *Union Now: A Proposal for a Federal Union of the Leading Democracies* (New York: Harpers, 1938), pp. 88, 90–92. D. V. Babst performed a quantitative study of this phenomenon of "democratic peace"; "A Force for Peace," *Industrial Research,* April 1972, pp. 55–58. And R. J. Rummel did a similar study of "libertarianism" (in the sense of laissez-faire), focusing on the postwar period, in "Libertarianism and International Violence," *Journal of Conflict Resolution* 27 (1983): 27–71. I use *liberal* in a wider (Kantian) sense in my discussion of this issue in "Kant, Liberal Legacies, and Foreign Affairs, Part 1," *Philosophy and Public Affairs* 12 (1983): 205–35. In that essay, I survey the period from 1790 to the present and find no war among liberal states. Recent work supporting the

thesis of democratic or liberal pacification includes Zeev Maoz and Nasrin Abdolali, "Regime Types and International Conflict, 1816–1976," *Journal of Conflict Resolution* 33 (March 1989); Randall Schweller, "Domestic Structure and Preventive War," *World Politics* 44 (January 1992), who finds that liberal hegemons do not engage in preventive wars; Carol Ember, Melvin Ember, and Bruce Russett, "Peace between Participatory Polities," *World Politics* 44 (July 1992), who find that pacification extends to ethnographic evidence of preindustrial societies; and David Lake, "Powerful Pacifists," *American Political Science Review* 86, no. 1 (1992).

3

Woodrow Wilson, *The Messages and Papers of Woodrow Wilson,* ed. Albert Shaw (New York: Review of Reviews, 1924), p. 378.

4

Babst, "A Force for Peace," did make a preliminary test of the significance of the distribution of alliance partners in World War I. He found that the possibility that the actual distribution of alliance partners could have occurred by chance was less than one percent (p. 56). But this assumes that there was an equal possibility that any two nations could have gone to war with each other, and this is a strong assumption. Rummel has a further discussion of significance as it applies to his libertarian thesis; see "Libertarianism and International Violence."

5

There is a rich contemporary literature devoted to explaining international cooperation and integration. Karl Deutsch's *Political Community and the North Atlantic Area* (Princeton: Princeton University Press, 1957) develops the idea of a "pluralistic security community" that bears a resemblance to the "pacific union," but Deutsch limits it geographically and finds compatibility of values, mutual responsiveness, and predictability of behavior among decision-makers as its essential foundations. These are important but their particular content, liberalism, appears to be more telling. Joseph Nye, in *Peace in Parts*

(Boston: Little, Brown, 1971), steps away from the geographic limits Deutsch sets and focuses on levels of development; but his analysis is directed toward explaining integration—a more intensive form of cooperation than the pacific union.

6

David Hume, "Of the Balance of Power," in *Essays: Moral, Political, and Literary* ([1741–42] New York: Oxford University Press, 1963), pp. 346–47. With "imprudent vehemence," Hume referred to the English reluctance to negotiate an early peace with France and the total scale of the resources devoted to that war, which together were responsible for over half the duration of the fighting and an enormous war debt. Hume, of course, was not describing fully liberal republics as defined here; but the characteristics he describes do seem to reflect some of the liberal republican features of the English eighteenth-century constitution (the influence of both popular opinion and a representative—even if severely limited—legislature). He contrasts these effects to the "prudent politics" that should govern the balance of power and to the special but different failings characteristic of "enormous monarchies," which are prone to strategic overextension, bureaucratic corruption and ministerial intrigue, and praetorian rebellion (pp. 347–48).

7

See Steve Chan, "Mirror, Mirror on the Wall . . . : Are Freer Countries More Pacific?," *Journal of Conflict Resolution* 28 (December 1984): 617–48; and Erich Weede, "Democracy and War Involvement," *Journal of Conflict Resolution* 28 (December 1984): 649–64. Chan and Weede support the conclusions reached by M. Small and J. David Singer, "The War-Proneness of Democratic Regimes, 1816–1965," *Jerusalem Journal of International Relations* 1 (Summer 1976): 50–69. Chan and Weede also counter Rummel's view that libertarian states are less prone to violence than nonlibertarian states, which Rummel based on a sample of 1976–80 data not representative of the war-year

data of 1816–1980 of Chan or the 1960–80 data of Weede.

8

There are, however, serious studies that show that Marxist regimes have higher military spending per capita than non-Marxist regimes; see, e.g., James Payne, "Marxism and Militarism," *Polity* 19 (1986): 270–89. But this should not be interpreted as a sign of the inherent aggressiveness of authoritarian or totalitarian governments or—with even greater enthusiasm—the inherent and global peacefulness of liberal regimes. Marxist regimes, in particular, represent a minority in the current international system; they are strategically encircled, and, due to their lack of domestic legitimacy, they might be said to suffer the twin burdens of needing defenses against both external and internal enemies. Moreover, Stanislav Andreski argues that (purely) military dictatorships, due to their domestic fragility, have little incentive to engage in foreign military adventures; see "On the Peaceful Disposition of Military Dictatorships," *Journal of Strategic Studies* 3 (1980): 3–10.

9

Chan, "Mirror, Mirror," p. 636.

10

Walter Clemens, "The Superpowers and the Third World," in Charles Kegley and Pat McGowan, eds., *Foreign Policy: USA/USSR* (Beverly Hills, Calif.: Sage, 1982), pp. 117–18.

11

Barry Posen and Stephen VanEvera, "Overarming and Underwhelming," *Foreign Policy* 40 (1980): 99–118, and Posen and VanEvera, "Reagan Administration Defense Policy," in Kenneth Oye, Robert Lieber, and Donald Rothchild, eds., *Eagle Defiant* (Boston: Little, Brown, 1983), pp. 86–89.

12

The following paragraphs build on arguments I presented in "Kant, Liberal Legacies, and Foreign Affairs, Part 2," *Philosophy and Public Affairs* 12 (1983): 323–53.

13
See memoranda by Mr. Eyre Crowe, 1 January 1907, and by Lord Sanderson, 25 February 1907, in G. P. Gooch et al., eds., *British Documents on the Origins of the War, 1898–1914,* vol. 3 (London: HMSO, 1928), pp. 397–431.

14
Herbert Hoover to President Wilson, 29 March 1919, excerpted in *Major Problems in American Foreign Policy,* vol. 2, ed. Thomas Paterson (Lexington, Mass.: D.C. Heath, 1978), p. 95.

15
U.S. Senate, *Hearings before the Committee on Foreign Relations on the Nomination of John Foster Dulles, Secretary of State Designate, 15 January 1953,* 83d Congress, 1st sess. (Washington, D.C.: GPO, 1953), pp. 5–6. John L. Gaddis has noted logistical differences between laissez-faire and social welfare liberals in policy toward the Soviet Union. In U.S. policy, until the advent of the Reagan administration, the fiscal conservatism of Republicans led them to favor a narrow strategy; the fiscal liberality of Democrats led to a broader strategy. See Gaddis, *Strategies of Containment* (New York: Oxford University Press, 1982).

16
Thirty-three divisions, the withdrawal of the Soviet bloc from the Mediterranean, political disarray in the Communist movement: these advantages called out for a quick and friendly response. An effective U.S. ambassador in place to present Tito's position to Washington, the public character of the expulsion from the Cominform (June 1948), and a presidential administration in the full flush of creative statesmanship (and an electoral victory) also contributed to Truman's decision to rescue Yugoslavia from the Soviet embargo by providing trade and loans (1949). Nonetheless (according to Yugoslav sources), this crisis was also judged to be an appropriate moment to put pressure on Yugoslavia to resolve the questions of Trieste and Carinthia, to cut its support for the guerrillas in Greece, to repay

prewar (prerevolutionary) debts, and to compensate the property owners of nationalized land and mines. Nor did Yugoslavia's strategic significance exempt it from inclusion among the countries condemned as "Captive Nations" (1959) or secure most-favored-nation trade status in the 1962 Trade Expansion Act. Ideological anticommunism and the porousness of the American political system to lobbies combined (according to George Kennan, ambassador to Yugoslavia at that time) to add these inconvenient burdens to a crucial strategic relationship. See John C. Campbell, *Tito's Separate Road* (New York: Council on Foreign Relations/Harper and Row, 1967), pp. 18–27; Suctozar Vukmanovic-Tempo, in Vladimir Dedijer, *The Battle Stalin Lost* (New York: Viking, 1970), p. 268; and George F. Kennan, *Memoirs, 1950–1963* (Boston: Little, Brown, 1972), chap. 12.

17
See Robert A. Packenham, *Liberal America and the Third World* (Princeton: Princeton University Press, 1973), for an interesting analysis of the impact of liberal ideology on American foreign aid policy, esp. chap. 3 and pp. 313–23.

18
Alexis de Tocqueville, *Democracy in America,* vol. 1 (New York: Vintage, 1945), p. 351. De Tocqueville describes how European settlement destroys the game; the absence of game reduces the Indians to starvation. Both then exercise their rights to self-defense. But the colonists are able to call in the power of the imperial government. Palmerston once declared that he would never employ force to promote purely private interests—whether commercial or settlement. He also declared that he would faithfully protect the lives and liberty of English subjects. In circumstances such as those de Tocqueville described, Palmerston's distinctions were irrelevant. See Kenneth Bourne, *Palmerston: The Early Years* (New York: Macmillan, 1982), pp. 624–26. Other colonial settlements and their dependence on imperial expansion are examined in Ronald Robinson, "Non-European Founda-

tions of Imperialism," in Roger Owen and Bob Sutcliffe, eds., *Studies in the Theory of Imperialism* (London: Longmans, 1972).

19

Gladstone had proclaimed his support for the equal rights of all nations in his Midlothian Speeches. Wilfrid Scawen Blunt served as a secret agent in Egypt keeping Gladstone informed of the political character of Arabi's movement. The liberal dilemma in 1882— were they intervening against genuine nationalism or a military adventurer (Arabi)?—was best expressed in Joseph Chamberlain's memorandum to the Cabinet, 21 June 1882, excerpted in J. L. Garvin and J. Amery, *Life of Joseph Chamberlain,* vol. 1 (London: Macmillan, 1935), p. 448. And see Peter Mansfield, *The British in Egypt* (New York: Holt, Rinehart and Winston, 1971), chaps. 2–3; Ronald Hyam, *Britain's Imperial Century, 1815–1914* (London: Batsford, 1976), chap. 8; and Robert Tignor, *Modernization and British Colonial Rule in Egypt* (Princeton: Princeton University Press, 1966).

20

The Platt Amendment is excerpted in Thomas Paterson, ed., *Major Problems in American Foreign Policy,* vol. 1 (Lexington, Mass.: D.C. Heath, 1978), p. 328.

21

During the Alliance for Progress era in Latin America, the Kennedy administration supported Juan Bosch in the Dominican Republic in 1962; see also William P. Bundy, "Dictatorships and American Foreign Policy," *Foreign Affairs* 54 (October 1975). See Samuel Huntington, "Human Rights and American Power," *Commentary* 72 (September 1981), and George Quester, "Consensus Lost," *Foreign Policy* 40 (Fall 1980), for argument and examples of the successful export of liberal institutions in the postwar period.

22

Kirkpatrick, "Dictatorships and Double Standards," 34–45. In 1851 the liberal French historian Guizot made a similar argument in a letter to Gladstone urging that Gladstone appreciate that the despotic government of Na-

ples was the best guarantor of liberal law and order then available. Reform, in Guizot's view, meant the unleashing of revolutionary violence; see Philip Magnus, *Gladstone* (New York: Dutton, 1964), p. 100.

23

Richard Barnet, *Intervention and Revolution: The United States in the Third World* (New York: Meridian, 1968), chap. 10; and on Nicaragua, see *The New York Times,* 11 March 1982, for a description of the training, direction, and funding ($20 million) of anti-Sandinista guerrillas by the United States.

24

Arthur Schlesinger, *A Thousand Days* (Boston: Houghton Mifflin, 1965), p. 769, and quoted in Richard Barnet, *Intervention and Revolution,* p. 158.

25

See L. Simon and J. Stephen, *El Salvador Land Reform, 1980–1981* (Boston: Oxfam-America, 1981), p. 38.

26

Charles Kindleberger, *The World in Depression* (Berkeley: University of California Press, 1973); Robert Gilpin, *U.S. Power and the Multinational Corporation* (New York: Basic Books, 1975); and Fred Hirsch and Michael Doyle, "Politicization in the World Economy," in Hirsch, Doyle, and Edward Morse, *Alternatives to Monetary Disorder* (New York: Council on Foreign Relations/McGraw-Hill, 1977).

27

Kirkpatrick, "Dictatorships and Double Standards," points out our neglect of the needs of the authoritarians. Theodore Lowi argues that Democratic and Republican policies toward the acquisition of bases in Spain reflected this dichotomy; "Bases in Spain," in Harold Stein, ed., *American Civil-Military Decisions* (Tuscaloosa, University of Alabama Press, 1963), p. 699. In other cases where both the geopolitical and the domestic orientation of a potential neutral might be influenced by U.S. aid, liberal institutions (representative legislatures) impose delay or public constraints and conditions on diplomacy that allow the Soviet Union to steal a march. Warren Christopher has suggested that this occurred in U.S. relations with Nicaragua in 1979; "Ceasefire between the Branches," *Foreign Affairs* 60 (Summer 1982): p. 998.

28

Ideological formulations often accompany these policies. Fear of Bolshevism was used to excuse not forming an alliance with the Soviet Union in 1938 against Nazi aggression. And Nazi and fascist regimes were portrayed as defenders of private property and social order. But the connection liberals draw between domestic tyranny and foreign aggression may also operate in reverse. When the Nazi threat to the survival of liberal states did require a liberal alliance with the Soviet Union, Stalin became for a short period the liberal press's "Uncle Joe."

29

The first formulation (classical realism) is that of Hans Morgenthau, *Politics among Nations* (New York: Knopf, 1967); the second (neorealism) is that of Kenneth Waltz, *Man, the State, and War* (New York: Columbia University Press, 1954).

30

Thomas Hobbes, *Leviathan* (Harmondsworth, Eng.: Penguin, 1980), pp. 186, 268. Other classic sources of the realist, or statist, or nationalist approach include Thucydides, *The Peloponnesian Wars,* trans. Rex Warner (Harmondsworth, Eng.: Penguin, 1954); Waltz, *Man, the State, and War,* and Waltz, *Theory of International Politics* (Reading, Mass.: Addison-Wesley, 1979); Rousseau's "Essay on St. Pierre's Peace Project" and his "State of War" in *A Lasting Peace* (London: Constable, 1917); E. H. Carr, *The Twenty Years' Crisis: 1919–1939* (London: Macmillan, 1951); and the works of Hans Morgenthau, most notably, *Politics among Nations.*

31

Hobbes, "De Cive," *The English Works of Thomas Hobbes* (London: J. Bohn, 1841), 2:13.8. Kenneth Waltz, *Theory of International Politics,* chap. 8; and Edward Gulick,

Europe's Classical Balance of Power (New York: Norton, 1967), chap. 3.

32

Robert Jervis, "Cooperation under the Security Dilemma," *World Politics* 30 (January 1978).

33

Ibid., pp. 186–210, 212. Jervis examines incentives for cooperation, not the existence or sources of peace.

34

Raymond Aron, *Peace and War* (New York: Praeger, 1968), pp. 151–54.

35

Karl Kautsky's views on ultraimperialism can be found in Lenin, *Imperialism: The Highest Stage of Capitalism* (New York: International Publishers, 1939), pp. 117–18. Lenin's response to Kautsky is in chap. 9 of the same work.

36

Charles Louis de Secondat de Montesquieu, *Spirit of the Laws* (New York: Hafner, 1949), trans. T. Nugent, vol. 1, bk. 20, chap. 1. The incompatibility of democracy and war is forcefully asserted by Paine in *The Rights of Man*. The connection between liberal capitalism, democracy, and peace is argued by, among others, Joseph Schumpeter in *Imperialism and Social Classes* (New York: Meridian, 1955). This literature is surveyed and analyzed by Albert Hirschman, "Rival Interpretations of Market Society: Civilizing, Destructive, or Feeble?" *Journal of Economic Literature* 20 (December 1982).

37

A partial list of significant studies on Kant's international theory includes A. C. Armstrong, "Kant's Philosophy of Peace and War," *Journal of Philosophy* (1931) 28: 197–204; Karl Friedrich, *Inevitable Peace* (Cambridge, Mass.: Harvard University Press, 1948); W. B. Gallie, *Philosophers of Peace and War* (Cambridge: Cambridge University Press, 1978); William Galston, *Kant and the Problem of History* (Chicago: University of

Chicago Press, 1975); Pierre Hassner, "Immanuel Kant," pp. 554–93 in Leo Strauss and Joseph Cropsey, eds., *History of Political Philosophy* (Chicago: Rand McNally, 1972); F. H. Hinsley, *Power and the Pursuit of Peace* (Cambridge: Cambridge University Press, 1967); Stanley Hoffmann, "Rousseau on War and Peace," pp. 45–87 in Hoffmann, *The State of War* (New York: Praeger, 1965); George A. Kelly, *Idealism, Politics, and History* (Cambridge: Cambridge University Press, 1969); Patrick Riley, *Kant's Political Philosophy* (Totowa, N.J.: Rowman and Littlefield, 1983); Kenneth Waltz, "Kant, Liberalism, and War," *American Political Science Review* 56 (1962): 331–40; Yirmiahu Yovel, *Kant and the Philosophy of History* (Princeton: Princeton University Press, 1980).

38
Kant, *Perpetual Peace*, pp. 99–102; and see Riley, chap. 5. I cite *Perpetual Peace* (1795), *The Idea for a Universal History with a Cosmopolitan Purpose* (1784), *The Contest of Faculties* (1798), and *The Metaphysics of Morals* (1797) from Hans Reiss, ed., and H. B. Nisbet, trans., *Kant's Political Writings* (Cambridge: Cambridge University Press, 1970).

39
I think Kant meant that the peace would be established among liberal regimes and would expand by ordinary political and legal means as new liberal regimes appeared. By a process of gradual extension the peace would become global and then perpetual; the occasion for wars with nonliberals would disappear as nonliberal regimes disappeared.

40
Riley, *Kant's Political Philosophy*, chap. 5.

41
Kant's *foedus pacificum* is thus neither a *pactum pacis* (a single peace treaty) nor a *civitas gentium* (a world state). He appears to have anticipated something like a less formally institutionalized League of Nations or United Nations. One could argue that these two institutions in practice worked for liberal states and only for liberal states. But no specifically liberal "pacific union" was institutionalized. Instead, liberal states have behaved for the past 180 years as if such a Kantian pacific union and treaty of perpetual peace had been signed.

42
In the *Metaphysics of Morals* (the *Rechtslehre*) Kant seems to write as if perpetual peace is only an epistemological device; to strive toward peace is an ethical duty, yet perpetual peace is empirically merely a "pious hope" (*Kant's Political Writings*, pp. 164–75). (Though even here Kant finds that the pacific union is not "impracticable," p. 171.) In the *Idea for a Universal History*, Kant writes as if the brute force of physical nature drives mankind toward inevitable peace. Yirmiahu Yovel argues that *Perpetual Peace* reconciles the two views of history, from a postcritical (post–*Critique of Judgment*) perspective; see Yovel, *Kant and the Philosophy of History* (Princeton: Princeton University Press, 1980), pp. 168ff. "Nature" is human-created nature (culture or civilization). Perpetual peace is the "a priori of the a posteriori" (a critical perspective that then enables us to discern causal, probabilistic patterns in history). Law and the "political technology" of republican constitutionalism is separate from ethical development. But both interdependently lead to perpetual peace: the first through force, fear, and self-interest; the second through progressive enlightenment; and both together through the widening of the circumstances in which engaging in right conduct poses smaller and smaller burdens.

43
This view is defended by Yovel, *Kant and the Philosophy of History*, pp. 153–54.

44
See Kelly, *Idealism, Politics, and History*, pp. 106–13 for a further explanation.

45
Hassner, "Kant," pp. 583–86. The Kantian pacific union has in fact expanded steadily, but whether we can anticipate its continued expansion much beyond the current numbers

of liberal democracies has been called into question by Samuel Huntington, "Will More Countries Become Democratic?," *Political Science Quarterly* 99 (Summer 1984): 193–218.

46
See Hume, *Essays,* pp. 347–48, and note 6 above.

47
For a confident reading of democratic capacities both to defer to prudent leadership and to make prudent judgments in this regard, see Kenneth Waltz, *Foreign Policy and Democratic Politics* (Boston: Little, Brown, 1967), pp. 288–97. Joseph Nye concludes that the U.S. record in postwar diplomacy is more mixed, finding that nuclear war has been successfully avoided but that containing Soviet power and fostering moderation in and by the Soviet Union have been less successful; "Can America Manage Its Soviet Policy?" in Joseph S. Nye, Jr., ed., *The Making of Amer-*

ica's Soviet Policy (New Haven: Yale University Press, 1984), pp. 325–29.

48
Karl Polanyi, *The Great Transformation* (Boston: Beacon Press, 1944), chaps. 1–2; Zbigniew Brzezinski and Samuel Huntington, *Political Power: USA/USSR* (New York: Viking Press, 1963), chap. 9; Robert Keohane and Joseph Nye, *Power and Interdependence* (Boston: Little, Brown, 1977), chap. 7; Richard Neustadt, *Alliance Politics* (New York: Columbia University Press, 1970).

49
Kenneth Waltz, "The Stability of a Bipolar World," *Daedalus* 93 (Summer 1964): 881–909; and Albert Carnesale, Paul Doty, Stanley Hoffmann, Samuel Huntington, Joseph Nye, and Scott Sagan, *Living with Nuclear Weapons* (New York: Bantam, 1983), p. 44.

50
Michael Walzer, *Spheres of Justice* (New York: Basic Books, 1983), p. 5.

Part Three

*Judging
the Kantian
Legacy*

Chapter 9

What Is Living and What
Is Dead in Kant's Practical
Philosophy?

William A. Galston

Fifty years ago, the influence of Kant's moral and political philosophy extended scarcely further than a few German professors and their disciples. Today, evidence of Kant-inspired practical philosophy is pervasive. From Robert Nozick on the libertarian right to Jürgen Habermas on the participatory left come appeals to Kantian concepts and premises, variously interpreted. John Rawls is of course the chief representative of this tendency within liberal thought.

Kant's startling comeback, I suggest, is neither an accident nor a fad. Rather, it is rooted in basic features of our contemporary experience.

To begin with, totalitarianism raised the prestige of philosophical positions that enable individuals to recognize and resist collective evil. In Germany it did not escape notice that Kant's followers were far less open to Nazi appeals than were either existentialists or legal positivists. And the recognition of the actual character of the former Soviet regime compelled most European thinkers to discard the illusion that the realization of Enlightenment hopes is somehow immanent in the historical process. As Bernard Crick has summed up the lesson of this experience, "Theories of socialism without a critical moral philosophy are as undesirable as they are impossible."[1] (Habermas's recent work may be viewed as a direct response to this imperative.)

In Anglo-American circles, utilitarianism was the first beneficiary of this felt need for a critical moral philosophy. But utilitarianism proved unequal to the demands placed upon it. Even before the Rawlsian critique, doubts grew steadily among professional philosophers that the utilitarian approach could yield determinate and plausible answers to the key questions of practical philosophy. Concrete political events only fed these doubts. The major domestic issues (at least in the United States) came to be focused on the long-frustrated claims of those groups whose interests were not necessarily served by the calculus of aggregation or by majoritarian procedures reflective of that calculus. This convergence of philosophy and social reality engendered the second source of the Kantian revival: for many of those who felt impelled to "take rights seriously," Kant seemed to provide the most nearly adequate foundation for their undertaking.

This return to Kant was facilitated by the broad compatibility of his approach with contemporary elite beliefs. Kant spurns both the appeal to divine authority and the reliance on any form of naturalism. At the same time, he provides philosophical support for the distinctiveness and self-respect of the human species. (For those reasons, Kant may well be regarded as the godfather of "secular humanism" and, therefore, as a key figure in the moral controversies now wracking American society.)

Finally, from the standpoint of these contemporary beliefs, not only is Kantian practical philosophy the right type of moral theory; it also leads to the right moral conclusions. Kant's account of moral personality is thoroughly egalitarian. As Judith Shklar has noted, "Anyone can in principle aspire to become a Kantian good character. It requires no special gifts of intelligence, beauty, wealth, or good luck. . . . This is a thoroughly democratic liberal character, built to preserve his own self-respect and that of others, neither demanding nor enduring servility."[2] Kantian moral theory thus provides a foundation for deriving principles of legitimate authority and rational social organization from freedom, equality, and consent—the predominant values of our democratic age.

This renewed interest in Kantian moral philosophy has gone through two distinct phases, corresponding to the two main waves of moral discussion since World War II. During the first, when "metaethical" considerations were paramount, attention focused on Kant's universalizability criterion. During the second, when substantive moral propositions regained some measure of philosophical respectability, the emphasis shifted to what was taken to be the key premise of Kantian moral philosophy—the requirement that the humanity of every person be treated as an end in itself, never as means alone. This premise has proved remarkably adaptable, with appeal to anarchists and libertarians on the one hand, and welfare liberals and socialists on the other.

The contemporary appropriation of Kant's practical philosophy has been partial at best, however. Kantian ethics has been detached from its place in the critical architectonic. Kant's search for a moral stance valid for "all rational beings" has not been resumed, and his insistence on the normative irrelevance of "anthropology" has been disregarded. Key teleological and intuitionist elements of his moral philosophy have been repudiated or ignored. Kant's moral rigor has been relaxed, in part because human freedom is regarded as prior to (rather than as the manifestation of) the moral law, and in part because *fiat justitia, pereat mundus* is no longer regarded as a sensible or sustainable moral stance. And finally, large pieces of Kant's social and political philosophy have been rejected on the grounds that they are inconsistent with the egalitarian thrust of his moral philosophy and too responsive to the socially stratified conditions of his own times.

There are two possible explanations of this highly selective appropriation. One is that modern theorists have in fact rummaged discerningly through the rubble of Kant's system, discarding the crumbled mortar and rotten beams while carting away the solid bricks out of which less ambitious but sturdier structures may be erected. The other possibility is that our approach to Kant has been unduly narrowed by our prejudices—by moral metaphysical skepticism, by our deep distrust of teleological arguments, and by a kind of easygoingness that elevates rights above duties and unbounded freedom above rational constraint.

In short, our selective appropriation raises the question: What is living and what is dead in Kant's practical philosophy?

I want to focus on three aspects of this question. First, how are universal moral judgments possible? Second, in what sense do "objective ends" enter into such judgments? And finally, what is the relation between these moral judgments and political theory?

Universal Moral Judgments

As children of a historical and anthropological century, we are impressed by the diversity of moral sentiments among cultures, and we tend to move from the consciousness of diversity to the conclusion that moral judgments binding across cultures are not in the last analysis defensible. At the philosophical level, this disposition is expressed in conventionalist theories of moral meaning and obligation and in the generalized "postmodern" critique of theories that purport to transcend rootedness in particular circumstances.

Yet at the very threshold of the *Foundations,* we encounter just the reverse— Kant's implacable insistence on the need for universally valid moral judgments and his imperturbable confidence that such judgments are possible. Kant demands "a pure moral philosophy which is completely freed from everything which may be only empirical," freed, that is, from propositions about "the nature of man or . . . the circumstances in which he is placed."[3] It is commonly observed that this requirement excludes reference to passions and emotions in fundamental moral principles (although, obviously, these principles may subsequently be applied to such sentiments). It is less frequently observed but equally true that Kant's requirement also excludes reference to history and culture in fundamental principles.

Kant argues that this demand flows from the very concept of morality itself: "Unless we wish to deny all truth to the concept of morality and renounce its application to any possible object . . . we must grant that it must be valid with absolute necessity and not merely under contingent conditions and with exceptions. . . . How could laws of the determination of our will be held to be laws of the determination of a rational being in general and of ourselves in so far as we are rational beings, if they were merely empirical and did not have their origin completely *a priori* in pure, but practical, reason?" (*Foundations*, pp. 28–29). To put this in contemporary terms: Kant denies that a proposition with moral meaning and force only within a particular context can function as a genuinely moral proposition, because the individual agent can always call into question the basic presuppositions of that context. Kant's argument, in short, is this: no morality without obligation, no obligation without necessity, no necessity without universality, no universality without an appeal to pure reason.

There are at least two possible lines of objection to this argument. The first was formulated by Aristotle, who contended that it is a mistake to think of morality as grounded in reason alone. Unlike contemplation, which is shared by humans and gods and is therefore an attribute of all "rational beings" in Kant's sense, the exercise of moral virtue is "confined to man." Aristotle argues that "it is in our dealings with one another that we perform just, courageous, and other virtuous acts, when we observe the proper kind of behavior toward each man in private transactions, in meeting his needs, in all manner of actions, and in our emotions, and all of these are, as we see, peculiarly human. Moreover, some moral acts seem to be determined by our bodily condition, and virtue or excellence of character seems in many ways closely related to the emotions. . . . The fact that these virtues are also bound up with the emotions [as well as with practical reason] indicates that they belong to our composite nature, and the virtues of our composite nature are human virtues" (*Ethics* 1178a 8–21).[4] Kant's rejoinder, of course, is that it is a fundamental mistake to accord moral weight to our bodies and emotions; our "peculiarly human" constitution is irrelevant from a moral point of view.

The second line of objection to the Kantian link between morality and universality asserts the moral significance of particular human associations and communities. As members of specific families and polities, we undertake special obligations that differ from family to family and polity to polity. It may be possible to offer a highly formalized, abstract description of what these obligations have in common. But at the level of moral content, they will differ fundamentally, without losing their prescriptive force. On this account, universality is not a condition of obligation.

The Kantian response to this theory of moral particularism is that so-called special obligations are at most rebuttable presumptions that must ultimately be weighed in light of universal criteria. If someone asks you why you lie to McCoy and you reply, "It's my duty, I'm a Hatfield," a Kantian would try to convince you that your responsibility to your family was subordinated to a higher moral law. (The Aristotelian distinction between the good man and the good citizen points in the same direction.)

To which it might be said, Kant's criterion of universality would be unobjectionable if a transcommunity, transhistorical moral principle were available. But what amounts to a post-Kantian critique of pure reason shows that no such principle exists. Reason is situated and rooted in a particular time and place. Its products will reflect that context. Universality is either a delusive myth (if put forward as actually achieved) or a destructive dream (if posited as the only worthy goal of rational striving). Reason may well be able to negate our sense of obligation to our community, but it can put nothing in its place. Thus (this line of argument concludes), just as Kant limited the pretensions of theoretical reason, so must we limit the pretensions of practical reason, in order to clear a space for the more modest kind of moral understanding that is truly attainable.

There are two kinds of replies to this argument. The first (to which I subscribe) is that a moment of universality is built into every moral proposition. To trace moral obligation (or, for that matter, the virtues) to the beliefs and practices of a specific community is to invite the objection, "Why am I obliged to take my bearings from my community?" In an age that is so conscious of global political and moral variety, this question is natural and unavoidable. The Platonic myth of the Cave does not guarantee the existence of the Sun, but it does characterize the nature of the Cave in ways that we are not free to ignore. There is, I suggest, no easy resting point ("situated morality," or whatever) between moral universality and moral skepticism. (For reasons that are not hard to understand, the search for such an intermediate point is a major element of contemporary political and moral theory.)

The second reply to the antiuniversalist argument, which Kant offers explicitly, is that moral universality is not only necessary, but also possible, for it is grounded in human reason, which is identical in, and shared by, all human beings. Thus, at the beginning of the first section of the *Foundations* Kant declares that the basic principle of morality "dwells already in the natural sound understanding and does not need so much to be taught as only to be brought to light" (p. 15). And at the end of that section he affirms that he has found that principle "within the moral knowledge of common human reason." To be sure, he continues, human reason is not always fully conscious of this principle. But reason "always has it in view and uses it as the standard of its judgments" (p. 23).

But why isn't human reason an aspect of the "human nature" from which Kant refuses to take any moral bearings? To answer this question, Kant distinguishes sharply between theoretical and practical reason. Theoretical reason "may permit and even sometimes find [it] necessary" to "depend upon the particular nature of human reason" (p. 33). Thus, it is possible to imagine ways of knowing the world theoretically that do not depend on the categories of experience explored in the first *Critique*. God's knowledge of Creation is direct, not mediated through these categories. Practical reason, on the other hand, includes no admixture of human particularity, but rests on the "universal concept of a rational being generally" (*Foundations*, p. 33). It is therefore impossible even to imagine modes of moral judgment that differ from human moral judgment. Kant carries this reasoning to its logical conclusion when he equates divine with human judgment and insists that "even the Only One of the Gospel must be compared with our ideal of moral perfection before he is recognized as such" (ibid., p. 29). Conversely, the divine judgment of human conduct must proceed in accordance with this same ideal: "Even the one and only absolute legislator would . . . have to be conceived as judging the worth of rational beings only by the disinterested conduct which they prescribe to themselves. . . . A man must be judged only by what constitutes his absolute worth; and this is true whoever his judge is, even if it be the Supreme Being" (ibid., pp. 65–66). (Kant thus inverts Aristotle's argument. For Aristotle, *theoria* is what we share with God, while practical reason is an aspect of our distinctive humanity. For Kant, precisely the reverse is true. It is difficult to determine the extent to which Kant's view secularizes the Judeo-Christian conception of God as engaged in praxis—that is, in creation and moral judgment.)

To locate morality in universal reason is not to say that individual moral judgments are universally correct. Kant points to an ineffaceable tension between the moral law and our "needs and inclinations"—a tension that tempts us to equivocate and to water down the rigorous purity of moral commands. Hedonism and eudaemonism are not just philosophical errors, but practical evasions. Yet this all-too-human flight from morality is in Kant's view fully consistent with its actual (not just potential) universality. The moral law within us is a voice that cannot be wholly stilled: "The moral law is given, as an apodictically certain fact, as it were, of pure reason, a fact of which we are *a priori* conscious, even if it be granted that no example could be found in which it had been followed exactly."[5] Thus, moral philosophy does not teach us right from wrong but, "in the manner of Socrates," reminds us of what we already know (*Foundations*, p. 23). At the same time, it helps us do battle against the inclinations that both weaken our incentive to obey the moral law and (more dangerously) obscure our awareness of its dictates.

In principle, then, Kant's thesis of moral universality is consistent with the actually observed diversity of moral belief and behavior. Kant's assertion is that whatever the point of departure, every individual can be led to the same conclusion, the recognition of moral obligation, through an appeal to the inner voice of practical reason. (Whether everybody—or anybody—can be led to actual moral conduct is an entirely different question. As Kant stresses throughout the *Foundations*, it is impossible to be sure that any act has ever been motivated purely by respect for the moral law.)

The experience of the twentieth century has not exactly inspired confidence in Kant's position. Even setting aside the issue of deep cultural differences, there seem to be individuals whose conscience has been altogether stilled, or who were born monsters, without conscience.

Kant's position can also be challenged from the standpoint of classical philosophy. At the end of the *Ethics,* Aristotle contends that

> the natural tendency of most people is to be swayed not by a sense of shame but by fear, and to refrain from acting basely not because it is disgraceful, but because of the punishment it brings. Living under the sway of emotion, they pursue their own proper pleasures and the means by which they can obtain them, and they avoid the pains that are opposed to them. But they do not even have a notion of what is noble and truly pleasant, since they have never tasted it. . . .
>
> Some people believe that it is nature that makes men good, others that it is habit, and others again that it is teaching. Now, whatever goodness comes from nature is obviously not in our power, but is present in truly fortunate men as the result of some divine cause. Argument and teaching, I am afraid, are not effective in all cases: the soul of the listener must first have been conditioned by habits to the right kind of likes and dislikes. . . . Emotion does not yield to argument but only to force. Therefore, there must first be a character that somehow has an affinity for excellence or virtue, a character that loves what is noble and feels disgust at what is base.
>
> To obtain the right training from youth up is difficult, unless one has been brought up under the right laws. (*Ethics* 1179b 22–32)

Aristotle fully acknowledges the role of the competent judge in determining the content of morality. But he denies that all human beings are equally competent and insists that for all except a happy few, the *paideia* of family and polity is essential for the achievement of even rudimentary moral competence. Where Kant sees a universal moral conscience, Aristotle sees at most a widely shared moral aptitude. As he says in the *Ethics,* "we are by nature equipped with the ability to receive [virtue], and habit brings this ability to completion" (1103a 25). On this basis Aristotle can readily account for the diversity of moral practices among various communities. He does not, however, infer moral skepticism from this diversity, in large measure because in his theory the evidentiary role of actual moral belief and behavior is circumscribed by an independent metaphysics and philosophical psychology.

Midway between Kant's "conscience" theory of morality and Aristotle's "blank slate" thesis is the Socratic dialectical route to moral insight. The Socratic argument, presented in classic form in the *Gorgias,* is that all human beings who are committed both to the rational justification of action and to the honest discussion of their opinions will converge on the same moral conclusions. The reason for this is not that everyone begins with the same moral intuitions (morality is not a "fact of reason" in that sense). Rather, and this is at bottom a metaphysical position, all false opinions contradict either themselves or some aspect of our experience.

The commitment to the rational justification of action may appear to be a minimal and unobjectionable requirement. In fact, it represents a fundamental choice among possible ways of life. It is a moral imperative rather than a logical truth, because the rejection of the imperative "Never perform an act for which an acceptable reason cannot be provided" does not lead to a contradiction. The *Gorgias* demonstrates this graphically. Callicles cannot formulate an acceptable principle that justifies the course of action on which he is embarked. But rather than reject this course, he rejects the process of rational justification, retreating into stubborn silence in the face of Socrates' arguments.

The lesson of this example has an important bearing on Kant's moral philosophy. As we have seen, Kant grounds the universality of moral judgments in the universal force of practical reason, taken as a "fact." But it seems more realistic to regard the power of practical reason as a *decision* than as a fact, for the rejection of reason is a real human possibility. Animals act without justification and without sensing this absence as a lack or defect. We can seek to become animals in this sense, and some of us can succeed. We can close ourselves off from the appeal to reason, allowing force and fraud to determine our relations with others. Locke perfectly describes the consequences of this course: "A criminal . . . having renounced reason—the common rule and measure God has given to mankind—has . . . declared war against all mankind, and therefore may be destroyed as a lion or tiger, one of those wild savage beasts with whom men can have no society nor security."[6]

The rejection of practical reason is neither inconceivable nor incoherent. But it is rarer than one might think. This is an underlying strength of the Kantian position: the tendency toward moral justification is deeply embedded in what makes us human, and the general commitment to the process of justification implies some substantive limits on acceptable moral beliefs. Still, no argument can prevent someone determined to shed this portion of his or her humanity from becoming what Aristotle feared, "the worst of all animals." Practical reason requires a commitment for which no further ground can be provided. It is where rational justification comes to an end.

Objective Ends

If the commitment to Kantian practical reason amounts to placing a certain conception of being human at the center of our moral decisions, then it would seem to follow that Kantian moral philosophy rests, not on empty formalism, but rather on a substantive telos of human action. It would also follow that the arguments Kant uses to render this telos plausible are critical to an adequate understanding of his moral philosophy.

Patrick Riley has done as much as any scholar in our generation to restore teleology to its proper place in the interpretation of Kant's thought. In so doing, he has cast doubt on the contemporary tendency to find in Kant the priority of the "right" to the "good" and to regard binding principles of conduct as "constructed" products of "rational agreement."[7]

The concept of teleology must, however, be deployed with care. There are three distinct teleological conceptions, the relations among which determine the kind of teleological doctrine a thinker actually embraces.

There is, to begin with, *intrinsic teleology*—the purposive construction of a specific entity. This kind of teleology describes the internal relations among the different parts of the entity in question and defines the proper activity of each part. A classic example of this occurs in the *Ethics* (Book I, chaps. 7 and 13), when Aristotle reviews the various aspects of human activity, fastens on the "activity of the soul in conformity with a rational principle" as the specifically human function, and sketches the different ways in which the soul may be said to conform with reason.

Second, there is *extrinsic teleology*—the hierarchical relation among different entities. The means/ends relation is an example of this: if X is for the sake of Y, then Y is held to be higher, more choiceworthy, or more valuable than X. But the means/ends relation does not exhaust the realm of hierarchy. In *Ethics* VI, for example, Aristotle argues that "man is not the best thing in the universe" because there are "other things whose nature is much more divine than man's." This judgment, however, does not rest on—or entail—the proposition than man is a means to (or for the sake of) those other things.

Finally, there is the *teleology of striving*—the ends of action, together with the analysis of action insofar as it is structured by purposiveness. It is in this sense that Aristotle begins the *Ethics* teleologically: "Every art or applied science and every systematic investigation, and similarly every action and choice, seem to aim at some good; the good, therefore, has been well defined as that at which all things aim." The point of departure for ethical inquiry is the goal that human beings regard as the ultimate and complete end of all striving. And the aim of ethical inquiry is to distinguish among more and less adequate accounts of that end.

What is most dramatic and distinctive about Aristotle's practical philosophy is the way in which these three aspects of teleology converge. Action in accordance with a rational principle amounts to the imitation of the highest and most divine, which in turn is the goal of human striving, properly understood.

While Aristotle offers a unified teleology, Kant argues for what may be called a bifurcated teleology. He employs a combination of intrinsic and extrinsic teleology to point toward rational being (in particular, practical reason) as an end in itself. At the same time, he detaches this end from the actual objects of human striving. Early in section 1 of the *Foundations,* for example, Kant invokes intrinsic teleology in arguing that our reason properly serves morality rather than the inclinations: "In the natural constitution of an organized being, i.e., one suitably adapted to life, we assume as an axiom that no organ will be found for any purpose which is not the fittest and best adapted to that purpose" (p. 13). And in section 2, he employs extrinsic teleology (in the form of means/ends analysis) to argue that rational being has "absolute worth": "Beings [that] are not rational beings have only a relative worth as means and are therefore called 'things'; on the other hand, rational beings are designated 'persons' because their nature indicates that they are ends in themselves, i.e., things which may not be used merely as means" (p. 53). But for Kant, there is no relation between this source of absolute worth and the objects of our desire. There is no ladder, no dialectical path that leads us from the valley of inclination to the peak of practical reason. Indeed, Kant argues, "the principle of one's own happiness is the most objectionable of all," because it "supports morality with incentives which undermine and destroy all its sublimity, for it puts the motives to virtue and those to vice in the same class, teaching us only to make a better calculation while obliterating the specific difference between them" (p. 69).

In Kant's concept of personality, therefore, harmony is ruled out; morality is at war with desire. And, as so often happens in war, each combatant develops an ideology of annihilation. The pursuit of happiness engenders what Kant calls "misology": reason comes to be hated as the force that prevents us from reveling wholeheartedly in our animality (*Foundations,* p. 14). The correlative response of reason to the desires is what might be called purgative asceticism: "The inclinations . . . are so lacking in absolute worth that the universal wish of every rational being must be indeed to free himself completely from them" (ibid., pp. 52–53). But, Kant concludes, this wish is vain. Because man is "always dependent with respect to what he needs for complete satisfaction with his condition, he can never be wholly free from desires and inclinations which, because they rest on physical causes, do not of themselves agree with the moral law, which has an entirely different source" (*Practical Reason,* p. 86). Thus, the highest possible moral condition for human beings is "virtue, i.e., moral disposition in conflict, and not holiness in the supposed possession of perfect purity of the intentions of the will" (ibid., p. 87).

Although Kant is clearly a partisan of reason in this struggle, he ultimately recognizes that asceticism is no less misguided than is misology. Thus, he draws back from a simply negative stance toward the inclinations and finds a place for the teleology of striving within his moral philosophy. The desire for happiness, excluded from permissible moral motivation, is restored as a legitimate moral hope. Virtue, he acknowledges, is the "supreme" good but not the "complete" good. To achieve the comprehensive human good, "happiness is also required, and indeed not merely in the partial eyes of a person who makes himself his own end but even in the judgment of an impartial reason, which impartially regards persons in the world as ends-in-themselves. For to be in need of happiness and also worthy of it and yet not to partake of it could not be in accordance with the complete volition of an omnipotent rational being" (*Practical Reason*, pp. 114–15). In this fashion, Kant's inability to deny all weight to the teleology of striving leads him to his controversial doctrine of the highest good.[8]

It is not difficult to agree with Kant's argument for the necessity of objective ends in moral philosophy. For as he says, "without them, nothing of absolute worth could be found, and if all worth is conditional and thus contingent, no supreme practical principle for reason could be found anywhere" (*Foundations*, p. 53). (This argument is parallel to Aristotle's point of departure in the *Ethics*. If there is no "end in the realm of action which we desire for its own sake," then we will "make all our choices for the sake of something else" and "the process will go on indefinitely so that our desire would be futile and pointless" [1094a 18–21].)

The difficulty comes rather in the attempt to identify such an end. Kant's radical humanism, which designates practical reason as the objective end and locus of absolute worth, will not be acceptable to those who believe that man was created to serve God and that God, separated from man by an unbridgeable gulf, is the sole absolute. Nor will Kant's proposal appeal to those who believe that the relation of other animals to human beings is not simply that of means to ends—to say nothing of those skeptics who profess to find animals superior to human beings. Even for those who accept Kant's humanist perspective, it is not self-evident that we should give one aspect of our nature such pronounced priority over others. It might well be argued that Kant's strict dualism of (human) reason and (animal) inclination is both disfiguring and unwarranted, that reason suffuses the full range of our sentiments in a way that makes them, too, aspects of our distinctive humanity.

Nevertheless, Kant's proposal is far from unattractive. He urges us to arrive at a reasoned recognition of what is highest and best within us, and to make that recognition the polestar of our moral life. Here again he is in broad agreement with Aristotle: "We should . . . do our utmost to live in accordance with what is highest in us. For though this is a small portion [of our nature], it far surpasses everything else in power and value. One might even regard it as each man's true self, since it is the controlling and better part" (*Ethics* 1177b 33–1178a 2).

It is easy to interpret Kant's teleological injunction statically, as simple assent to a "fact of reason" already present, fully formed. But there is, as well, a dynamic dimension to Kantian teleology: "It is not sufficient that [moral] action not conflict with humanity in our person as an end in itself; it must also harmonize with it. Now in humanity there are capacities for greater perfection which belong to the end of nature with respect to humanity in our own person; to neglect these might perhaps be consistent with the preservation of humanity as an end in itself but not with the furtherance of that end" (*Foundations,* p. 55). If the humanity that constitutes Kant's end in itself were simply given as a fact, Kantian morality would be the radical quasi-Stoic individualism, indifferent to circumstances, that it is sometimes made out to be. But because Kantian humanism is in part a developmental perfectionism, it is at least possible to ask whether all social orders are equally hospitable to this perfectionist ideal and, thus, to move from Kant's moral philosophy to the realm of politics.

From Morality to Politics

At first glance it might appear that Kant's political philosophy cannot accommodate—or is designed precisely to exclude—the teleological strand of his moral philosophy. Three lines of argument would seem to build a wall of separation between his morality and his politics: first, that the (phenomenal) world of public life cannot affect the (noumenal) world of the moral life; second, that public life need not seek to create virtue because a decent political order does not—as a practical matter—require it; and finally, that even if it were possible to foster morality through public institutions, it would be a breach of individual freedom for the state to do so.

The first line of argument—the impact of Kant's dualism on the relation between his moral and political doctrines—has been examined exhaustively and in my view definitively by Pierre Hassner.[9] Suffice it to say here that to the extent that individual morality is to be understood as developmental rather than static, the full theoretical rigor of Kant's distinction between freedom and nature must be relaxed more decisively than he acknowledges, even in the *Critique of Judgment.* Or, to put it differently, at some point one must decide whether to approach Kantian morality theoretically, in which case it will not be possible to give a wholly satisfactory account of moral development, or rather phenomenologically, in which case it will not be possible to maintain a wholly Kantian account of moral freedom.

This first argument reduces to the proposition that public life cannot really foster virtue. The second line of argument amounts to the claim that it need not do so, because the proper functioning of decent republican institutions is in no way dependent on a virtuous citizenry. Kant, so to speak, casts his lot with Mandeville and Adam Smith against Montesquieu and the civic republican tradition:

> The *republican* constitution is the only one which does complete justice to the rights of man. But it is also the most difficult to establish, and even more so to preserve, so that many maintain that it would only be possible within a state of *angels,* since men, with their self-seeking inclinations, would be incapable of adhering to a constitution of so sublime a nature. But

in fact, nature comes to the aid of the universal and rational human will, so admirable in itself but so impotent in practice, and makes use of precisely those self-seeking inclinations in order to do so. It remains only for men to create a good organization for the state, a task which is well within their capability, and to arrange it in such a way that their self-seeking energies are opposed to one another, each thereby neutralizing or eliminating the destructive effects of the rest. And as far as reason is concerned, the result is the same as if man's selfish tendencies were non-existent, so that man, even if he is not morally good in himself, is nevertheless compelled to be a good citizen. As hard as it may sound, the problem of setting up a state can be solved even by a nation of devils (so long as they possess understanding).[10]

This "invisible hand" theory of republican politics, in which institutional contrivances make good what James Madison called the defect of better motives, has had a substantial if controversial influence on political practice, especially in the United States. It raises a host of larger issues, which I have discussed elsewhere.[11] To summarize a lengthy argument: I know of no instance in which a republican polity, whatever its theoretical foundations, has been able in practice to remain indifferent to the moral character of its citizenry. Institutions can make a big difference, but they cannot wholly substitute for loyalty, integrity, fairmindedness, and a host of other necessary virtues. In rejecting the basic tenet of classical republicanism, Kant embraced its extreme—and equally untenable—antithesis.

It is Kant's third argument—that the state should not endeavor to foster virtue even if it could—on which I wish to dwell, for it is here that the inner tensions of his politico-moral stance become most manifest. In his political writings, especially *The Metaphysical Elements of Justice* and "Theory and Practice," he propounds a doctrine of the neutral state. The state is not in the business of teaching or enforcing morality, nor can it promote a specific conception of happiness. A paternalistic government, Kant insists, is the "greatest conceivable despotism." The substance of politics is neither virtue nor happiness, but rather "freedom in the mutual external relationships of human beings." And the leading principle of politics is "right," defined as the "restriction of each individual's freedom so that it harmonizes with the freedom of everyone else."[12]

Kant does not—indeed, cannot—simply posit external freedom as a value. Rather, he seeks to derive it from what is for him the unconditional value, moral freedom. This effort is bedeviled, however, by structural differences between these two senses of freedom. Kantian moral freedom is, in Isaiah Berlin's terms, a kind of positive freedom. We are morally free when our will is open to, and determined by, practical reason. Kantian external freedom, on the other hand, is a kind of negative freedom. We are externally free to the extent that we are not constrained by other human beings in the pursuit of our individual purposes. While one individual's exercise of moral freedom can never conflict with another individual's moral freedom, the exercise of external freedom can and will engender conflict. Thus, unlike moral freedom, the political freedom of each individual must be limited if the multiplicity of wills is to be harmonized. Kantian practical philosophy is, I suggest, the uneasy attempt to combine an ethics of positive freedom with a politics of negative freedom.

This tension between positive and negative freedom is reflected in Kant's theory of the state. The strain shows in two ways. First, state policies compatible with negative freedom are nevertheless ruled out if they contradict positive freedom. Kant asks, for example, whether a people can impose on itself an ecclesiastical constitution "whereby certain accepted doctrines and outward forms of religion are declared permanent, [thus preventing] its own descendants from making further progress in religious understanding or from correcting any past mistakes." No, it cannot, he replies: "It is clear that any original contract of the people which established such a law would itself be null and void, for it would conflict with the appointed aim and purpose of mankind."[13] With this ringing appeal to the teleological understanding of individual rational perfection, Kant breaks through the limits of external freedom and of the neutral state. For if human beings cannot, as individuals, deliberately undercut their potential for rational development, they cannot do so collectively, as citizens.

Second, Kant's arguments against the paternalistic state turn out, on close inspection, to constitute no real barrier to the tutelary state that is directly engaged in the moral education of its citizens. Kant defines paternalism as state enforcement of an arbitrary conception of happiness, but given his sharp distinction between happiness and virtue, this definition can have no bearing on the issue of moral education. Equally, his insistence that morality cannot be coerced is irrelevant, for he distinguishes between coercion and education. And in spite of his emphasis on practical reason as a "fact," Kant affirms both the possibility and the necessity of moral education: "The fact that virtue must be acquired (and is not innate) is contained already in the concept of virtue. . . . That virtue can and must be taught follows from the fact that it is not innate."[14]

In the end, then, Kant gives no compelling arguments against the tutelary state. This is not terribly surprising for, as George Kelly has pointed out, there is a tutelary ideal at work in Kantian politics. Membership in civil society and participation in an advancing culture discipline our natural inclinations even as they help us to attain our ends. Political life, especially in a polity that heeds the precepts of republican legitimacy and liberates the life of the mind, is a preparation for morality.[15] Kant's teleological doctrine of human perfection thus exerts an irresistible pressure on the limits of the neutral state.

This result is not just an idiosyncrasy of Kantian theory. To say that rational knowledge of the good life is available is to imply both that one ought to strive to lead that life and that one is harmed by deviating from it. It is to open up the possibility that B may understand what is good for A better than A does. It is to concede that negative freedom is not the only, or highest, value and that its exercise may impede the attainment of the human good.[16]

It may be argued, however, that this abstract conclusion is willfully blind to the experience of the seventeenth-century religious wars that gave rise to the liberal settlement. In circumstances of religious or moral diversity, the superiority of one specific doctrine—even if that superiority can be demonstrated—is irrelevant. The cruelty of the coercion that would be required to render that doctrine publicly binding far outweighs any possible benefits from such an establishment. What reader of history or, for that matter, what observer of contemporary "holy wars" could underestimate the force of this argument?

And yet: regarding cruelty as the "first vice," which must be avoided above all, is not the same as neutrality among competing moral and political doctrines. It is itself a specific doctrine, which Judith Shklar has labeled the "liberalism of fear." It tacitly regards the avoidance of pain and violent death as the supreme good. It sees negative freedom as a zone of protection around each individual that can help ward off dangerous intrusions by other individuals as well as by the state. And it creates a system of institutions that tolerates other practices only insofar as they are compatible with these purposes. While it is certainly the case that "as a matter of liberal policy we must learn to endure enormous differences in the relative importance that various individuals and groups attach to the vices," our endurance is circumscribed by a prior decision to give one rank-order pride of place.[17]

The structure and dynamic of this argument is instructive. As I have argued elsewhere, there are two broad strategies for justifying the liberal state. The first may be called substantive justification. It begins by arguing for the worth of the way of life characterized by distinctively liberal virtues and goals. The liberal state is justified, according to this view, because it is designed to foster liberal virtues, to allow the maximum scope for their exercise, and to permit, so far as possible, the unhindered pursuit of liberal goals. The second strategy for justifying liberalism may be called formal justification. According to this view, the liberal state is desirable not because it promotes a specific way of life but precisely because it alone does not do so. The liberal state is neutral concerning different ways of life; it presides benignly over them, intervening only to adjudicate conflicts and to prevent any particular way of life from tyrannizing over others.

In my judgment, the strategy of formal justification necessarily fails. The concept of the state as the tamer of conflict rests on a substantive judgment about the worth of civil tranquility relative to the worth of any of the contending parties. One may defend this conclusion as Hobbes does—by positing a *summum malum* while impugning the rational status of conflicting claims about the *summum bonum*. Or one may do it as Rawls does, by arguing that the evils of coercion necessarily override the benefits of publicly promoting even rationally justified claims about virtue or the good. But in each case, I conclude, the state neutrality thesis comes to rest on some substantive view of the human good.[18]

It is important to be clear about what this argument does and does not mean. I am not suggesting that the scope for diversity in liberal societies is no greater than in closed or theocratic communities; that contention would be absurd on its face (although it has been advanced—recall Herbert Marcuse's shrill charge of "repressive tolerance"). But I am suggesting that liberalism has a characteristic tendency, imparted to the members of liberal societies both directly (through systems of education and training) and indirectly (through the tacit norms conveyed by political and social practices). And I am also suggesting that the moral commitments of liberalism influence—and in some cases circumscribe—the ability of individuals to engage fully in particular ways of life. If, to be wholly effective, a religious doctrine requires control over the totality of an individual's life, including the formative social and political environment, then the classic liberal demand that religion be practiced "privately" amounts to a substantive restriction on that religion. The manifold blessings of liberal social orders come at a price, and we should not be surprised that those who pay the most occasionally grow restive.

My argument has another implication as well. If liberal societies do embody substantive commitments, then it would seem to follow that their viability is threatened by declining adherence to those commitments—which implies that liberal societies, like all others, must concern themselves with strengthening and passing on their core beliefs. To return to our earlier example: if liberal societies rest on a decision to regard cruelty as the worst vice, then anything that tends to legitimate cruelty or even reduce the horror with which it is regarded would weaken those societies. From this standpoint, it might well make sense to engage in moral instruction through public schools, or even to censor forms of culture that seem likely to increase the propensity to commit acts of cruelty.

There is, in short, a tension, prefigured in Kant's political thought, between the moral underpinnings of liberalism and the tolerance of diversity that stands at the core of liberal society. Liberal politics is in part the maintenance of proper balance between these tendencies—avoiding the extremes of moral intrusion, which unduly restricts diversity, and moral abdication, which gives illiberal tendencies full scope for development. Somewhere between coercion and nonintervention stands education. Liberal education is in part a training in liberal virtues, for liberal societies, by liberal states. This conclusion may be against the letter of Kant's practical philosophy, but it is, I submit, very much in its spirit.

Notes

1

Bernard Crick, quoted in Norman Daniels, ed., *Reading Rawls* (New York: Basic Books, 1975), p. xvi.

2

Judith Shklar, *Ordinary Vices* (Cambridge, Mass.: Harvard University Press, 1984), p. 233.

3

Kant, *Foundations of the Metaphysics of Morals,* ed. Robert Paul Wolff (Indianapolis: Bobbs-Merrill, 1969), pp. 5–6. Subsequent references in the text to *Foundations* are to this edition.

4

Aristotle, *Nicomachean Ethics,* trans. Martin Ostwald (Indianapolis: Bobbs-Merrill, 1962). Subsequent references to *Ethics* are to this edition.

5

Kant, *Critique of Practical Reason,* trans. Lewis White Beck (Indianapolis: Bobbs-Merrill, 1956), p. 48. Subsequent references in the text to *Practical Reason* are to this edition.

6

John Locke, *The Second Treatise of Government,* 3d ed., ed. J. W. Gough (Oxford: Blackwell, 1966), sect. 11.

7

See especially Patrick Riley, *Kant's Political Philosophy* (Totowa, N.J.: Rowman and Littlefield, 1982).

8

For an analysis, see William A. Galston, *Kant and the Problem of History* (Chicago: University of Chicago Press, 1975), pp. 251–55.

9

See especially Pierre Hassner, "Immanuel Kant," in Leo Strauss and Joseph Cropsey, eds., *History of Political Philosophy,* 3d ed. (Chicago: University of Chicago Press, 1987).

10

Kant, *Perpetual Peace,* in Hans Reiss, ed., *Kant's Political Writings* (Cambridge: Cambridge University Press, 1970), p. 112.

11

See Galston, "Liberal Virtues," *American Political Science Review* 82 (1988): 1277–90.

12

"On the Common Saying, 'This May Be True in Theory, But It Does Not Apply in Practice,'" in *Kant's Political Writings,* p. 73.

13

Kant, "Theory and Practice," in *Kant's Political Writings,* p. 85.

14

Kant, *The Metaphysical Principles of Virtue,* trans. James Ellington (Indianapolis: Bobbs-Merrill, 1964), p. 145.

15

George Kelly, *Idealism, Politics and History: Sources of Hegelian Thought* (Cambridge: Cambridge University Press, 1969), pp. 170–74.

16

The preceding discussion of the state's role in fostering virtue is based on my article "Defending Liberalism," *American Political Science Review* 76:621–29.

17

The quotation is from Shklar, *Ordinary Vices,* pp. 4–5.

18

See Galston, "Defending Liberalism."

Chapter 10

The Problem with Kantian
Liberalism

Bernard Yack

There are two very different ways in which we can identify with others and attempt to see the world from their point of view. We can, on the one hand, try to abstract from what is peculiar to our own perspective in the hope of identifying a perspective that others share with us. On the other hand, we can seek to identify what distinguishes others' perspectives from our own and then make an effort to look at things from their point of view. Since there will inevitably remain aspects of our own particular identity from which we cannot abstract, as well as aspects of others' perspectives that we cannot fathom, neither of these strategies will ever be completely successful. Nevertheless, they represent two ideals that can guide us when we attempt to identify with others.

Liberalism, as a set of aspirations and practices that encourages the coexistence of very different perspectives within one political community, requires its supporters to make at least some effort at identifying with very different kinds of individuals. Kantian liberalism, by which I mean the liberalism elaborated by Kant and contemporary reinterpreters such as John Rawls, concentrates all its moral weight on the first of the two means of identification. Critics of Kantian liberalism have argued that its requirement that we abstract from our particular identity in making moral and/or political judgments renders Kantian liberalism untenable as a political theory and, moreover, manifests the limitations of liberalism in general. Michael Sandel, for example, complains that because of its demand for abstraction Kantian liberalism unnecessarily cuts us off from the communities that we actually share with others.[1]

In this chapter, I put forward the opposite criticism of Kantian liberalism. The problem with Kantian liberalism, I argue, is not that it unrealistically assumes too little community among individuals, but rather that it unrealistically assumes too much of a common identity among individuals. To be more precise, Kantian liberals assume that all individuals within our political community share a minimal but essential common identity as moral actors. This assumption creates two kinds of problems for Kantian liberalism. The first problem is theoretical: the need to justify a relatively unrealistic claim about our common identity as moral actors. The second problem is more practical: the promotion of a set of moral dispositions that makes us relatively insensitive to the depth and breadth of the differences that exist among us. Kantian liberalism leads us to associate a moral perspective on the world with abstraction from these differences. By placing all its moral weight on abstraction from differences as a means of identifying with others, Kantian liberalism, I argue, diminishes the very openness to differences that liberals set out to protect. The problem with Kantian liberalism is thus not a problem with liberalism per se, but rather a problem with a particular, one-sided version of liberalism, a version that may, unintentionally, diminish the value of liberal pluralism and toleration.

Kantian liberalism represents a particular way of formulating and justifying some of the aspirations and institutions favored by most liberals. It has been described by some of its critics as "deontological liberalism," that is, as a theory that claims that if we proceed "deontologically" in our political reasoning, if we subordinate our various and controversial conceptions of the good to our conception of rightness, we will come to recognize the legitimacy of a variety of liberal practices and institutions.[2] While it is undeniable that the two most influential Kantian liberals, Kant and Rawls, both insist upon the priority of the right to the good, this deontological assertion follows for them from a prior claim about our identities as moral actors. It is this claim, I shall argue, that most distinguishes Kantian liberalism from other forms of liberalism.

Kantian versions of liberalism are based on the following four claims and assumptions. (1) All individuals, or at least all individuals in our political community,[3] share a common identity as free and equal moral actors. (2) We can discern this identity by abstracting from the social and natural contingencies that ordinarily shape our social and political judgments. (3) Just political principles and institutions are those that we would select were we to reason primarily from the common ground provided by our identity as free and equal moral actors, rather than from the various grounds provided by our conceptions of the good. (4) Proper reasoning from this common ground will lead us to approve of certain liberal practices, especially those that assert and protect universally held legal and political rights.

Critics of deontological liberalism have focused their attention on the third of these claims, the priority of a universal conception of rightness to our various conceptions of goodness. But that claim is valid for Kantian liberals only because they make a prior claim about our shared identity. Kantian liberals do not merely insist that we *ought* to take up a neutral standpoint toward conceptions of the good when making political judgments. They insist that we do, in fact, share such a standpoint, and that such a standpoint is essential to our identity as moral actors.

Consequently, far from resting upon claims about the extreme dissociation of individuals, Kantian liberalism rests upon claims about shared identity and membership in a community of free and equal rational actors.

The reason that Kantian liberalism appears (to supporters as well as critics) to demand the dissociation of individuals is that we tend to associate community with particular and usually irrational affective ties. But as Robert Paul Wolff points out in his own critique of liberalism, "affective" community only represents one possible form of community. Among the other forms, Wolff suggests, is "rational" community, the form of community celebrated by Kant, among others. Rational community is the community defined by mutual recognition of our shared identity as free and equal moral actors, a form of community toward which, according to Wolff, we should all aspire.[4] Kantian liberals rely heavily on this notion of rational community. But they differ from Wolff in making rational community the foundation rather than the goal of their arguments. They claim that our shared identity as moral persons makes us part of such a community, at least implicitly, even before we have done anything to realize it in our social and political institutions.

That Kant himself makes such a claim is undeniable. Our capacity for moral freedom, which, according to Kant's critical philosophy, no empirical or theoretical evidence can disprove, provides all individuals with an extraempirical or "noumenal" identity as moral actors. This capacity for moral freedom—for Kant, the capacity of unconditioned reason to be the determining ground of the will[5]—provides all rational beings with a particular kind of identity, one that establishes them all as ends-in-themselves rather than as mere means to another's ends. This identity is what Kant and many moral philosophers who follow him call moral personality.[6] Kant exhorts us to honor the moral personality that we share with other rational creatures. We owe duties to others because we must endeavor to treat them as ends or moral persons rather than merely as means to our own ends. But we also owe duties to ourselves: we must act so as to respect the moral person we bear within us, as well as the moral personality borne by others.[7]

Moral action, in Kant's view, thus requires that we acknowledge the identity we share with all rational beings. Consequently, far from dissociating ourselves from each other, Kantian moral personality makes rational beings members of the rational community described by Kant as the "kingdom of ends."[8] This kingdom of ends represents the community of free and equal rational actors who relate to others only as bearers of moral personality. Our political communities, at least in Kant's account, can never take the form of the kingdom of ends, given that human beings do not *only* relate to each other as ends-in-themselves or as free and equal moral actors.[9] Nevertheless, the kingdom of ends is, for Kant, not merely an ideal toward which we should strive. It is, instead, a real community that all rational creatures share to the extent that they possess moral personality. Much the greatest effort in

Kant's critical moral philosophy is to present and justify his understanding of our shared moral personality.

This understanding of our shared moral identity provides the foundation for Kant's arguments about legal and political authority in *The Metaphysical Elements of Justice*. "People constitute themselves a state," Kant declares, by means of an "original contract." But Kant does not derive the terms of that contract from what actual citizens do or would agree to under particular conditions. Instead, he derives these terms, which define just legal and political institutions, from what we all as free and equal moral actors implicitly accept. Kant's original contract is thus an "idea" of an agreement deduced from his conception of moral personality, rather than an actual agreement of any sort. [10] However much our experience of social life may have taught us about our need for legal and political institutions, "it is not experience that makes public, lawful coercion necessary. The necessity of public, lawful coercion does not rest on a fact, but on an *a priori* idea of reason." Proper reasoning about fundamental political principles thus must proceed, according to Kant, from the common a priori ground provided by our shared identity as free and equal rational actors. Such reasoning establishes an a priori "idea of the state as it ought to be according to pure principles of justice," an idea that "provides an internal guide and standard for every actual union of men in a commonwealth."[11]

The basic principle that, according to Kant, free and rational beings would choose to govern their association with each other is a relatively liberal one. "Every action is just that in itself or in its maxim is such that the freedom of the will of each can coexist together with the freedom of everyone in accordance with a universal law." Consequently, legal coercion is just only "inasmuch as it is the prevention of a hindrance to freedom."[12] On the basis of this fundamental principle, Kant justifies a variety of recognizably liberal political practices and institutions. Kant's liberal theory thus rests on the foundation provided by his understanding of our shared identity as moral actors. He argues that just political principles and institutions are those that free and rational moral actors would choose and that, if we reason consistently, we will conclude that such actors would choose relatively liberal principles of justice. But the hypothetical choice of these factors is binding on us only because we do actually share, whether we recognize it or not, a noumenal identity as free and rational moral actors.

Rawls, in contrast to Kant, devotes much less attention to establishing and justifying a claim about our shared identity. Indeed, with his later emphasis on the "fact of pluralism," Rawls makes it quite difficult to see that his arguments rest upon a claim about our shared identity as moral actors. [13] He devotes much the greater part of his effort, both in *A Theory of Justice* and his later revisions of that work, to the reasoning that should lead us to choose liberal principles and practices. Moreover, he is quite anxious to avoid the metaphysical assumptions and connotations of

Kant's claims about moral personality. Nevertheless, careful examination of Rawls's arguments from *A Theory of Justice* onward reveals his reliance upon a claim about our shared identity as moral actors very similar to Kant's.

In defending what he calls a "Kantian interpretation of justice as fairness," Rawls suggests that "we think of the original position as the point of view from which noumenal selves see the world." The parties to the original position, as noumenal selves, possess "a desire to express their nature as rational equal members of the intelligible realm" by choosing principles that "most fully reveal their independence from natural contingencies and social accident."[14] Rawls is not suggesting here that the parties in the original position, stripped as they are of all particular features of their identities, exist in this or any other world. As he emphasizes in his responses to criticism of the original position, the original position is simply a "device of representation" rather than a description of a deeper noumenal reality.[15] Nevertheless, when we ask just what it is that the "device" of the original position represents, it becomes clear that, his denials notwithstanding, Rawls is, at least implicitly, making a claim about our identity as rational human beings.

Rawls suggests that the "parties" in the original position "are to be seen as representatives of free and equal citizens who are to reach an agreement under conditions that are fair."[16] The original position thus represents two things: something about the freedom and equality of citizens and something about fair conditions of choice for such individuals. But what is it about the freedom and equality of citizens that the original position represents? In *A Theory of Justice* it clearly serves to represent to ourselves "our nature as free moral persons."[17] All mature individuals share, according to Rawls, the nature of "free moral persons." The original position is a regulative idea that helps us represent our nature as moral persons to ourselves.[18] It demands that we abstract from the natural and social contingencies that shape our particular identities because Rawls, like Kant, identifies moral personality with "independence from natural contingencies and social accident."[19] We should regulate our principles of justice according to the constraints provided by the original position because that device allows us to represent our true identity as free and equal moral actors in our deliberations. In *A Theory of Justice* Rawls assumes, like Kant, that all human beings share a common identity and that our political reasoning should proceed from the premises provided by that common identity.

In his later essays Rawls replaces this universalistic understanding of moral personality with a more restricted, "political conception of the person." Such a conception of moral personality follows from his insistence in these essays that "justice as fairness is intended as a political conception of justice," by which Rawls means that "it tries to draw solely upon basic intuitive ideas that are embedded in the political institutions of a constitutional democratic regime and the public traditions of their interpretation." A political conception of justice thus "starts within a certain political tradition." The conception of citizens as free and equal moral actors, Rawls insists, is derived from ideas "embedded" in the public culture of liberal democracies, rather than from a more universal and "comprehensive" theory of moral identity.[20]

Rawls's political conception of moral personality certainly eliminates the Kantian universalism implicit in *A Theory of Justice*. It is valid only for participants in a liberal democratic public culture, a group that, Rawls assumes, includes us. Nevertheless, in important ways, Rawls's "political" conception of moral personality is even more Kantian than the conception advanced in his book.[21] For Rawls finds "embedded" in our public culture a conception of persons as possessing two moral powers over their actions that no empirical evidence can challenge, as well as a "highest-order interest in realizing and exercising these powers." He now suggests that the primary goods of *A Theory of Justice* are merely the "all-purpose means to enable human beings to realize and exercise their moral powers." All of these claims about persons he "assume[s] to be implicit in the public culture of a democratic society."[22] His aim is to locate and recover "the deeper bases of agreement" corresponding to "our deeper understanding of ourselves and our aspirations" as a basis for public principles of justice. If we avoid controversial philosophic or comprehensive claims about justice and the good, we can find in our public culture and its implicit conception of moral personality the basis for an "overlapping consensus" among very different and otherwise contradictory positions.[23]

Rawls rightly insists that his political conception of moral personality "need not involve . . . questions of philosophical psychology or a metaphysical doctrine of the self."[24] Instead, it raises questions about whether he is justified in attributing such a highly specific and, indeed, highly Kantian conception of moral personality to our democratic public culture, questions we shall consider in the following section. Nevertheless, Rawls is still resting his defense of liberal principles and institutions on a claim about our shared identity, and thus he continues to follow the basic theoretical model of Kantian liberalism. Just as the original position served to represent to ourselves our "nature" as free and equal rational beings in *A Theory of Justice,* so, in Rawls's later essays, it serves to represent the deeper conception of moral personality that we actually share, even in the midst of our most basic disagreements, as participants in a democratic public culture. Rawls remains a Kantian liberal even as he eschews Kantian universalism for a more pragmatic approach.[25]

Social contract theories all try to justify substantive political principles and institutions by deriving them from the reasoning imputed to individuals shorn of the conventional hierarchies and prejudices created by their current political institutions and practices. Typically, contractarians derive these substantive conclusions from relatively neutral premises in three ways: by means of specific characterizations of rationality, of fair conditions of choice, or of the actors themselves who choose principles in these fair conditions. Rawls tries to make the characterization of fair initial conditions of choice do most of the work in his contractarian theory. But in the end, he, like Kant, relies on a highly specific characterization of the person who chooses to derive the liberal conclusions of his social contract theory.

The success of Kantian liberal theories depends, among other things, upon the persuasiveness of their claim that we do indeed share and can reason from a common identity as free and equal moral actors. Kant clearly devoted the bulk of his efforts to establishing and justifying his claims about our shared moral personality. Compared to the arguments in Kant's critiques of pure and practical reasons, the contractarian argument that supports the relatively liberal conclusions of his *Metaphysical Elements of Justice* seems rather hurried and schematic. Rawls, in contrast, took for granted key elements of his understanding of our shared moral identity in *A Theory of Justice,* preferring instead to concentrate upon the contractarian reasoning that would yield liberal conclusions.[26] It is only in response to criticisms of his arguments in the book that he has devoted much attention to the articulation and justification of his conception of moral personality.

That Kant's claim about our shared moral identity is unrealistic I do not think even Kant himself would deny. There is no way to measure this claim against reality. Kant devoted much of his effort in the *Critique of Pure Reason* to demonstrating that no empirical evidence can prove or disprove our moral freedom, the foundation of our shared moral identity. "I have found it necessary to deny knowledge" of things-in-themselves, Kant writes, "in order to make room for *faith*" in freedom and the moral dignity of human beings. It is not unreasonable or contradictory, according to Kant, to think of ourselves both as free beings who participate in the universal community of the kingdom of ends and as bodies buffeted about by natural laws of cause and effect.[27] But in order to do so we must have faith in the existence of a kind of causality and a noumenal reality beyond that which we do and can experience. Kant insists that when we act morally we affirm such a faith and make claims that necessarily lack empirical confirmation. In the end, Kant's claim about our shared moral identity requires a leap of faith, though not an unreasonable one, beyond the reality we experience and can judge theoretically.

It is precisely this leap beyond empirical reality that Rawls wants to avoid in his version of Kantian liberalism. He claims to have reformulated Kant's arguments in a way that brings them into line with "the canons of a respectable empiricism." The original position, Rawls claims, provides "a procedural interpretation of Kant's conception of autonomy and the categorical imperative" that makes Kant's metaphysical faith in a noumenal order unnecessary.[28] The popularity and influence of Rawls's version of liberalism surely owe something to acceptance of his claim that, unlike Kant, he need not rely on unrealistic and disrespectable metaphysical assumptions about human beings to justify his liberal conclusions.

But does Rawls actually succeed in bringing his Kantian arguments into line with "the canons of a respectable empiricism"? In response to criticism that his theory of justice implicitly relies on metaphysical assumptions about human identity, Rawls has rightly argued that the original position provides "a device of representation" or a metaphor, rather than a description of a deeper noumenal reality. But, as I noted in the previous section, this device allows us to represent to ourselves the forms of reasoning that best "express our nature as a free and rational being." We should accept the constraints on our political reasoning imposed by the original position because they represent to us the conditions under which we can "express most fully what we are or can be, namely free and equal beings with a liberty to choose." We do indeed share an identity, according to Rawls, not as the dissociated individuals of the original position, but rather as the free and equal beings who possess the liberty to choose principles of justice that "most fully reveal [our] independence from natural contingencies and social accident."[29] In the end, Rawls makes *A Theory of Justice* as broad and controversial a claim about our shared moral identity as Kant did. He differs from Kant only in his failure to recognize his need to justify that claim.

The implied justification of this claim seems to be that the description "free and equal rational being" somehow corresponds to our "nature" as human beings. Such an argument about human nature has, of course, a long and distinguished history in the development of liberal and democratic political conceptions. But it represents precisely the kind of metaphysical assertion that fails, one would think, to meet the canons of a respectable empiricism.[30]

It is no wonder then that Rawls has spent so much effort revising his account of moral personality since the publication of *A Theory of Justice*. Rawls denies that he ever meant to offer an account of moral personality rooted in a universal account of human nature. The original position, he insists, "has no metaphysical implications concerning the nature of the self." When "we simulate being in this position, our reasoning no more commits us to a metaphysical doctrine about the nature of the self than our playing a game of Monopoly commits us to thinking that we are landlords engaged in a desperate rivalry, winner take all."[31] The original position still remains a device whereby Rawls represents a particular conception of moral personality. But he now argues that this conception corresponds to "deeper understandings of ourselves and our aspirations . . . embedded in our public life" rather than to human nature per se.

Rawls is certainly correct in suggesting that his revised theory of justice commits us to no "*metaphysical* doctrine about the nature of the self." But it seems rather disingenuous to compare its requirements to those of "a game of Monopoly."[32] For the revised theory of justice commits us to a very specific political (if not metaphysical) conception of the self. Rawls is arguing that if we are true to the "deeper understandings of ourselves and our aspirations . . . embedded in our public life," then we will formulate our principles according to the rules and constraints provided by the original position. The rules of Monopoly merely represent the constraints that we must impose on ourselves if we choose to play a particular game. In contrast, the rules contained in the original position represent something more: our deepest understanding of ourselves as participants in a democratic culture. These rules represent, for Rawls, the constraints that we must impose on ourselves if we are to be true to our moral selves as Rawls believes our moral selves to be.

This revision of *A Theory of Justice* clearly reflects and responds to the increasing dissatisfaction with which American moral philosophers have come to view universalistic and foundationalist arguments in the last decade. It is not surprising then that the most influential American antifoundationalist, Richard Rorty, has hailed Rawls's reformulation of his theory of justice as a demonstration of "how liberal democracy can get along without philosophical presuppositions."[33] Rawls can now explicitly acknowledge that his argument was rooted in an initial assertion about the shared moral identity of the individuals that he addresses. But unlike Kant and other foundationalist philosophers he need not ground that assertion in universalistic claims about human nature or noumenal reality. Instead, he need merely refer us to something seemingly much more tangible and empirically respectable than human nature or noumenal reality: "the public culture of a democratic society."

On further reflection, however, one begins to wonder whether Rawls has not simply replaced an unrealistic conception of human nature with an equally unrealistic conception of democratic "public culture." That suspicion grows stronger when one recognizes, as noted in the previous section, that the conception of moral personality he finds embedded in democratic public life is even more Kantian in content than the conception he once grounded in human nature.[34]

Even if we grant Rawls the rather questionable assumptions that he makes about the homogeneous and coherent structure of our democratic public culture, there are good reasons to doubt his claims about the conception of moral personality embedded in democratic public culture. Surely talk of freedom and equality will appear in any account of a democratic public culture. But why should we think that the account of freedom and equality contained in Rawls's rather Kantian conception of moral personality is embedded in some way in our liberal democratic practices and institutions? Since Rawls offers no description and analysis of the particular shared political practices, institutions, or aspirations within which the moral personality is embedded, it is hard to avoid the conclusion that he simply writes his conception of moral personality into democratic public culture, rather than discovers it there.

Rawls's later theory desperately needs an extended examination of democratic public culture, especially since so many of the implications of his conception of moral personality seem, at least at first glance, at odds with powerful currents in American political culture. For example, Rawls's claim that justice reflects general agreements rather than inherent desert follows directly from his Kantian view of personality as the free and rational constructor of moral constraints. This claim continues as a crucial element of the theory of justice defended in his later revisions. But it hardly reflects the predominant view in American political culture. It would not require much study to demonstrate that most Americans think that justice rewards desert in some way and our agreements should, accordingly, seek to reward desert in some way. Yet Rawls states that this separation between desert and justice "seems perfectly obvious," without even considering how widely and strongly Americans are attached to contrary convictions.[35]

In *A Theory of Justice* Rawls also gives short shrift to "considered convictions" that do not agree with his own or with those of most moral philosophers. But in that work he did not explicitly set out to recover the conceptions embedded in an empirically examinable public culture. Once he rests his argument upon such conceptions, then his failure to consider the depth and breadth of un-Kantian and, for that matter, un-Rawlsian principles in our public culture seriously undermines his attempt to provide a more pragmatic grounding for his theory.

Sometimes, however, Rawls waffles and suggests that his "Kantian view . . . hopes to bring to awareness a conception of the person and of social cooperation conjectured to be implicit in that [democratic] culture, *or at least congenial to* its deepest tendencies when properly expressed and presented" (emphasis added).[36] It is a far weaker claim to suggest his moral conceptions are "congenial to" rather than latent, implicit, or embedded in democratic public culture. It implies no precommitment on our part to Rawls's Kantian interpretation of the democratic conception of moral personality. It merely suggests that Rawls's moral conceptions fit well with a democratic public culture. Such a qualification absolves Rawls of the obligation to offer evidence that we do indeed accept a particular conception of moral identity as participants of a democratic public culture. He can then simply offer his theory as a reconstruction of democratic public life that he expects or hopes most citizens will find persuasive.

But by watering down in this way his claims about the conceptions and principles embedded in our public life, Rawls loses his claim upon the attention of those, and there are many, who do not find his reconstruction of their public life congenial. The reason for saying that moral conceptions are "embedded in" rather than merely "congenial to" our public life is to suggest that even those who explicitly deny those conceptions implicitly rely on them while participating in our public life. Rawls can count on finding a "deeper basis of agreement" among us only because he assumes that we do indeed implicitly rely on these conceptions. Without the claim that these conceptions are actually embedded in our public life, Rawls would have to await the reaction to his philosophic reconstruction of democratic practice in order to judge whether there is any deeper basis of agreement among us. Rawls's argument rests upon reminding us of something we already are, rather than persuading us to become something we might be. He calls on us to revise our judgments about what we should be and do in light of our deepest convictions about who we are as participants in a democratic public culture.

In principle at least, Rawls's conception of our shared moral identity is more realistic than Kant's: it can, unlike Kant's conception, be subject to empirical examination and confirmation. But Rawls himself neither derives that conception from reflection upon our public culture nor seeks to examine public practices in order to confirm his claim. He merely superimposes his philosophically designed conception upon something he calls our public culture. Like so many philosophers who have turned in recent years from abstract argument to social practice in order to justify their claims, Rawls miraculously rediscovers philosophic conceptions in nonphilosophic practices.[37] His turn to social practice was dictated at least in part by a desire to avoid the unrealistic and a priori picture of moral personality advanced by Kant. But in its place, Rawls simply advances an equally unrealistic and a priori conception of democratic public culture.

The theoretical problem with Kantian liberalism, I have argued, lies in its unrealistic assumptions about our shared identity rather than in unrealistic assumptions about our dissociation from each other. As a result, far from fearing that Kantian liberalism promotes and reinforces the dissolution of our sense of community, I fear instead that it promotes and reinforces a set of moral dispositions that tends to make us insensitive to the different ways in which various members of our political community conceive of themselves.

Kantian liberals believe that by abstracting from natural and social contingencies we can reach an identity that we truly share with others. In representing our own moral identity, they believe, we can represent the identity of others as well. This assertion about our ability to reach a common moral identity represents the Kantian liberals' most characteristic contribution to social contract theory. Earlier contractarians argue that, if we do not accept their conclusions about the principles and practices we would choose were we free of actual social and political constraints, we are either illogical and imprudent in our reasoning or we are still constrained by reliance on actual political practices and institutions. Kantian liberals like Kant and Rawls build on this approach but add another claim against their opponents. Those who fail to accept their conclusion are not only irrational, they are also untrue to themselves, that is, to their true identity as free and equal moral actors. Kantian liberals argue that if we make rational judgments from the standpoint provided by our shared moral identity, then we will choose liberal principles and practices. Individuals who disagree do not know their true moral selves. They fail to recognize what Rawls calls their "highest-order" interest in the realization of the powers they possess as moral persons.

Since, as Montesquieu pointed out long ago, "in all countries and governments, people wish for morality," such an appeal to our shared moral identity as the grounding for political principles has considerable rhetorical appeal, especially in a democracy.[38] Who would want to deny that they and their fellow citizens are equal moral actors? Unfortunately, however, this appeal can inspire unjustified confidence that widely held or socially dominant viewpoints do not represent impositions upon those who protest against them. One need not worry as much about imposing one's conclusions on others if one thinks that, after abstracting from one's own particular characteristics, one reaches an identity that one shares with others and that provides an uncontroversial starting point for political reasoning.

Moreover, Kantian liberals assume that we can reach this shared identity on our own, rather than through shared deliberation with others who might remind us of the ways in which moral identities and perceptions may differ among individuals with different backgrounds and social experiences. This is a necessary assumption for Kantian liberals, if they wish to maintain their substantive claims about moral identity. If we could not reach our shared moral identity on the basis of our own efforts at abstraction, then it would make little sense to describe this identity as that of free and equal actors expressing their independence from natural and social contingencies. If one needed a favorable setting—a setting that required, for example, relative self-sufficiency or familiarity with the variety of moral perspectives in one's community—in order to reach our shared moral identity, then moral personality would be contingent upon social and natural circumstances.[39] Kantian liberals thus must resist the introduction of any social prerequisites for the achievement of the proper moral standpoint for political reasoning, even if these prerequisites aim at increasing their openness to the kinds of differences they affirm and set out to protect.

Kantian liberals insist that we base our fundamental political structures upon a minimal conception of moral personality precisely because they do not want to impose their conceptions on others. Indeed, their claim that they avoid imposing their conceptions on others contributes to the popularity of their theories. For example, even Susan Moeller Okin, who criticizes Rawls for ignoring the gender bias in his language and concepts, celebrates "the brilliant idea of the original position" as a conception that "forces us to question our shared understandings from all points of view" and requires "a greater capacity to identify with others than is normally characteristic of liberalism."[40] Rawls has simply failed, in Okin's analysis, to go far enough in identifying and abstracting from the consequences of contingent social and natural characteristics such as gender.

I suggest, on the contrary, that the limitations Okin discovers in Rawls's approach represent the limitations of the one-sided approach to identifying with others characteristic of Kantian liberalism, rather than a failure to carry this approach to its logical conclusion. In his influential essay on equality, Bernard Williams rightly suggests that the notion that every individual is "owed the effort at identification" is a key element of contemporary, liberal conceptions of moral equality. But in what does such an "effort at identification" consist? Each individual, Williams suggests, "is to be abstracted from certain conspicuous structures of inequality" and each individual is owed an effort at "seeing the world from his perspective."[41]

Williams presents this elaboration of the "effort at identification" we owe each other without noting that they represent two kinds of mental effort, not a single one. One way of identifying with others is to abstract from their and our particular identities so that we can imagine ourselves experiencing the treatment they receive. This form of identification with others plays a major role in some of the most familiar liberal practices and institutions. Nevertheless, it does not allow us to "see the world from [the] perspective" of other individuals. It merely allows us to imagine ourselves receiving the treatment we see others receiving. In order to see the world from their perspective, rather than merely sympathetically experience their suffering, we would have to identify the most salient differences between our ways of looking at the world and theirs and then proceed to examine our own conceptions from their perspective. By abstracting from particularity, we try to avoid imposing things on others we would not want imposed on ourselves. By trying to view our own conceptions from the particular perspective of others we try to identify things that might amount to impositions on others even though we do not ordinarily recognize them as impositions. The "effort at identification" that Williams and most liberals recommend demands both of these approaches to identifying with others.

Rawls's original position, like Kantian liberalism in general, commends itself to social critics like Okin because it demands that a great effort be made to identify and abstract from the particular features of our own identity. But Kantian liberals and their followers usually fail to recognize that this is an inherently one-sided approach to identifying with others.[42] Kantian liberals do not rule out efforts at sympathetic reconstruction of others' perspectives on the world. But they do give a privileged moral place to abstraction from particularity in political reasoning. They insist that we occupy a *moral* perspective on the world only when we abstract from particularity in order to reach our common moral identity. We may also want to identify the distinctive features of others' perspectives on the world in order to be more sensitive in the way we deal with others. But such sensitivity has no place in the determination of moral judgments on basic political questions, according to the Kantian liberal view. It represents, at best, a postmoral corrective to the judgments we make from a moral perspective.

Okin sees Rawls's original position as a means of encouraging individuals, especially the males who ordinarily dominate theoretical and practical discussion of political principles, to consider hitherto ignored conceptions that grow out of women's perspective on the world. I agree that by making an effort to occupy the particular standpoints held by members of different classes, races, cultures, and genders, liberals could improve their conceptions. Moreover, such improvement need not only be negative in character, such as the removal of otherwise unnoticed forms of social exclusion. As Okin herself encourages us to recognize, it can also be positive—for example, the discovery of otherwise ignored and valuable means of promoting political cohesion. To improve our moral and political conceptions in this way requires that we take the particular perspectives of different groups in our community as a source of moral insight.

But that is precisely what Kantian liberalism rules out. For Kantian liberals such as Rawls, moral conceptions (or at least those moral conceptions that ground political principles) are those that we derive from our universal and shared identity as free and equal moral actors. Insights derived from efforts to occupy diverse standpoints within our community represent, at best, practical correctives to moral insights. By privileging abstraction from particularity as a path to moral insight, Kantian liberalism erects an important barrier to the broadening and improvement of our conceptions that Okin wants to use Rawls's theory to promote. As long as they identify the moral point of view per se with abstraction from particular features of our identities, then it will only be with great reluctance that individuals who seek moral insight will make an effort to occupy the specific standpoints held by members of different groups. They may seek to identify with others by abstracting from their own identity in order to imagine experiencing the treatment that others receive. But they will not be inclined to seek moral insight by trying to see their own conceptions from the particular perspective of others, since their principles teach them that universality is the only legitimate path to the construction of moral conceptions.

Moreover, Kantian liberals' moral privileging of abstraction from particularity diminishes the value of conclusions they draw from their attempts to reason from a universally shared standpoint. For we cannot abstract from contingent features of our own identity unless we recognize them as such. But it is very often the case that we can only recognize them as such by examining our own conceptions from another's point of view. If we feel morally constrained not to dwell on the distinctive features of our own and others' perspectives on the world, then we will be much more likely to treat particular conceptions we hold as part of our common moral identity. Abstraction from particularity thus works hand in hand with the identification and consideration of particularity to avoid unreasonable impositions of our conceptions on others. Any approach that morally privileges one over the other is bound to increase such impositions and thus work against one of liberalism's major goals.

It might seem that I am demanding far more from Kantian liberals than we should reasonably expect in the construction of a liberal theory, such as neutral political outcomes as well as neutral political procedures. Rawls, following a suggestion made by Charles Larmore, wisely eschews claims about neutral outcomes for his theory of justice. He insists, instead, that he aims merely at procedural neutrality, the avoidance of controversial conceptions of the good in the construction and justification of liberal practices and institutions.[43]

I agree that neutrality of outcome is a chimera. Nevertheless, there is a problem with the way in which Rawls and Kant conceive of and construct neutral procedures. Clearly, if neutrality of procedure is to have any worth, then we cannot limit it merely to avoidance of explicit reference to controversial conceptions of the good. We must also seek out the implicit and often unrecognized ways in which procedures can exclude individuals who identify themselves in other ways than our own. But to uncover these implicit forms of exclusion, we must hear the voices of others who do not find themselves in our conceptions—in our conceptions of the *right* as well as of the good—and try to see how our conceptions look from their perspective. The construction of neutral procedures is a task that requires ever-renewed effort and adjustment. In fact, it is through such efforts, through continuing readjustment as new voices are heard and understood, that we go about building the kind of procedures that we describe as neutral in contemporary liberal democracies.

Kantian liberalism treats procedural neutrality as if it is something we can achieve by individual acts of will whereby we abstract from our particular identities. Kant suggests that we can reach such neutrality at any place and time by testing our maxims against the requirements of the categorical imperative. Rawls suggests "that we can, as it were, enter this [the original] position simply by reasoning for principles of justice in accordance with the enumerated restrictions."[44] But if we cannot know what is truly our own without understanding what belongs to others, then even procedural neutrality requires a continuing effort to identify and to occupy perspectives that differ from our own. Kantian liberalism's moral privileging of abstraction from differences thus threatens to diminish the value of the procedural neutrality so important to liberal practices and institutions.

The basic practical problem with Kantian liberalism stems not only from its unrealistic and unjustified assumptions about our shared identity, but from its unrealistic assumptions about the ability of individuals to abstract from their particular identities. Given our greater familiarity with our own conceptions and identity, we are all understandably inclined to treat the points where others differ from us as the deviations from the universal, especially when, consciously or not, we identify our own standpoint with that of a dominant group in the community. Skepticism about the ability of individuals to reach a neutral standpoint on important moral and political issues is one of the reasons that led earlier liberal theorists to try to ground their contractarian theories in shared self-interest rather than on a shared moral identity. The Kantian liberals' move to shared moral identity as the basis for political judgment, however flattering it may be to our self-esteem, introduces the possibility of forms of domination excluded by earlier forms of liberal contractarianism.

Those who disagree with the conclusions of earlier contractarian theorists are told that they are reasoning improperly. It is at least open to them to argue that liberal theories fail to express a universal form of reasoning because such theories exclude what is fundamental to their own identity as individuals. In contrast, opponents of Kantian liberal theories are told that they do not know *who they are* as moral beings. They receive a figurative pat on the back informing them that they really do share the moral identity ascribed to them and would recognize that fact if they kept their minds open and stuck around long enough to be persuaded.[45]

There is, of course, a considerable risk that we are imposing an identity on others anytime we make the slightest suggestion that we know others better than they know themselves. That risk becomes enormous when we make our determinations about the identity of others without even considering their own opinions about their identities. In effect, this is what Kantian liberals do. By means of a process of internal and solitary deliberation, they determine the fundamental moral identity shared by all members of their community. Consideration of the opinions of others about their moral identity plays no role in that determination. How could those who do not see themselves in the Kantian liberals' conception of moral personality convince their opponents that this conception is an imposition upon them? Only by getting them to view this conception through their eyes. But that is precisely what the Kantian liberals' approach to moral and political deliberation cannot allow.

Were Kantian liberals to allow voices expressing different particular perspectives on their moral conceptions to enter into their moral deliberations, they might discover that their own conception of moral identity is far more particular and exclusive than they think it is. Does the Kantian liberals' association of morality with universality itself represent a shared conception in our political community? Not, for example, if Carol Gilligan and other students of women's moral experience are correct. For they suggest a very different conception of moral reasoning is common among many American women.[46] Does the Kantian liberal conception of moral identity rest upon a relatively male Protestant cultural experience? It may or may not. But we cannot even begin to answer such questions if we are not allowed to consider the unique perspectives of men and women—or Protestants, Catholics, and Jews—in our fundamental moral deliberation.

Kantian liberals are certainly skeptical about the universality of conceptions of the good. But they abandon such skepticism when it comes to questions of moral identity and conceptions of the right. Nevertheless, the same reasons that lead us to be skeptical about the possibility of reaching some common conception of the good by abstracting from our particular conceptions should lead us to be skeptical about reaching a common conception of rightness and moral identity by the same means. Such skepticism, I believe, is an important support for liberal theories and practices that Kantian liberalism abandons. I am thinking here of the liberalism of Montaigne, Montesquieu, and Mill, a liberalism that was deeply aware of the distasteful consequences of human pretensions to moral certainty. Precisely because they recognized the variety of ways in which different kinds of experiences shape our moral identities, these thinkers insisted that our moral conceptions should always be kept open to correction on the basis of others' opinions. Moreover, such skepticism need not be merely negative in its effects. It can help justify liberal institutions and practices that create opportunities to give at least some voice to the protests of those who experience our conceptions as an imposition rather than as a liberation.

Kant, for one, fought skepticism about moral freedom and our shared noumenal identity precisely because he feared it would lead to diminished respect for human beings and their rights. But Kant's well-known "admiration and awe" for our "invisible self" or moral "personality"[47] can also lead us to ignore ways in which we disrespect and dominate other human beings, unless it is balanced by a skeptical disposition that leads us to recognize our need of others to correct the limitations of our own conceptions. Rawls's conception of moral personality lacks Kant's poetic reverence. But it needs a similar kind of balancing precisely in order to serve Rawls's genuinely liberal goals.

Liberals need to promote dispositions toward both abstracting from particularity and recognizing it as a valuable corrective to our own limitations. We can derive the need for these two kinds of dispositions from the claim, accepted by most liberals, that we owe each other, at least, an "effort at identification." Kantian liberals, I believe, accept this claim, but pursue it in a one-sided and potentially self-defeating fashion. In this chapter I have sought to identify and suggest ways of correcting their one-sided account of liberal theory and practice.

Notes

1

Michael Sandel, *Liberalism and the Limits of Justice* (Cambridge: Cambridge University Press, 1982), p. 174 and passim.

2

Sandel, *Liberalism and the Limits of Justice*, 1; Victor Seidler, *Kant, Respect, and Injustice* (London: RKP, 1986), pp. 13–14.

3

I add this qualification to take into account Rawls's revisions of his theory of justice in his recent essays, which I shall discuss at some length below.

4

Robert Paul Wolff, *The Poverty of Liberalism* (Boston: Beacon, 1969), pp. 191–92.

5

Kant, *Critique of Practical Reason,* trans. Lewis White Beck (Indianapolis: Bobbs-Merrill, 1956), pp. 15–35.

6

See, especially, H. E. Jones, *Kant's Principle of Personality* (Madison: University of Wisconsin Press, 1971).

7

This distinction between forms of duty supports the dichotomy between justice and virtue that Kant uses to divide his *Metaphysics of Morals* into two parts: *The Metaphysical Elements of Justice* and *The Doctrine of Virtue*.

8

Kant, *Fundamental Principles of the Metaphysics of Morals,* trans. T. K. Abbot (Indianapolis: Bobbs-Merrill, 1949), pp. 50–52.

9

Kant's followers, especially Fichte, Schiller, Schelling, and the young Hegel, whom I have described as "left Kantians," did not accept this limitation. They sought, unlike Kant, to try to "realize," that is, bring into the phenomenal world, Kant's conceptions of autonomy and the kingdom of ends. See Bernard Yack, *The Longing for Total Revolution* (Princeton: Princeton University Press, 1986), chap. 3.

10

Kant, *The Metaphysical Elements of Justice,* trans. John Ladd (Indianapolis: Bobbs-Merrill, 1965), p. 80.

11

Ibid., pp. 76–77.

12

Ibid., pp. 35–36.

13

John Rawls, "The Priority of the Right and Ideas of the Good," *Philosophy and Public Affairs* 17 (1988): 251–76.

14

John Rawls, *A Theory of Justice* (Cambridge, Mass.: Harvard University Press, 1971), p. 255. There is a lively controversy about the degree to which Rawls is correct in giving his theory of justice a Kantian interpretation. See, among other articles, Andrew Levine, "Rawls's Kantianism," *Social Theory and Practice* 3 (1974–75): 47–64; O. Johnson, "The Kantian Interpretation of the Original Position," *Ethics* 85 (1974–75): 58–66; and Stephen Darwell, "A Defence of the Kantian Interpretation of the Original Position," *Ethics* 86 (1975–76): 164–70. More recently, see David Heyd, "How Kantian Is Rawls's 'Kantian Constructivism,'" in Yirmiahu Yovel, ed., *Kant's Practical Philosophy Reconsidered* (Dordrecht: Kluwer, 1989), pp. 196–212. Rawls himself has suggested that we think of his theory of justice as analogous to Kantian moral theory, rather than in agreement with it; see especially "Kantian Constructivism in Moral Theory," *Journal of Philosophy* 77 (1980): 515–72. Unfortunately, when describing the similarity of his position to Kant's theory, Rawls reverts to the language of agreement, as when he suggests that his doctrine "sufficiently resembles Kant's in enough fundamental respects so that it is far closer to his view than to the other traditional moral conceptions" (ibid., p. 517). It seems to me that Rawls is right to suggest that his theory of justice is merely analogous to Kant's moral theory, but that Rawls himself has not thought through the analogy and thus can only point to the apparent agreement of the two doctrines. In this chapter I try to show what is truly analogous in the two doctrines: a structure whereby we move from a universally shared identity, arrived at by means of abstraction from particularity, to liberal political conclusions.

15

John Rawls, "Justice as Fairness: Political Not Metaphysical," *Philosophy and Public Affairs* 15 (1985): 223–51, esp. pp. 237–39.

16

Ibid., p. 237.

17

Rawls, *A Theory of Justice,* pp. 574, 255. Rawls insists at one point (p. 560) that it is "not aims, but principles that reveal our nature."

18

David Heyd, relying on Rawls's later interpretation of these claims, suggests that Rawls tries to distinguish himself from Kant by describing our conceptions of moral personality rather than our "nature" as moral persons. See Heyd, "How Kantian is Rawls's 'Kantian Constructivism'?," p. 202. It seems to me, however, that Rawls in his later essays is, at best, correcting the clear implications of the language he used to describe our moral "nature" in *A Theory of Justice*. In any case, as I argue below, even with such a correction, Rawls still bases his arguments upon a claim about a shared moral identity that preexists our deliberations about principles of justice. He merely shifts the source of that identity from our nature as moral persons to our "democratic public culture."

19

Rawls, *A Theory of Justice,* p. 255.

20

Rawls, "Justice as Fairness," pp. 223–25, 231; "The Priority of Right," p. 255.

21

This is also noted by Richard Arneson in his introduction to a recent *Ethics* symposium on Rawls's later work. See Arneson, "Introduction," *Ethics* 99 (1989): 695–710.

22

Rawls, "Kantian Constructivism," pp. 525–26, 533, 547; "Justice as Fairness," p. 334.

23

Rawls, "Kantian Constructivism," pp. 518–19; "Justice as Fairness," p. 226; "The Idea of an Overlapping Consensus," *Oxford Journal for Legal Studies* 1 (1987); "The Priority of the Right," p. 256.

24

Rawls, "Kantian Constructivism," p. 531.

25

In other words, the structure of Rawls's liberal theory still remains analogous to Kant's in that it proceeds from a shared moral identity reached by means of abstraction from particularity to liberal conclusions. Rawls's theory of justice remains analogous in form to Kant's liberal theory even while it departs from Kantian universalism.

26

This emphasis also reflects the origins of Rawls's theory in a solution to a rational choice bargaining game. See Robert Paul Wolffe, *Understanding Rawls* (Princeton: Princeton University Press, 1977).

27

Kant, *Critique of Pure Reason,* trans. N. K. Smith (New York: St. Martin's Press, 1965), pp. 28–29.

28

Rawls, "The Basic Structure as Subject," *American Philosophical Quarterly* 14 (1977): 159–65, and *A Theory of Justice,* p. 256.

29

Rawls, *A Theory of Justice,* pp. 255–56.

30

Moreover, assertions about our nature as human beings are a particularly inappropriate way of justifying Rawls's claim about our identity as free and equal moral actors, since, following Kant, Rawls understands that identity as being based upon independence from natural contingencies and social accident. In effect, Rawls justifies making independence from natural contingencies central to our identity as moral actors by telling us to be true to our nature. But if it is independence from natural contingencies that characterizes moral personality, then why should we treat the contingency of our species' natural constitution as an authoritative guide to what we should be? Rawls does not examine such problems because, it seems to me, his assertions about human nature act in his theory more as a placeholder for an absent justification than as that justification itself.

31
Rawls, "Justice as Fairness," pp. 238–39.

32
Rawls, "Kantian Constructivism," pp. 519, 517; "Justice as Fairness," p. 239.

33
Richard Rorty, "The Priority of Democracy to Philosophy," in M. Peterson and R. Vaughan, eds., *The Virginia Statute for Religious Freedom* (Cambridge: Cambridge University Press, 1988), p. 261.

34
Rawls is careful to distinguish his position on our highest-order interest in realizing our moral powers from Kant's position on autonomy. Kant, he suggests, made the pursuit of moral autonomy a "comprehensive" principle against which we should measure the value of every practice and aspiration. Rawls, in contrast, limits his claim about our desire to realize our moral powers as autonomous personalities to a claim about the identity of persons who judge the suitability of basic political principles. Nevertheless, his "political" conception of moral personality is decidedly more Kantian in the privileged place accorded development of our moral powers than his prepolitical conception in *A Theory of Justice* with its amoral conception of the primary goods all individuals seek.

35
Rawls, "Kantian Constructivism," p. 551.

36
Ibid., p. 569.

37
Rawls is certainly not alone in reading philosophic conceptions into social practice even while turning to social practice as the basis of moral and political conceptions. Alasdair MacIntyre, for example, does not hesitate to interpret contemporary political debate about justice as a debate between followers of Rawls and Nozick. Likewise, MacIntyre describes fifth-century political debate in Athens as a confrontation between "the goods of excellence and the goods of cold effectiveness"—which he glosses as a debate between Thucydidean expediency and Platonic moralism—rather than as the more obvious and less philosophical confrontation between oligarchs and democrats we find in the historical record. See Alasdair MacIntyre, *After Virtue,* 2d ed. (Notre Dame: University of Notre Dame Press, 1984), chap. 17, and *Whose Justice, Which Rationality?* (Notre Dame: University of Notre Dame Press, 1988), p. 42. Like Rawls, MacIntyre simply assumes, without actually examining actual social and political conflicts such as that between oligarchs and democrats in Athens, that the conflicts between philosophic conceptions he describes actually arise out of social and political practice.

38
Charles Louis de Secondat de Montesquieu, *L'esprit des lois,* in *Oeuvres complètes,* 2 vols. (Dijon: Gillimard, 1951), 2:227–28. Intellectuals, however, unlike most people, do not always "wish for morality." They tend to go through cycles of rejection and celebration of reliance on moral principles. The success of Rawls's theory of justice and the revival of Kantian liberalism owes something to the turn in the cycle to celebration of moral principle among Anglo-American intellectuals that occurred during the late 1960s and 1970s.

39
Victor Seidler perceptively notes that Kant, in spite of his philosophic premises, recognized the importance of social prerequisites for autonomy in his much-reviled doctrine of passive citizenship for servants and others who

lack social independence. See Seidler, *Kant, Respect, and Injustice,* pp. 111–20.

40
Susan Moeller Okin, "Justice and Gender," *Philosophy and Public Affairs* 16 (1987): 65; Okin, *Justice, Gender, and the Family* (New York: Basic Books, 1989), pp. 101–09.

41
Bernard Williams, "The Idea of Equality," in *Problems of the Self* (Cambridge: Cambridge University Press, 1973), pp. 236–37.

42
Okin assumes that this one-sidedness can be corrected by adding an awareness of the differences in perspective shaped by gender roles and identities (*Justice, Gender, and the Family,* pp. 102, 108–09). But to bring such an awareness into a Kantian liberal approach, like Rawls's, would threaten its basic method (abstraction from particular identities) of reaching a shared moral identity upon which to ground our principles of justice. Okin's suggestions, I agree, would improve Rawls's conception of moral deliberation, but they would also require him to give up the Kantian form of liberalism to which he seems so strongly attached.

43
Rawls, "The Priority of the Right," pp. 262–63; Charles Larmore, *Patterns of Moral Complexity* (Cambridge: Cambridge University Press, 1987), pp. 42–47.

44
Rawls, "Justice as Fairness," pp. 238–39.

45
"It is natural to ask why . . . we should take any interest in these principles, moral or otherwise. The answer is that the conditions embodied in the description of the original position are ones that we do in fact accept. Or if we do not, then perhaps we can be persuaded to do so by philosophic reflection" (Rawls, *A Theory of Justice,* p. 21; see also p. 257).

46
Carol Gilligan, *In a Different Voice: Psychological Theory and Women's Development* (Cambridge, Mass.: Harvard University Press, 1982). See also Gilligan, et al., *Mapping the Moral Domain* (Cambridge, Mass.: Harvard University Press, 1989), p. xvii.

47
Kant, *Critique of Practical Reason,* p. 166.

Chapter 11

The Limits of Autonomy:
Karl Marx's Kant Critique

William James Booth

In an earlier work I set out Kant's moral and political thought as a viable alternative to the "Promethean humanism" of Marx and his twentieth-century followers.[1] Among my contentions was that Kant, in placing a credible theory of the autonomy of the person at the foundation of his contractarian political thought, provided a solid foundation for liberalism as well as the means by which to reveal the failings of a theory that had as its central informing vision the idea of a virtually complete human mastery over nature and society. In this chapter I shall turn the tables—that is, provide a sympathetic reconstruction of Marx's critique of Kantian practical philosophy and argue that there may in fact be good reasons to acknowledge the force of its direction, if not of its details.

Marx's few pronouncements on Kant do not seem at first glance to be very promising as a starting point for a philosophical critique of the Kantian idea of autonomy. Consider first Marx's statement in an early (1842) piece, *The Philosophical Manifesto,* that Kant's philosophy "must be rightly regarded as the *German* theory of the French Revolution."[2] This claim is not quite as straightforward as it might appear. When Marx writes that Kant is the "German" philosopher of the French Revolution he intends this as the beginning of a critique of him, a critique fully set out in the following passage from *The German Ideology:*

> The state of affairs in Germany at the end of the last century is fully re-
> flected in Kant's *Critik der practischen Vernunft*. While the French bour-
> geoisie, by means of the most colossal revolution that history has ever
> known, was achieving domination and conquering the Continent of Europe,
> while the already politically emancipated English bourgeoisie was revolu-
> tionising industry . . . the impotent German burghers did not get any fur-
> ther than "good will." Kant was satisfied with "good will" alone, even if it
> remained entirely without result. . . . Kant's good will fully corresponds to
> the impotence, depression and wretchedness of the German burghers. . . .
> Neither he [Kant], nor the German middle class, whose whitewashing

spokesman he was, noticed that these theoretic ideas of the bourgeoisie had as their material basis interests and a *will* that was conditioned and determined by the material relations of production. . . . He made the materially motivated determinations of the will of the French bourgeoisie into *pure* self-determination of "free will," of the will in and for itself.[3]

On its face what this passage offers us is a fairly crude historical materialist account of Kant's political and moral philosophies that seeks their roots in the limitations of eighteenth-century Prussian society and, insofar as it is critical of them, its weapon consists of an unflattering comparison between the audacious exploits of the French and English bourgeoisie and their "impotent" German confreres. No doubt Marx's intention in the above-quoted remarks is precisely an explanation of the ideology of Germany in light of its economic and political undevelopment. I do not wish, however, to follow that well-traveled, and not very useful, path into the debate over philosophy as ideology. Rather, I intend to pursue a different theme: to tease out of Marx's praise of the English and French bourgeoisie and his mockery of the good, free will of German philosophy the sense of his critique of the Kantian concept of autonomy. This endeavor involves, of course, a voyage considerably beyond the small compass of the *German Ideology* passage and, I suspect, beyond arguments that can be said with certainty to be canonically Marxist. Nevertheless, his critique serves as a beginning and, as I hope to show, a valuable one for understanding the limits of the Kantian idea of autonomy. In the pages that follow, then, I shall sketch the Marxist and Kantian ideas of autonomy and suggest some of the critical paths that flow from their encounter. I shall then elaborate upon two of those strands, namely, the critique of Kantian autonomy as it is reflected in his theory of nature and freedom and in his understanding of coercion and autonomy.

Autonomy

That Kant and Marx are both moving within a philosophical tradition concerned with the concept of autonomy has been observed by commentators as have also some of the substantial differences in their notions of freedom and will. Consider the following statements by Marx: "The criticism of religion ends with the teaching that *man is the highest being for man,* hence with the *categorical imperative to overthrow all relations* in which man is a debased, enslaved, forsaken, despicable being" and "The criticism of religion disillusions man to make him think and act and shape his reality like a man who . . . has come to reason, so that he will revolve round himself and therefore round his true sun."[4] The latter passage sets out what Marx elsewhere alludes to as a "Copernican" revolution, that man must "revolve round himself," that is, no longer live under the tutelage of an imagined higher being but rather be guided by his own, human, reason.[5] The first passage describes the "categorical imperative" that flows from the Copernican revolution, "to overthrow all relations" in which man is a debased and enslaved creature. The Copernican insight, then, that man is the highest being for man leads to the imperative to remove those conditions that degrade and enslave him: the criticism of religion (like the critique of pure reason) brings about the former conclusion, but there it also reaches its limits. What is required therefore is a critique of practice (or practical reason), for only in the practical sphere is the individual's autonomy and his status as the highest being fully realized.[6]

However textually thin and rare Marx's pronouncements on freedom may be, we must venture here to draw out their sense, if only to establish a background for his comparatively rich discussion of the various ways in which that freedom is limited. In a passage (crossed out by Marx) of the *German Ideology,* we find the following remarks on freedom, materialist and idealist: materialist freedom, Marx writes, is "power, as domination over the circumstances and conditions in which an individual lives"; the idealist conception of freedom speaks of "self-determination, riddance of the real world, as merely imaginary freedom of the spirit."[7] Freedom, then, is "power," but power of a certain kind, that exercised over the world, its "circumstances and conditions" and not the mere "negative power to avoid this or that."[8] Moral freedom, on the other hand, by which Marx means both Christian and Kantian morality, seeks the "riddance of the world" and the autonomy of the "spirit"—it is, Marx writes in *The Holy Family,* "impuissance mise en action."[9] Freedom is power over external circumstances, but it is not, Marx makes clear, an end in itself. It is rather the prerequisite to the self-affirmation or realization of the individual: "the positive power to assert his true individuality," just as the Christian/Kantian freedom of the spirit issues only in self-denial, the restricting of nature in man.[10]

This notion of freedom seems (Marx does not develop explicitly the following ties) related to a sketchy philosophical anthropology that views the human as a purposive, tool-using being. Man's life activity is an object of his will, Marx asserts, and only as such is it capable of being free activity. To be an object of his will, this activity must be subject to his purposes, something that he deliberates about, decides upon, and then acts out. The characteristic life activity in Marx's writings is labor, by which is meant not merely the economically productive expenditure of time and effort but, in a broader sense, creative activity generally. Tools are the medium by which our purposiveness (the more or less constrained capacity of setting the ends of our activities) and power over nature, the external circumstances of our existence, are united. Tool-using labor, then, is an expression of the will, of the ability to set purposes (to determine one's activity as if it were an object), and of the mastery of the external environment which, to the degree that it is more or less extensive, expands or restricts the compass of purposive activity.[11]

The conjunction of these three elements, purposiveness, control over the external world, and self-realization, may best be seen in Marx's celebrated description of communist society: "in communist society, where nobody has one exclusive sphere of activity, but each can become accomplished in any branch he wishes, society regulates the general production and thus makes it possible for me to do one thing today and another tomorrow, to hunt in the morning, . . . criticise after dinner, just as I have a mind to."[12] The social regulation of production indicates control over economic life and that in turn refers to planning in place of the apparent anarchy of the capitalist mode of production and, as is plain throughout Marx's writings, mastery over nature, that is, the growth of human productive forces. This control creates a context in which the person "can do one thing today and another tomorrow," which is to say that the individual's activity is determined neither by natural necessity (gender, physical prowess, and the like) nor by her place in the structure of the capitalist economy (such as the worker with nothing to sell but her labor-power). Self-actualization thus becomes for the first time a real possibility. I can do "as I have a mind to": the characteristic purposiveness of human activity has its restraining bridles removed and becomes an effective force in the world, one whose horizon is not tightly constrained by nature or the social order.

The notion of tool using provides us a key to Marx's concepts of will and freedom. The tool is an instrument of purposive activity, of the capacity that distinguishes persons from animals, that is, the setting of ends or, in short, self-determination, activity as an object of the human will. As an instrument of labor, the tool is also part of the armament of the will ("die Arbeit . . . ist . . . eine Bethätigung, die von seinem Willen abhängt, zugleich Willensäusserung desselben ist"), a means by which it establishes the primacy of man over constraining nature, which struggle is itself among the main negative liberty conditions of self-determination (effective purposiveness) and self-actualization.[13] And, finally, the tool (or, to keep with Marx's vocabulary, the means of production) decisively shapes the social relations of the persons for whom it is the historically given, dominant form of production. The conscious control of the means of production suggests, therefore, that the tool is at once an instrument of liberation (from nature) and something endowed with a history of its own, a force which shapes society quite apart from the will of the latter, until the day arrives when individuals shall become the masters not only of nature but also of the means by which they have established their sovereignty over nature, namely their technology and the edifice of social relations that it molds.

The preceding reconstruction points to some central elements of Marx's idea of autonomy. They are, on the one hand, a notion of autonomy understood as the capacity to set ends for oneself or, in somewhat different words, the ability to make one's activity the object of deliberation. On the other hand, this theory invokes the language of self-realization as the proper end (the positive content) of freedom in an *almost* Aristotelian manner; I say "almost" because the hierarchy of activities at the core of the Aristotelian account finds no expression in Marx, that is, there is no single best life against which others are to be measured.[14] As to the former constellation of ideas, it is possible, if one knits together Marx's notions of labor as an expression of the will and as purposive activity (understood as meaning activity as the object of effective deliberation), to conclude that Marx did indeed have an (inchoate) theory of the freedom of the will as autonomy or self-determination. What I wish to underscore is the image of tool using as the central metaphor in Marx's thinking on autonomy. The reasons for doing so will become more evident as we proceed, but for the present I shall only repeat that the tool-using idea points to a notion of autonomy as a faculty essentially relational in character—between humans and nature, and between themselves—and one therefore fundamentally oriented toward the external environment. This is not to say that Marx entirely neglects what might be called the inner dimension of autonomy, self-mastery. Quite the contrary, in one passage comparing the slave and the wage laborer, Marx writes in praise of the latter: "He *learns to control himself, in contrast to the slave,* who needs a master."[15] Rather, it is to suggest (indirectly) that Marx's view of the constraints placed on human autonomy draws principally on external barriers: nature, time, and relations between persons.

If Marx's idea of autonomy is best seen in the image of man as tool-user, Kant's core concept of autonomy must surely be expressed in the idea of the "morality of intention," of the good will. *Self*-mastery here becomes the ideal, the task set before persons: "to bring all his powers and inclinations under his (that is, reason's) control—hence the command of self-mastery. For unless reason holds the reins of government in its own hands, man's feelings and inclinations assume mastery over him."[16] The capacity to have government over one's own actions rests in the first instance on negative freedom, that is, mere independence from empirical conditions or, to be more exact, on freedom of choice, meaning that one's actions are not directly determined by sensual impulse but are preceded by a choice that reasons in the silence of the passions.[17] The proof of the possibility of an ability to initiate spontaneously (freely) a course of events in a world whose lawlike coherence precludes uncaused causes is the task of the *Critique of Pure Reason,* especially its Third Antinomy and Kant's subsequent commentaries on that Antinomy. I shall not rehearse those arguments here, except to draw attention to Kant's contention that the temporal domain, the forum of man's empirical existence and actions, is bound by the laws of nature in which no room is allowed for the recognition of free causality (the "ought" as a law given independently of nature.) This is one of the powerful philosophical motivations driving Kant's argument back from the world and toward the inner morality of intention.

What Kant terms the positive concept of freedom is the power of a rational being to act according to concepts and, in particular, in accordance with the idea of law. That is, the will is able to determine itself, drawing its direction from the intrinsic legislation of practical reason. Autonomy, in short, is "the property the will has of being a law to itself."[18] And it is just that power, the capacity for self-legislation, that endows man with personality (a notion of central importance both for Kant's moral and political philosophy), that is, the quality of being the subject of attribution, the proper owner, so to speak, of one's own actions.

This idea of the human as an end in him/herself in virtue of his/her autonomy does not, as we shall see (and as has already been intimated in the earlier remark on the Third Antinomy), carry with it the thought that humans are completely or even largely free of determination by nature or that they need become so. Kantian autonomy has a special legislative domain that may best be grasped by considering its opposite condition, namely, heteronomy. The heteronomy of the will is the condition under which the will does not prescribe law for itself but rather has nature make the law. The latter idea, unpacked, amounts to the following: the will is determined to choose a certain action under the "impulsion which the anticipated effect of the action exercises on the will."[19] The object of legislation, then, whether successfully governed by the self or, in cases of the failure of the will, by nature (the anticipated effect), is choice itself. Choice, even of the perverse, heteronomous kind, is free in the sense that it selects among the possible determinants of its operations as well as among the varied strategies for achieving those goals. Humans are, accordingly, distinguished from other creatures by their capacity for strategic behavior (what Kant calls hypothetical imperatives), which indicate an ability both to select ends and to determine optimal routes for the attainment of those ends. But, as George Kelly notes, the person who places himself under the causality of nature is, for Kant, evil.[20] At the very least, in making the object of desire the determinant of his choice, he has abused that freedom by denying it its full, self-legislative, use. If the significant restraint on autonomy is, as Kant maintains, choice made under the "impulsion" of "anticipated effects," then autonomy, the release from that constraint, amounts to self-mastery understood as self-legislation. Or, to say much the same thing in different words, "inner freedom requires two things of the agent: to be *in control* of himself . . . —that is, to *tame* his agitations and to have *mastery* over himself . . . —that is, to *govern* his obsessions."[21]

Kantian autonomy is concerned above all with the nature of choice and the provenance of the law that is selected as the determining ground of choice.[22] The consequences of this view are twofold. On the one side, it suggests that whatever the barriers may be to action, however effective the external environment may be in thwarting the intentions of agents, autonomy remains unaffected because it is not conceived of as effective causality in the world but as control over the maxims of one's actions. On the other side, this notion of autonomy removes from the consideration of actions any account of their antecedent causes other than, of course, the maxims lying behind them. The former point Kant expresses in these words: "The essence of things does not vary with their external relations; and where there is something which, without regard to such relations, constitutes by itself the absolute worth of man, it is by this that man must be judged. . . . Thus *morality* lies in the relation of actions to the autonomy of the will—that is, to a possible making of universal law by means of its maxims."[23] Autonomy, in brief, is the special character of legislation over choice, the "essence of things" that remains unaffected by external barriers or consequences. The second point is illustrated in Kant's example from the *Critique of Pure Reason,* in which the behavior of a liar is examined. That his behavior may be traced to a variety of preceding causes—bad education, coarse friends, and so forth—is not denied by Kant. Nevertheless, this individual is held fully culpable for his deed because "we regard reason as a cause that irrespective of all the above mentioned empirical conditions *could* have determined, and *ought* to have determined, the agent to act otherwise." The "causality of reason," Kant concludes, is "complete in itself."[24]

The governing concept of autonomy that emerges from Kant's line of reasoning is one profoundly indifferent to the constraining impact of the world upon the will's causality. One reason for this we have already suggested: that given the particular, law-governed character of all phenomenal events (nature, human and inanimate), Kant's analysis is forced to search for the possibility of freedom in a domain that is not determined by the laws that rule space and time. What this means is that the world of the empirical agent must be put aside in order to disclose his or her true autonomy. We are now in a position to suggest a second Kantian motivation: it is the faculty of choice and self-legislation that marks human beings as distinctive in relation to the rest of nature. The great dividing line between the sort of being that man is and the rest of creation is the good will, the proper form of intention—that rule of conduct which is self-determined rather than being set by nature. This good will is fully self-sufficient: it is its own cause and is not subordinate to further purposes or objects. Kant does not argue that humans can or ought to be indifferent to the course of events in the world. Rather, it is his contention that the "essence of things," as it pertains to the capacities of human will, is contained in the idea of free and self-legislated choice. The uprightness of the will, to play on a phrase from Kant's appropriately Jobian essay *The Failure of All Philosophical Theodicies,* can, because of its self-sufficiency, withstand inefficacy and it *must* (and can), at the other end of the causal spectrum, resist efforts to reduce its deliberations to antecedent empirical causation.

The understanding of autonomy as internal legislation over choice, overcoming the "fetters" of "impulse,"[25] is one target of Marx's mocking attack on the Kantian good will. Marx argues that there are other fetters, external ones, which severely restrict human autonomy and that the latter cannot be fully realized without control over the world as well as over the maxims of choice. This critique is particularly evident in his counter to Kant's notion of the relationship between man and nature. Where Kant's concept of autonomy ventures beyond its principal location in the legislative activity of the will and moves into relations between persons, Marx's critique is that Kant's theory leads him to dismiss a major source of compulsion that is compatible with (or, more strongly, emerges from) contractual freedom.

The Impact of the World: The Constraints of Nature

Marx's aversion to the idea of the "actus purus,"[26] to pure undetermined activity, is misconstrued if it is taken simply as one facet of his materialism, and its meaning is perverted if it is read as praise of the determined condition of the human will. Marx's point is rather that the more that will is understood as the good will, as a force undetermined and omnipotent within its own small compass, the more we are blinded to the natural and other limits placed on the will, and consequently we are rendered incapable of discovering (and overcoming) the true source of these restraints.[27] Clearly implicit in Marx's image of man as a tool-using being is the thought that nature is one such constraint and that the confrontation between man and nature is an elemental characteristic of human existence. This notion is not only a central part of Marx's explanatory apparatus, but it also forms a key moment in what might (loosely) be called his normative vision, for only when the "impact of the world . . . is under the control of the individuals themselves" will the "realization of the individual" cease to be a mere ideal.[28]

The idea of man as a tool-using creature suggests, then, a picture of the human being as engaged in an unceasing struggle with nature, in which the level of the latter's power is directly a consequence of the state of development of the productive forces, that is, the instruments with which humans seek to govern their metabolism with nature. Where that technology is weak, which is especially the case when the productive forces are themselves natural (for example, fields and oxen in agrarian societies), individuals are "subservient to nature," that is, subject to its vagaries and laws.[29] In a striking passage, Marx applies this notion to Indian rural society: "They subjugated man to external circumstances instead of elevating man the sovereign of circumstances. . . . They transformed a self-developing social state into never changing natural destiny, and thus brought about a brutalising worship of nature, exhibiting its degradation in the fact that man, the sovereign of nature, fell down on his knees in adoration of Kanuman, the monkey, and Sabbala, the cow."[30]

The "impact of the world," as Marx calls it, amounts, of course, to more than the degrading worship of nature by its rightful sovereign. In premodern societies, it imposes a natural division of labor on society based typically on gender and physical prowess, and thereby nature assigns, as it were, a position (class membership corresponding to the various divisions of labor) to individuals.[31] Limited productive forces or, what is the same thing, a condition in which nature determines man also yields what Marx terms a natural economy, one with a surplus so small that it is not a market or trading economy but an inward-looking autarkic community. In short, the mastery of nature over human beings leads to a determination of the lives of individuals by criteria not of their own design or choosing and to the forging of a stagnant, nonuniversal community.

Capitalism, in which production and the unlimited expansion of productive forces replace mere survival (or self-perpetuation) as the end of human activity, is, on this view, the full development of human mastery over nature and hence the precondition of their autonomy.[32] Nature, for the first time, becomes an object, subjected by science and technology to the satisfaction of human needs. Labor is freed from natural necessity; the division of labor loses its natural character and becomes rather an artifact of a particular (and corrigible) organization of economic activity. Notwithstanding the grand irony at the center of Marx's project—that man under capitalism has subjugated nature only to be ruled in turn by the instruments of that power—it is his contention that the optimal utilization of those forces will bring about a condition in which the negative liberty of the (greatest possible) freedom from nature will be translated into society's and individuals' full conscious control over their activity.

For our purposes what is of interest in the preceding account is not the detail of Marx's analysis nor the plausibility of his vision of communist society. Rather, what needs to be underscored is the intuitively credible idea that where technology is primitive, man's struggle with nature is decided significantly in favor of the latter. In somewhat more concrete terms, we can say that, for example, the amount of time dedicated to survival, to activity required for the bare maintenance of life, is greater where productive forces are weak and that discretion over time is correspondingly smaller. To the extent that technology is typically labor-saving and seeks to supplant muscle-power by instruments, where that technology is primitive we might also expect to find tasks assigned among the community's members according to their physical prowess, the person being, under those circumstances, the principal instrument of production. The division of labor, in short, is there a sort of fate assigned by nature, over which humans exercise only modest control. Relations of subordination within the community are powerfully shaped by these conditions of scarcity and by the necessity (for some large part of the population) of prolonged physical labor. On the face of it, the possibility of subjecting to human choice key features of their existence, that is, time, activity, and relations among themselves, depends if not entirely then at least in some important measure on the ability to control their metabolism with nature. Put in this manner, the conquest of nature is not a Promethean adventure, the transformation of humans into gods and the relentless pursuit of worldly power for its own sake, but is rather the necessary condition of the exercise of choice, of the extension of discretion (and, thereby, autonomy) to manifestly important areas of human existence. The tool, then, is emblematic of the abiding fact of our necessary interchange with nature *and* of our potential to free ourselves from nature's tutelage, that is, to increase the scope of our autonomy.

The Kantian autonomy of intention or choice is not oblivious to the struggle between man and nature. Kant writes movingly of man's initial tutelage and slavish servitude to nature and of the hardships imposed on him by nature.[33] And, in what might be taken as an early version of Marx's notion of man as the "sovereign of nature," Kant speaks of the human destiny as the free exercise of its own powers and indeed of man as the "lord of nature."[34] Yet for all the apparent similarities, Kant's understanding of the relationship between man and nature and of the meaning of that relationship for the question of autonomy is sharply different from Marx's. To grasp the heart of this distinction, let us begin by considering the following sentences from Kant's *Critique of Practical Reason:* "Two things fill the mind with ever new and increasing admiration and awe, the oftener and more steadily we reflect on them: the starry heavens above me and the moral law within me. . . . The former begins at the place I occupy in the external world of sense. . . . The latter begins at my invisible self, my personality. . . . The former view of a countless multitude of worlds annihilates, as it were, my importance as an animal creature. . . . The latter, on the contrary, infinitely raises my worth . . . [as] a life independent of all animality and even of the whole world of sense."[35] The two viewpoints expressed in this passage neatly sum up the relationship of human beings and nature in Kant's thought: on the one hand, as an empirical being, an "animal creature," the human is by no means the most potent or best favored of natural beings; on the other hand, as moral personality man is raised above all nature. Both standpoints, in their different ways, drive Kant to ignore the question of autonomy as it arises from reflection upon the human metabolism with nature.

The first of the above themes, the modesty of the human being as an animal creature in relation to nature, is present throughout Kant's works, precritical and critical alike. Indeed, it is most starkly set out in two early essays on the cataclysmic earthquakes of 1755. There Kant, adopting the spectator's standpoint that characterizes much of his writing on other great events (for example, the French Revolution), asks what is to be learned from such events. And he answers: modesty, that mankind has been taught by these catastrophes not to expect comfort from nature. His pretensions of being only a part of nature while "wanting to be the whole of it," that is, to have its laws subordinated to his wishes, are thereby reduced, and he learns that he must adapt to nature rather than expect it to adapt to him, for example, by reducing (as Kant says the Peruvians had done) the size of the structures he constructs on the earth's surface. But if modesty is one lesson, there is a second and more important one: that humans have a higher purpose than happiness or comfort here in the world.[36]

The "irresistibility" of nature, Kant writes in the third *Critique,* makes us "recognize our own physical impotence, considered as beings of nature."[37] Our "higher purpose," to which we are destined by virtue of our personality, that is, our capacity for freedom, raises us above and makes us independent of nature. But independent in what sense? Consider Kant's analysis of the aesthetic experience of the sublime. The sublime is a feeling awakened in us as we face the mightiest and most terrible exertions of nature. Confronted by these terrors, and in the absence of any moral faculty, that is, a sense of a higher purpose or destiny, the experience would be one of simple fear, a recognition of man as a mere speck on the planet, a vanishing quantity.[38] Now if nature were superior to our ability to resist it, it would have "dominion" over us; but what the experience of the sublime reveals to us, according to Kant, is just such a faculty of resistance, "of judging independently of and a superiority over nature."[39] Our superiority over nature consists in the capacity to judge its exertions independently of our physical relation to it, to subject our impotent physical person to the intelligible person within us, to be courageous in the face of nature. Thus, Kant concludes, "humanity in our own person remains un-humiliated . . . [for] a power is called up in us of regarding as small the things about which we are solicitous (goods, health, life) and of regarding its [nature's] might (to which we are no doubt subjected in respect of these things) as nevertheless without any dominion over us."[40]

This thread binds Kant's aesthetic theory of the sublime and his moral philosophy: that autonomy is principally a function of judgment and that the fetters threatening that autonomy are the "natural impulses" of our own and not external nature, that is, the tendency to submit our exercise of choice to the guidance of such objectives as happiness, prosperity, and so forth. Kant is able consistently to acknowledge the dominion of nature over us in regard to worldly goods, to recognize our trivial position in creation, and, at the same time, to assert the fullness of our autonomy and superiority over nature. This point can be recast in the language of freedom and time. Man as a temporal being is wholly governed by the laws of causality which rule that domain; his actions, in their phenomenal guise, are as law-bound (and determined by the same law) as those of any natural thing, and with sufficient scientific insight we could, Kant maintains, exhaustively predict his actions and map out their antecedent causal conditions.[41] Viewed as a being outside time, as a supersensible being, or *causa noumenon,* the human stands above natural necessity and is the sole author of her actions and therefore an autonomous being. Note that Kant does not deny the might of nature in controlling goods of value to humans. Indeed, that is just the thought underlying the "starry heavens" passage cited above: man, as a phenomenal being, is an insignificant, dominated creature. Mankind's counter to nature is our unassailable capacity to choose and specifically to determine ourselves according to self-prescribed law. This position is vulnerable to a variety of objections, but in the discussion that follows I shall focus on those that could have been penned by Marx.

The first move in such a critique would be the objection that in order for Kant to make his idea of autonomy credible in the light of the dominion of nature (which he himself acknowledges), he must adopt a particularly cramped theory of the self who legislates. One might say that Kant almost concedes this charge when he argues that the legislative self cannot have a history, that it is "temporal unity," a life viewed as a single, freely determined act. The self, on this account, is dissolved into the abstract (universal) self of pure practical reason; it allows of no individuation, no consideration of the rich texture of the person who must act and who most certainly has a history. One consequence of this is a robust (almost exhilarating in its severity) conception of imputation and hence accountability: because one is always capable of choosing the maxim for one's actions, every act is freely committed and thus the agent never bears less than full responsibility for it. That the self who acts in, let us say, an evil manner is a needy being, a creature with a "history" (an antecedent and causally important story) is something that Kant grants; but having allowed for what he might term an empirical anthropology, Kant is forced, by both his theory of knowledge and his attempt to preserve a strenuous concept of freedom against the weakening admixture of empirical incentives and apologies, to an idea of the self that is radically implausible—one that, to use Wittgenstein's phrase, is the "limit of the world—not a part of it."

The Marxist self, such as it can be teased out of his writings, is most definitely a part of the world, the bearer of a history and the subject of constraints. This is not to say that the individual is conceived of as determined in every important regard. While Marx's analysis of the behavior of individuals could be seen, from a Kantian perspective, as far too exculpatory ("I do not by any means depict the capitalist . . . in rosy colours. . . . [But] my standpoint . . . can less than any other make the individual responsible for relations whose creature he remains")[42] because based on a less radical idea of freedom, it is evident that he saw (and sought) a progressive diminution of the constraints on the self as agent: the slave's recognition that he cannot be an article of property, the proletarian's realization that he is master (of a sort) over himself, and, of course, communist man doing "as he has a mind to." Even clearer is that for Marx abstract conceptions of the self are both theoretically ill-founded and, in a sense, normatively perverse. They are theoretically ill-founded precisely because of their universality and their consequent neglect of the specific, malleable determinants of the self: "A Negro is a Negro. He only becomes a slave in certain relations. A cotton-spinning jenny is a machine for spinning cotton. It becomes capital only in certain relations."[43] A proper understanding of the self can only be the endpoint of a dense description of his history, just as social formations, epochs, can only adequately be grasped as the inheritors of their preceding societies and as constrained by the productive forces available to them. The normative objections to abstract conceptions of man are rooted in Marx's most radical individualism and not, I would suggest, in an antihumanism (the Althusserian reading). The textual foundation for this claim is principally the *Critique of the Gotha Program,* where Marx advances the case that doctrines of "equal right" damage persons precisely because their universality must cause them to pass over the irreducible particularity of the individual. But indirect evidence is also to be had across the breadth of Marx's works: from the early critique of the solventlike qualities of money to the crowd of abstract characters (the "bearers" or "functionaries of capital") who populate his political economy and who, in their very abstractness, reveal according to Marx the perverseness of an order that subordinates individuals to the valorization process of capital.

The self of Marxian autonomy is a richer one than that of Kantian moral philosophy: richer in the sense that it is embedded in a world, that it interacts with nature and with other persons; richer also in that it corresponds to the agent that we recognize in the everyday activities of choice that constitute the stuff of moral life, an agent with a formative history, acting within constraints. Marx, like Aristotle—his teacher in so many things—reminds us that the practical is concerned above all with the particular, that man is not by nature self-sufficient, and that the "impact of the world" is a central and inescapable part of human agency. To abstract from the external conditions of freedom may yield a more exalted idea of the self, but when it is that self in its moral life that we wish to understand, the Kantian starting point seems barren.

Let us now turn to the second element of the idea of autonomy, legislation or law. We saw that, for Kant, the realm over which the self legislates, or has clear dominion, is broadly in the choice of maxims by which its behavior is to be determined. By dividing the possible set of maxims into two species, categorical and hypothetical, and binding them to two types of legislation, autonomous and heteronomous—the latter bundle constituting determination by nature, the former self-determination—Kant is able to deploy a concept of choice that abstracts entirely from its preconditions (the self as historical, that is, embedded in a world that exercises an antecedent causal power, of greater or lesser degree, over the activity of the self) as well as from its present constraints. The possibility of freedom of choice is perhaps thereby preserved, but again at a considerable cost, namely its restriction to a completely internal event, the selection of maxims.

Marx's discussion of nature and of the various ways in which it determines human activity provides one alternative to the Kantian approach. We might say that, for Marx, a vital part of autonomy is the magnitude of the choice set, the numbers of areas of importance to human beings over which they exercise effective control. The exclusion of worldly goods from that set on the grounds that they are one and all the objects of heteronomous, that is, base, maxims appears compelling only when it is forgotten that, by conceding them to the dominion of nature, one also constricts the sphere of choice, which is itself an essential part of human independence from nature. Now according to Kant, the only natural fetters that matter are those "impulses" or "sensuous attachments," the perversions of judgment brought about by an attachment to the objects of desire, to the too-much-loved world; correspondingly, freedom of choice is understood as independence from these impulses.[44] Marx, in illuminating the importance of nature's power over man, shows the many ways in which the exercise of choice is substantially restricted by nature, and human autonomy thereby reduced in its scope. His scant portrait of communist society reveals a world in which the power of nonhuman forces has been markedly reduced and the magnitude, the range of autonomy, of human legislation over its own affairs correspondingly increased.

Cast in this manner, the debate between Marx and Kant is not one over "external goods" but rather over the character of choice and whether choice, autonomy, and independence can adequately be grasped apart from a consideration of the extent of the domain over which they are legislative. That restrictions on the choice set are restrictions on autonomy is a plausible assertion, and it underpins Marx's understanding of the human metabolism with nature. Kant's indifference to the choice set beyond that required for the adoption of maxims for behavior cannot be adequately defended against objections of the Marxist sort unless one can make the case (strongly implied by, but not extensively developed in, Kant's own arguments) that freedom of choice construed as the power to select one type of maxim (the categorical imperative) over another (heteronomous maxims) is in some sense so clearly superior to the power of control over other constraints on one's independence that the latter issue can readily be put to one side, with no damage done to the concept of autonomy. I suspect that an effort to make the above argument on Kantian grounds would involve incorporating the conclusion (the distinction between autonomy as command over the adoption of maxims and as command over other constraints on one's independence, coupled with the claimed, though unspecified, superiority of the former over the latter) in the premises of the argument. However that may be, the Kantian notion of legislation as a component of the concept of autonomy appears thin. It is implausibly restricted to judgment as the selection of the right type of maxim, and it embraces neither the variety of ways in which our self-determination is substantially constrained by forces other than our own impulses nor the ways in which we are, or could become, legislative over many of those same forces.

We may accept or reject the detailed catalog of the ways in which, according to Marx, humans are determined by nature at certain stages in the growth of their productive forces. And we may also choose to reject as fantastic or unpalatable (or both) his vision of communist society as the overcoming of many of these restraints. Yet in the former part of his project, Marx's analysis gives rise to serious questions as to whether Kant's according of a privileged (almost exclusively so) position to "impulse" as the principal natural fetter over human's freedom is a coherent or credible understanding of the sources of unfreedom. The second part of that same project, the positive concept of autonomy, suggests that Kant's observation that man is only a part of nature but wants to be the whole of it is perhaps truer than its author realized. Or, more exactly: that the wish to govern nature arises not from a will to power nor from a desire for a merely commodious life or a surfeit of material comforts but from the certainty that autonomy embraces more than self-mastery and must be extended to control over, so far as possible, all those external forces that determine us.

The Impact of the World: Coercion and Freedom

Kant's concept of the person, cast as the foundation for relations of external freedom, contains the following central elements: freedom, equality, and independence. By freedom is understood, in this context, "independence from the constraint of another's will, insofar as it is compatible with the freedom of everyone else."[45] Equality in external relations is taken to mean the reciprocal nature of coercion, that no person can be bound to do more than he in turn can bind others to do or, what amounts to much the same thing, no individual has a prior (natural) and unilateral entitlement to coercive power over others.[46] The third principle, independence, means for Kant the right of each to be her own master in the sense of not owing her existence to others.[47] This latter principle is, as we shall see, laden with consequences for Kant's political thought, and in the form in which he typically presents it, it is an attribute of one type of citizenship (full) and not part of the natural endowment of every member of society, nor is it something to which they are positively entitled (though legislated obstacles to independence would seem, in Kant's argument, to be unjust). Insofar as equality and independence flow from the one innate right, freedom, I shall interpret independence here as stating the principle that since all are born free (and, derivatively, equal) there are no masters or servants by nature; each is his own master because he is not born into a rightful hierarchy of persons.

The *summum malum* which stands behind these three characteristics of the person and against which they are meant to secure individuals is coercion, which Kant defines (as we saw above) as the condition of being subject to the "arbitrary will of another." With Robert Nozick, we may say that to be coerced is, in general terms, to be in a situation where choice is "not fully [one's] own" or, seen from the other side of the relation, it is a condition in which "the will of another is operating or predominant."[48] Since there is no natural rank ordering of humans by which the superior may justly exercise their wills upon the inferior, the wielding of such power is an evil, a violation of the innate right to freedom and its corollaries, unless, among other conditions, it is consented to. Given the propensity of humans to dominate one another a "master" is needed, a public authority to secure individuals against the violence of others, that is, to guarantee their external freedom. This public authority is itself coercive, but since the force it employs is guided by the idea of what the people could have consented to, it counts according to Kant as authorized coercion and hence not the imposition of an arbitrary will on others. Similarly, in relations among members of the society (rather than in their relations to the legislative authority), it is the contractual passing of power from one person to another that constitutes one of the principal sources of the legitimacy of that power, and of its consistency with their status as persons, as free, equal, and independent beings.

Consider now one of Kant's applications of his contract theory: the analysis of the relationship between the household master and his servants. The household in all its relations is, Kant writes, a *Gemeinschaft* of free persons, and yet within that community there is found a property right over persons: the possession of them as external objects, as things, and the "use of them as persons."[49] More precisely, this personal right is "the possession of the will of another" and the capacity to command it to perform specific actions. In light of Kant's concept of the person, it is plain that such a right cannot be innate, that no one is by birth entitled to the power of command over another's will. Rather, that right can only be justly acquired by contract, by the voluntary (and limited) passing of self-mastery from servant to employer. The form of this acquisition is just as it would be in the case of material property right (a situation of ownership), but since it is the will of a person (the servant) that is the object of the transfer by contract, ownership cannot be unconditional. The household master can never acquire, by contract, rights over his servant that would destroy the latter's personhood. Thus he does not have the right to abuse the servant nor to perpetual ownership of him.

The power wielded by this master over his servant does not necessarily differ in its application from the coercive power of someone who subjects another to the commands of his "arbitrary will." What does distinguish it from mere coercion is (a) that the relation of the two wills is established by the consent of both parties and (b) that the contractual origins of their relationship impose certain restrictions on the powers otherwise inherent in ownership, restrictions pertaining both to the use and duration of ownership. Nevertheless, within these restrictions, Kant acknowledges that the will of another is owned, or controlled, by the household head. This can only be reasonably construed as a loss of autonomy in external relations on the part of the servant, though the limited (if indeterminate) time during which the relationship endures and the restrictions on the use of the servant's labor ensure, Kant argues, that the servant does not lose his status as a person. Yet if he does not lose that status, he is nevertheless ineligible to participate fully in the legislative activity of his broader community. The servant is not "his own master"; he "allows someone else to make use of him" and so he is not (in the civil sense) independent, one of the crucial qualifications for full or active citizenship.[50]

The servant, or hired laborer, suffers a twofold loss of autonomy: in his relationship to the master and, derivatively, in his relation to the political community. This Kant clearly recognizes, and his explanation is that the condition of servitude is not incompatible with the freedom and equality that humans possess as persons.[51] There are standards that dictate how persons, even if passive and not self-determining in any active sense, must be treated—for example, that rich and poor, master and day laborer are all equal (as subject) before the law. In seeking to render the status of personhood (with its three attributes, freedom, equality, and independence) consistent with the condition of servitude, Kant can succeed only by stripping the idea of the person of much of the sense of autonomy that it at first seemed to carry. If to be made passive in relation to one's political community and subject to the rule of the employer within the household is a state compatible with the inalienable freedom of the person, then we are entitled to ask how we are to understand this Kantian conception of freedom.

The preceding paragraphs surveyed some of the consequences of Kant's contractarianism for the concepts of the person and autonomy. But the rejoinder might be made that, notwithstanding those consequences, the origins of contractual servitude are to be found in choice and thus are voluntary. I shall leave aside here the issue of whether the voluntary or noncoercive origins of a situation render the direct consequences of that first act of consent also voluntary (the most radical affirmative answer is Hobbes's theory of authors and actors) in order to focus on the question of choice, constraint, and freedom in the original act of consent. Let us return to Kant's servant. His condition is, according to Kant, free in this sense: it is chosen and therefore is not the result of coercion. This is so for two related reasons: (1) to be able to choose means (at a minimum level) having the right or power of veto over the event,[52] the right, in other words, to withdraw altogether from the purposed exchange and (2) as a (in fact, the principal) specification of (1) it requires that one not be under the arbitrary will of the other (the Kantian definition of coercion). Perhaps not surprisingly, it was Hobbes who set this argument out most boldly: a prisoner being dragged in chains by his captor has not consented to his position and is consequently in no way obliged to his master. But that same prisoner, offered the choice between servitude and death, in choosing the former has contracted, that is, acted freely, and he thus assumes voluntarily all the responsibilities pertaining to that contract. He could (at some considerable cost) decline the contractual offer of his life for his liberty, in contrast to the prisoner in chains who is not even given the option of declining but is instead placed under the absolute dominion of his captor.

In more general terms, we might express these conditions as saying that the only significant (for the theory) constraints on choice are those that are the result of coercion as defined above; the scope of the choice set has no bearing on the characterization of the resulting condition as a freely chosen one, so long as the parties have the power to decline the offer. One final example (drawn from Nozick) will serve to illustrate these points.[53] Imagine twenty-six females (A–Z) and the same number of males (A'–Z'). Together these fifty-two persons constitute the set of those who are to be married. Now further postulate that they have identical preferences as to whom they would wish to marry: A' prefers A most of all (and vice versa), B second, and so on down to Z; similarly B' most likes A et cetera. A marries her first choice, A', while B', being denied his first choice (A) selects B, and so forth until at last Z' gets his turn: since only Z remains, Z' has no choice among spouses, but only the choice to pick either his least desired partner or not to marry at all. The question is, does Z' make a free choice? On Kantian grounds the answer must be yes. First, there is no coercion in this scenario. Neither A' nor any other actor attempts to subordinate others to his will; each makes a fair choice pertaining to his private sphere and having only indirect consequences for the rest of the players. Second, in the most extreme case of Z', he does have a choice: he may marry Z or he can remain celibate. However unpalatable his choice may be and however restricted his alternatives, he is not compelled to marry Z in the sense implied in much contract theory: he is not subject to another's will by being denied the right to decline that party's offer.

Now let us look back once more at Kant's servant. Why does he arrive at his future master's door, seeking employment? Perhaps because he has no other way of providing for his daily needs. We might speculate that the land on which he formerly worked has been purchased and indeed that all the land, once the commons, has come into private hands. The process of transfer, however effected, is (we postu-late) legitimate—none of the landowners have come by their property through theft or unjust violence. The cumulative result of this series of transfers is that some now find themselves sustained by the land they have acquired, while others have no means of support save that of selling their labor, of entering the master's household and submitting their wills (conditionally) to his. Neither this master nor any other has coerced them, has bound them without choice to service. Their fate (like that of the women and men in Nozick's illustration) is the result of the impact of the world, of the fact that the legitimate exercise by others of their freedom (the acquisition of land) has, as an unintended consequence, fixed the world (exhausted, by our hypothesis, the sole source of independent labor) in such a way that the choice set of some members of that community is reduced to a decision between work for one master or another and whatever the results of unemployment might be. By the criteria sketched in the preceding paragraphs, this choice is free and consistent with autonomy of the person. The resulting subordination of the servant's will to that of the master is thus freely assumed by both sides and, while there is clearly some considerable loss of independence involved in the servant's activity, his relationship to the household head is a just one between persons (free, equal, and independent) because of the restrictions placed on the use of the laborer's time and activity. One consequence of the loss of independence within the household is that the laborer is made ineligible for active or full citizenship; hence, his contractually assumed loss of autonomy in the one sphere leads to the denial of it in his standing within the broader community. Yet there too Kant argues, as we have seen, that the servant/citizen suffers no diminution in his status as a person; he must always be treated as the bearer of certain fundamental and inalienable qualities. In sum, what emerges at the conclusion of Kant's analysis is an application of the idea of personhood to private and public relations. This application recognizes only one significant source of unfreedom: the unauthorized dominion of an "arbitrary will" over other wills. The concept of the person seeks to guarantee against this unfreedom by (in private relations) requiring the consent, together with other restrictions implied by the act of consent, of the one who is to be subordinated to the will of his master.

Marx's central critique of contract theory can be formulated in these words: the prevalence of genuine contractual relations, that is, agreements not produced by coercion as discussed above, is entirely consistent with continued unfreedom and the denial of autonomy. It is this key paradox—that social relations can be accurately described as flowing from voluntary contracts or exchanges between individuals *and* that domination nevertheless remains a governing feature of society—that Marx tries to unravel in his political economic writings. For Marx, the transition (to use Sir Henry Maine's classic phrase) from status to contract did not amount to a move from unfreedom to freedom but rather from one form of domination to a radically new one. His analysis of the coexistence of contract and domination, while framed largely in economic terms and directed toward a world quite different from Kant's, nevertheless provides some direction for a critique of the latter's contract theory, and it is those signposts, rather than an overview of Marx's economic writings, that will be the subject of the following paragraphs.

For Marx, the transition from precapitalist to capitalist society involved the substitution of the dominion of material or objective forces over man for that of direct personal domination: "What was the domination of person over person is now the general domination of the *thing* over the person."[54] Precapitalist compulsion was principally of an extraeconomic kind, intended to be sure to extract a surplus from the producing population, but characterized by direct relations of personal domination legitimized through various explanations of natural superiority and inferiority. Capitalist society, conversely, rests on and can only exist in the presence of the "personal freedom" of the (formerly subordinate) producing classes, a claim which has many roots in Marx's economic analysis but which is based on his understanding of the pervasiveness of the market (and the commodification of labor power) under capitalism.[55] When the employer and the worker meet in the marketplace, status and personal compulsion are absent from their exchange: both are equal (as commodity owners), independent of one another, and free. Their situation and the transaction between them seems little different from the one between master and servant that Kant describes.

This summary presents us with an idealized picture of social relations in which coercion, understood as forcible assertions of one will over another, plays no role. Yet Marx's argument is just that the absence of personal coercion (which, as we shall see below, is not actually entirely absent) conceals the forced or compelled nature of human activity. Indeed, it is Marx's claim that the "slaveowner's whip" never produced the same high degree of compulsion that is to be found under capitalism. But whereas the Roman slave's chains were readily apparent, those that bind now are "invisible." They are invisible precisely because they appear in the form of chance, or fate, events that befall one but do not originate in the will of another person. These new chains are not apparent to a pretheoretical, naive view of society, because in grasping coercion as the efflux of the will and seeking its corrective in nonstatus contractual relations, liberalism failed to understand other sources of unfreedom and, more, failed to appreciate the seemingly paradoxical coexistence of personal freedom and compulsion greater than that enforced by the Roman slaveowner.[56]

The personal, coercive power of the lord has been replaced, Marx argues, by the "cold blooded" inevitability of economic laws, by capital—a "lord at once autocratic and barbarous."[57] Capital is conceived by Marx not as a thing and only derivatively as a person, the capitalist. Its principal meaning is rather the set of social relations that constitute the metamorphosis of value, the process whereby surplus value is produced and the circuit of value-creation renewed. It is this process, or capital, not individual persons, that is set free, made autonomous, in a market economy directed toward the production of an ever-expanding surplus.[58] Indeed, on one reading of Marx, it is the very independence of persons from one another, their atomistic and not consciously regulated encounters, that creates an autonomous economic sphere, one which (to speak metaphorically) legislates for its human occupants.[59] I say "on one reading" because Marx, particularly in the third volume of *Capital*, tends to speak of the market as epiphenomenal or, more accurately, as simply the expression of the underlying laws of capital. This dispute need not detain us, however; on either reading the essential point is clear: under capitalism, the economy takes on a life of its own, independent of the conscious control of society and acting as a compelling force on all persons, capitalist and worker alike.

This is not to claim that personal freedom in capitalist society is, for Marx, a fraud or an illusion. Personal freedom, meaning freedom from the arbitrary will of others, is the answer to one form of coercion, that of personal dominion and inequality found in precapitalist societies. But it does not address (indeed it is implicated in) a new form of compulsion, that exercised by an autonomous economic process. What this means, in general terms, is that even in the absence of personal coercion, the compulsion generated by the reproduction circuit of capital is so great that contracting individuals can only be said to be free (this will be modified below) in relation to each other. Individually, their roles in the contract situation are assigned to them; they are, Marx says, the "bearers" or "functionaries" of their respective roles in the reproduction of value, and those roles are set before they encounter one another in the market. Their bargaining advantages, the purpose, and the consequences of their contracts are all determined for them by the capital circuit, and even if one allows that they are personally free (not coerced) it is difficult, on Marx's account, to understand the sense in which they can be called autonomous.

The above constitutes an overview of Marx's analysis of the limits of autonomy in capitalist society. What I now wish to proceed to is an examination of some key details of his critique of contractarianism. Recall the example, from our discussion of Kant, of the servant arriving at his prospective employer's door. Under Kant's theory of choice and coercion, the fact that the servant, being deprived of land, is compelled to sell his labor does not alter the freely made character of the bargain he strikes with his new master. Marx's analysis of the labor market—specifically, why workers appear at the factory gates—has three components: (1) the creation of the working class has its origins not in a voluntary transfer of the means of an independent existence (land, tools, and so forth) but in the violent, coercive expropriation of the rural population; (2) the first point notwithstanding, the selling of one's labor can only be construed as voluntary when that latter condition of free choice or voluntary action is deemed compatible with a choice set that is reduced to wage labor or misery; and (3) the character of capitalist production continually reproduces those restrictive conditions under which labor virtually *must* be sold.

The first argument demands little consideration here. It is a historical point, capital's original sin as Marx likes to call it, which suggests that far from being a tranquil exchange of land for the right to labor in factories, the creation of the European working class was a coercive, often state-led, expropriation of independent rural producers. Were Marx's account accurate, subsequent and apparently just contracts whose origins were nevertheless dubious, being located in an act of clear coercion, would have their legitimacy placed in question (on Nozick's historical principle of justice in acquisition). What interests us here is not so much the historical accuracy of Marx's charge, nor its implications for the theory of justice, but rather an intriguing issue that it raises about autonomy. According to Marx, it is an essential condition of capitalism that the worker be compelled in the present (noncoercively) to sell his labor. That in turn requires that at some earlier point he be denied (by whatever means) those conditions under which he could, so to speak, opt out, for example, by staying on his land as a yeoman. Capitalism, insofar as it requires a producing class, also demands the separation of formerly independent persons from the material sources of their independence.[60] Thus the precondition of the labor contract is precisely the loss of independence by one of the parties. When the servant meets her master, there may well be no relation of coercion or inequality between them—both are free and juridically equal persons—but the very fact of their meeting implies compulsion, and that compulsion originates in a loss of independence.[61] Put briefly, a labor contract occurs because the servant no longer has the means to avoid such a contract situation.

Let us look at this same situation, the labor contract, but now from the perspective of choice and opting out and not from the point of view of the contract's antecedent conditions. The textual basis for the following discussion is chapter 33 of *Capital,* entitled "The Modern Theory of Colonization." In fact, the chapter has very little to do with colonization, being rather an attempt to illuminate the nature of compulsion in capitalist society. In the developed capitalist world, Marx says, the compulsion of the labor market is hidden: the voluntary contract is the means by which labor is sold and purchased, and the compulsion that stands behind it appears as a "natural law," that is, a dictate not emanating from any particular will. The worker is "compelled to sell himself of his own free will."[62] But in the colonies, Marx continues, where land is readily and cheaply available, migrants do not choose to become industrial laborers. They prefer instead to return to the condition of independent producers. The worker "vanishes from the labour-market—but not into the workhouse," the latter being his choice set in mature capitalist societies.[63] In the end, Marx concludes, the conditions that "naturally" populate the labor market with applicants must, in the colonies, be artificially instituted—for example, by increasing land prices. It is, then, only as a result of a highly constrained choice set, labor or the workhouse, that the labor contract, so essential to capitalism, occurs at all. Alter the boundaries of that set, and individuals opt out. Marx, we may thus say, is not being ironic when he describes as voluntary the worker's sale of his labor power. It is not coerced in the sense that precapitalist labor was forced; the capitalist does not and, except in atypical cases, cannot order laborers to appear at his factory gate. But Marx is also not speaking metaphorically when he writes that the worker is "compelled" to sell himself of his own free will: he is compelled by the fixity of the social world that, in denying him access to the means of production, has forced upon him a condition in which the sale of his labor is the only reasonable choice. Marx's question to Kant is again: if autonomy is a good, and perhaps the principal one, and if the restraints on its flourishing are many, including both the coercive will and objective constraints, then how can it be satisfactory to rectify unfreedom in only one of its guises and to claim thereby that autonomy has been realized?

We now come to a brief consideration of the third point mentioned above, namely the reproduction of those (compelling) conditions that make the labor contract necessary. Marx's argument here is that capitalist production, in which labor power is applied in order to expand capital or embodied value, recreates those circumstances in which the worker must reappear at his master's door. Labor power, that is, is consumed in such a way that "objectified labour," standing over against its living counterpart, grows while the latter remains in its state of dependency.[64] The separation of persons from the external means of providing for their independence first creates the labor market, and that separation is continually reproduced by the labor contract itself. Whatever validity Marx's argument may have as a piece of economic analysis, it raises this question: what are we to make of a contract that originates in a certain kind of compulsion and recreates through its fulfillment those original compulsory conditions? The worker, in this account, is constrained by the narrow choice set to offer his labor power for sale, and that act of sale and purchase initiates a production process that preserves those constraints and thereby compels him to sell his labor anew. Something like this would presumably be true of Kant's servant, yet his appearance at the master's door out of necessity and the fact that his contract there is certain to reproduce that necessity seem not to have led Kant to question the idea of the servant's autonomy.

I now wish to turn to another element of Marx's critique of contractarianism: the consequences of the labor contract for relations between employer and employed. Marx maintains that out of the labor/capital exchange there emerges a master/servant relation, but one of a radically new type. Formerly, status and birth were at the foundation of relations of servitude among persons, but this new relationship arises from the specific nature of the commodity being sold, that is, labor power.[65] The contract is between persons, free and equal, but the transfer that is thus brought about consists of a person's activity and time. That transfer brings the worker into the factory and places him under the direction of the capitalist. This direction or superintendence Marx describes as "despotic" and "autocratic," a world in which the laborer loses his independence to the will of the capitalist.[66] Marx's point is sufficiently plain here: the "Garden of Eden" of the innate rights of man— his freedom, equality, and independence—comes to an end as soon as worker and capitalist close the factory door behind them, to be replaced by the largely unrestricted exercise of the capitalist's authority over his employees. The contract that produces such a condition is of questionable value in achieving its (tacitly) stated end: to put relations between persons on a footing of equality and independence. Here is another feature of Marx's account of this new master/servant relation, one which further highlights the specific (nonpersonal) character of compulsion under capitalism. The capitalist, as we noted earlier, is for Marx only a "functionary" of capital, subject to the laws of its production. His power over his workers stems not from his "arbitrary will," not from his political or social position, but from the particular function that he has in the "metabolism" of capital.[67] Thus, for example, Marx argues that the pressure of the employer on his staff to work ever-longer hours arises from the requirements of the production process of surplus value, not from his good or bad will. It is clear that Marx thought personal coercion to be a derivative and secondary source of unfreedom in capitalist society. The principal focus of his critique of contractarianism is, therefore, to be found in the idea of the compulsion that originates in an economic process: "objective" compulsion, as he sometimes called it, on the model (but by analogy only) of the laws of nature, meaning not by human design and not under man's conscious control.

Conclusion

Marx's Kant critique rests on a conception of autonomy that has humans as purposive beings at its center and that sees in the impact of the world the principal source of constraints on human autonomy. That impact is of two kinds: the struggle for mastery over nature, a struggle whose sense is not, for Marx, mastery for its own sake but rather the creation of those conditions under which humans will be as fully legislative as possible over their own affairs; and limitations that arise from social relations between persons, whether those are of the directly coercive, precapitalist variety or of the objective compulsion of the valorization process. Marx's derision of the Kantian "good will," its impotence and wretchedness, amounts to the assertion that neither in its reflection on man and nature nor in its social philosophy does Kant's idea of autonomy address the central forms of constraint arrayed against human freedom. Or, more precisely, it acknowledges the existence of those constraints, the human being as a trifle in the face of nature or the servant's loss of independence, but judges and by and large dismisses them by invoking an idea of autonomy so emaciated that it is consistent even with very servile conditions.

Thus in Kant's writings on humans and their relation to nature, it is plain that as physical beings they occupy an insignificant place in creation, insignificant in that even though they may fancy themselves (or wish to be) its legislators, they are constantly reminded of its sovereignty over them. Their stature in creation is, conversely, heightened when their power to select the maxims for their behavior is recognized. This core of the Kantian idea of autonomy, from which the political version is derivative, involves on the one side a rejection of antecedent causation as a factor diminishing freedom and, on the other side, the claim that the "impulsion" of the anticipated effect, if allowed to determine action, nullifies the greatest freedom of which humans are capable. The result is a severe theory of moral imputation and accountability according to which, whatever the external constraints may be, the person is always fully the author of his actions. While such a theory may well claim to have shown man's independence of nature, the cost is high: the idea of independence that the theory supports is thin, being restricted to the exercise of a choice between maxims; the systematic abstraction from the particularity of the self and of the context in which it acts renders that self pale and bloodless, a creature without a causally important history or determinants. One need not accept the details of Marx's analysis of man and nature, nor even less the theory of historical movement that arises on that foundation, in order to see how the Kantian good will would have appeared paltry to him, both in its relation to the natural constraints that determine human activity and in relation to the more expansive sphere of autonomy made possible by the conquest of nature. The underlying notion that self-legislation demands, among other things, the greatest possible control over all competing centers of legislation, including the reduction of nature's impact upon human choices and action, is not a peculiarly Marxist insight. But its pervasive presence and centrality in Marx's writings make those works a useful beginning point for understanding the limits of this aspect of Kantian autonomy.

If the moral good will finds refuge from the compulsion of nature in its capacity for free choice among maxims, the will in its political expression seems to be denied even that small area for its activity. Here the concept of the jural person, whose central characteristics are civil freedom, equality, and independence, is transformed into an imperative for rulers to treat citizens in a manner consistent with their status as persons and not to enact laws for them other than those to which they could, as jural persons, have agreed. Kant's political contractarianism strips the idea of autonomy of any behavioral specification save that of being a guide for the treatment of citizens. Still more striking is that, for Kant, a legitimate contract (the manner of interaction among persons by which one can become voluntarily subordinate to another) does not preclude antecedent compulsion (economic necessity), considerable loss of private independence (to the household master), or the civil loss of full citizenship. That a contract emerging out of necessity and resulting in a diminution of independence across the range of human relations, private and public, can nevertheless be judged legitimate suggests that the autonomy it is said to preserve must be slight indeed, if it is compatible with so much compulsion.

The above difficulties in Kant's political philosophy can be discerned directly from a reading of his works, and the recognition of them requires no external critical apparatus. A deeper challenge to his contractarianism can, however, be distilled from Marx's critique of capitalism. By *contractarianism* we refer here not to a metaphorical language used to describe the limits of governmental authority, but to the claims of a society to have set relations between persons on a free and equal footing, through the substitution of contract for coercion. Marx's attack on this claim has a number of facets, the least important of which is the argument that capitalism has merely replaced personal power based on status by that same power based on economic advantages. I call this the least important of Marx's claims because, cast in this manner, it works within contractarian theory—that coercion is personal, arbitrary power is the evil to be remedied—but asserts that the "despotic lords" of old have been replaced by new and equally despotic lords, the capitalists. A more fundamental and intriguing challenge can be composed from other elements of Marx's analysis: (1) contractarianism recognizes only one source of unfreedom, coercion or personal domination; (2) objective compulsion, the power of forces consisting of the actions of persons but not under their control and taking on a dynamic independent of those agents, is the dominant form under capitalism but because it does not involve the direct subordination of one will to another the necessity it imposes appears to be something natural, a fate, and hence unobjectionable to a view that sees coercion as the summum malum; (3) not only can contractual relations coexist with objective compulsion, they are (broadly construed as the core of a free market economy) at the root of the latter; (4) autonomy, individual or political, is under those circumstances largely, though not entirely, illusory.

Let me note again that this presentation of Marx's challenge does not attack contractarianism by asserting the continued existence of the despotic lords, by claiming that wage labor is no different than slavery, or by advancing the view that liberal democracy is a sham behind which stands the real power of the bourgeoisie, whose dictatorship is enforced by the state, its executive committee. That line of reasoning would in effect grant that the contractarian argument had accurately identified the major source of unfreedom, personal domination and arbitrary political power, but had failed to identify the continued existence of these evils. Marx (at times) set himself a rather more difficult task: to allow that coercion has virtually disappeared, that individuals confront one another as free and equal contracting agents, that the modern state has incorporated this freedom and equality in its practice of citizenship, yet then to show that autonomy remains radically curtailed. This way of framing the debate also has the effect of making the challenge to the contractarian position more intriguing, for it engages the latter not by counterposing to it end-pattern claims resting on principles of distributive justice (for example, that a different social arrangement, perhaps one curtailing individual property rights, would result in a more equitable distribution of society's economic assets) but by seeking to show that the exercise of certain freedoms causes a significant loss of freedom, including a reduction in the autonomy imputed to the contracting agents themselves.

The heart of this challenge is that by doing away with the personal (extra-economic) coercion of precapitalist society and by replacing these openly coercive relations of production with new ones based on the personal freedom of individuals acting in an all-embracing market oriented toward the production of ever-greater quantities of surplus value, the economy comes to generate its own laws that are beyond the control of individuals and that subordinate those persons to a discipline more potent than the master's whip. A new type of unfreedom is thus born, one not easily recognized because, unlike previous forms, it does not originate in the wills of dominant persons but precisely in the interaction of formally free and equal individuals. Autonomy in its struggle against the legislative power of nature requires technology; against the lawgiving capacity of the unhindered economy, autonomy requires the conscious control of individuals regulating their own inter-change rather than having it determined for them by the valorization process of capital. It should perhaps be underlined here that this challenge to (a much revised version of) Kant's theory does not rest on the wildly anachronistic assertion that Kant did not understand capitalism. Kant, in a general way, certainly did grasp economic compulsion, as did Rousseau and Locke, but insofar as it could not be reduced to the illegitimate exercise of the arbitrary will of one person over another Kant chose not to see in it a threat to human autonomy—and it is that latter thought to which Marx's objections are addressed.

However ill-suited Marx's writings are as a guide to the understanding of will and autonomy, they excel in their ability to disclose forms of compulsion and to turn those "discoveries," whether of the violent expropriative origins of capitalism or of the independent laws of the market economy, against the proponents of the contrac-tarian conception of liberty. And in their concern, indeed almost their preoccupa-tion, with the power of nature over man and the liberating effects of technology, Marx's writings point to yet another source of unfreedom. The impact of the world—of economic and natural compulsion—is what is of importance to us in Marx's analysis. Critically employed, that analysis shows us the limits of a concep-tion of autonomy that can allow significance only to the compulsion of heterono-mous maxims or of the coercive will. Such a conception must, in the end, pass over the many ways in which aspects of the world beyond the individual's will (in the selection of its maxims or in relations between wills) conspire to restrict autonomy. Marx, always more a philosopher of compulsion than of freedom, has nevertheless done us the service of showing the limits of a theory of autonomy too much centered on the will alone.

Notes

1

William James Booth, *Interpreting the World: Kant's Philosophy of History and Politics* (Toronto: University of Toronto Press, 1986).

2

Karl Marx, "The Philosophical Manifesto," in Karl Marx and Frederick Engels, *Collected Works* (hereafter CW with volume and page numbers; New York: International Publishers, 1975–), 1:206.

3

Marx and Engels, *The German Ideology,* CW 5:193, 195.

4

Marx, "Contribution to the Critique of Hegel's *Philosophy of Right,*" CW 3:182, 176.

5

Marx, "The Leading Article in No. 179 of the Kölnische Zeitung," CW 1:201.

6

Compare Marx's eleventh thesis on Feuerbach and Immanuel Kant, *Critique of Judgment,* trans. J. H. Bernard (New York: Hafner, 1951), p. 293 (5:442–43). Subsequent references to *Critique of Judgment* are to the Bernard translation, with the Academy citation provided parenthetically.

7

Marx and Engels, *German Ideology,* CW 5:301.

8

Marx and Engels, *The Holy Family,* CW 4:131, and *The German Ideology,* CW 5:306, 315.

9

Marx and Engels, *The Holy Family,* CW 4:201, and *The German Ideology,* CW 5:254.

10

See Marx and Engels, *The Holy Family,* CW 4:131, and *The German Ideology,* CW 5:302. In an earlier piece (1842), "Comments on the Latest Prussian Censorship," Marx praises Kant for separating morality from religion (CW 1:119).

11

See Marx, *Manuskript, 1861–1863* in *Karl Marx. Friedrich Engels Gesamtausgabe* (hereafter MEGA with volume and page numbers; Berlin: Dietz Verlag, 1982), 3.1:51, 63, 69, 127. Marx, *Capital,* vol. 1, trans. Ben Fowkes (New York: Vintage, 1977), pp. 284ff; and *Capital,* vol. 3, trans. David Fernbach (New York: Vintage, 1981), p. 964.

12

Marx and Engels, *The German Ideology,* CW 5:47.

13

Marx, MEGA, 3.2:83.

14

Much recent scholarly attention has been devoted to the Aristotelian dimension of Marx's concept of self-realization. See Terence Ball, "Marxian Science and Positivist Politics," in Terence Ball and James Farr, eds., *After Marx* (Cambridge: Cambridge University Press, 1984), p. 243, and Alan Gilbert, "Marx's Moral Realism," in that same volume. See also Jon Elster, *Making Sense of Marx* (Cambridge: Cambridge University Press, 1985), pp. 219, 515, and G. A. Cohen, *Karl Marx's Theory of History: A Defense* (Princeton: Princeton University Press, 1978), chap. 11.

15
Marx, *Results of the Immediate Process of Production,* published as an appendix to *Capital,* 1:1033; see also MEGA 3.6:2133, 2135.

16
Immanuel Kant, *The Doctrine of Virtue: Part Two of the Metaphysics of Morals,* trans. Mary J. Gregor (New York: Harper and Row, 1964), p. 70 (Academy ed., 6:408).

17
See Kant, *Critique of Pure Reason,* trans. N. K. Smith (New York: St. Martin's, 1965), A553/B581. (For the *Critique of Pure Reason,* I again follow the standard scholarly practice and give only the Prussian Academy pagination in the form of A-/B-. This pagination is provided in the margins of Smith's translation.) See also Kant, *Critique of Practical Reason,* trans. Lewis White Beck (Indianapolis: Library of Liberal Arts, 1956), p. 33 (Academy ed., 5:33) and *Groundwork of the Metaphysic of Morals,* trans. H. J. Paton (New York: Harper and Row, 1964), p. 114 (Academy ed., 4:446). For further analysis see George A. Kelly, *Idealism, Politics and History* (Cambridge: Cambridge University Press, 1969), pp. 107ff.; Patrick Riley, *Will and Political Legitimacy* (Cambridge, Mass.: Harvard University Press, 1982), pp. 145–46; and Lewis White Beck, "Kant's Two Conceptions of the Will in Their Political Context," chap. 2 this volume.

18
Kant, *Groundwork,* p. 108 (4:440).

19
Kant, *Groundwork,* p. 111 (4:444).

20
Kelly, *Idealism, Politics and History,* p. 108.

21
Kant, *The Doctrine of Virtue,* p. 69 (6:407).

22
See Beck, "Kant's Two Conceptions," chap. 2 above.

23
Kant, *Groundwork,* p. 107 (4:439). See also Kant, *Critique of Practical Reason,* pp. 18–19, 59–60, 74 (5:20–21, 57–58, 71).

24
Kant, *Critique of Pure Reason,* A554/B582ff.; emphasis added.

25
Kant, *Critique of Judgment,* p. 282 (5:432).

26
Marx and Engels, *The German Ideology,* CW 5:465.

27
Marx, "Critical Marginal Notes," CW 3:199.

28
Marx and Engels, *The German Ideology,* CW 5:292. For a powerful argument in favor of including nature among the sources of unfreedom see Harry G. Frankfurt, "Coercion and Moral Responsibility," in Ted Honderick, ed., *Essays on the Freedom of Action* (London: Routledge and Kegan Paul, 1973), especially pp. 83–84.

29
Marx and Engels, *The German Ideology,* CW 5:63.

30
Marx, "The British Rule in India," CW 12:132.

31
Marx, *The Poverty of Philosophy,* CW 6:184, and *The German Ideology,* CW 5:44, 76.

32
Marx, *Capital,* 1:649; *Grundrisse,* trans. Martin Nicholaus (New York: Vintage, 1973), pp. 409–10, 488; *Capital,* 3:358–59, 368.

33
See Kant, "Conjectural Beginning of Human History," in *On History,* ed. Lewis White

Beck (Indianapolis: Library of Liberal Arts, 1963), pp. 58, 60, 65 (Academy ed., 8:113, 115, 120).

34
Kant, "On the Common Saying, 'This May Be True in Theory But Does Not Apply in Practice,'" in Hans Reiss, ed., *Kant's Political Writings* (Cambridge: Cambridge University Press, 1971), p. 91 (Academy ed., 8:312), and *Critique of Practical Reasons*, p. 281 (5:431).

35
Kant, *Critique of Practical Reason*, p. 166 (5:161–62).

36
Kant, *Geschichte und Naturbeschreibung der merkwürdigsten Vorfälle des Erdbebens*, Academy ed., 1:431, 456, 460.

37
Kant, *Critique of Judgment*, p. 101 (5:261).

38
Kant, *Critique of Judgment*, p. 105 (5:265).

39
Kant, *Critique of Judgment*, pp. 96, 99–101 (5:257, 260–62).

40
Kant, *Critique of Judgment*, p. 101 (5:262), and *Critique of Practical Reason*, p. 89 (5:86–87).

41
Kant, *Critique of Pure Reason*, A549–50/B577–78, and *Religion within the Limits of Reason Alone*, trans. T. M. Greene and H. H. Hudson (New York: Harper and Row, 1960), p. 64n (Academy ed., 6:70n).

42
Marx, *Capital*, 1:92.

43
Marx, *Wage Labour and Capital*, CW 9:211.

44
See Kant, *Critique of Judgment*, p. 282 (5:432); *Critique of Practical Reason*, p. 156

(5:152); *Doctrine of Virtue*, p. 10 (6:213–14).

45
Kant, *The Metaphysical Elements of Justice: Part One of the Metaphysics of Morals*, trans. John Ladd (Indianapolis: The Library of Liberal Arts, 1965), pp. 43–44 (Academy ed., 6:237).

46
Kant, *Metaphysical Elements of Justice*, p. 44 (6:237–38).

47
Kant, *Metaphysical Elements of Justice*, p. 79 (6:314).

48
Robert Nozick, "Coercion," in Sidney Morgenbesser, ed., *Philosophy, Science and Method: Essays in Honor of Ernest Nagel* (New York: St. Martin's, 1969), pp. 459, 463.

49
Kant, *Die Metaphysik der Sitten. Rechtslehre*, Academy ed., 6:276 (not translated in *Metaphysical Elements of Justice*).

50
Kant, "On the Common Saying," p. 78n (8:295n), and *Metaphysical Elements of Justice*, p. 79 (6:314).

51
Kant, *Metaphysical Elements of Justice*, pp. 79–80 (6:315).

52
See Serge-Cristophe Kolm's definition of contractual liberty: "*Libre* signifie ici que chaque personne a le droit de s'abstenir d'échanger: chacun . . . a un droit de *veto* sur cet acte"; *Justice et Equité* (Paris: Éditions du Centre National de la Récherche Scientifique, 1972), p. 31.

53
Robert Nozick, *Anarchy, State and Utopia* (New York: Basic Books, 1974), pp. 263ff. A valuable critique of Nozick is to be found in G. A. Cohen, "The Structure of the Prole-

tarian Unfreedom," in John Roemer, ed., *Analytical Marxism* (Cambridge: Cambridge University Press, 1986).

54
Marx, "Comments on James Mill," CW 1:221, and *The German Ideology,* CW 5:77, 78–79. For further analysis of this way of thinking about compulsion see Jeffrey H. Reiman, "The Fallacy of Libertarian Capitalism," *Ethics* 92 (October 1981): 85–95.

55
Marx, *Theories of Surplus Value,* vol. 3 (Moscow: Progress Publishers, 1971), p. 431. See also *Capital,* 3:926, and *Results of the Immediate Process of Production,* in *Capital,* 1:1021.

56
See Marx, MEGA, 3.1:174; MEGA, 3.6:2131; *The German Ideology,* CW 5:80–81.

57
Marx, "Moralizing Criticism," CW 6:336, and *Wage Labour and Capital,* CW 9:228.

58
Marx, *Grundrisse,* p. 650.

59
Marx, *Grundrisse,* pp. 196–97, 652; *Capital,* 1:187, 202–03.

60
Marx, *Capital,* 1:272, 284; *Theories of Surplus Value,* vol. 1 (Moscow: Progress Publishers, 1963), p. 78.

61
Marx, MEGA, 3.1:32–33; *Results of the Immediate Process of Production,* p. 1017.

62
Marx, *Capital,* 1:932.

63
Marx, *Capital,* 1:936.

64
See Marx, MEGA, 3.1:126; *Capital,* 1:723–24.

65
Marx, MEGA, 3.1:93–94.

66
Marx, MEGA, 3.6:2023–24; *Capital,* 1:450, 477, 481, 549. This aspect of Marx's theory of domination is set out, perhaps with too much emphasis, in Robert Tucker, *The Marxian Revolutionary Idea* (New York: W. W. Norton, 1969), pp. 81ff.

67
See Marx, *Capital,* 3:1021; *Theories of Surplus Value,* 1:390; *Capital,* 1:739.

Chapter 12

Kant, the Sublime, and
Nature

Ronald Beiner

As is well known, the core of Heidegger's challenge to the philosophical tradition that runs from Plato to Nietzsche is his charge that the history of metaphysics represents a cumulative process of ever-increasing subjectivization of our experience of being. In Heidegger's novel reading, Western philosophy as a whole represents one continuous, integral process of the unfolding and consolidation of an all-consuming subjectivism—that is, an interpretation of being in general founded upon the exaltation of the human subject, in relation to which Being itself consists merely of objects to be conceptually apprehended or "represented." Heidegger's middle and later work is a relentless exposé and critique of Western subjectivism, running, as Heidegger thinks, from Plato to Nietzsche. This critique takes the form of a brilliant series of commentaries on the history of philosophy. This Heideggerian reading of the metaphysical tradition reaches its climax in an understanding of contemporary technology as the outcome of a fateful turn in Western ontology first initiated by Plato and confirmed by each of his successors in what we now accept as the history of philosophy.

In this chapter I draw upon Heidegger's subjectivization thesis in order to illuminate one notable case within the intellectual heritage of the West, namely, an important but neglected dimension of Kant's moral vision. Kant is obviously one of the axes of our moral tradition. His philosophical account of the nature of morality informs contemporary thinking in far-reaching ways. Yet, as far as I am aware, there is very little attention, if any, given to the stunning implications that Kantian moral thinking has for our practical stance toward nature as a whole. Perhaps the reason for this oversight is that Kant's clearest statement of this underlying attitude toward nature is situated in a rather unlikely location: his analysis of aesthetic judgments of the sublime in sections 23–30 of the *Critique of Judgment*. I shall focus on this segment of Kant's work, which will provide us with one radical illustration of Heidegger's thesis of the progressive unfolding of Western subjectivism, culminating in a concept of being that finds embodiment in the achievements of modern technology.

We all know the famous passage from the conclusion to the *Critique of Practical Reason:* "Two things fill the mind with ever new and increasing admiration and awe, the oftener and the more steadily we reflect on them: the starry heavens above and the moral law within."[1] It might appear from this passage that our experience of nature possesses a dignity equal (or at least comparable) to our moral experience; that nature occupies a stature commensurate with that of the moral law. Strikingly enough, however, it is the very task of Kant's analytic of the sublime, as we shall see, to offer a rendering of our most exalted experience of nature *in terms of* our moral experience, that is, *to reduce* "the starry heavens above" *to* "the moral law within." To the extent that Kant succeeds in this endeavor, we are left with only *one* thing that excites awe in us, namely, our own capacity for recognizing the dictates of practical reason. The apparent parallel between nature's capacity to incite awe and reason's capacity to do the same turns into a decided triumph of awesome reason over awesome nature.

One might say that the chief purpose of Kant's analysis is to *subjectivize* our understanding of the experience of the sublime.

> We express ourselves on the whole inaccurately if we term any *Object of nature* sublime. . . . All that we can say is that the object lends itself to the presentation of a sublimity discoverable in the mind. For the sublime, in the strict sense of the word, cannot be contained in any sensuous form, but rather concerns ideas of reason which, although no adequate presentation of them is possible, may be excited and called into the mind by that very inadequacy itself which does admit of sensuous presentation. Thus the broad ocean agitated by storms cannot be called sublime. Its aspect is horrible, and one must have stored one's mind in advance with a rich stock of ideas, if such an intuition is to raise it to the pitch of a feeling which is itself sublime—sublime because the mind has been incited to abandon sensibility.[2]

Let us see how Kant arrives at this conception. In §25 he offers two definitions of the sublime. The first is this: *"Sublime* is the name given to what is *absolutely great"* (*Critique of Judgment,* p. 94; 5:248). Later he gives another formulation of the same definition: "that is sublime in comparison with which all else is small" (p. 97; 5:250). Now, it should be obvious that nothing available in the empirical world is sublime in this sense, that is, is "absolutely great" or renders all else small by comparison. All empirical things are great in relation to some things and small in relation to others. Moreover, they actually appear to shift in magnitude as we vary our perspective. As Kant says, even the greatest magnitude may be "degraded to the level of the infinitely little" by being looked at through a telescope, or conversely, the infinitely little "enlarged to the greatness of a world" by being looked at through a microscope (ibid.). All empirical magnitudes are merely relative. At most, then, any particular empirical spectacle can give us only *intimations* of what is sublime in this sense. (In other words, the sensible gives us intimations of what is supersensible: "a sublimity discoverable in the mind" or, as Kant terms it, "ideas of reason.") Thus the very definition of sublimity points us toward that which can find no location in empirical reality. Rather, the purpose of Kant's discussion of the sublime is to *detach* us from all that is merely empirical; as he says, the reference to nature finds its only significance "in the possible *employment* of our intuitions of it in inducing a feeling in our own selves of a finality quite independent of nature" (p. 93; 5:246). Intuitions of the sublime in nature do not adhere to nature itself but refer ultimately to what *transcends* nature.

By this line of argument, Kant arrives at the conclusion that the idea of the sublime as that which is absolutely, unconditionally great *cannot* find embodiment in nature (it is a conceptual impossibility), and this in turn yields an understanding of sublimity that can be linked up with the notion of autonomy: for that which is beyond all comparison great, "it is not permissible to seek an appropriate standard outside itself, but merely in itself. It is greatness comparable to itself alone. Hence it comes that the sublime is not to be looked for in the things of nature, but only in our own ideas."[3] (Compare §23: for the sublime, in contrast to the beautiful, one must not "seek a ground external to ourselves" but "one merely in ourselves"; *Critique of Judgment,* p. 93; 5:246.) If the sublime therefore realizes a kind of autonomy, we have further confirmation that it must lie beyond all that is natural, which—as we know—is confined to strict heteronomy. All objects of sense can be imagined as greater and greater, but never absolutely great. Yet reason demands absoluteness. It is precisely the "inability on the part of our faculty for the estimation of the magnitude of things of the world of sense" that leads to "the awakening of a feeling of a supersensible faculty within us; and it is the use to which judgment naturally puts particular objects on behalf of this latter feeling, and not the object of sense, that is absolutely great. . . . Consequently it is the disposition of soul evoked by a particular representation engaging the attention of the reflective judgment, and not the Object, that is to be called sublime." Hence Kant ends §25 with a third, and definitive, definition of the sublime: "The sublime is that, the mere capacity of thinking which evidences a faculty of mind transcending every standard of sense" (pp. 97–98; 5:250).

Kant's formula, defining the sublime in terms of what is "absolutely great" (*schlechthin groß*) or great without qualification, cannot help but remind us of another famous formula of his, at the beginning of the *Foundations of the Metaphysics of Morals:* that "which could be called good without qualification" (*was ohne Einschränkung für gut könnte gehalten werden*), or absolutely good. The similarity between these two formulas is deliberate, not accidental. Both formulas yield for Kant a notion of "respect"; more to the point, they actually define the strictly conceived Kantian notion of respect. If we say of an object, without qualification, that it is great, "we then always couple with the representation a kind of respect" (*Critique of Judgment,* p. 96; 5:249). In contrast to the experience of the beautiful, which positively delights and attracts us, delight in the sublime, according to Kant, involves almost a kind of wondrous aversion ("negative pleasure") that Kant associates with admiration or respect (p. 91; 5:245).[4] The question then becomes: Can we "respect" objects of nature, or is this experience confined to persons or the feeling of our own personhood? It is obvious from the whole orientation of Kant's moral writings what his answer *must* be to such a question (an answer made explicit in his formulation of the distinction between persons and things in the *Foundations of the Metaphysics of Morals*): We can only respect "persons," who lie outside the domain of empirical reality.[5] The conclusion is inescapable: if sublimity elicits respect, the experience of sublime objects must not attach us to those objects themselves, but must rather draw us away from anything merely empirical or "sensible" (that is, available to sensibility) and instead direct us toward that which lies beyond the empirical—our own personhood.

Kant's appeals to notions of autonomy and respect in his account of the sublime indicate the ultimate destination of his theory of sublimity. What the imagination reaches out for (but cannot grasp) in intimations of the sublime is nothing pertaining to the world of sense; rather, it is a representation of our moral vocation as supersensible beings. Hence, "a feeling for the sublime in nature is hardly thinkable unless in association with an attitude of mind resembling the moral" (*Critique of Judgment,* p. 120; 5:268). The experience of sublimity generates respect, not for any natural object that is only relatively great, but for our moral nature, which alone is absolutely great. He concludes: "the feeling of the sublime in nature is respect for our own vocation, which we attribute to an Object of nature by a certain subreption (substitution of a respect for the Object in place of one for the idea of humanity in our own self—the Subject)" (p. 106; 5:257).

The fact that the sense of our own sublime vocation ultimately triumphs over the sublimity that is not our own might help clarify a very important puzzle in Kant's account. He consistently emphasizes that experience of the sublime, no less than beauty, is productive of delight, or is intrinsically pleasing (*für sich selbst gefällt*). But why should the apprehension of what is awesome or terrible in nature be experienced as pleasing or delightful? Sublime objects, after all, both attract and repel us; what we experience is an "alternation" of attraction and repulsion (pp. 90–91; 5:244–45). It is, as he says in §27, an amalgam of pleasure and displeasure. He even refers to it as "a vibration" (*Erschütterung*), "a rapidly alternating repulsion and attraction produced by one and the same Object" (p. 107; 5:258).[6] The question is, how is it possible that this queer sensation is felt to be intrinsically pleasing? How can something that Kant describes as half pleasure, half displeasure, be nonetheless an occasion for pure delight (*Wohlgefallen*)? The answer, Kant suggests, is that the pleasure is an indirect one, a pleasure mediated by pain, so to speak (*Lust* mediated by *Unlust*), where we experience the thrill of coming to realize that the terrors of nature are less formidable than we had originally feared. So the pleasure that we derive from the experience of sublimity consists, Kant says, in a "judgment of the inadequacy of the greatest faculty of sense being in accord with ideas of reason." We "esteem as small in comparison with ideas of reason everything which for us is great in nature as an object of sense," and that begets delight. In short, it is for us a source of pleasure "to find every standard of sensibility falling short of the ideas of reason" (p. 106; 5:257–58). The very thing that displeases us, the frustration of the senses in their striving to comprehend absoluteness, is simultaneously the ground of the pleasure.

This may also help explain why Kant refers to respect as "negative pleasure": not a positive pleasure in the wonders of nature, but a pleasure in apprehending nature's deficiency measured against our own supersensible powers (p. 91; 5:245; see also p. 120; 5:269). This reading is supported by §68 of the *Anthropology*, where Kant writes that the feeling aroused by the sublime becomes an agreeable one insofar as "it continuously triumphs over pain"—namely, the pain of apprehending that in comparison with physical nature "we shall shrink into insignificance in our own estimation," our fear that we shall fail "to make our forces equal to it," "our anxiety about not being able to rise to its greatness."[7] When we come to see that this fear is misplaced (which it is in principle), the outcome is delight, albeit the negative delight of appreciating, to our immense relief, that we are not the infinitely small creatures that nature makes us seem to be.

It is the sense of our independence of nature, indeed our superiority to it, that confers an experience of sublimity, for the greater the display of nature's power, the more intense our feeling of our supremacy over nature. Here the Stoic theme in Kant's moral thinking reaches its highest pitch. The "might" of nature humbles us as beings of nature, but at the same time it exalts us because we know that we are beings "independent of nature," possessing "a pre-eminence above nature." As Kant puts it, "This saves humanity in our own person from humiliation." The mightiness of nature serves merely to impress upon the mind "the appropriate sublimity of the sphere of its own being, even above nature" (*Critique of Judgment,* pp. 111–12; 5:261–62). The mind's representation of the might of nature draws forth a consciousness of "our superiority over nature," and the greater the might that nature presents to our gaze, the greater our sense of being able to transcend fear of that might and thus "of regarding our estate as exalted above it" (p. 114; 5:264). According to Kant's Stoic understanding, our ability to survey nature's mightiness without cowering in fear before it serves to express our independence of nature.

Again, the sense of respect elicited is directed not toward nature but toward ourselves as moral subjects.[8]

This way of thinking finds its most decisive expression in §29. In the experience of the sublime as a moral experience, the faculty of imagination acknowledges its ultimate subordination to ideas of reason, that is, moral feeling gives us an awareness of imagination's inadequacy to reason, except in the service of "the mind's supersensible province" (p. 119; 5:268). In this extremity, our power of imagination itself becomes what Kant calls "an instrument of reason" in the dominion of reason over sensibility. It thereby acquires "a might enabling us to assert our independence as against the influences of nature, to degrade what is great in respect of the latter to the level of what is little, and thus to locate the absolutely great only in the proper estate of the Subject" (p. 121; 5:269).[9] This, indeed, marks an apotheosis of Western subjectivism, as Heidegger might say. It is difficult to imagine a more total abasement of natural being as such in the face of our autonomy in relation to nature.

To sum up: the moral problem that the idea of the sublime poses for Kant is that to regard objects of nature as supremely sublime is a kind of insult to our own nature as rational beings (beings whose dignity reposes *above and beyond* nature). As Kant puts it, our most urgent need is to "save humanity in our own person from humiliation" (p. 111; 5:262). Kant's solution to this problem was to construe sublime objects of nature as mere projections of a sublimity actually located within ourselves as moral persons. Thus Kant exactly *inverts* the meaning of the sublime—from a token of our awe before nature to a token of our autonomy, that is, our superiority to nature!

Let us return to the passage with which we started, the conclusion to the *Critique of Practical Reason*. Even there we see already that nature and morality, despite their seeming parity, are actually ranked in a way that is to the unconditional advantage of the latter over the former. The former, Kant says, "begins from the place I occupy in the external world of sense," whereas the second "begins from my invisible self, my personality": "The former view of a countless multitude of worlds annihilates as it were my importance as an *animal creature*. . . . The second, on the contrary, infinitely elevates my worth as an *intelligence* by my personality, in which the moral law reveals to me a life independent of animality and even of the whole sensible world."[10] Kant begins the conclusion by stating that "the starry heavens above" and "the moral law within" both incite awe (*Ehrfurcht*). But the subsequent commentary shows that they do so in ways that serve quite different, yet inseparable, functions. The awesomeness of nature "annihilates" the sensible side of our being, while the awesomeness of morality "infinitely elevates" the supersensible side of our being.[11] The implicit ranking of these two opposed functions is perfectly evident. If Kant's tacit purpose is to disrupt the apparent symmetry of outer sublimity and inner sublimity, the text achieves this purpose by subverting the symmetry from both directions at once: depressing the sensible and elevating the supersensible.

Kant's theme in this passage is "what gives awe" or "what compels awe." What the analytic of the sublime has shown us is that it is theoretically intolerable for Kant that the starry heavens above should give awe or compel awe in a way that matches the awesomeness of the moral law within. This is so troubling for Kant that he is driven not merely to *rank the one above* the other (as he does even at the end of the *Critique of Practical Reason*), but to *reduce the one to* the other (as he does in the *Critique of Judgment*), so that nature actually ceases to be an independent source of awe. (In that sense, the position defined in the third *Critique* goes beyond, and is far more radical than, that implied in the second *Critique*.) If one reads the first sentence of the conclusion in abstraction from what follows, or in abstraction from the overall context of Kant's philosophy, one fails to see that the two perspectives, that of the heavens above and that of the moral law within, are radically opposed, in fact at war with each other. It is impossible for both to be genuinely awesome, for the true awesomeness of the physical universe would abrogate man's moral worth, while, conversely, the true awesomeness of man as a moral being would render nugatory the apparent sublimity of nature. The analytic of the sublime has the merit of bringing out this point in its furthest implications; what it does is to reinterpret the genuinely felt aesthetic experience of awe toward physical nature so as to be consistent with the doctrine of a single ultimate source of awe, thereby solving the problem.

In order to comprehend more fully what is at stake in Kant's devaluation of the sublimity of nature, let us reconsider his account in relation to two other philosophic sources, one dating from a century prior to Kant, the other from a century after Kant, both of which formulate equally radical statements of the problem. In a memorable passage in the *Pensées,* Pascal writes: "When I consider the short duration of my life, swallowed up in the eternity before and after, the little space which I fill and even can see, engulfed in the infinite immensity of spaces of which I am ignorant and which know me not, I am frightened and am astonished at being here rather than there; for there is no reason why here rather than there, why now rather than then."[12] Similarly, Nietzsche begins his early essay "On Truth and Lie in an Extra-Moral Sense" with a reflection on the paltriness of earthly existence: "In some remote corner of the universe, poured out and glittering in innumerable solar systems, there once was a star. . . ."[13] One is strongly tempted to read Kant on the sublime as a response to Pascal's perception of our insignificance in relation to *l'infini immensité des espaces.* One must respond to this challenge to human dignity if one is to avoid the extreme conclusion of Nietzsche, who likens man's conceits to the self-importance of the mosquito, "feeling within itself the flying centre of the world," and Kant's comparison of the sublimity of nature to the sublimity of moral experience, it would appear, supplies this response.

Like Pascal, Kant speaks of "worlds upon worlds and systems of systems," as well as the "limitless times of their periodic motion"; like Nietzsche, he refers to the earth as "a mere speck in the universe."[14] The problem is that in all three accounts, nature is no longer understood as enfolding man within a more comprehensive, rationally meaningful order—and yet nature continues to appear no less awesome. In fact, the boundlessness of nature in its cosmological aspect, or more specifically its "centerlessness," renders nature more awesome than ever, as Pascal and Nietzsche express with supreme effect. It is of course no coincidence that Kant introduces his philosophy with his famous reference to the astronomical revolution of Copernicus, for it is the need to come to terms with the sense of cosmological dislocation, displacement from the center, that Copernicus's revolution instilled that at least in part elicited Kant's philosophical reflection in the first place.[15] As Nietzsche very strikingly put it, "Since Copernicus man has been rolling from the centre toward X."[16] For Pascal, the post-Copernican universe was a source of terror and desperation. For Nietzsche, the Copernican revolution was perceived as a tremendous liberation.[17] For Kant, it posed a consummate challenge—a challenge that was ultimately met in the analytic of the sublime in the *Critique of Judgment*.[18] To give a name to Kant's solution, one might call it, somewhat provocatively, the "anthropological narcissism" of Kant's account of the sublime: man gazes up at the heavens and apprehends . . . himself.

Hannah Arendt's book *The Human Condition* contains a critique of Kant focused on the extreme "anthropocentrism" of his thought and the sorry implications that this has for man's relation to what is nonhuman: "The anthropocentric utilitarianism of *homo faber* has found its greatest expression in the Kantian formula that no man must ever become a means to an end, that every human being is an end in himself. . . . The same operation which establishes man as the "supreme end" permits him . . . to degrade nature and the world into mere means, robbing both of their independent dignity."[19] The textual basis for this line of criticism is to be found not only in the "Critique of Teleological Judgment" (§84), which Arendt cites, but also in the *Foundations of the Metaphysics of Morals:* "Beings whose existence does not depend on our will but on nature, if they are not rational beings, have only a relative worth as means and are therefore called 'things'; on the other hand, rational beings are designated 'persons' because their nature indicates that they are ends in themselves, i.e., things which may not be used merely as means. Such a being is thus an object of respect."[20] The ethical implications of this distinction between instrumental things and respectworthy persons are drawn in Kant's *Lectures on*

Ethics: "So far as animals are concerned, we have no direct duties. Animals are not self-conscious and are there merely as a means to an end. That end is man. We can ask, 'Why do animals exist?' But to ask, 'Why does man exist?' is a meaningless question. Our duties towards animals are merely indirect duties towards humanity."[21] Morally speaking, there are only two classes of entities in the universe: things and persons, means and ends. Since animals are not persons, they must be morally considered as things; that is, they admit of the question "for what end?," a question that would be illegitimate for a rational being whose end was located within itself. The same applies to inanimate nature: "No man ought to mar the beauty of nature," not because to do so would be a violation of nature itself, but rather because "what he has no use for may still be of use to someone else. He need, of course, pay no heed to the thing itself."[22] Within this framework of thought, the notion of an extrahuman standard that limits the uses to which we may put nature in submission to our own ends is simply unintelligible.[23]

Arendt's censure of this aspect of Kant's thought leads us back to Heidegger, for Arendt's critique is derived in large measure from Heidegger's indictment of "humanism," especially in the *Letter on Humanism,* and his attempt to refute the conception of man as *sovereign* over other beings on account of the privileged character of his metaphysical properties as a "rational animal." Heidegger seeks an alternative understanding of human essence that does not yield these consequences for man's relation to other beings: "the highest determinations of the essence of man in humanism still do not realize the proper dignity of man. . . . Humanism is opposed because it does not set the *humanitas* of man high enough. . . . Man is the shepherd of Being."[24] In "The Question Concerning Technology," Heidegger analyzes the ontological "narcissism" that has come to fruition in modernity. He shows how technological man negates the very autonomy of the object as such to the point where "the object disappears into . . . objectlessness." In the midst of this objectlessness, "the impression comes to prevail that everything man encounters exists only insofar as it is his construct. This illusion gives rise in turn to one final delusion: It seems as though man everywhere and always encounters only himself." Under these circumstances, it is hardly very surprising that man conducts himself as "lord of the earth."[25]

I believe that the "antihumanistic" or antianthropocentric analyses of Heidegger and Arendt can be well illustrated by reflecting critically on Kant's account of the sublime: namely, the manner in which that account intimates the sovereignty of man over nature.[26] The question of the sublime, *das Erhabene,* is in essence the issue of what is raised or elevated (*erhaben*) to the utmost height, the human or the nonhuman; or, to employ the terms that Kant elects in §84 of the *Critique of Judgment,* it is the issue of the "final end" in relation to which all else is subordinated as means. It is precisely in considering that experience of nature where we are most subject to its power and feel driven to acknowledge our own lowliness ("the prospect of mountains ascending to heaven, deep ravines and torrents raging there, deep-shadowed solitudes that invite to brooding melancholy"; *Critique of Judgment,* p. 121; 5:269) that we can perceive in the clearest way the contrary impulse in man to assert that he is, not the shepherd of Being, but "the lord of beings."[27] It is this that is disclosed for us in Kant's magisterial effort to transpose the sublimity of objective nature into the even higher sublimity of man's inner subjectivity.[28]

Notes

1
Immanuel Kant, *Critique of Practical Reason and Other Works on the Theory of Ethics,* trans. Thomas Kingsmill Abbott (London: Longmans, Green, 1898), p. 260; *Kant's gesammelte Schriften,* ed. Königlich Preussischen Akademie der Wissenschaften (Berlin, 1902–), 5:161. (In all subsequent notes, with the exception of those referring to the *Critique of Pure Reason* and *Lectures on Ethics,* references to an English translation is followed by a citation of the Academy edition.)

2
Immanuel Kant, *The Critique of Judgment,* trans. James Creed Meredith (Oxford: Clarendon Press, 1952), part 1, pp. 91–92; 5:245–46. Subsequent citations to *Critique of Judgment,* part 1 (both the Meredith translation and the Academy edition) appear in the text.

3
Ibid., p. 97; 5:250. One may compare—as well as contrast—Plato, *Republic* 523e–524c, where Socrates argues that the physical eye can see only bigness mixed with littleness (big in relation to what is littler, little in relation to what is bigger); it is the eye of the intellect alone that can conceive pure, unmixed bigness. (Plato's version of Kant's statement might read: the sublime is not to be looked for in the things of nature, but only in *the* ideas.)

4
It is important to note that the correlation between sublimity and moral respect is also very notably present in Kant's pre-Critical period. Cf. *Observations on the Feeling of the Beautiful and Sublime* (1763), §2—e.g., "Erhabene Eigenschaften flößen Hochachtung, schöne aber Liebe ein" (Academy ed., 2:211).

5
See Kant, *Foundations of the Metaphysics of Morals,* trans. Lewis White Beck (Indianapolis: Bobbs-Merrill, 1959), p. 46; Academy ed., 4:428.

6
Cf. Susan Shell's chapter in this volume, note 23. See also Hans-Georg Gadamer, *The Relevance of the Beautiful and Other Essays,* ed. Robert Bernasconi (Cambridge: Cambridge University Press, 1986), p. 168: "the sublime in nature . . . excites a paradoxical pleasure in something unpleasant." Relevant here is Plato's discussion of composite pleasure-pains in *Philebus,* 46ff.

7
Kant, *Anthropology from a Pragmatic Point of View,* ed. Mary J. Gregor (The Hague: Martinus Nijhoff, 1974), pp. 110–11; Academy ed., 7:243. It may be noted that the Kantian term for awe in this text already subsumes fear and anxiety: *Ehrfurcht,* literally "respectful fright."

8
It is worth noting that the correlative relationship between sublimity and morality developed in the *Critique of Judgment* is already expressed in Kant's invocation, in the *Grund-*

legung, of the *Erhabenheit* of the person: Academy ed., 4:439–40; see also the reference to the *Erhabenheit* of *Sittlichkeit,* 4:442.

9

The all-important verb *abwürdigen* (= *herabwürdigen*) in this passage can also be rendered: to belittle, demean, abase, debase. Cf. the usage of the same verb in the passage quoted above (Academy ed., 5:250).

10

Kant, *Critique of Practical Reason,* p. 260; 5:162. Note the use of the German verb *erheben* in Kant's description of the effect of the moral law; this verb is the etymological root of the German term for the sublime, *das Erhabene.* Cf. the use of the adjective *erhaben* (elevated, exalted) in, for instance, *Critique of Judgment,* 5:264.

11

Cf. Kant, *The Conflict of the Faculties,* trans. Mary J. Gregor (New York: Abaris Books, 1979), p. 105; Academy ed., 7:58): "there is something in us that we cannot cease to wonder at when we have once seen it, the same thing that raises *humanity* in its Idea to a dignity we should never have suspected in *man* as an object of experience. . . . This ascendancy of the supersensible man in us over the *sensible,* such that (when it comes to a conflict between them) the sensible is *nothing,* though in its own eyes it is *everything,* is an object of the greatest *wonder.*" The same double motion of simultaneous diminution and elevation recurs in *The Conflict of the Faculties:* man is both "but a trifle" and "the ultimate purpose of creation itself" (p. 161; 7:89).

12

Blaise Pascal, *Pensées,* trans. W. F. Trotter (New York: Modern Library, 1941), pp. 74–75. Cf. Montesquieu, *Persian Letters,* Letter 76.

13

The Portable Nietzsche, ed. Walter Kaufmann (New York: Viking, 1968), p. 42.

14

Kant, *Critique of Practical Reason,* p. 260, 5:162.

15

Kant, *Critique of Pure Reason,* Bxvi–xvii, Bxxii note. For further discussion, see Karl Löwith, *Nature, History, and Existentialism,* ed. Arnold Levison (Evanston: Northwestern University Press, 1966), pp. 24–29 and 102–15. Löwith writes: "how can one feel at home in a universe . . . which is said to have come into existence through an explosion?" (p. 28). It is not coincidental that Kant was both one of the earliest progenitors of modern cosmological speculation and the source of one of the deepest attempts to address (even in his aesthetics) the philosophical challenge of man's cosmic homelessness. (Cf. ibid., pp. 105–06.) See Kant, *Universal Natural History and Theory of the Heavens,* in *Kant's Cosmogony,* ed. Willy Ley, trans. W. Hastie (Westport, Conn.: Greenwood, 1968); and William R. Shea, "Filled with Wonder," in *Kant's Philosophy of Physical Science,* ed. Robert E. Butts (Dordrecht: D. Riedel, 1986), pp. 95–124.

16

Friedrich Nietzsche, *The Will to Power,* ed. Walter Kaufmann (New York: Vintage, 1968), p. 8. Cf. *Genealogy of Morals,* Third Essay, section 25, where Nietzsche explicitly cites the passage in the conclusion of the *Critique of Practical Reason* discussed above. For extended discussion of Kant and Copernicus, see James Booth, *Interpreting the World* (Toronto: University of Toronto Press, 1986). For an account of how the waning of the idea of natural teleology implicit in the demise of pre-Copernican cosmology is integral to the problems that govern Kant's *Critique of Judgment,* in a way that joins together the critique of aesthetic judgment with the critique of teleological judgment, see Ernst Cassirer, *Kant's Life and Thought* (New Haven: Yale University Press, 1981), pp. 278ff. See also Hans-Georg Gadamer, *Truth and Method* (New York: Seabury Press, 1975), p. 47, on "the dissolution of ancient cosmological thought" and its relevance to Kant's aesthetics; and p. 50, on the relation between Kant's account of the beautiful and the sublime in nature and his treatment of teleology.

17

The Will to Power, p. 47.

18

See Richard L. Velkley, *Freedom and the End of Reason* (Chicago: University of Chicago Press, 1989), p. 111: "it may be the greatest 'interest' of this supposedly 'disinterested' morality to provide a confirmation of the human need for a sense of 'worth' within the natural whole. . . . To provide an answer to [the question of what death means] is unavoidable for any philosophy that dares to be responsible for the whole human condition." The same may be said to apply to what is at stake in Kant's account of the sublime.

19

Hannah Arendt, *The Human Condition* (Chicago: University of Chicago Press, 1958), pp. 155–56.

20

Kant, *Foundations of the Metaphysics of Morals,* p. 46; 4:428. Cf. Kant, *The Doctrine of Virtue,* trans. Mary J. Gregor (Philadelphia: University of Pennsylvania Press, 1964), pp. 22, 99, 132; 6:223, 434, 462.

21

Kant, *Lectures on Ethics,* trans. Louis Infield (New York: Harper and Row, 1963), p. 239. The corresponding discussion of this topic in *The Metaphysics of Morals* is *The Doctrine of Virtue,* pp. 108–09; 6:442–43. Cf. Kant, *On History,* ed. Lewis White Beck (Indianapolis: Bobbs-Merrill, 1963), pp. 58–59 (Academy ed., 8:114); and *Critique of Judgment,* part 2, pp. 86–88, 98–100; 5:425–27, 434–36.

22

Kant, *Lectures on Ethics,* p. 241.

23

Cf. Hans Jonas, *The Imperative of Responsibility* (Chicago: University of Chicago Press, 1984), pp. 88–90, where Jonas ob-

serves that Kant's ethics enjoins a feeling of reverence (*Ehrfurcht*) only for the moral law itself, that is, the form of willing by which we, as moral subjects, impose law upon ourselves, and thereby precludes, on grounds of heteronomy, reverence for Being. Against this, Jonas commends the possibility of experiencing reverence for "things rather than states of my will." Although he does not necessarily mean by Being exactly what Heidegger means by it, such a challenge clearly adds weight to a Heideggerian critique of Kant.

24

Martin Heidegger, *Basic Writings,* ed. David Farrell Krell (New York: Harper and Row, 1977), p. 120.

25

Heidegger, *The Question Concerning Technology,* trans. William Lovitt (New York: Harper and Row, 1977), pp. 19, 27. Kant actually refers to man as the "titular lord of nature" in *Critique of Judgment,* part 2, p. 94; 5:431.

26

Cf. Nietzsche, *The Will to Power,* p. 85: "All the beauty and sublimity we have bestowed upon real and imaginary things I will reclaim as the property and product of man." For discussion of this text, see Heidegger, *Nietzsche,* vol. 3, ed. David Farrell Krell (New York: Harper and Row, 1987), p. 228; and Heidegger, *Nietzsche,* vol. 4, ed. David Farrell Krell (New York: Harper and Row, 1982), pp. 81, 83. More generally, see *Nietzsche,* vol. 3, pp. 122, 154–55, and vol. 4, pp. 28–29, 80, 83, 85, 183, for an especially trenchant statement by Heidegger of how Western metaphysics consummates itself in the most extreme anthropomorphism.

27

Heidegger, *Basic Writings,* p. 221.

28

Notwithstanding his distinction between persons and things, Kant was at least still able to appreciate the starry heavens as an object of reverential awe. This appears not to have been the case for Kant's successors within the

German Idealist tradition, who in this respect applied all the more rigorously Kant's dualism of nature and freedom: "Marx liked to quote Hegel's remark that the most criminal thought is more magnificent and sublime than all the wonders of the starry skies because the criminal, as mind, is conscious of his thoughts whereas nature does not know itself. Marx is no longer astonished by those things which are by nature what they are and cannot be otherwise" (Löwith, *Nature, History, and Existentialism,* p. 141). Cf. p. 201: Hegel's disdain for nature "led him to describe the stars as only a sort of 'light-eruption, no more astonishing than a crowd of men or a mass of flies.'" For further expressions of Kant's wonder, see *Kant's Cosmogony,* pp. 52–53, 123, and 131; 1:255–56, 306, 312.

Part Four

Contemporary

Debates

Chapter 13

Themes in Kant's
Moral Philosophy

John Rawls

I shall discuss several connected themes in Kant's moral philosophy, in particular, what I shall refer to as moral constructivism and the fact of reason, and how that fact connects with the authentication of the moral law and the moral law as a law of freedom. These are each large topics, and I can only survey them; but perhaps something can be gained from a brief synoptic view. I should like to have concluded with some comments about what Kant means by the practical point of view, but that has proved impossible for lack of space.

To set the background for these topics, I begin with a schematic outline of how Kant understands the moral law, the categorical imperative, and the procedure by which that imperative is applied. Some account of that procedure is an essential preliminary to understanding his constructivism. Plainly a full account is out of the question but I believe many intriguing details of interpretation are not crucial so long as the account meets certain conditions (see §1.5). My hope is that the reading suggested is accurate enough to bring out the more central elements of Kant's constructivism and to connect this doctrine with the other topics.

My discussion has five parts: the first covers the procedure for applying the categorical imperative, or the CI-procedure, as I shall call it; the second surveys six conceptions of the good, and how these conceptions are constructed in an ordered sequence; whereas the third, based on the preceding two parts, examines the aspects of Kant's doctrine that make it constructivist and specify a conception of objectivity. The fourth and fifth parts take up, respectively, the kind of justification, or authentication, that can be given for the moral law, and how the moral law as an idea of reason is seen as a law of freedom and how this connects with Kant's idea of philosophy as defense.

Reprinted from *Kant's Transcendental Deductions: The Three "Critiques" and the "Opus Postumum,"* edited by Eckart Förster, with the permission of the publishers, Stanford University Press. © 1989 by the Board of Trustees of the Leland Stanford Junior University.

§1. The Four-Step CI-Procedure

1. I begin with a highly schematic rendering of Kant's conception of the categorical imperative.[1] I assume that this imperative is applied to the normal conditions of human life by what I shall call the "categorical imperative procedure," or the "CI-procedure" for short. This procedure helps to determine the content of the moral law as it applies to us as reasonable and rational persons endowed with conscience and moral sensibility, and affected by, but not determined by, our natural desires and inclinations. These desires and inclinations reflect our needs as finite beings having a particular place in the order of nature.

Recall that the moral law, the categorical imperative, and the CI-procedure are three different things. The first is an idea of reason and specifies a principle that applies to all reasonable and rational beings whether or not they are like us finite beings with needs. The second is an imperative and as such it is directed only to those reasonable and rational beings who, because they are finite beings with needs, experience the moral law as a constraint. Since we are such beings, we experience the law in this way, and so the categorical imperative applies to us. The CI-procedure adapts the categorical imperative to our circumstances by taking into account the normal conditions of human life and our situation as finite beings with needs in the order of nature.

Keep in mind throughout that Kant is concerned solely with the reasoning of fully reasonable and rational and sincere agents. The CI-procedure is a schema to characterize the framework of deliberation that such agents use implicitly in their moral thought. He takes for granted that the application of this procedure presupposes a certain moral sensibility that is part of our common humanity.[2] It is a misconception to think of it either as an algorithm that yields more or less mechanically a correct judgment or, on the other hand, as a set of debating rules that will trap liars and cheats, cynics and other scoundrels, into exposing their hand.

2. The CI-procedure has four steps as follows.[3] At the first step we have the agent's maxim, which is, by assumption, rational from the agent's point of view: that is, the maxim is rational given the agent's situation and the alternatives available together with the agent's desires, abilities, and beliefs (which are assumed to be rational in the circumstances). The maxim is also assumed to be sincere: that is, it reflects the agent's actual reasons (as the agent would truthfully describe them) for the intended action. Thus the CI-procedure applies to maxims that rational agents have arrived at in view of what they regard as the relevant features of their circumstances. And, we should add, this procedure applies equally well to maxims that rational and sincere agents might arrive at given the normal circumstances of human life. To sum up: the agent's maxim at the first step is both rational and sincere. It is a

particular hypothetical imperative (to be distinguished later from *the* hypothetical imperative) and it has the form:

(1) I am to do X in circumstances C in order to bring about Y. (Here X is an action and Y a state of affairs.)

The second step generalizes the maxim at the first to get:

(2) Everyone is to do X in circumstances C in order to bring about Y.

At the third step we are to transform the general precept at (2) into a law of nature to obtain:

(3) Everyone always does X in circumstances C in order to bring about Y (as if by a law of nature).

The fourth step is the most complicated and raises questions that I cannot consider here. The idea is this:

(4) We are to adjoin the law of nature at step (3) to the existing laws of nature (as these are understood by us) and then calculate as best we can what the order of nature would be once the effects of the newly adjoined law of nature have had a chance to work themselves out.

It is assumed that a new order of nature results from the addition of the law at step (3) to the other laws of nature, and that this new order of nature has a settled equilibrium state the relevant features of which we are able to figure out. Let us call this new order of nature a "perturbed social world" and let's think of this social world as associated with the maxim at step (1).

Kant's categorical imperative can now be stated as follows. We are permitted to act from our rational and sincere maxim at step (1) only if two conditions are satisfied: first, we must be able to intend, as a sincere, reasonable, and rational agent, to act from this maxim when we regard ourselves as a member of the perturbed social world associated with it (and thus as acting within that world and subject to its conditions); and second, we must be able to will this perturbed social world itself and affirm it should we belong to it.

Thus, if we cannot at the same time both will this perturbed social world and intend to act from this maxim as a member of it, we cannot now act from the maxim even though it is, by assumption, rational and sincere in our present circumstances. The principle represented by the CI-procedure applies to us no matter what the consequences may be for our rational interests as we now understand them. It is at this point that the force of the priority of pure practical reason over empirical practical reason comes into play. But let's leave this aside for the moment.

3. To illustrate the use of the four-step procedure, consider the fourth example in the *Grundlegung* (Gr 4:423). The maxim to be tested is one that expresses indifference to the well-being of others who need our help and assistance. We are to decide whether we can will the perturbed social world associated with this maxim

formulated as follows: I am not to do anything to help others, or to support them in distress, unless at the time it is rational to do so, given my own interests.

The perturbed social world associated with this maxim is a social world in which no one ever does anything to help others for the sake of their well-being. And this is true of everyone, past, present, and future. This is the relevant equilibrium state; and we are to imagine that this state obtains, like any other order of nature, in perpetuity, backward and forward in time. Kant takes for granted that everyone in the perturbed social world knows the laws of human conduct that arise from generalized maxims and that everyone is able to work out the relevant equilibrium state. Moreover, that everyone is able to do this is itself public knowledge. Thus, the operation at step (3) converts a general precept at step (2) into a publicly recognized law of (human) nature. That Kant takes these matters for granted is clearest from his second example, that of the deceitful promise.

Now Kant says that we cannot will the perturbed social world associated with the maxim of indifference because many situations may arise in that world in which we need the love and sympathy of others. In those situations, by a law originating from our own will, we would have robbed ourselves of what we require. It would be irrational for us to will a social world in which everyone, as if by a law of nature, is deaf to appeals based on this need. Kant does not say much about how the idea of a rational will works in this example. In addition, the test as he applies it to the maxim of indifference is too strong: that is, the same test rejects those maxims that lead to any form of the precept (or duty) of mutual aid. The reason is this: any such precept enjoins us to help others when they are in need. But here also, in the perturbed social world associated with a precept to help others in need, situations may arise in which we very much want not to help them. The circumstances may be such that helping them seriously interferes with our plans. Thus, in these cases too, by a law originating from our own will, we would have prevented ourselves from achieving what we very much want. The difficulty is clear enough: in any perturbed social world all moral precepts will oppose our natural desires and settled intentions on at least some occasions. Hence the test of the CI-procedure, as Kant apparently understands it, is too strong: it appears to reject all maxims that lead to moral precepts (or duties).

4. One way out, I think, but I don't say the only one, is to try to develop an appropriate conception of what we may call "true human needs," a phrase Kant uses several times in the *Metaphysics of Morals* (MM 6:393, 432; see also 452–58).[4] Once this is done, the contradiction in the will test as illustrated by the fourth example might be formulated as follows: Can I will the perturbed social world associated with the precept of indifference rather than the perturbed social world associated with a precept of mutual aid, that is, a maxim enjoining me to help others in need? In answering this question I am to take account only of my true human

needs (which by assumption, as part of the CI-procedure, I take myself to have and to be the same for everyone).

Thus, in applying the procedure as now revised we understand that any general precept will constrain our actions prompted by our desires and inclinations on some and perhaps many occasions. What we must do is to compare alternative social worlds and evaluate the overall consequences of willing one of these worlds rather than another. In order to do this, we are to take into account the balance of likely effects over time for our true human needs. Of course for this idea to work, we require an account of these needs. And here certain moral conceptions, rooted in our shared moral sensibility, may be involved.

I believe that Kant also assumes that the evaluation of perturbed social worlds at step (4) is subject to at least two limits on information. The first limit is that we are to ignore the more particular features of persons, including ourselves, as well as the specific content of their and our final ends and desires (Gr 4:433). The second limit is that when we ask ourselves whether we can will the perturbed social world associated with our maxim, we are to reason as if we do not know which place we may have in that world (see the discussion of the Typic in *Critique of Practical Reason,* CP 5:69–70). The CI-procedure is misapplied when we project into the perturbed social world either the specific content of our final ends or the particular features of our present or likely future circumstances. We must reason at step (4) not only on the basis of true human needs but also from a suitably general point of view that satisfies these two limits on particular (as opposed to general) information. We must see ourselves as proposing the public moral law for an ongoing social world enduring over time.

5. This brief schematic account of the CI-procedure is intended only to set the background for explaining the sequence of conceptions of the good in §2 and Kant's moral constructivism in §3. To serve this purpose, the procedure must meet two conditions: (1) it must not represent the requirements of the moral law as merely formal (otherwise, the moral law lacks sufficient content for a constructivist view); and (2) it must have features that enable us to see what Kant means when he says that the moral law discloses our freedom to us (considered in §5 below), for this, too, is an essential part of Kant's constructivism, since freedom of moral thought and action is required if the constructivist procedure is to be authenticated as objective, as the work of reason (considered in §4).

It turns out that for the second condition to be met, the CI-procedure must display in how it works, on its face as it were, the way in which pure practical reason is prior to empirical practical reason. This enables us to understand the distinctive structure of Kant's moral conception and how it is possible for our freedom to be made manifest to us by the moral law.

What this priority means will become clearer as we proceed. For the present let's say that pure practical reason restricts empirical practical reason and subordinates it absolutely. This is an aspect of the unity of reason. The way in which pure practical reason restricts and subordinates empirical practical reason is expressed in imperative form by the CI-procedure: this procedure represents the requirements of pure practical reason in the manner appropriate for the conditions of human life. Empirical practical reason is the principle of rational deliberation that determines when particular hypothetical imperatives are rational. The CI-procedure restricts empirical practical reason by requiring the agent's rational and sincere deliberations to be conducted in accordance with the stipulations we have just surveyed. Unless a maxim passes the test of that procedure, acting from the maxim is forbidden. This outcome is final from the standpoint of practical reason as a whole, both pure and empirical. The survey of six conceptions of the good in Kant's doctrine in the next part will supplement these remarks about how the two forms of practical reason are combined in the unity of practical reason.

6. Before turning to this survey, a few comments on the sketch of the CI-procedure. In characterizing human persons I have used the phrase "reasonable and rational." The intention here is to mark the fact that Kant uses *vernünftig* to express a full-bodied conception that covers the terms *reasonable* and *rational* as we often use them. In English we know what is meant when someone says: "Their proposal is rational, given their circumstances, but it is unreasonable all the same." The meaning is roughly that the people referred to are pushing a hard and unfair bargain, which they know to be in their own interests but which they wouldn't expect us to accept unless they knew their position is strong. *Reasonable* can also mean judicious, ready to listen to reason, where this has the sense of being willing to listen to and consider the reasons offered by others. *Vernünftig* can have the same meanings in German: it can have the broad sense of *reasonable* as well as the narrower sense of *rational* to mean, roughly, furthering our interests in the most effective way. Kant's usage varies but when applied to persons it usually covers being both reasonable and rational. His use of *reason* often has the even fuller sense of the philosophical tradition. Think of what *Vernünft* means in the title of the *Critique of Pure Reason!* We are worlds away from "rational" in the narrow sense. It's a deep question (which I leave aside) whether Kant's conception of reason includes far more than reason.

It is useful, then, to use *reasonable* and *rational* as handy terms to mark the distinction that Kant makes between the two forms of practical reason, pure and empirical. The first is expressed as an imperative in *the* categorical imperative, the second in *the* hypothetical imperative. These forms of practical reason must also be distinguished from particular categorical and hypothetical imperatives—the particular maxims at step (1)—that satisfy the corresponding requirements of practical reason in particular circumstances. The terms *reasonable* and *rational* remind us of the fullness of Kant's conception of practical reason and of the two forms of reason it comprehends.

7. I conclude with some remarks about the relation between Kant's three different formulations of the categorical imperative. Some may think that to rely, as I shall, on the first formulation alone gives an incomplete idea of the content of the categorical imperative. It may be incomplete, but nevertheless I believe it is adequate for our purposes. Kant says (Gr 4:436–37) that the three formulations are "so many formulations of precisely the same law." He also says that there is a difference between the formulations, which is only subjectively rather than objectively practical. The purpose of having several formulations is to bring the idea of reason (the moral law) nearer to intuition in accordance with a certain analogy and so nearer to feeling. At the end of the passage (pars. 72–75 of chap. 2), Kant says that if we wish to gain access (or entry) for the moral law[5] it is useful to bring one and the same action under all three formulations, and in this way, so far as we can, to bring "it [the action] nearer to intuition." We are also instructed that it is better when making a moral judgment to "proceed always in accordance with the strict method and take as our basis the universal formula of the categorical imperative." This imperative we have interpreted in accordance with the law of nature formula (Gr 4:421); we noted also the *Critique of Practical Reason* with its account of the Typic at CP 5:67–71.

There are certain obscurities in Kant's view here. I shall not discuss them but simply state what I regard as his two main points. First, we are to use the four-step CI-procedure whenever we are testing whether our maxim is permitted by the categorical imperative. The other formulations cannot add to the content of the moral law as it applies to us. What is important here is that, however we interpret them, the second and third formulations must not yield any requirement that is not already accounted for by the CI-procedure. In particular, this holds for the second formulation concerning treating persons always as ends and never as means only (see Gr 4:429). With its use of the term *humanity* (*Menschheit*), this formulation seems strikingly different from the first and third. This appearance is misleading, since it is clear from the Introduction to the *Metaphysics of Morals* that *humanity* means the powers that characterize us as reasonable and rational beings who belong to the natural order. Our humanity is our pure practical reason together with our moral sensibility (our capacity for moral feeling). These two powers constitute moral personality and include the power to set ends (MM 6:392); they make a good will and moral character possible. We have a duty to cultivate our natural capacities in order to make ourselves worthy of our humanity (MM 6:387). Thus, the duty to treat humanity, whether in our own person or in the person of others, always as an end and never simply as a means is the duty to respect the moral powers both in ourselves and in other persons, and to cultivate our natural capacities so that we can be worthy of those powers. Modulo shifts of points of view as described in the next paragraph, what particular duties are covered by this duty are ascertained by the first formulation of the categorical imperative. The first principle of the doctrine of virtue (MM 6:395) is a special case of this formulation. I think we cannot discern what Kant means by the second formulation apart from his account in the *Metaphysics of Morals*.

8. A second point about the relation of the three formulations: I believe that the purpose of the second and third formulations is to look at the application of the CI-procedure from two further points of view. The idea is this: each formulation looks at this procedure from a different point of view. In the first formulation, which is the strict method, we look at our maxim for our point of view. This is clear from how the procedure is described. We are to regard ourselves as subject to the moral law and we want to know what it requires of us. In the second formulation, however, we are to consider our maxim from the point of view of our humanity as the fundamental element in our person demanding our respect, or from the point of view of other persons who will be affected by our action. Humanity both in us and in other persons is regarded as *passive:* as that which will be affected by what we do. As Kant says (CP 5:87), in an apparent reference to the second formulation of the *Grundlegung*, the autonomy of a reasonable and rational being is to be "subjected to no purpose which is not possible by a law which could arise from the will of the passive subject itself." But when this passive subject considers which laws can arise from its will, it must apply the CI-procedure. The point is simply that all persons affected must apply that procedure in the same way both to accept and to reject the same maxims. This ensures a universal agreement that prepares the way for the third formulation.

In this formulation we come back again to the agent's point of view, but this time we no longer regard ourselves as someone who is subject to the moral law but as someone who makes that law. The CI-procedure is seen as the procedure adherence to which with a full grasp of its meaning enables us to regard ourselves as legislators, as those who make universal public law for a possible moral community. This community Kant calls a realm of ends—a commonwealth and not a kingdom—the conception of which is also an idea of reason.

Finally, using all three formulations of the moral law is subjectively practical in two ways: first, having these formulations deepens our understanding of the moral law by showing how it regards actions from different points of view, and, second, our deeper understanding of that law strengthens our desire to act from it. This is what Kant means, I think, by gaining entry or access for the moral law.[6]

§2. *The Sequence of Six Conceptions of the Good*

1. In order to understand Kant's constructivism and how he thinks that the moral law discloses our freedom to us, we need to look at the priority of pure practical reason over empirical practical reason and to distinguish six conceptions of the good in Kant's doctrine. These conceptions are built up in a sequence one by one from the preceding ones. This sequence can be presented by referring to the four steps of the CI-procedure, since each conception can be connected with a particular step in this procedure. This provides a useful way of arranging these conceptions and clarifies the relations among them. It also enables us to explain what is meant by calling the realm of ends the necessary object of a will determined by the moral law, as well as what is meant by saying of this realm that it is an object given a priori to such a pure will (CP 5:4).

The first of the six conceptions of the good is given by unrestricted empirical practical reason. It is the conception of happiness as organized by the (as opposed to a particular) hypothetical imperative. This conception may be connected with step (1) of the CI-procedure, since the maxim at this step is assumed to be rational and sincere given that conception. Thus the maxim satisfies the principles of rational deliberation that characterize the hypothetical imperative, or what we may call the rational. There are no restrictions on the information available to sincere and rational agents either in framing their conceptions of happiness or in forming their particular maxims: all the relevant particulars about their desires, abilities, and situation, as well as the available alternatives, are assumed to be known.

The second conception of the good is of the fulfillment of true human needs. I have suggested that at the fourth step of the CI-procedure we require some such idea. Otherwise the agent going through the procedure cannot compare the perturbed social worlds associated with different maxims. At first we might think this comparison can be made on the basis of the agent's conception of happiness. But even if the agent knows what this conception is, there is still a serious difficulty, since Kant supposes different agents to have different conceptions of their happiness. On his view, happiness is an ideal, not of reason but of the imagination, and so our conception of our happiness depends on the contingencies of our life and on particular modes of thought and feeling we have developed as we come of age. Thus, if conceptions of happiness are used in judging social worlds at step (4), then whether a maxim passes the CI-procedure would depend on who applies it. This dependence would defeat Kant's view. For if our following the CI-procedure doesn't lead to approximate agreement when we apply it intelligently and conscientiously against the background of the same information, then that law lacks objective content. Here objective content means a content that is publicly recognized as correct, as based on sufficient reasons and as (roughly) the same for all reasonable and sincere human agents.

Observe that this second conception of the good based on true human needs is a special conception designed expressly to be used at step (4) of the CI-procedure. It is formulated to meet a need of reason: namely, that the moral law have sufficient objective content. Moreover, when this procedure is thought of as applied consistently by everyone over time in accordance with the requirement of complete determination (Gr 4:436), it specifies the content of a conception of right and justice that would be realized in a realm of ends. This conception, as opposed to the first, is restricted: that is, it is framed in view of the restrictions on information to which agents are subject at step (4).

The third conception of the good is the good as the fulfillment in everyday life of what Kant calls "permissible ends" (MM 6:388), that is, ends that respect the limits of the moral law. This means in practice that we are to revise, abandon, or repress desires and inclinations that prompt us to rational and sincere maxims at step (1) that are rejected by the CI-procedure. Here it is not a question of balancing the strength and importance to us of our natural desires against the strength and importance to us of the pure practical interest we take in acting from the moral law. Such balancing is excluded entirely. Rather, whenever our maxim is rejected, we must reconsider our intended course of action, for in this case the claim to satisfy the desires in question is rejected. At this point the contrast with utilitarianism is clear, since for Kant this third conception of the good presupposes the moral law and the principles of pure practical reason. Whereas utilitarianism starts with a conception of the good given prior to, and independent of, the right (the moral law), and it then works out from that independent conception its conceptions of the right and of moral worth, in that order. In Kant's view, however, unrestricted rationality, or the rational, is framed by and subordinated absolutely to a procedure that incorporates the constraints of the reasonable. It is by this procedure that admissible conceptions of the good and their permissible ends are specified.

2. The first of the three remaining conceptions of the good is the familiar conception of the good will. This is Kant's conception of moral worth: a completely good will is the supreme (although not the complete) good of persons and of their character as reasonable and rational beings. This good is constituted by a firm and settled highest-order desire that leads us to take an interest in acting from the moral law for its own sake or, what comes in practice to the same thing, to further the realm of ends as the moral law requires. When we have a completely good will, this highest-order desire, however strongly it may be opposed by our natural desires and inclinations, is always strong enough by itself to ensure that we act from (and not merely in accordance with) the moral law.

The next conception of the good is the good as the object of the moral law, which is, as indicated above, the realm of ends. This object is simply the social world that would come about (at least under reasonably favorable conditions) if everyone were to follow the totality of precepts that result from the correct application of the CI-procedure. Kant sometimes refers to the realm of ends as the necessary object of a will, which is determined by the moral law, or, alternatively, as an object that is given a priori to a will determined by that law (CP 5:4). By this I think he means that the realm of ends is an object—a social world—the moral constitution and regulation of which is specified by the totality of precepts that meet the test of the CI-procedure (when these precepts are adjusted and coordinated by the requirement of complete determination). Put another way, the realm of ends is not a social world that can be described prior to and independent of the concepts and principles of practical reason and the procedure by which they are applied. That realm is not an already given, describable object the nature of which determines the content of the moral law. This would be the case, for example, if this law were understood as stating what must be done in order to bring about a good society the nature and institutions of which are already specified apart from the moral law. That such a teleological conception is foreign to Kant's doctrine is plain from chap. 2 of the Analytic of the *Critique of Practical Reason*. The burden of that chapter is to explain what has been called Kant's Copernican revolution in moral philosophy (CP 5:62–65).[7] Rather than starting from a conception of the good given independently of the right, we start from a conception of the right—of the moral law—given by pure (as opposed to empirical) practical reason. We then specify in the light of this conception what ends are permissible and what social arrangements are right and just. We might say: a moral conception is not to revolve around the good as an independent object, but around a conception of the right as constructed by our pure practical reason into which any permissible good must fit. Kant believes that once we start from the good as an independent given object, the moral conception must be heteronomous, and this is as true of Leibniz's perfectionism as it is of the psychological naturalism that underlies Hume's utilitarianism. In these cases what determines our will is an object given to it and not principles originating in our pure reason as reasonable and rational beings.

Finally, there is Kant's conception of the complete good. This is the good that is attained when a realm of ends exists and each member of it not only has a completely good will but is also fully happy so far as the normal conditions of human life allow. Here, of course, happiness is specified by the satisfaction of ends that respect the requirements of the moral law and so are permissible ends. Often Kant refers to this complete good as the highest good. This is his preferred term after *Grundlegung,* especially when he is presenting his doctrine of reasonable faith in the second *Critique.* I shall use the secular term "realized realm of ends," and I assume that this complete good can be approximated in the natural world, at least under reasonably favorable conditions. In this sense it is a natural good, one that can be approached (although never fully realized) within the order of nature.

Kant holds that in the complete good, the good will is the supreme good, that is, we must have a good will if the other goods we enjoy are to be truly good and our enjoyment of them fully appropriate. This applies in particular to the good of happiness, since he thinks that only our having a good will can make us worthy of happiness. Kant also believes that two goods so different in their nature, and in their foundations in our person, as a good will and happiness are incommensurable; and, therefore, that they can be combined into one unified and complete good only by the relation of the strict priority of one over the other.

3. The preceding sketch of conceptions of the good in Kant's view indicates how they are built up, or constructed, in an ordered sequence one after the other, each conception (except the first) depending on the preceding ones. If we count the second (that of true human needs) as part of the CI-procedure itself, we can say that beginning with the third (that of permissible ends), these conceptions presuppose an independent conception of right (the reasonable). This conception of right is represented by the CI-procedure as the application of pure practical reason to the conditions of human life. Only the first conception of the good is entirely independent of the moral law, since it is the rational without restriction. Thus the sequence of conceptions beginning with the second exemplifies the priority of pure practical reason over empirical practical reason and displays the distinctive deontological and constructivist structure of Kant's view. We start with two forms of practical reason, the reasonable and the rational. The unity of practical reason is grounded in how the reasonable frames the rational and restricts it absolutely. Then we proceed step by step to generate different conceptions of the good and obtain at the last two steps the conceptions of the good will and of a complete good as a fully realized realm of ends. The contrast between the deontological and constructivist structure of Kant's doctrine and the linear structure of a teleological view starting from an independent conception of the good is so obvious as not to need comment.

§3. Kant's Moral Constructivism

1. We are now in a position to see what is meant in saying that Kant's moral doctrine is constructivist and why the term *constructivist* is appropriate.

One way to bring out the features of Kant's moral constructivism is to contrast it with rational intuitionism. The latter doctrine has, of course, been expressed in many ways; but in some form it dominated moral philosophy from Plato and Aristotle onward until it was challenged by Hobbes and Hume, and, I believe, in a very different way, by Kant. To simplify things, I take rational intuitionism to be the view exemplified in the English tradition by Samuel Clarke and Richard Price, Henry Sidgwick, and G. E. Moore, and formulated in its minimum essentials by W. D. Ross. With qualifications, it was accepted by Leibniz and Christian Wolff in the guise of perfectionism, and Kant knows of it in this form.

For our purposes here, rational intuitionism may be summed up in three theses, the first two of which it has in common with a number of other views, including Kant's. First, the basic moral concepts of the right and the good, and the moral worth of persons, are not analyzable in terms of nonmoral concepts (although possibly they are analyzable in terms of one another). Second, first principles of morals (whether one or many), when correctly stated, are true statements about what kinds of considerations are good reasons for applying one of the three basic moral concepts: that is, for asserting that something is (intrinsically) good, or that a certain institution is just or a certain action right, or that a certain trait of character or motive has moral worth. Third (and this is the distinctive thesis for our purposes), first principles, as statements about good reasons, are regarded as true or false in virtue of a moral order of values that is prior to and independent of our conceptions of person and society, and of the public social role of moral doctrines.

This prior moral order is already given, as it were, by the nature of things and is known by rational intuition (or in some views by moral sense, but I leave this possibility aside). Thus, our agreement in judgment when properly founded is said to be based on the shared recognition of truths about a prior order of values accessible to reason. Observe that no reference is made to self-evidence; for although intuitionists have often held first principles to be self-evident, this feature is not essential.

It should be observed that rational intuitionism is compatible with a variety of contents for the first principles of a moral conception. Even classical utilitarianism, which Sidgwick in his *Methods of Ethics* was strongly inclined to favor, was sometimes viewed by him as following from three more fundamental principles, each grasped by rational intuition in its own right. Of the recent versions of rational intuitionism, the appeal to rational intuition is perhaps most striking in Moore's so-called ideal utilitarianism in *Principia Ethica*. A consequence of Moore's principle of organic unity is that his view is extremely pluralistic: there are few if any useful first principles, and distinct kinds of cases are to be decided by intuition as they arise. Moore held a kind of Platonic atomism[8]—moral concepts (along with other concepts) are subsisting and independent entities grasped by the mind. That pleasure and beauty are good and that different combinations of them alone or together with other good things are also good, and to what degree, are truths known by intuition: by seeing with the mind's eye how these distinct objects (universals) are (timelessly) related.

Now my aim in recalling these familiar matters is to indicate how rational intuitionism, as illustrated by Sidgwick, Moore, and Ross, is distinct from a constructivist moral conception. That Kant would have rejected Hume's psychological naturalism as heteronomous is clear. But I believe that the contrast with rational intuitionism, regardless of the specific content of the view (whether utilitarian, perfectionist, or pluralist), is even more instructive. It has seemed less obvious that for Kant rational intuitionism is also heteronomous. Perhaps the reason is that in rational intuitionism basic moral concepts are conceptually independent of natural concepts, and first principles as grasped by rational intuition are viewed as synthetic a priori and so independent of any particular order of nature. They give the content of an ethics of creation, so to speak: the principles God would use to ascertain which is the best of all possible worlds. Thus, it may seem that for Kant such principles are not heteronomous.

Yet in Kant's moral constructivism it suffices for heteronomy that first principles obtain in virtue of relations among objects the nature of which is not affected or determined by our conception of ourselves as reasonable and rational persons (as possessing the powers of practical reason), and of the public role of moral principles in a society of such persons. Of particular importance is the conception of persons as reasonable and rational, and, therefore, as free and equal, and the basic units of agency and responsibility. Kant's idea of autonomy requires that there exist no moral order prior to and independent of those conceptions that is to determine the form of the procedure that specifies the content of first principles of right and justice among free and equal persons. Heteronomy obtains not only when these first principles are fixed by the special psychological constitution of human nature, as in Hume, but also when they are fixed by an order of universals, or of moral value grasped by rational intuition, as in Plato's realm of forms or in Leibniz's hierarchy of perfections.

Thus an essential feature of Kant's moral constructivism is that the first principles of right and justice are seen as specified by a procedure of construction (the CI-procedure) the form and structure of which mirrors our free moral personality as both reasonable and rational. This conception of the person he regards as implicit in our everyday moral consciousness. A Kantian doctrine may hold (as Kant did) that the procedure by which first principles are specified, or constructed, is synthetic a priori. This thesis, however, must be properly understood. It simply means that the form and structure of this procedure express the requirements of practical reason. These requirements are embedded in our conception of persons as reasonable and rational, and as the basic units of agency and responsibility. This conception is found in how we represent to ourselves our free and equal moral personality in everyday life, or in what Kant in the second *Critique* calls the fact of reason.

It is characteristic of Kant's doctrine that a relatively complex conception of the person plays a central role in specifying the content of his moral view. By contrast, rational intuitionism requires but a sparse conception of the person, based on the idea of the person as knower. This is because the content of first principles is already given, and the only requirement is that we be able to know what these principles are and to be moved by this knowledge. A basic psychological assumption is that the recognition of first principles as true of a prior and antecedent order of moral values gives rise, in a being capable of rationally intuiting those principles, to a desire to act from them for their own sake. Moral motivation is defined by reference to desires that have a special kind of causal origin, namely, the intuitive grasp of first principles. This sparse conception of the person together with this psychological assumption characterizes the moral psychology of Sidgwick, Moore, and Ross. Of course, intuitionism is not forced to so sparse a conception. The point is rather that, since the content of first principles is already given, it is simply unnecessary to have a more elaborate moral psychology or a fuller conception of the person of a kind required to specify the form, structure, and content of a constructivist moral view.

2. So much for explaining Kant's moral constructivism by the contrast with rational intuitionism. Let's turn to a more specific account of the constructivist features of his view. But I should mention first that the idea of constructivism arises within moral and political philosophy. The term *constructivist* is not used because of analogies with constructivism in the philosophy of mathematics, even though Kant's account of the synthetic a priori nature of arithmetic and geometry is one of the historical sources of constructivist accounts of mathematical truth. There are also important constructivist elements in Kant's account of the basis of Newtonian mechanics.[9] The roots of constructivism lie deep in Kant's transcendental idealism, but these parallels I cannot discuss here.

My aim is to see the way in which Kant's moral doctrine has features that quite naturally lead us to think of it as constructivist, and then how this connects with the themes of the unity of reason and the moral law as an idea of freedom. To this end, let's consider three questions.

First, in moral constructivism, what is it that is constructed? The answer is, the *content* of the doctrine.[10] In Kant's view this means that the totality of particular categorical imperatives—general precepts at step (2)—that pass the test of the CI-procedure are seen as constructed by a procedure worked through by *rational* agents subject to various *reasonable* constraints. These agents are rational in that, subject to the reasonable constraints of the procedure, they are guided by empirical practical reason, or the principles of rational deliberation that fall under *the* hypothetical imperative.

A second question is this: is the CI-procedure itself constructed? No, it is not. Rather, it is simply *laid out*. Kant believes that our everyday human understanding is implicitly aware of the requirements of practical reason, both pure and empirical; as we shall see, this is part of his doctrine of the fact of reason. So we look at how Kant seems to reason when he presents his various examples and we try to lay out in procedural form all the conditions he seems to rely on. Our aim in doing this is to incorporate into that procedure all the relevant criteria of practical reasonableness and rationality, so that the judgments that result from a *correct* use of the procedure are themselves correct (given the requisite true beliefs about the social world). These judgments are correct because they meet all the requirements of practical reason.

Third, what, more exactly, does it mean to say, as I said a while back, that the form and structure of the CI-procedure *mirror* our free moral personality as both reasonable and rational? The idea here is that not everything can be constructed and every construction has a basis, certain materials, as it were, from which it begins. While the CI-procedure is not, as noted above, constructed but laid out, it does have a basis; and this basis is the conception of free and equal persons as reasonable and rational, a conception that is mirrored in the procedure. We discern how persons are mirrored in the procedure by noting what powers and abilities, kinds of beliefs and wants, and the like, they must have as agents who are viewed as implicitly guided by the procedure and as being moved to conform to the particular categorical imperatives it authenticates. We look at the procedure as laid out, and we consider the use Kant makes of it, and from that we elaborate what his conception of persons must be. This conception, along with the conception of a society of such persons, each of whom can be a legislative member of a realm of ends, constitutes the basis of Kant's constructivism. Thus, we don't say that the conceptions of person and society are constructed. It is unclear what that could mean. Nor do we say they are laid out. Rather, these conceptions are *elicited* from our moral experience and from what is involved in our being able to work through the CI-procedure and to act from the moral law as it applies to us.

To illustrate: that we are both reasonable and rational is mirrored in the fact that the CI-procedure involves both forms of reasoning. We are said to be rational at step (1), and indeed at all steps, since the deliberations of agents within the constraints of the procedure always fall under the rational. We are also said to be reasonable, since if we weren't moved by the reasonable, we would not take what Kant calls a pure practical interest in checking our maxims against the procedure's requirements; nor when a maxim is rejected would we have such an interest in revising our intentions and checking whether our revised maxim is acceptable. The deliberations of agents *within* the steps of the procedure and subject to its reasonable constraints mirror our rationality; our motivation as persons in caring about those constraints and taking an interest in acting in ways that meet the procedure's requirements mirrors our being reasonable.

The conception of free and equal persons as reasonable and rational is the basis of the construction: unless this conception and the powers of moral personality it includes—our humanity—are animated, as it were, in human beings, the moral law would have no basis in the world. Recall here Kant's thought that to commit suicide is to root out the existence of morality from the world (MM 6:422–23).

3. It is important to see that the contrast between rational intuitionism and Kant's moral constructivism is not a contrast between objectivism and subjectivism. For both views have a conception of objectivity, but each understands objectivity in a different way.

In rational intuitionism a correct moral judgment, or principle, is one that is true of a prior and independent order of moral values. This order is also prior to the criteria of reasonableness and rationality as well as prior to the appropriate conception of persons as autonomous and responsible, and free and equal members of a moral community. Indeed, it is that order that settles what those reasonable and rational criteria are, and how autonomy and responsibility are to be conceived.

In Kant's doctrine, on the other hand, a correct moral judgment is one that conforms to all the relevant criteria of reasonableness and rationality, the total force of which is expressed by the way they are combined into the CI-procedure. He thinks of this procedure as suitably joining together all the requirements of our (human) practical reason, both pure and empirical, into one unified scheme of practical reasoning. As we saw, this is an aspect of the unity of reason. Thus, the general principles and precepts generated by the correct use of that procedure of deliberation satisfy the conditions for valid judgments imposed by the form and structure of our common (human) practical reason. This form and structure is a priori, rooted in our pure practical reason and thus for us practically necessary. A judgment supported by those principles and precepts will, then, be acknowledged as correct by any fully reasonable and rational (and informed) person.

A conception of objectivity must include an account of our agreement in judgments, how it comes about. Kant accounts for this agreement by our sharing in a common practical reason. For this idea to succeed, we must suppose, as Kant does, that whoever applies the CI-procedure, roughly the same judgments are reached, provided the procedure is applied intelligently and conscientiously, and against the background of roughly the same beliefs and information. Reasonable and rational persons must recognize more or less the same reasons and give them more or less the same weight. Indeed, for the idea of judgment even to apply, as opposed to the idea of our simply giving voice to our psychological state, we must be able to reach agreement in judgment, not of course always but much of the time. And when we can't do so, we must be able to explain our failure by the difficulties of the question, that is, by the difficulties of surveying and assessing the available evidence or the delicate balance of the competing reasons on opposite sides of the issue, either or both of which lead us to expect that reasonable persons may differ. Or, alternatively, the disagreement arises from lack of reasonableness or rationality or conscientiousness on the part of one or more persons involved, where of course the test of this lack cannot simply be the fact of disagreement itself or the fact that other persons disagree with us. We must have independent grounds for thinking these causes of disagreement are at work.

Finally, to prevent misunderstanding, I should add that Kant's constructivism does not say that moral facts, much less all facts, are constructed. Rather, a constructivist procedure provides principles and precepts that specify *which* facts about persons, institutions, actions, and the world generally are relevant in moral deliberation. Those norms specify which facts are to *count* as reasons. We should not say that the moral facts are constructed, since the idea of constructing the facts seems odd and may be incoherent; by contrast, the idea of a constructivist procedure generating principles and precepts singling out the facts to count as reasons seems quite clear. We have only to recall how the CI-procedure accepts some maxims and rejects others. The facts are there already, so to speak, available in our everyday experience or identified by theoretical reason, but apart from a constructivist moral conception they are simply facts. What is needed is a way to single out which facts are relevant from a moral point of view and to determine their weight as reasons. Viewed this way, a constructivist conception is not at odds with our ordinary idea of truth and matters of fact.

§4. What Kind of Authentication Has the Moral Law?

1. In the first appendix to chap. 1 of the Analytic of the *Critique of Practical Reason,* Kant says that the moral law can be given no deduction, that is, no justification of its objective and universal validity, but rests on the fact of reason. This fact (as I understand it) is the fact that in our common moral consciousness we recognize and acknowledge the moral law as supremely authoritative and immediately directive for us. Kant says further that the moral law needs no justifying grounds; to the contrary, that law proves not only the possibility but also the actuality of freedom in those who recognize and acknowledge that law as supremely authoritative. The moral law thus gives objective, although only practical, reality to the idea of freedom and thereby answers to a need of pure speculative reason, which had to assume the possibility of freedom to be consistent with itself. That the moral law does this is sufficient authentication, or credential, as Kant says, for that law. And this credential takes the place of all those vain attempts to justify it by theoretical reason, whether speculative or empirical (CP 5:46–50).

This is a fundamental change from the *Groundwork,* where in the last part Kant tries to derive the moral law from the idea of freedom. Now what is the significance of this change?[11] It signals, I believe, Kant's recognition that each of the four forms of reason in his critical philosophy has a different place and role in what he calls the unity of reason. He thinks of reason as a self-subsistent unity of principles in which every member exists for every other and all for the sake of each (see Bxxiii, and CP 5:119–21). In the most general sense, the authentication of a form of reason consists in explaining its place and role within what I shall call the constitution of reason as a whole. For Kant there can be no question of justifying reason as such, for reason must answer all questions about itself from its own resources (A476–84/B504–12), and it must contain the standard for any critical examination of every use of reason (CP 5:16): the constitution of reason must be self-authenticating.

Now, once we regard the authentication of a form of reason as an explanation of its role within the constitution of reason, then, since the forms of reason have different roles, we should expect their authentications to be different. Each fits into the constitution of reason in a different way, and the more specific considerations that explain their role in that constitution will likewise be different. The moral law will not have the same kind of authentication that the categories do, namely, the special kind of argument Kant gives for them in the transcendental deduction of the first *Critique*, an argument designed to show the concepts and principles in question are presupposed in some kind of experience, or consciousness, in contrast, for example, to their being regulative of the use of a faculty.

Pure speculative reason also has what Kant calls a deduction (A670/B698), that is, a justification (or authentication) of the objective validity of its ideas and principles as transcendental principles (A651/B679). But what is important here is that the moral law as an idea of pure practical reason has an even different authentication than pure speculative reason. To elaborate: for Kant, pure reason, as opposed both to the understanding and to empirical practical reason, is the faculty of orientation.[12] Whereas reason's work in both spheres is similar, it performs its work differently in the theoretical than in the practical sphere. In each sphere, reason provides orientation by being normative: it sets ends and organizes them into a whole so as to guide the use of a faculty, the understanding in the theoretical sphere, the power of choice in the practical. In the theoretical sphere, pure reason is regulative rather than constitutive; the role of its ideas and principles is to specify an idea of the highest possible systematic unity and to guide us in introducing this necessary unity into our knowledge of objects and our view of the world as a whole. In this way the work of reason yields a sufficient criterion of empirical truth (A651/B679).[13] Without pure reason, general conceptions of the world of all kinds—religion and myth, and science and cosmology—would not be possible. The ideas and principles of reason that articulate them, and that in the case of science provide a criterion of empirical truth, would not exist, for their source is reason. The role of speculative reason in regulating the understanding and organizing into a unity our empirical knowledge authenticates its ideas and principles.

By contrast, in the practical sphere, pure reason is neither constitutive nor regulative but directive: that is, it immediately directs the power of choice, which does not provide independent material of its own to be organized, as the understanding does. In this sphere, it is empirical practical reason that is regulative; for empirical practical reason organizes into a rational idea of happiness, by the principle of the hypothetical imperative, the various desires and inclinations belonging to the lower faculty of desire (CP 5:120). In contrast, the power of choice, as the higher faculty of desire, is directed *immediately* by pure reason's idea of the moral law, a law by which reason constructs for that power its practically necessary object, the realm of ends.

In a way suitable to the theoretical and the practical spheres, pure reason tries to fashion what Kant calls the unity of reason. There are three such unities: the first, in the theoretical sphere, is the greatest possible systematic unity of the knowledge of objects required for a sufficient criterion of empirical truth; the second, in the practical sphere, is the greatest possible systematic unity of ends in a realm of ends. The third unity is that of both theoretical and practical reason in one constitution of reason with theoretical reason subordinate to practical reason, so that practical reason has primacy (CP 5:119–21).

2. I turn from these general remarks to consider why Kant might have given up the attempt to give an argument from theoretical reason for the moral law by examining several forms such an argument might take.

During the 1770s, Kant made a number of efforts in this direction. Dieter Henrich divides them into two groups.[14] In the first, Kant tries to show how the theoretical use of reason, when applied to the totality of our desires and ends of action, necessarily gives rise in a rational agent not only to the characteristic approval of moral judgment but also to incentives to act from that judgment. In the second group, Kant tries to derive the essential elements of moral judgment from what he takes to be a necessary presupposition of moral philosophy, but a presupposition that can be seen to be necessary by the use of theoretical reason alone, namely, the concept of freedom.

For each group, Henrich describes a few examples. I leave aside these details. The relevant point is that Kant tries to ground the moral law solely in theoretical reason and the concept of rationality. He tries to derive the reasonable from the rational. He starts from a conception of a self-conscious rational (versus reasonable) agent with all the powers of theoretical reason and moved only by natural needs and desires. These arguments bear witness to Kant's effort over a number of years to find a derivation of the moral law from theoretical reason.

Another kind of argument for the moral law, one resembling the kind of argument Kant gives for the categories, might be this: we try to show the moral law to be presupposed in our *moral consciousness* in much the same way that the categories are presupposed in our *sensible experience* of objects in space and time.[15] Thus, we might argue that no other moral conception can specify the concepts of duty and obligation, or the concepts needed to have the peculiarly moral feelings of guilt and shame, remorse and indignation, and the like. Now, that a moral conception include the necessary background for these concepts is certainly a reasonable requirement. But the argument tries for too much: it is implausible to deny that other conceptions also suffice for this background. The conceptions of two societies may differ greatly even though people in both societies are capable of moral consciousness. Many doctrines satisfy this condition besides that specified by the moral law.

A fault in this kind of argument is that it assumes the distinction between concept and pure intuition, whereas in moral consciousness there is not such distinction. Theoretical reason concerns the knowledge of objects, and sensory experience provides its material basis. But practical knowledge concerns the reasonable and rational grounds for the production of objects. The complete good is the realization of a constructed object: the realm of ends as the necessary object of a will immediately determined by the moral law. Moral consciousness is not sensible experience of an object at all, and this kind of argument has no foothold.

Consider a further argument. One might say: since the deduction of the categories shows that their objective validity and universal applicability is presupposed in our unified public experience of objects, a parallel argument for the moral law might show it to constitute the only possible basis for a unified public order of conduct for a plurality of persons who have conflicting aims and interests. The claim is that without the moral law, we are left with the struggle of all against all as exemplified by the pledge of Francis I (CP 5:28). This would allow us to say that the moral law is constitutive of any unified public order of a social world.[16]

This approach, I think, is likewise bound to fail. The requirement that a moral conception specify a unified and shared public order of conduct is again entirely reasonable. The obvious difficulty is that utilitarianism, perfectionism, and intuitionism, as well as other doctrines, can also specify such an order. The moral law is, as we have seen, a priori with respect to empirical practical reason. It is also a priori as an idea of reason, but it is not a priori in the further sense that any unified public order of conduct must rest on it.

Kant does not, I believe, argue that the moral law is a priori in this further sense. What, in effect, he does hold is that the moral law is the only way for us to construct a unified public order of conduct without falling into heteronomy. Kant uses the idea of autonomy implicit in a constructivist conception of moral reason to eliminate alternative moral doctrines. Although Kant never discusses utilitarianism,[17] perfectionism, and intuitionism as we view them today, it is clear that he would also regard these contemporary doctrines as forms of heteronomy. His appeal would be to the moral law as a principle of free constructive reason.

3. Finally, let's return briefly to the second *Critique,* where Kant explains why the moral law has no deduction (CP 5:46–50). Here he stresses the differences between theoretical and practical reason. Theoretical reason is concerned with the knowledge of objects given to us in our sensible experience; whereas practical reason is concerned with our capacity as reasonable and rational beings to bring about, or to produce, objects in accordance with a conception of those objects. An object is understood as the end of action, and for Kant all actions have an object in this sense. Acting from pure practical reason involves, first, bringing about an object the conception of which is framed in the light of the ideas and principles of pure practical reason, and, second, our being moved (in the appropriate way) by a pure practical interest in realizing that conception. Since it is in virtue of our reason that we can be fully free, only those actions meeting these two conditions are *fully* free.

Now from what we have said the authentication of the moral law can seem highly problematic. This sets the stage for Kant's introducing the doctrine of the fact of reason in the second *Critique.* For the moral law cannot be derived from the concepts of theoretical reason together with the concept of a rational agent; nor is it presupposed in our moral experience or necessary to specify a unified order of public conduct. It cannot be derived from the idea of freedom since no intellectual intuition of freedom is available. Moreover, the moral law is not to be regulative of a faculty with it own material. This kind of authentication holds for speculative reason and, within the practical sphere, for empirical practical reason, which regulates the lower faculty of desire. Yet there is still a way, Kant now holds, in which the moral law is authenticated: "The moral law is given, as an apodictically certain fact, as it were, of pure reason, a fact of which we are a priori conscious, even if it be granted that no example could be found in which it has been followed exactly, [while] the objective reality of the moral law can be proved through . . . no exertion of the theoretical reason, whether speculative or empirically supported. . . . Nevertheless, it is firmly established of itself." He adds: "Instead of this vainly sought deduction of the moral principle, however, something entirely different and unexpected appears: the moral principle itself serves as a principle of the deduction of an unscrutable faculty which no experience can prove but which speculative reason had to assume as at least possible (in order not to contradict itself . . .). This is the faculty of freedom, which the moral law, itself needing no justifying grounds, shows to be not only possible but actual in beings that acknowledge the law as binding upon them" (CP 5:47).

To conclude: each form of reason in Kant's critical doctrine has its own distinctive authentication. The categories and principles of the understanding are presupposed in our experience of objects in space and time, and pure speculative reason is authenticated by its role in organizing into a systematic unity the empirical knowledge of the understanding, thereby providing a sufficient criterion of empirical truth. Empirical practical reason has a similar role with respect to our lower faculty of desire, organizing its inclinations and wants into a rational conception of happiness. It is *pure* practical reason the authentication of which seems the most elusive: we long to derive its law, as Kant did for many years, from some firm foundation, either in theoretical reason or in experience, or in the necessary conditions of a unified public order of conduct, or, failing all of these, from the idea of freedom itself, as Kant still hopes to do in the *Grundlegung*.

But none of these authentications are available within Kant's critical philosophy. In the second *Critique,* Kant recognizes this and accepts the view that pure practical reason, with the moral law as its first principle, is authenticated by the fact of reason and in turn by that fact's authenticating, in those who acknowledge the moral law as binding, the objective reality of freedom, although always (and this needs emphasis) only from a practical point of view. In the same way the moral law authenticates the ideas of God and immortality. Thus, along with freedom, the moral law is the keystone of the whole system of pure reason (CP 5:3). Pure practical reason is authenticated finally by assuming primacy over speculative reason and by cohering into and, what is more, by *completing* the constitution of reason as one unified body of principles: this makes reason self-authenticating as a whole (CP 5:119–21).

Thus by the time of the second *Critique* Kant has developed, I think, not only a constructivist conception of practical reason but a coherentist account of its authentication. This is the significance of his doctrine of the fact of reason and of his abandoning his hitherto vain search for a so-called deduction of the moral law. This doctrine may look like a step backward into intuitionism, or else into dogmatism. Some have tried to interpret it away so as to make it continuous with Kant's earlier views; others have lamented it. Here I think that Kant may be ahead of his critics. A constructivist and coherentist doctrine of practical reason is not without strengths as a possible view; and as such it is part of the legacy Kant left to the tradition of moral philosophy.

§5. *The Moral Law as a Law of Freedom*

1. The distinctive feature of Kant's view of freedom is the central place of the moral law as an idea of pure reason; and pure reason, both theoretical and practical, is free. For Kant there is no essential difference between the freedom of the will and

freedom of thought. If our mathematical and theoretical reasoning is free, as shown in free judgments, then so is our pure practical reasoning as shown in free deliberative judgments. Here in both cases free judgments are to be distinguished from verbal utterances that simply give voice to, that are the (causal) upshot of, our psychological states and of our wants and attitudes. Judgments claim validity and truth, claims that can be supported by reasons. The freedom of pure reason includes the freedom of practical as well as of theoretical reason, since both are freedoms of one and the same reason (Gr 4:391; CP 5:91, 121). Kant's approach requires that the moral law exhibit features that disclose our freedom, and these features should be discernible in the CI-procedure, on its face, so to speak. The moral law serves as the *ratio cognoscendi* of freedom (CP 5:4n). Our task is simply to recall the features of this procedure (surveyed in §1), which Kant thinks enables us to recognize it as a law of freedom.[18]

Consider first the features through which the CI-procedure exhibits the moral law as unconditional. These are evident in the ways that the reasonable restricts the rational and subordinates it absolutely. The CI-procedure (the reasonable) restricts empirical practical reason (the rational) by requiring that unless the agent's rational and sincere maxim is accepted by the procedure, acting from that maxim is forbidden absolutely. This outcome is final from the standpoint of practical reason as a whole, both pure and empirical. Thus, the moral law, as represented by the CI-procedure, specifies a scope within which permissible ends must fall, as well as limits on the means that can be adopted in the pursuit of these ends. The scope and limits that result delineate the duties of justice. The moral law also imposes certain ends as ends that we have a duty to pursue and to give some weight to. These duties are duties of virtue. That the moral law as represented is unconditional simply means that the constraints of the CI-procedure are valid for all reasonable and rational persons, no matter what their natural desires and inclinations.

We might say: pure practical reason is a priori with respect to empirical practical reason. Here the term *a priori* applies, of course, to pure practical knowledge and not to the knowledge of objects given in experience. It expresses the fact that we know in advance, no matter what our natural desires may be, that the moral law imposes certain ends as well as restrictions on means and that these requirements are always valid for us. This fits the traditional epistemological meaning of *a priori* once it is applied to practical knowledge, and it accords with Kant's definition of the a priori at CP 5:12. Kant uses the unconditional and a priori aspects of the moral law to explain the sense in which our acting from that law shows our independence of nature and our freedom from determination by the desires and needs aroused in us by natural and psychological causes (so-called negative freedom).

2. Next, let's ask how the CI-procedure exhibits the moral law as sufficient of itself to determine the will. Here we should be careful not to interpret this feature too

strongly. I do not think Kant wants to say, and certainly he does not need to say, that the moral law determines all the relevant aspects of what we are to do. Rather, the moral law specifies a scope *within* which permissible ends must fall and also *limits* the means that may be used in their pursuit, and this goes part way to make the moral law sufficient of itself to determine the will. (Of course, particular desires determine which permissible ends it is rational for us to pursue, and they also determine, within the limits allowed, how it is rational for us to pursue them. This leeway I view as compatible with Kant's intentions.)

But beyond specifying a scope for permissible ends and limiting means in their pursuit, the moral law must further provide sufficient grounds to determine the will by identifying certain ends that are also duties and by requiring us to give at least some weight to those ends. Since the moral law determines both aspects of action, both ends and means, pure practical reason, through the moral law as an idea of reason, is *sufficient* to determine the will.[19] The point here is that for Kant action has an end; if the moral law failed to identify certain ends as also duties, it would not suffice to determine an essential feature of actions.

What is crucial for Kant's view is that the moral law must not be merely formal but have enough content to be, in a natural meaning of the word, sufficient of itself to determine ends: pure reason is not merely finding the most effective way to realize given ends but criticizing and selecting among proposed ends. Its doing this is what Kant has in mind when he says that the moral law specifies a positive concept of freedom. We are free not only in the sense that we are able to act independently of our natural desires and needs but also free in the sense that we have a principle regulative of *both* ends and means from which to act, a principle of autonomy appropriate to us as reasonable and rational beings.

3. So much for the way in which the CI-procedure exhibits the moral law as unconditional and sufficient of itself to determine the will. In addition to this procedure exhibiting how the moral law imposes ends that are also duties, it exhibits that law as doing reason's work in setting ends and in securing their ordered unity, so that it is not merely a principle of rationality. We can also see how the moral law constructs the realm of ends and thereby specifies the conception of its object. In short, the CI-procedure in its constructions models all the essential features of a principle doing the work of pure reason in the practical sphere.

This procedure also clarifies the more general aspects of pure practical reason to which Kant refers in a passage from the first *Critique*. "Reason does not . . . follow the order of things as they present themselves in appearance, but frames for itself with perfect spontaneity an order of its own according to ideas [of pure reason], to which it adapts the empirical conditions, and according to which it declares actions to be [practically] necessary" (A548/B576).

We can grasp what Kant has in mind: namely, that pure practical reason constructs out of itself the conception of the realm of ends as an order of its own according to ideas of reason; and given the historical and material circumstances under which society exists, that conception guides us in fashioning institutions and practices in conformity with it.

The particular characteristics of a realm of ends are, then, to be adapted to empirical, that is, to historical and social conditions. What in particular is the content of citizens' permissible ends, and what specific institutions are best suited to establish a moral community regulated by the moral law, must wait upon circumstances. But what we do know in advance are certain general features of such a moral community: the nature of ends that are also duties, and the arrangement of these ends under the duty to cultivate our moral and natural perfection, and the duty to further the happiness (the permissible ends) of others. We also know that under favorable conditions, a realm of ends is some form of constitutional democracy.

4. Now consider the two examples Kant presents in chap. 1 of the Analytic (CP 5:30). Kant's first example is that of a man who claims to have a natural desire so overwhelmingly strong that if the object desired were vividly placed before him, this desire would be irresistible. Kant thinks that the man must be exaggerating or else mistaken. If he knew that he would be executed immediately upon satisfying his desire, and the instruments of execution (for example, the gallows) were as vividly placed before him as the attractive object, surely he would realize that there are other desires, if necessary his love of life—the sum total of all natural desires as expressive of life—which would intervene to resist this alleged irresistible desire. In the last resort the love of life, when equally vividly aroused, is able to control all other natural desires. Kant thinks that as purely rational and natural beings we cannot act against the love of life.

The second example is that of a man who is ordered by his sovereign to make a false deposition against an honorable subject whom the sovereign wishes to be rid of on some plausible pretext. This order, we are to assume, is backed up by a threat of sudden death as vividly present as in the previous case. This time, however, it is the desire to act from the moral law that opposes the love of life. Here Kant thinks that while perhaps none of us would want to say what we would do in such a situation, we do know, as this man would know of himself, that it would be *possible* for us to disobey the sovereign's order. Of this man Kant says: "He judges . . . that he can do something because he knows that he ought, and he recognizes that he is free—a fact which, without the moral law, would have remained unknown to him" (CP 5:30).

Kant's aim in these examples is to convince us that although as purely natural beings, endowed with the powers of the rational but not the reasonable, we cannot oppose the love of life, nevertheless we can do so as natural beings endowed with *humanity,* that is, the powers of the reasonable in union with moral sensibility.[20] Moreover, our consciousness of the moral law discloses to us that we can stand fast against the totality of our natural desires; and this in turn discloses our capacity to act independently of the natural order. Our consciousness of the moral law could not do this unless that law was not only unconditional and sufficient of itself to determine our will but also had all the features of a principle of pure practical reason. These features must be exhibited in our moral thought and feeling in some such manner as the CI-procedure represents them. Knowledge that we *can* act from a law of that kind—a law that is a principle of autonomy—is what discloses our freedom to us.

5. To conclude, one other passage should be mentioned. It is found at CP 5:94: here Kant says that there are writers who think they can explain freedom by empirical principles. They regard it as a psychological property that can be accounted for by an exact investigation of the mind and the incentives of the will as discerned in sense experience. Those writers do not regard freedom as a transcendental predicate of the causality of persons who also have a place in the natural order but who, Kant implies, are not entirely of it. He writes: "They deprive us of the great revelation which we experience through our practical reason by means of the moral law—the revelation of an intelligible world through realization of the otherwise transcendent concept of freedom; they deprive us of the moral law itself, which assumes absolutely no empirical ground of determination. Therefore, it would be necessary to add something here as a protection against this delusion and to expose empiricism in its naked superficiality."

This severe passage expresses the depth of Kant's conviction that those without a conception of the moral law and lacking in moral sensibility could not know they were free. They would appear to themselves as purely natural creatures endowed with rationality, without the essentials of humanity. If by some philosophical or other doctrine we were to be convinced that the moral law is a delusion, and our moral sensibility simply an artifact of nature to perpetuate the species or a social contrivance to make institutions stable and secure, we would be in danger of losing our humanity, even though we cannot, Kant thinks, lose it altogether. The empiricist "delusion," as Kant calls it, must not be allowed to take from us the glorious disclosure of our autonomy made known to us through the moral law as an idea of pure reason. Philosophy as defense (apology in the traditional sense)—the role Kant gives it—is to prevent this loss.

Notes

This chapter draws upon three lectures circulated at Johns Hopkins University in the summer of 1983, where discussions of Kant's moral philosophy were held. The presentation here is considerably abbreviated in parts and at places much revised. In making these changes, I am especially grateful to Stephen Engstrom, Michael Friedman, Michael Hardimon, Barbara Herman, Wilfried Hinsch, and T. M. Scanlon. Discussion with them has been enormously helpful, and their criticisms led to many improvements.

1

Modulo a few minor variations, my account of the CI-procedure in §1 follows closely that of Onora (Nell) O'Neill in her *Acting on Principle* (New York, 1975). See also Paul Dietrichson, "When Is a Maxim Universalizable?" *Kant-Studien* 56 (1964). I have followed Barbara Herman in supposing that when we apply the CI-procedure we are to assume that the agent's maxim is rational. See her "Morality as Rationality: A Study in Kant's Ethics," Ph.D. diss., Harvard, 1976. All references to Kant are to the volume and page number of the Academy edition (Berlin, 1902–).

2

On this presupposition, see the instructive discussion by Barbara Herman, "The Practice of Moral Judgment," *Journal of Philosophy* 82 (1985).

3

In describing these steps many refinements are glossed over. I am indebted to Reinhard Brandt for illuminating discussions on this score. But as I have said, the account need only be accurate enough to set the stage for the themes of moral constructivism and the authentication of the moral law, and the rest.

4

In adopting this way out we are amending, or adding to, Kant's account. It is, I think, Kantian in spirit provided that, as I believe, it doesn't compromise the essential elements of his doctrine.

5

The German is: "Will man aber dem sittlichen Gesetze zugleich Eingang verschaffen." Kant's meaning here is obscure; see below at last paragaraph of §1.

6

I am indebted to Michael Friedman for clarification on this point.

7

John Silber, "The Copernican Revolution in Ethics: The Good Re-examined," *Kant-Studien* 51 (1959).

8

This description is Peter Hylton's.

9

For this, see Michael Friedman, "The Metaphysical Foundations of Newtonian Science," in *Kant's Philosophy of Science,* ed. R. E. Butts (Dordrecht, 1986).

10

It should be noted that this content can never be specified completely. The moral law is an idea of reason, and since an idea of reason can never be fully realized, neither can the content of such an idea. It is always a matter of approximating thereto, and always subject to error and correction.

11

For the importance of this change I agree with much of Karl Amerik's valuable discussion in his *Kant's Theory of Mind* (Oxford, 1982), chap. 6. He discusses the views of Lewis White Beck and H. J. Paton, who have tried to preserve the continuity of Kant's doctrine and have denied the fundamental nature of the change.

12

For this view, and in my account of Kant's conception of the role of reason generally, I have been much indebted for some years to Susan Neiman. See Neiman, "The Unity of Reason: Rereading Kant," Ph.D. diss., Harvard, 1986.

13

See A644/B672: "Reason has . . . as its sole object the understanding and its effective application. Just as the understanding unifies the manifold in the object by means of ideas, positing a certain collective unity as the goal of the activities of the understanding." Observe here that reason is *normative* in relation to the understanding and sets a goal for its activities. The understanding itself has no grasp of this goal; indeed, it cannot set goals for itself at all. Moreover, whereas the activities of the understanding are spontaneous in the sense that it operates by applying its own concepts and categories in constituting the experience of objects and it is not, as Hume thinks, governed by natural psychological laws (for example, the laws of association of ideas), the understanding is, nevertheless, not free. It is pure reason that is free. See also A669–95/B697–723.

14

Dieter Henrich has made a study of these arguments in the *Nachlaß*, and he suggests that when Kant speaks of "this vainly sought deduction" of the moral law he has his own failure in mind. See "Der Begriff der sittlichen Einsicht und Kants Lehre vom Faktum der Vernunft," in *Die Gegenwart der Griechen im neuern Denken*, ed. Dieter Henrich et al. (Tübingen, 1960), pp. 239–47. I am much indebted to this essay.

15

As Lewis White Beck says, we might expect Kant to carry out a critical regression on the presuppositions of moral experience; see *A Commentary on Kant's Critique of Practical Reason* (Chicago, 1960), p. 171.

16

This way of deducing the moral law seems to be suggested by Ernst Cassirer in *Kant's Life and Thought* (New Haven, 1981), pp. 238–47, esp. pp. 239–43, but it is not very far developed.

17

At CP 5:36–38 (in the last remark of §8), there is some critical discussion of utilitarianism but it does not, I think, affect what is said in the text.

18

There are three ideas of freedom in Kant that need to be distinguished and related in an account of the practical point of view: those of acting under the idea of freedom, of practical freedom, and of transcendental freedom. Unhappily, I cannot consider them here.

19

The third and strongest way in which the moral law might suffice to determine the will would seem to be this: we read Kant to say in the *Doctrine of Virtue* that the ends of all our actions must be ends that are also duties. The only leeway that now remains is in the weight we are allowed to give to these ends and in the choice of the most effective means to achieve them. The ordinary pleasures of life are permissible only insofar as they are required to preserve our self-respect and sense of well-being and good health, essential if we are conscientiously and intelligently to fulfill our duties. This is one interpretation of Kant's so-called rigorism, but I shall not pursue it here.

20

Kant is not everywhere consistent in his use of *humanity*, but usually it means what is indicated in the text. Recall that, when Kant's doctor, then rector of the university, came to visit him in his last days, Kant, wasted and enfeebled, struggled from his chair to his feet. When the rector asked him to sit down, he seemed reluctant to do so. E. A. C. Wasianski, who knew Kant's courteous way of thinking and highly proper manners, assured the rector that Kant would sit down as soon as the rector, the visitor, did. The rector seemed dubious about this reason, but was quickly convinced when Kant said with great effort after collecting his strength: "Das Gefühl für Humanität hat mich noch nicht verlassen." By which he implied: "I can still act as I should, so I must stand until my visitor sits." This well-known incident (described in Cassirer, *Kant's Life and Thought*, p. 412) nicely illustrates the meaning of humanity.

Chapter 14

*Morality and Ethical Life: Does
Hegel's Critique of Kant
Apply to Discourse Ethics?*

Jürgen Habermas

Translated by Christian Lenhardt
and Shierry Weber Nicholsen

In recent years Karl-Otto Apel and I have begun to reformulate Kant's ethics by grounding moral norms in communication, a venture to which I refer as "discourse ethics."[1] In this chapter I hope to accomplish two things: first, to sketch the basic idea of discourse ethics and then to examine Hegel's critique of Kantian moral philosophy. In part one I deal with two questions: What is discourse ethics? and What moral intuitions does discourse ethics conceptualize? I address the complicated matter of how to justify discourse ethics only in passing.

In part two, I turn to the question of whether Hegel's critique of Kantian ethics applies to discourse ethics as well. The criticisms Hegel leveled against Kant as a moral philosopher are many. From among them I single out four which strike me as the most trenchant. These are as follows: (1) Hegel's objection to the *formalism* of Kantian ethics. Since the moral principle of the categorical imperative requires that the moral agent abstract from the concrete content of duties and maxims, its application necessarily leads to tautological judgments.[2] (2) Hegel's objection to the *abstract universalism* of Kantian ethics. Since the categorical imperative enjoins separating the universal from the particular, a judgment considered valid in terms of that principle necessarily remains external to individual cases and insensitive to the particular context of a problem in need of solution.[3] (3) Hegel's attack on the *impotence of the mere ought.* Since the categorical imperative enjoins a strict separation of "is" from "ought," it necessarily fails to answer the question of how moral insight can be realized in practice.[4] (4) Hegel's objection to the terrorism of

Reprinted from Jürgen Habermas, *Moral Consciousness and Communicative Action,* translated by Christian Lenhardt and Shierry Weber Nicholsen (Cambridge, Mass.: MIT Press, 1990), pp. 195–216.

pure conviction (*Gesinnung*). Since the categorical imperative severs the pure postulates of practical reason from the formative process of spirit and its concrete historical manifestations, it necessarily recommends to the advocates of the moral worldview a policy that aims at the actualization of reason and sanctions even immoral deeds, so long as they serve higher ends.[5]

I

(*1*) *What Is Discourse Ethics?*

First I want to comment briefly on the general nature of Kantian moral philosophy. It has all of the following attributes: it is deontological, cognitivist, formalist, and universalist. Wanting to limit himself strictly to the class of justifiable normative judgments, Kant was forced to choose a narrow concept of morality. Classical moral philosophies had dealt with *all* the issues of the "good life." Kant's only deals with problems of right or just action. To him, moral judgments serve to explain how conflicts of action can be settled on the basis of rationally motivated agreement. Broadly speaking, they serve to justify actions in terms of valid norms and to justify the validity of norms in terms of principles worthy of recognition. In short, the basic phenomenon that moral philosophy must explain is the normative validity (*Sollgeltung*) of commands and norms of action. This is what is meant by saying that a moral philosophy is *deontological*. A deontological ethics conceives the rightness of norms and commands on analogy with the truth of an assertoric statement. It would be erroneous, though, to equate the moral "truth" of normative statements with the assertoric validity of propositional statements, a mistake made by intuitionism and value ethics. Kant does not make this mistake. He does not confuse theoretical with practical reason. As for myself, I hold the view that normative rightness must be regarded as a claim to validity that is analogous to a truth claim. This notion is captured by the term *cognitivist* ethics. A cognitivist ethics must answer the question of how to justify normative statements. Although Kant opts for the grammatical form of an imperative ("Act only according to that maxim by which you can at the same time will that it should become a universal law"), his categorical imperative, in fact, plays the part of a principle of justification that discriminates between valid and invalid norms in terms of their universalizability: What every rational being must be able to will is justified in a moral sense. This is what one means when one speaks of an ethics as being *formalist*. Discourse ethics replaces the Kantian categorical imperative by a procedure of moral argumentation. Its principle postulates that

> — only those norms may claim to be valid that could meet with the consent of all affected in their role as participants in a practical discourse.[6]

While retaining the categorical imperative after a fashion, discourse ethics scales it down to a principle of universalization (U). In practical discourses, (U) plays the part of a rule of argumentation:

— (U) For a norm to be valid, the consequences and side effects of its general observance for the satisfaction of each person's particular interests must be acceptable to all.

Finally, an ethics is termed *universalist* when it alleges that this (or a similar) moral principle, far from reflecting the intuitions of a particular culture or epoch, is valid universally. As long as the moral principle is not justified—and justifying it involves more than simply pointing to Kant's "fact of pure reason"—the ethnocentric fallacy looms large. I must prove that my moral principle is not just a reflection of the prejudices of adult, white, well-educated, Western males of today. This is the most difficult part of ethics, a part that I cannot expound in this paper. Briefly, the thesis discourse ethics puts forth on this subject is that anyone who seriously undertakes to participate in argumentation implicitly accepts by that very undertaking general pragmatic presuppositions that have a normative content. The moral principle can then be derived from the content of these presuppositions of argumentation if one knows at least what it means to justify a norm of action.[7] These, then, are the deontological, cognitivist, formalist, and universalist assumptions that all moral philosophies of the Kantian type have in common. Let me make one more remark concerning the procedure I call practical discourse.

The viewpoint from which moral questions can be judged *impartially* is called the "moral point of view." Formalist ethical theories furnish a rule explaining how something is looked at from the moral point of view. John Rawls, for example, recommends an original position, where those concerned meet as rational and equal partners who decide upon a contract, not knowing their own or each other's actual social positions.[8] G. H. Mead for his part recommends a procedure that he calls ideal role taking. It requires that any morally judging subject put itself in the position of all who would be affected if a problematic plan of action were carried out or if a controversial norm were to take effect.[9] As a procedure, practical discourse is different from these two constructs, the Rawlsian and the Meadian. Argumentation ensures that all concerned in principle take part, freely and equally, in a cooperative search for truth, where nothing coerces anyone except the force of the better argument. Practical discourse is an exacting form of argumentative decision making. Like Rawls's original position, it is a warrant of the rightness (or fairness) of any conceivable normative agreement that is reached under these conditions. Discourse can play this role because its idealized, partly counterfactual presuppositions are precisely those that participants in argumentation do in fact make. That is why I think it unnecessary to resort to Rawls's fictitious original position with its "veil of ignorance." Practical discourse can also be viewed as a communicative process *simultaneously* exhorting *all* participants to ideal role taking. Thus practical discourse transforms what Mead viewed as *individual, privately enacted* role taking into a *public* affair, practiced intersubjectively by all involved.[10]

(2) *What Moral Intuitions Does Discourse Ethics Conceptualize?*

How can it be argued that the *procedural* explanation discourse ethics gives of the moral point of view—in other words, of the impartiality of moral judgment—constitutes an adequate account of moral intuitions, which are after all *substantive* in kind? This is an open question that needs to be addressed.

Moral intuitions are intuitions that instruct us on how best to behave in situations where it is in our power to counteract the extreme vulnerability of others by being thoughtful and considerate. In anthropological terms, morality is a safety device compensating for a vulnerability built into the sociocultural form of life. The basic facts are the following: Creatures that are individuated only through socialization are vulnerable and morally in need of considerateness. Linguistically and behaviorally competent subjects are constituted as individuals by growing into an intersubjectively shared lifeworld, and the lifeworld of a language community is reproduced in turn through the communicative actions of its members. This explains why the identity of the individual and that of the collective are interdependent; they form and maintain themselves together. Built into the consensus-oriented language use of social interaction is an inconspicuous necessity for participants to become more and more individuated. Conversely, everyday language is also the medium by which the intersubjectivity of a shared world is maintained.[11] Thus, the more differentiated the structures of the lifeworld become, the easier it is to discern the simultaneous growth of the autonomous individual subject and his dependence on interpersonal relationships and social ties. The more the subject becomes individuated, the more he becomes entangled in a dense woven fabric of mutual recognition, that is, of reciprocal exposedness and vulnerability. Unless the subject externalizes himself by participating in interpersonal relations through language, he is unable to form that inner center that is his personal identity. This explains the almost constitutional insecurity and chronic fragility of personal identity—an insecurity that is antecedent to cruder threats to the integrity of life and limb.

Moral philosophies of sympathy and compassion (Schopenhauer) have discovered that this profound vulnerability calls for some guarantee of mutual consideration.[12] This considerateness has the twofold objective of defending the integrity of the individual and of preserving the vital fabric of ties of mutual recognition through which individuals *reciprocally* stabilize their fragile identities. No one can maintain his identity by himself. Consider suicide, for example. Notwithstanding the Stoic view that held that this final, desperate act reflects the imperious self-determination

How does discourse ethics
get around looking at

of the lone individual, the responsibility for suicide can never be attributed to him or her alone. This seemingly loneliest of deeds actually enacts a fate for which others collectively must take some of the blame, the fate of ostracism from an intersubjectively shared lifeworld.

Since moralities are tailored to suit the fragility of human beings individuated through socialization, they must always solve *two* tasks *at once*. They must emphasize the inviolability of the individual by postulating equal respect for the dignity of every one. But they must also protect the web of intersubjective relations of mutual recognition by which these individuals survive as members of a community. To these two complementary aspects correspond the principles of justice and solidarity, respectively. The first postulates equal respect and equal rights for the individual, whereas the second postulates empathy and concern for the well-being of one's neighbor. Justice in the modern sense of the term refers to the subjective freedom of inalienable individuality. Solidarity refers to the well-being of associated members of a community who intersubjectively share the same lifeworld. W. K. Frankena distinguishes a principle of justice or equal treatment from a principle of beneficence, which commands us to advance the common weal, to avert harm, and to do good.[13] In my view, it is important to see that both principles have one and the same root: the specific vulnerability of the human species, which individuates itself through sociation. Morality thus cannot protect the one without the other. It cannot protect the rights of the individual without also protecting the well-being of the community to which he belongs.

The fundamental motif of an ethics of compassion can be pushed to the point where the link between the two moral principles becomes clear. In the past, these principles have served as core elements of two contrary traditions in moral philosophy. Theories of duty have always centered on the principle of justice, whereas theories of the good have always emphasized the common weal. Hegel was the first to argue that we misperceive the basic moral phenomenon if we isolate the two aspects, assigning opposite principles to each. His concept of ethical life (*Sittlichkeit*) is an implicit criticism of two kinds of one-sidedness, one the mirror image of the other. Hegel opposes the abstract universality of justice manifesting itself in the individualist approaches of the modern age, in rational natural right theory, and in Kantian moral philosophy. No less vigorous is his opposition to the concrete particularism of the common good that pervades Aristotle and Thomas Aquinas. The ethics of discourse picks up this basic Hegelian aspiration to redeem it with Kantian means.

This idea is not so stunning if one keeps in mind that discourses, treating as they do problematic validity claims as hypotheses, represent a reflective form of communicative action. To put it another way, the normative content of the pragmatic presuppositions of argumentation is borrowed from that of communicative action,

[Handwritten margin note, top: Specific ideas of the good life? (Is moral content possible w/o them? What moral weight should we give intuitions?)]

onto which discourses are superimposed. This is why all moralities coincide in one respect: The same medium, linguistically mediated interaction, is both the reason for the vulnerability of socialized individuals and the key resource they possess to compensate for that vulnerability. Every morality revolves around equality of respect, solidarity, and the common good. Fundamental ideas like these can be reduced to the relations of symmetry and reciprocity presupposed in communicative action. In other words, the common core of all kinds of morality can be traced back to the reciprocal imputations and shared presuppositions actors make when they seek understanding in everyday situations.[14] Admittedly, their range in everyday practice is limited. While equal respect and solidarity are present in the mutual recognition of subjects who orient their actions to validity claims, normative obligations usually do not transcend the boundaries of a concrete lifeworld, be it that of a family, a neighborhood, a city, or a state. There is only one reason why discourse ethics, which presumes to derive the substance of a universalistic morality from the general presuppositions of argumentation, is a promising strategy: Discourse or argumentation is a more exacting type of communication, going beyond any particular form of life. Discourse generalizes, abstracts, and stretches the presuppositions of context-bound communicative actions by extending their range to include competent subjects beyond the provincial limits of their own particular form of life.

[Handwritten margin note, right: H. answers that "all moralities coincide" in communicative action]

These considerations address the issue of whether and why discourse ethics, though organized around a concept of procedure, can be expected to say something relevant about substance as well and, more important perhaps, about the hidden link between justice and the common good, which have traditionally been divorced, giving rise to separate ethics of duty and the good. On the strength of its improbable pragmatic features, practical discourse, or moral argumentation, serves as a warrant of insightful will-formation, ensuring that the interests of individuals are given their due without cutting the social bonds that intersubjectively unite them.[15]

In his capacity as a participant in argumentation, everyone is on his own and yet embedded in a communication context. This is what Apel means by an "ideal community of communication." In discourse, the social bond of belonging is left intact despite the fact that the consensus required of all concerned transcends the limits of any actual community. The agreement made possible by discourse depends on two things: the individual's inalienable right to say yes or no, and his overcoming of his egocentric viewpoint. Without the individual's uninfringeable freedom to respond with a yes or no to criticizable validity claims, consent is merely factual rather than truly universal. Conversely, without empathetic sensitivity by each person to everyone else, no solution deserving universal consent will result from the deliberation. These two aspects—the autonomy of inalienable individuals and their embeddedness in an intersubjectively shared web of relations—are internally connected, and it is this link that the procedure of discursive decision making takes into account. The equal rights of individuals and the equal respect for the personal dignity of each depend upon a network of interpersonal relations and a system of mutual recognition. On the other hand, while the degree of solidarity and the growth of welfare are indicators of the quality of communal life, they are not the only ones. Just as important is that *equal* consideration be given to the interests of every individual in defining the general interest. Going beyond Kant, discourse ethics extends the deontological concept of justice by including in it those structural aspects of the good life that can be distinguished from the concrete totality of specific forms of life.

II

For all its affinities with Kant's moral theory, discourse ethics is rather different. Before going on to consider Hegel's objections to Kant's ethics, I want to focus briefly on three differences that strike me as important.

First, discourse ethics gives up Kant's dichotomy between an *intelligible* realm comprising duty and free will and a *phenomenal* realm comprising inclinations, subjective motives, political and social institutions, et cetera.[16] The quasi-transcendental necessity with which subjects involved in communicative interaction orient themselves to validity claims is reflected only in their being *constrained* to speak and act under idealized conditions. The unbridgeable gap Kant saw between the intelligible and the empirical becomes, in discourse ethics, a mere tension manifesting itself in *everyday communication* as the factual force of counterfactual presuppositions. Second, discourse ethics rejects the monological approach of Kant, who assumed that the individual tests his maxims of action *foro interno* or, as Husserl put it, in the loneliness of his soul. The singularity of Kant's transcendental consciousness simply takes for granted a prior understanding among a plurality of empirical egos; their harmony is preestablished. In discourse ethics it is not. Discourse ethics prefers to view shared understanding about the generalizability of interests as the *result* of an intersubjectively mounted, public discourse. There are no shared structures preceding the individual, except the universals of language use. Third, discourse ethics improves upon Kant's unsatisfactory handling of a specific problem of justification when he evasively points to the alleged "fact of pure reason" and argues that the effectiveness of the "ought" is simply a matter of experience. The latter solves this problem by deriving (U) from the universal presuppositions of argumentation.

(1) On the Formalism of the Moral Principle

a) Neither Kantian ethics nor discourse ethics lays itself open to the charge that, since it defines the moral principle in formal or procedural terms, it can only make tautological statements about morality. Hegel was wrong to imply that these principles postulate logical and semantic consistency, and nothing else. In fact they postulate the employment of a substantive moral point of view. The issue is not whether normative statements must have the grammatical form of universal sentences. The issue is whether we can *all* will that a contested norm gain binding force under given conditions. [17] The content that is tested by a moral principle is generated not by the philosopher but by real life. The conflicts of action that come to be morally judged and consensually resolved grow out of everyday life. Reason as a tester of maxims (Kant) or actors as participants in argumentation (discourse ethics) *find* these conflicts. They do not create them. [18]

b) There is a somewhat different sense in which Hegel's charge of formalism does ring true. Any procedural ethics must distinguish between the structure and the content of moral judgment. Its deontological abstraction segregates from among the general mass of practical issues precisely those that lend themselves to rational debate. They alone are subjected to a justificatory test. In short, this procedure differentiates *normative* statements about the hypothetical "justice" of actions and norms from *evaluative* statements about subjective preferences that we articulate in reference to what our notion of the good life happens to be, which in turn is a function of our cultural heritage. Hegel believed it was this tendency to abstract from the good life that made it impossible for morality to claim jurisdiction over the substantive problems of daily life. He has a point, but his criticism overshoots its aim. To cite an example, human rights obviously embody generalizable interests. As such they can be morally grounded in terms of what all could will. And yet nobody would argue that these rights, which represent the moral substance of our legal system, are irrelevant for the ethics (*Sittlichkeit*) of modern life.

In the back of Hegel's mind was a theoretical question that is rather more difficult to answer: Can one formulate concepts like universal justice, normative rightness, the moral point of view, and the like independently of any vision of the good life, that is, independently of an intuitive project of some privileged but concrete form of life? Noncontextual definitions of a moral principle, I admit, have not been satisfactory up to now. Negative versions of the moral principle seem to be a step in the right direction. They heed the prohibition of graven images, refrain from positive depiction, and, as in the case of discourse ethics, refer negatively to the damaged life instead of pointing affirmatively to the good life. [19]

(2) *On the Abstract Universalism of Morally Justified Judgment*

a) Neither Kantian ethics nor discourse ethics lays itself open to the objection that a moral point of view based on the generalizability of norms necessarily leads to the neglect, if not the repression, of existing conditions and interests in a pluralist society. As interests and value orientations become more differentiated in modern societies, the morally justified norms that control the individual's scope of action in the interest of the whole become ever more general and abstract. Modern societies are also characterized by the need for regulations that impinge *only* on particular interests. While these matters do require regulation, a discursive consensus is not needed; compromise is quite sufficient in this area. Let us keep in mind, though, that fair compromise in turn calls for morally justified procedures of compromising.

Hegel's objection sometimes takes the form of an attack on rigorism. A rigid procedural ethics, especially one that is monologically practiced, fails to take account, so the argument goes, of the consequences and side effects that may flow from the generalized observance of a justified norm. Max Weber was prompted by this objection to counterpose an ethics of responsibility to what he termed Kant's ethics of conviction. The charge of rigorism applies to Kant. It does not apply to discourse ethics, since the latter breaks with Kant's idealism and monologism. Discourse ethics has a built-in procedure that ensures awareness of consequences. This comes out clearly in the formulation of the principle of universalization (U), which requires sensitivity to the results and consequences of the general observance of a norm for every individual.

b) Hegel is right in another respect, too. Moral theories of the Kantian type are specialized. They focus on questions of *justification,* leaving questions of *application* unanswered. An additional effort is needed to *undo* the abstraction (from particular situations and individual cases) that is, initially at least, an inevitable part of justification. No norm contains within itself the rules for its application. Yet moral justifications are pointless unless the decontextualization of the general norms used in justification is compensated for in the process of application. Like any moral theory, discourse ethics cannot evade this difficult problem: Does the application of rules to particular cases necessitate a separate and distinct faculty of *prudence* or judgment that would tend to undercut the universalistic claim of justificatory reason because it is tied to the parochial context of some hermeneutic starting point? The neo-Aristotelian way out of this dilemma is to argue that practical reason should forswear its universalistic intent in favor of a more contextual faculty of judgment.[20] Since judgment always moves within the ambit of a more or less accepted form of life, it finds support in an evaluative context that engenders *continuity* among questions of motivation, empirical issues, evaluative and normative issues.

In contrast to the neo-Aristotelian position, discourse ethics is emphatically opposed to going back to a stage of philosophical thought prior to Kant. Kant's achievement was precisely to dissociate the problem of justification from the application and implementation of moral insights. I argue that even in the prudent application for norms, principles of practical reason take effect. Suggestive evidence is provided by classical topoi, for instance, the principles that all relevant aspects of a case must be considered and that means should be proportionate to ends. Principles such as these promote the idea of *impartial* application, which is not a prudent but a moral point of view.

(3) On the Impotence of the "Ought"

a) Kant is vulnerable to the objection that his ethics lacks practical impact because it dichotomizes duty and inclination, reason and sense experience. The same cannot be said of discourse ethics, for it discards the Kantian theory of the two realms. The concept of practical discourse postulates the inclusion of all interests that may be affected; it even covers the critical testing of interpretations through which we come to recognize certain needs as in our own interests. Discourse ethics also reformulates the concept of autonomy. In Kant, autonomy was conceived as freedom under self-given laws, which involves an element of coercive subordination of subjective nature. In discourse ethics, the idea of autonomy is intersubjective. It takes into account that the free actualization of the personality of one individual depends on the actualization of freedom for all.

b) In another respect Hegel is right. Practical discourse does disengage problematic actions and norms from the substantive ethics (*Sittlichkeit*) of their lived contexts, subjecting them to hypothetical reasoning without regard to existing motives and institutions. This causes norms to become removed from the world (*entweltlicht*)—an unavoidable step in the process of justification, but also one for which discourse ethics might consider making amends. For unless discourse ethics is undergirded by the thrust of motives and by socially accepted institutions, the moral insights it offers remain ineffective in practice. Insights, Hegel rightly demands, should be transformable into the concrete duties of everyday life. This much is true: Any universalistic morality is dependent upon a form of life that *meets it halfway*. There has to be a modicum of congruence between morality and the practices of socialization and education. The latter must promote the requisite internalization of superego controls and the abstractness of ego identities. In addition there must be a modicum of fit between morality and sociopolitical institutions. Not just any institutions will do. Morality thrives only in an environment in which postconventional ideas about law and morality have already been institutionalized to a certain extent.

Moral universalism is a *historical result*. It arose, with Rousseau and Kant, in the midst of a specific society that possessed corresponding features. The last two or three centuries have witnessed the emergence, after a long seesawing struggle, of a *directed* trend toward the realization of basic rights. This process has led to, shall we cautiously say, a less and less selective reading and utilization of the universalistic meaning that fundamental-rights norms do have; it testifies to the "existence of reason," if only in bits and pieces. Without these fragmentary realizations, the moral intuitions that discourse ethics conceptualizes would never have proliferated the way they did. To be sure, the gradual embodiment of moral principles in concrete forms of life is not something that can safely be left to Hegel's absolute spirit. Rather, it is chiefly a function of collective efforts and sacrifices made by sociopolitical movements. Philosophy would do well to avoid haughtily dismissing these movements and the larger historical dimension from which they spring.

(4) On the Subject of Virtue and the Way of the World

a) Neither Kantian ethics nor discourse ethics exposes itself to the charge of abetting, let alone justifying, totalitarian ways of doing things. This charge has recently been taken up by neoconservatives. The maxim that the end justifies the means is utterly incompatible with both the letter and the spirit of moral universalism, even when it is a question of politically implementing universalistic legal and constitutional principles. A problematic role is played in this connection by certain notions held by philosophers of history, Marxists, and others. Realizing that the political practice of their chosen macrosubject of society is sputtering, if not paralyzed, they delegate revolutionary action to an avant-garde with proxy functions. The error of this view is to conceive of society as a subject writ large and then to pretend that the actions of the avant-garde need not be held any more accountable than those of the higher-level subject of history. In contrast to any philosophy of history, the intersubjectivist approach of discourse ethics break with the premises of the philosophy of consciousness. The only higher-level intersubjectivity it acknowledges is that of public spheres.

b) Hegel rightly sets off action *under* moral laws from political practice that aims to bring about, or at least to promote, the institutional prerequisites for general participation in moral reasoning of a posttraditional type. Can the realization of reason in history be a meaningful objective of intentional action? As I argued earlier, the discursive justification of norms is no guarantee of the actualization of moral insight. This problem, the disjunction between judgment and action on the output side, to use computer jargon, has its counterpart on the input side: Discourse cannot by itself ensure that the conditions necessary for the actual participation of all concerned are met. Often lacking are crucial institutions that would facilitate discursive decision making. Often lacking are crucial socialization processes, so that the dispositions and abilities necessary for taking part in moral argumentation cannot be learned. Even more frequent is the case where material living conditions and social structures are such that moral-practical implications spring immediately to the eye and moral questions are answered, without further reflection, by the bare facts of poverty, abuse, and degradation. Wherever this is the case, wherever existing conditions make a mockery of the demands of universalist morality, moral issues turn into issues of political ethics. How can a political practice designed to realize the conditions necessary for a dignified human existence be morally justified?[21] The kind of politics at issue is one that aims at changing a form of life from moral points of view, though it is not reformist and therefore cannot operate in accordance with existing laws and institutions. The issue of revolutionary morality (which incidentally has never been satisfactorily discussed by Marxists, Eastern or Western) is fortunately not an urgent one in our type of society. Not so moot are cognate issues like civil disobedience, which I have discussed elsewhere.[22]

III

In sum, I argue that Hegel's objections apply less to the reformulation of Kantian ethics itself than to a number of resulting problems that discourse ethics cannot be expected to resolve with a single stroke. Any ethics that is at once deontological, cognitivist, formalist, and universalist ends up with a relatively narrow conception of morality that is uncompromisingly abstract. This raises the problem of whether issues of justice can be isolated from particular contexts of the good life. This problem, I believe, can be solved. But a second difficulty makes its appearance, namely whether practical reason may be forced to abdicate in favor of a faculty of judgment when it comes to applying justified norms to specific cases. Discourse ethics, I think, can handle this difficulty too. A third problem is whether it is reasonable to hope that the insights of a universalistic morality are susceptible to translation into practice. Surely the incidence of such a morality is contingent upon a complementary form of life. This by no means exhausts the lists of consequent problems. I have mentioned only one more: How can political action be morally justified when the social conditions in which practical discourses can be carried on and moral insight can be generated and transformed do not exist but have to be created? I have so far not addressed two other problems that flow from the self-limitation of every nonmetaphysical point of view.

Discourse ethics does not see fit to resort to an objective teleology, least of all to a countervailing force that tries to negate dialectically the irreversible succession of historical events—as was the case, for instance, with the redeeming judgment of the Christian God on the Last Day. But how can we live up to the principle of discourse ethics which postulates the consent of *all,* if we cannot make restitution for the injustice and pain suffered by previous generations or if we cannot at least promise an equivalent for the day of judgment and its power of redemption? Is it not obscene for present-day beneficiaries of past injustices to expect the posthumous consent of slain and degraded victims to norms that appear justified to us in light of our own expectations regarding the future?[23] It is just as difficult to answer the basic objection of ecological ethics: How does discourse ethics, which is limited to subjects capable of speech and action, respond to the fact that mute creatures are also vulnerable? Compassion for tortured animals and the pain caused by the destruction of biotopes—these surely are manifestations of moral intuitions that cannot be fully satisfied by the collective narcissism of what in the final analysis is an anthropocentric way of looking at things.

At this point I want to draw only one conclusion from these skeptical considerations. Since the concept of morality is limited, the self-perception of moral theory should be correspondingly modest. It is incumbent on moral theory to explain and ground the moral point of view. What moral *theory* can do and should be trusted to do is clarify the universal core of our moral intuitions, and thereby to refute value skepticism. What it cannot do is make any kind of substantive contribution. By singling out a procedure of decision making, it seeks to make room for those involved, who must then find answers on their own to the moral-practical issues that come at them, or are imposed upon them, with objective historical force. Moral philosophy does not have privileged access to particular moral truths. In view of the four big moral-political liabilities of our time—hunger and poverty in the Third World, torture and continuous violations of human dignity in autocratic regimes, increasing unemployment and disparities of social wealth in Western industrial nations, and finally the self-destructive risks of the nuclear arms race—my modest opinion about what philosophy can and cannot accomplish may come as a disappointment. Be that as it may: Philosophy cannot absolve anyone of moral responsibility. And that includes philosophers; for like everyone else, they face moral-practical issues of great complexity, and the first thing they might profitably do is get a clearer view of the situation they find themselves in. The historical and social sciences can be of greater help in this endeavor than philosophy. On this note I want to end with a quote from Max Horkheimer from the year 1933: "What is needed to get beyond the utopian character of Kant's idea of a perfect constitution of humankind is a materialist theory of society."[24]

Notes

1

See the essays by K. O. Apel in K. O. Apel, D. Böhler, and G. Kadelbach, eds., *Praktische Philosophie/Ethik* (Frankfurt, 1984); and J. Habermas, "Discourse Ethics," in *Moral Consciousness and Communicative Action*, trans. Christian Lenhardt and Shierry Weber Nicholsen (Cambridge, Mass.: MIT Press, 1990).

2

"But the content of the maxim remains what it is, a specification or singularity, and the universality conferred on it by its reception into the form is thus a merely analytic unity. And when the unity conferred on it is expressed in a sentence purely as it is, that sentence is analytic and tautological." G. W. F. Hegel, *Natural Law*, trans. T. M. Knox (Philadelphia: University of Pennsylvania Press, 1975), p. 76. The same formalism manifests itself in the fact that any maxim at all can take the form of a universal law. "There is nothing whatever which cannot in this way be made into a moral law" (ibid., p. 77).

3

"The moral consciousness as the simple knowing and willing of pure duty is . . . brought into relation with the object which stands in contrast to its simplicity, into relation with the actuality of the complex case, and thereby has a complex moral relationship with it. . . . As regards the many duties, the moral consciousness heeds only the pure duty in them; the many duties qua manifold are specific and therefore as such have nothing sacred about them for the moral consciousness." G. W. F. Hegel, *Phenomenology of Spirit*, trans. A. V. Miller (New York: Oxford University Press, 1977), pp. 369–70. The counterpart to abstracting from the particular is hypostatizing the particular, for it becomes unrecognizable in the form of the universal: "By confusing absolute form with conditioned matter, the absoluteness of the form is imperceptibly smuggled into the unreal and conditioned character of the content; and in this perversion and trickery lies the

nerve of pure reason's practical legislation"; Hegel, *Natural Law*, p. 79.

4

"The moral consciousness . . . learns from experience that Nature is not concerned with giving it a sense of the unity of its reality with that of Nature. . . . The nonmoral consciousness . . . finds, perhaps by chance, its realization where the moral consciousness sees only an occasion for acting, but does not see itself obtaining, through its action, the happiness of performance and the enjoyment of achievement. Therefore it finds rather cause for complaint about such a state of incompatibility between itself and existence, and about the injustice which restricts it to having its object merely as pure duty, but refuses to let it see the object and itself realized"; Hegel, *Phenomenology*, p. 366.

5

In the *Phenomenology of Spirit* Hegel devotes a famous section entitled "Virtue and the Way of the World" to a discussion of Jacobin moral zeal (*Gesinnungsterror*). In it, he shows how morality can be turned into a means to bring "the good into actual existence by the sacrifice of individuality" (p. 233).

6

K. H. Ilting seems to have missed the fact that the notion of what can be consented to merely operationalizes what he himself calls the "imposability" of norms. Only those norms are imposable for which a discursive agreement among those concerned can be reached. See K. H. Ilting, "Der Geltungsgrund moralischer Normen," in W. Kuhlmann and D. Böhler, eds., *Kommunikation und Reflexion* (Frankfurt, 1982), pp. 629ff.

7

The concept of the justification of norms must not be too strong; otherwise the conclusion that justified norms must have the assent of all affected will already be contained in the premise. I committed such a *petitio principii*

in the essay on "Discourse Ethics" cited in n.
1 above. [Trans.: Habermas is referring here
to the first edition of *Moralbewusstsein und
kommunikatives Handeln*. In the second edition, on which this translation was based, the
appropriate changes were made. They occur
at the bottom of p. 92 of *Moral Consciousness and Communicative Action*.]

8
J. Rawls, *A Theory of Justice* (Cambridge,
Mass.: Harvard University Press, 1971), p.
136: "The idea of the original position is to
set up a fair procedure so that any principles
agreed to will be just."

9
G. H. Mead, *Mind, Self, and Society* (Chicago: University of Chicago Press, 1934),
"Fragments on Ethics," pp. 379–89. The concept of ideal role taking also underlies Kohl-
berg's theory of moral development. Cf. also
H. Joas, *G. H. Mead: A Contemporary Re-
examination of His Thought* (Cambridge,
Mass., 1985), pp. 121ff.

10
Practical discourse can fulfill functions other
than critical ones only when the subject matter to be regulated touches on generalizable
interests. Whenever exclusively particular interests are at stake, practical decision making
necessarily takes the form of compromise.
See J. Habermas, *Legitimation Crisis*, trans.
T. McCarthy (Boston: Beacon Press, 1975),
pp. 111ff.

11
J. Habermas, *The Theory of Communicative
Action*, vol. 2, *Lifeworld and System* (Boston:
Beacon Press, 1987), pp. 58ff.

12
Compare my critique of Arnold Gehlen: "The
profound vulnerability that makes necessary
an ethical regulation of behavior as its coun-
terpoise is rooted, not in the biological weaknesses of humans, not in the newborn infant's
lack of organic faculties and not in the risks
of a disproportionately long rearing period,
but in the cultural systems that are constructed as compensation. The fundamental
problem of ethics is guaranteeing mutual consideration and respect in a way that is effective in actual conduct. That is the core of
truth in any ethics of compassion." J. Habermas, "Imitation Substantiality," in J. Habermas, *Philosophical-Political Profiles*, trans.
Frederick G. Lawrence (Cambridge, Mass.:
MIT Press, 1983), p. 120.

13
W. Frankena, *Ethics* (Englewood Cliffs, N.J.:
Prentice-Hall, 1973), pp. 45ff.

14
This is an old topic of action theory. See
A. Gouldner, "The Norm of Reciprocity,"
American Sociological Review 25 (1960):
161–78.

15
Michael Sandel has justly criticized Rawls for
saddling his construct of an original position
with the atomistic legacy of contract theory.
Rawls envisions isolated independent individuals who, prior to any sociation, possess the
ability to pursue their interests rationally and
to posit their objectives monologically. Accordingly, Rawls views the basic covenant not
so much in terms of an agreement based on
argumentation as in terms of an act of free
will. His vision of a just society boils down to
a solution of the Kantian problem of how the
individual will can be free in the presence of
other individual wills. Sandel's own anti-
individualist conception is not without problems either, in that it further deepens the separation between an ethics of duty and an
ethics of the good. Over against Rawls's pre-
social individual, he posits an individual who
is the product of his community; over against
the rational covenant of autonomous individuals, he posits a reflective awareness of prior
social bonds; over against Rawls's idea of
equal rights, he posits the ideal of mutual solidarity; over against equal respect for the dignity of the individual, he posits the
advancement of the common good. With
these traditional juxtapositions Sandel blocks
the way to an intersubjectivist extension of
Rawls's ethics of justice. He roundly rejects
the deontological approach, returning to a

teleological conception that presupposes an objective notion of community. "For a society to be a community in the strong sense, community must be constitutive of the shared self-understandings of the participants and embodied in their institutional arrangements, not simply an attribute of certain of the participants' plans of life." Michael Sandel, *Liberalism and the Limits of Justice* (Cambridge: Cambridge University Press, 1982), p. 173. Clearly, totalitarian (i.e., forcibly integrated) societies do not fit this description, which is why Sandel would have to explicate carefully the normative content of such key notions as community, embodied, shared self-understanding. He does not do so. If he did, he would realize just how onerous the burden of proof is that neo-Aristotelian approaches must bear (as in the case of A. MacIntyre, *After Virtue* [London, 1981]). They must demonstrate how an objective moral order can be grounded without recourse to metaphysical premises.

16
K. O. Apel, "Kant, Hegel und das aktuelle Problem der normativen Grundlagen von Moral und Recht," in D. Henrich, ed., *Kant oder Hegel* (Stuttgart, 1983), pp. 597ff.

17
G. Patzig, "Der Kategorische Imperativ in der Ethikdiskussion der Gegenwart," in G. Patzig, *Tatsachen, Normen, Sätze* (Stuttgart, 1980), pp. 155ff.

18
The controversial subjects Kant focused upon, the stratum-specific "maxims of action" in early bourgeois society, were not produced by law-giving reason but simply taken up by law-testing reason as empirical givens. If one realizes this, then Hegel's attack on Kant's deposit example (*Critique of Practical Reason,* section 4, Remark) becomes groundless.

19
Conversely, one might critically ask what evidence there is for the suspicion that universal and particular are always *inextricably* interlocked. We saw earlier that practical discourses are not only embedded in complexes

of action but also represent, at a higher plane of reflection, continuations of action oriented to reaching understanding. Both have the same structural properties. But in the case of communicative action there is no need to extend the presuppositions about symmetry and reciprocity to actors *not* belonging to the particular collectivity or lifeworld. By contrast, this extension into universality does become necessary, indeed forced, when argumentation is at issue. No wonder that ethical positions starting from the ethics (*Sittlichkeit*) of such concrete forms of life as the polis, the state, or a religious community have trouble generating a universal principle of justice. This problem is less troublesome for discourse ethics, for the latter presumes to justify the universal validity of its moral principle in terms of the normative content of communicative presuppositions of *argumentation* as such.

20
E. Vollrath, *Die Rekonstruktion der politischen Urteilskraft* (Stuttgart, 1977).

21
Compare J. Habermas, *Theory and Practice,* trans. J. Viertel (Boston: Beacon Press, 1973), pp. 32ff.

22
J. Habermas, *Die neue Unübersichtlichkeit* (Frankfurt, 1985), and *The New Conservatism,* trans. Shierry Weber Nicholsen (Cambridge, Mass.: MIT Press, 1989). The only comment I want to make on this subject here is that problems of this kind do not lie on the same plane of complexity as the objections discussed earlier. First, the relation of morality, law, and politics has to be clarified. While these universes of discourse may overlap, they are by no means identical. In terms of justification, posttraditional ideas about law and morality are structurally similar. At the heart of modern legal systems are basic moral norms which have attained the force of law. On the other hand, law differs from morality, inter alia, in that the target group of a law— those who are expected to comply with a legal norm—are relieved of the burdens of jus-

tifying, applying, and implementing it. These chores are left to public bodies. Politics, too, has an intimate relation to morality and law. Basic political issues are moral issues. And exercising political power is tantamount to making legally binding decisions. Also, the legal system is for its part tied up with politics via the legislative process. As far as the field of public will-formation is concerned, the main thrust of politics is to pursue collective ends in an agreed-upon framework of rules rather than to redefine this framework of law and morality.

23

See H. Peukert, *Science, Action, and Fundamental Theology* (Cambridge, Mass., 1984); C. Lenhardt, "Anamnestic Solidarity," *Telos* no. 25 (1975).

24

M. Horkheimer, "Materialismus und Moral," in *Zeitschrift für Sozialforschung,* vol. 2 (1933), p. 175; English translation, "Materialism and Morality," *Telos* 69 (1986): 85–118.

Chapter 15

The Motivation behind a
Procedural Ethics

Charles Taylor

The foundational program of a discourse ethics advocated by Habermas and Apel renews the whole modern tradition of procedural ethics, and it is certainly the most interesting and most plausible attempt within a tradition that characterizes modern thought at least since Kant and, in my view, even earlier. Discourse ethics has overcome a set of inadequacies in the older theoretical projects, in particular, the monological character of Kant's theory.

There remains, nevertheless, the question of whether a procedural ethics as such can be convincing as a theory of moral life when it for the most part privileges the question of the right over the question of the good. In my view, this cannot be the case. But it is not my intention here to defend this thesis directly; what I am more interested in exploring is the *motivation* behind a procedural ethics. In fact, I initially abstain from answering the central question, but the considerations developed here should contribute indirectly to resolving the problem.

As the counter-thesis to a procedural ethics, the subsumption of the good under the right—an essential feature of procedural ethics, which I will discuss below in more detail—is in the final analysis untenable. According to this counter-thesis, every ethics is founded upon a fundamental concept of the good. Now it in no way follows from this that every type of procedural ethics is to be rejected, but merely that, as a theory of moral life, procedural ethics misconceives the specific nature and logic of what is moral. Should this counter-position succeed in validating itself, it would indeed force a procedural ethics to accept some significant reformulations, but the latter would not be refuted as such. I will have more to say below about the implications of my basic contention for discourse ethics.

The confrontation between procedural ethics and substantive ethics is closely bound up with the relation between ethical and metaethical questions. The subsumption of the good under the right implies a metaethical view, even in those cases

This essay originally appeared in *Moralität und Sittlichkeit: Das Problem Hegels und die Diskursethik*, edited by Wolfgang Kuhlmann (Frankfurt am Main: Suhrkamp, 1986), pp. 101–35.

where it seeks to evade a decision about the form of an ethical theory. Consistency then demands that one proceed on the assumption that metaphysical questions can be decided independently of assumptions about the good. If a procedural ethics must presuppose a concept of the good in order to be able to legitimate itself, it finds itself in a contradiction at the point where the priority of the right to the good can no longer be maintained. By the same logic, the defender of a procedural ethics will also uphold the independent status of metaethics, a position which its adversaries will almost without exception dispute.

In recent years, this has been an important theme of philosophical discussion in the Anglo-American world. There are, to be sure, different varieties of procedural ethics—for instance, Hare's utilitarian Kantianism, or the pure version of Rawls and Dworkin cleansed of metaphysical presuppositions—but in each case the question of the place value of metaethics plays a decisive role. Critics attempt to show, to the contrary, that a metaethic, as the form of the theory, rests upon a substantive basis that is not compatible with its putative status. For instance, central to Hare's critique is the metaethical supposition of a gulf between *is* and *ought,* and between facts and values. Habermas, on the other hand, accentuates, with reference to Weber, the differentiation between questions of factual truth and those of normative rightness. It is perhaps possible to overcome both positions by showing that they themselves require tacit assumptions about the good, which on the one hand places their logic in question and on the other hand renders it possible to bridge the supposed chasm.

In this sense, a historical-hermeneutical reconstruction of the motivation behind a procedural ethics should help to prepare this reformulation. In addition to justifying my approach, I anticipate a further theoretical payoff: namely, if procedural ethics is in fact secretly nourished by a concept of the good, then it obviously follows that the unacknowledged motivation also remains misunderstood, and this gives rise to various confusions. In my view, it is from this that procedural ethics draws a considerable portion of its appeal, which one hopes can be dissolved as soon as it source is exposed.

I have now revealed *my* motivation for undertaking this inquiry. In particular, disentangling the various confused motives is of primary concern to me here. For this purpose, I rely upon Alasdair MacIntyre's *After Virtue* (1981), one of the most important contributions to discussion within Anglo-American debates on the construction of ethical theories, and I begin with his discussion of the historical presuppositions of the fact/value dichotomy in order to pursue a closer examination of the roots of procedural ethics.

In chapter 5 of *After Virtue,* MacIntyre takes up the discussion of the fact/value dichotomy. Following Elizabeth Anscombe's path-breaking article, he shows how the growing sense among many different schools of modern philosophy that no "ought" can be derived from an "is" is not the slow dawning of a context-free logical truth but rather the correlate of the decline or rejection of the conception central to much ancient philosophy that human life was defined by a telos.[1] The sharp gap between the permissible ways to argue that something is a good watch and someone a good farmer, on one hand, and what one needs to say to show that someone is a good human being, on the other, just does not arise, for instance, in Aristotle's theory, which was undoubtedly the most powerful and widespread of ancient traditions at the dawn of the modern world (p. 56).

The crucial point that MacIntyre adds to this is that the decline of teleological conceptions cannot just be understood as an independent development in science and epistemology. It also reflects a new understanding of man's moral and spiritual predicament. He points here to the important role of Protestant and Jansenist theologies, with their sense of the powerlessness of fallen human reason (pp. 51–52). Because it will play a role in my later argument, I shall develop this connection more fully.

We might think that there are sufficient grounds to reject Aristotle's teleology once natural science has made the crucial transformation described as "the mechanization of the world-picture," wrought by Galileo, Descartes, and their successors. This seems radically to undercut teleological accounts in general, and particularly in biology. MacIntyre mentions the dependence of Aristotle's ethical views on his "metaphysical biology."

But this is not so. The notion that human beings have something like a telos qua human can be separated from the thesis that everything in nature belongs to some class or other, whose behavior is explained by some Form or Idea. Because we no longer explain the movements of stars and stones teleologically does not mean that we cannot explain humans in these terms. This is not to say that the demise of explanation by Form did not have a traumatic effect on the teleological outlook or that other big problems do not remain, notably that of relating human to natural science once they are seen to invoke quite different explanatory principles. But it does mean that the mechanization of natural science by no means makes inevitable the changes in moral outlook that have often been justified by it. (I shall argue below that the very tendency to exalt scientific reasoning—and to depreciate practical reason in relation to it—itself springs from the moral outlook of modernity.)

Rather, the thesis that MacIntyre puts forward here, which I support, is that the change in the understanding of morality is to be explained itself in terms of changing moral vision. Changed views about the very nature of moral discourse and thought—like the new no "ought" from "is" principle—spring from substantive changes in moral outlook. The new metaethics may indeed be assisted in its progress by new scientific theories, but then there is also a notorious line of influence in the other direction. It has been well documented, for instance, how one important motive for embracing the new mechanism in the seventeenth century was theological in nature. One very important tradition of thought in Christendom, which stressed the sovereignty of God and tended to be suspicious of Greek conceptions of a fixed cosmic order, was happy to embrace mechanism in the seventeenth century, particularly over against the more extravagant neopagan excesses (as they saw them) of high Renaissance animism, as we see it in figures like Bruno. Something like this was the motivation, for instance, of Mersenne, who played such an important role in the diffusion of the new scientific outlook.

A great deal of reciprocal action there certainly was between science and morality in these centuries, as at any time in our civilization. But it is quite wrong to fix on only one direction of causation and propound a story in which scientific discovery simply brings changes in moral outlook in its train.

Behind the fact/value split, which one sees emerging in Hume and then becoming a dominant theme in our century, lies a new understanding and valuation of freedom and dignity. MacIntyre points out its theological origins. These must be understood, I think, in terms of the strand of Christian thought I mentioned above. In fact, the Christian synthesis with Greek thought was always an uneasy one. For some thinkers the notion of a fixed and ordered cosmos, whose principles of justification could be found in itself, was incompatible with the sovereignty of God. Think of the nominalist rebellion against Thomism. The issue in one formulation concerned the relation in God of reason and will. Is God constrained by his own creation, so that he has to will a good that is, as it were, built into it? Occam and others offer a more voluntaristic view of God's power. Anything less seems to belittle God. The Reformers took this spiritual side, even where they did not always adopt the same intellectual formulations. The fight of Thomas versus Occam then carries down in Christendom in ever-new forms, through, for example, the battle between Jesuit and Jansenist, right up to our day.

We can see easily enough why the Occamite temper might welcome mechanism, as I mentioned above. Here at last is an utterly neutral view of the universe, waiting to have purposes given to it by sovereign fiat. The fact/value split is first a theological thesis, and God is at first the sole beneficiary. But at this stage the spiritual motivation of this view is evident. The thesis is propounded to defend God's freedom of choice.

Later something of this conception of freedom is transferred onto man. As against seeing our paradigm purposes as given to us by the nature of the cosmic order in which we are set, we find them rather in the nature of our own reasoning powers. These demand that we take control by objectifying the world, submitting it to the demands of instrumental reason. The purposes to which the surrounding world is instrumentalized are found within us. These are the purposes of life—self-preservation, and what was later called the pursuit of happiness—and as such they too are given by nature. But what confers dignity on their pursuit is that this is not to be carried on in a blind, licentious, or undisciplined fashion, but under the control of far-sighted, calculating reason.

The changes are well enough known: reason is no longer defined substantively, in terms of a vision of cosmic order, but formally, in terms of the procedures that thought ought to follow, and especially those involved in fitting means to ends, instrumental reason; the hegemony of reason is consequently redefined and now means not ordering our lives according to the vision of order, but rather controlling desires by the canons of instrumental reason. Freedom consequently takes on a new meaning, and this entails breaking loose from any external authorities in order to be governed solely by one's own reasoning procedures. And the notion of human dignity assumes a new importance, since now the source of obligation is no longer a cosmic order without but rather my own status as a sovereign reasoning being, which demands that I achieve rational control. I owe this, as it were, not to the order of things, but to my own dignity.

Descartes was one of the founding figures of this new outlook, and virtually all its themes are present in his work. In the *Meditations,* for instance, he makes clear that my coming to understand myself as I truly am, a thinking being, involves disengaging from the usual stance wherein I perceive things through the body—see the color as in the rose, for instance, or experience the pain as in the tooth. I must assume a stance from which I can recognize that both color and pain are really occurrences in the soul, albeit (we have reason to believe) caused by factors in rose and tooth respectively. This is the disengaged stance in which I see the body as a mechanism, mediating causal connections between world and soul. In his later writings on morality, the correspondence with Elisabeth, and *Le traité des passions,* Descartes reinterprets the ancient moral traditions (particularly the Stoic) in the light of this new ideal of disengaged rational control. The hegemony of reason over the passions is no longer a matter of seeing through the latter in order to render them inoperative (as for the Stoics) but of understanding them in order to make them instrumentally subordinate. The passions are no longer analyzed as opinions (*dogmata*), which have to be either quite exploded (Stoics) or aligned with my whole, reflective understanding of the good (Aristotle). Instead, Descartes offers a *functional* theory of the passions, showing us how they ought to be used. The crucial place of the new notion of dignity—which becomes explicit later with Kant—is already indicated in Descartes by the important status he accords generosity, which in its seventeenth-century meaning designated the aristocratic virtue one displays when one has a lively sense of one's own worth and rank and the demands it puts on one. Descartes does not, in fact, make a big thing of freedom, but it is clear how the later notion is implicit in his philosophy.

Descartes provides an excellent illustration of the crisscrossing motives I talked about above. Of course, he was moved by the tremendous potentiality of the mechanist reading of nature, as he found it in Galileo. This scientific/epistemological motive stands out clearly. But it is also clear that he was moved by the ideal of disengaged rational control. Anthropological ideal and scientific theory collaborate, as they have throughout the modern culture of which Descartes is one of the founders.

This brings us to the point where we can look at and perhaps raise questions about the structure of MacIntyre's argument in *After Virtue*. What we have seen so far is that the modern metaethics of the fact/value dichotomy does not stand as a timeless truth, at last discovered, like the inverse-square law or the circulation of the blood. It makes sense only within certain ethical outlooks. For an Aristotelian, the sharp division between factual and evaluative claims makes no sense. Of course, at this point the defender of the split is tempted to reply that this just shows the mistake of Aristotle, whose theories the progress of science has relegated to the trash heap. But the whole argument above has been designed to detach us from this way of seeing things. The progress of science may have refuted Aristotle's physics and his biology, but it does not rule out thinking of ethics in terms of telos or other similar concepts. The shift in ethical outlook is underdetermined by the scientific change. Rather, the split has to be seen as part of a new understanding of freedom and moral agency. The neutral world of nature waiting to have purposes imprinted on it is the correlate of the disengaged subject. Neutrality is the property he *ought* to perceive in the world, if he is to realize his potentiality as the free agent of dignity and rational control.

But then we are being sold a bill of goods by the theorists of the split. What is supposed to be an outlook-independent metaethical finding, setting the rules of reasoning for all possible moral positions, turns out to be just the preferred interpretation of one ideal among others. This stage of the argument is now relatively familiar to us all. It consists in unmasking the spuriously independent validity of certain metaethical propositions, which in fact outrageously fix the rules of discourse in the interests of one outlook, forcing rival views into incoherence.

But one can go further. One can argue back, with all the resources of moral phenomenology, to show that this metaethic is not only biased but also false. All sorts of arguments have been put forward. This book itself comprises arguments for this, in pitting Aristotle against Nietzsche, whose position is thought to be the only consistent conclusion for proponents of the split. In general these arguments, as deployed by MacIntyre and others, attempt to convince us that in what we have to recognize as our own moral reasoning we just could not do without modes of thinking that the split rules out, for example, using virtue terms that cannot be neatly segmented into descriptive and evaluative components. I refrain from going into this because I think these arguments are now relatively familiar and even, I hope, convincing to most scholars. The difficult issue is where we go from here.

Or perhaps better put, where have we got. People like MacIntyre and me want to accuse the Hares and the Stevensons of—to put it polemically and brutally— trying to ram through their own ethic of disengaged freedom under the guise of an independently established, rationally undeniable metaethic. Then we go on to argue for our own metaethic; let us call it for short Aristotelian. But this is tied to another range of moral views—not, of course, narrowly to Aristotle's own detailed theory; MacIntyre shows how diverse and susceptible of development the understanding in terms of the virtues is. Nevertheless, this also makes some views more coherently statable than others. Does that mean that arguing from one's substantive view through the connected metaethic—for one's moral position through the implied form of moral reasoning—is after all legitimate, that the only problem with the fact/value split was that their case was bad?

The simple answer to this question is yes. If moral positions and metaethical theories are closely interwoven, then one ought to be able to argue in either direction. But the detailed case is more complicated. Does it follow from this that (assuming our moral phenomenology is convincing) we ought to consider the ethics of modern disengaged freedom as refuted, as the proponents of the split considered Aristotle's? This would be too quick. All we would have shown is that in the form in which they have come down to us these moral positions are incoherent, namely, in ruling as impossible the forms of moral thinking that their protagonists nevertheless cannot help using. But perhaps the essence of the moral vision can be saved in a more sophisticated variant that takes account of this. And, of course, perhaps not; perhaps the ideal of modern freedom is so out of tune with what we are that it inevitably forces us into incoherence. But we cannot answer this question a priori. We have to give these ideals a run for their money.

And the need to try is made the more urgent by the fact that for many of us in the "Aristotelian" camp, some facets at least of the ideal of modern freedom have great appeal. Indeed, one might suspect that there is virtually no one in the modern age who is not committed to some of its facets. Can one build an identity in the modern world that has not to some extent been shaped by this understanding of freedom? Many of MacIntyre's critics have raised this worry. So the argument thus far, once we have denounced the credentials of the spuriously independent metaethic, and even once we have established a better metaethic, still leaves an important issue: what can/should be rescued of the moral vision that spawned the distortive metaethic?

And beyond this, another issue arises. If we are right and the Aristotelian metaethic is the right one, in the sense of offering the forms in which we cannot help but think and construe at least good parts of our moral lives, how possible is it in fact for people to escape its forms? Presumably they can do so at the cost of abandoning those aspects of moral lives that we cannot help casting in its terms. But how possible is this in practice? The answer we give to this question will have important consequences for our whole reading of our civilization.

Those who think that the Aristotelian metaethic in fact offers the inescapable categories for anyone's moral thought will see the rival package of views—say disengaged freedom, plus the metaethics of the fact/value dichotomy—as an unviable basis for an alternative life-form. In fact, people who aspire to live by this alternative will be deluding themselves. They will be unclear in many respects about the ways that they in fact think. They will always be in truth more Aristotelian than they believe, surreptitiously relying on notions like virtue and the good life, even while they repudiate them on the level of theory. On the other hand, those who think that the Aristotelian forms can be escaped will think that the modern package offers the basis for a coherent viable alternative.

Which way one goes on this has great importance for the critique he or she offers of modernity. Part of what one means to say in offering the moral phenomenology that issues in the Aristotelian metaethic is that these forms of thinking are closely tied to central features of our moral life. If one thinks that people who embrace the modern package in fact escape these forms, then the modernists will be seen as doing away with these features and, consequently, sacrificing essential parts of human life and departing from the human norm. If, on the other hand, one thinks that these forms of thought are not escapable, one will be ready to convict modern culture of muddle but will doubt that it actually departs as much from the norm as its theory would call for.

This is a very important issue for our entire understanding of modernity, once we engage in this critique of modern metaethics. MacIntyre seems to lean toward the view that there is a viable way of being outside of the Aristotelian forms of thought. Consequently, he tends to take modern society at the face value of its own dominant theories, as heading for runaway atomism and breakup. He speaks at times of a society organized around "emotivist" understandings of ethics. I, on the other hand, frankly lean in the other direction. I think that we are far more Aristotelian than we allow, and hence our practice is in some significant way based less on pure disengaged freedom and atomism than we realize. Of course, this does not mean that getting the right metaethic makes no practical difference; without doubt, seeing ourselves as atoms, for instance, distorts and inhibits the practices that embed the contrary understanding. This is notably the case for the practices of citizen participation in contemporary society. But these practices nevertheless survive. Our way of life never sinks to the full horror that would attend it (I believe) if we could be truly consistent Benthamites, for instance.

MacIntyre and I lean opposite ways on this issue. (He has been heavily criticized for his stand on this question too.) The truth may be somewhere between us. But my aim here is to bring this issue to the fore. There are thus two more questions that we have to address to the line of argument that MacIntyre offers in *After Virtue:* (1) is the substantive ethical vision that spawned the false metaethic to be just abandoned, or can/ought it to be rescued in some form? and (2) to the extent that it must be abandoned, is this package of inadequate views to be taken seriously in our diagnosis of modernity as what underlies a coherent but dangerous and destructive way of life, or should it be discounted in part at least as confusion, rendering us blind to our actual ways of thinking and reacting and hence no doubt potentially dangerous and destructive, but not precisely in the ways that the false theory indicates on its face?

Let me call these two questions the rescue question and the diagnostic questions, respectively, and plunge on to look at more serious issues of metaethics that MacIntyre raises.

I do not mean to imply that the fact/value split is not serious. In some way it is the most serious and fundamental claim that arises out of the new conception of modern freedom. That is why MacIntyre seems to give it pride of place in talking of our modern culture as "emotivist." It is emblematic of modern views, too, in that it issues both from the underlying ethic of freedom and from the felt pressure of that ethical skepticism that modern scientific culture tends to breed, from a mix of moral and epistemological considerations. But it is also familiar to us, and the arguments against it have been often rehearsed, to the point where many people will now agree in laying this particular thesis to rest.

There is, however, another issue that concerns the proper scope of ethical theories. In terms of the paradigm case of justice, it pits a group of thinkers of which John Rawls and Ronald Dworkin are key figures against another of which, say, Michael Walzer and Michael Sandel are important spokesmen. One holds that a theory of justice ought to be general, applying across all societies, or at least all of a certain level of development. The other believes that justice is at least partly relative to the particular culture and history of each society. Let's call these two views the universalist and communitarian, respectively.

Now, MacIntyre's book offers what appears to be a very good argument in favor of the communitarian case, and he specifically takes up the issue of justice in chapter 17. But the universalists might still be dissatisfied and think that their case is being sidestepped rather than confronted. What they consider the most important point of a theory of justice, its potential to criticize the existing reality, seems to be lost in what appears to be a derivation of goods from existing practices.

I think that this is a misreading of MacIntyre's thesis and that his book gives us an excellent basis to go at the issue between universalists and communitarians. But confusion has arisen from running together what I think are different strands of the argument—an elision to which proponents of modern disengaged freedom are prone. I want to try to separate them out here. Let me take up three issues that are or have been considered in some sense metaethical and that divide many communitarians from universalists.

1. At the end of chapter 9, posing the issue of Aristotle versus Nietzsche, MacIntyre speaks of an opposition between an ethic of rules and one of virtue. According to the former, "the rules of morality or law . . . are not to be derived from or justified in terms of some more fundamental conception of the good for man" (p. 112). The target here is Dworkin. Later MacIntyre quotes Rawls, to show that the latter has a fundamentally derived notion of the virtues: they are defined in terms of rules of right. He opposes this to a moral theory that would begin with the virtues.

This is my first issue, but I would like to put it in slightly different (though basically equivalent) terms. I oppose an ethic of rules to an ethic whose more basic concept is the good. In effect, this amounts to the same distinction. To see this, we should look briefly at the Aristotelian notion of the relation of virtue and the good. The term *virtue* is often used to pick out qualities of two kinds: either particular facets of what is seen as a good life, such as kindness or liberality, or else properties that have the effect of bringing about, preserving, or maintaining the good life, such as courage, temperance, constancy, and (on some readings) justice. Let's call these latter "preserving" qualities. It is central to Aristotle's theory that while he picks out a great many preserving virtues, these are also considered to fall into the first class, to be proper parts of the good life. Being a causal condition of the good does not rule out being constitutive of it.

There is a particular understanding of the good at work here, one in which the whole good life contains within it particular partial goods, but not just as an aggregation. Rather, the good life puts the partial goods together in their proper order, according to their proper rank, as it were. One needs the virtue of courage, and also the kind of insight he calls *phronēsis,* to discern and maintain allegiance to this order; but these qualities are also goods that have their place in it, a part of what the virtues are meant to sustain.

Now it is a feature of many modern theories, as MacIntyre points out, that they cannot abide this kind of relation, in which one element is both cause and constituent of another. It is a central demand of one influential construal of modern reason that one clearly sort out means from ends. For utilitarians, the good is happiness, and virtues can only be good instrumentally: they are preserving qualities without being part of what is to be preserved. And something similar goes for any theory that makes rules ultimate. If the basic point of morality is to do the right actions, then the virtues must be seen as purely executive. They cannot also be seen as part of the end, because the end is not defined that way.

So MacIntyre is right to see the place accorded the virtues as a kind of litmus test for discriminating Aristotelian from modern ethical theory. But I want to make the place of the good the central issue, because I think this enables us to get faster to the motivational core of these theories. It is the same mixture as before, of epistemological and moral concerns.

The epistemological consideration is easily described, even though rather harder to justify. A theory of ethics that takes as its basic concept a notion of the human good seems to presuppose metaphysical concepts that we can no longer justify, like that of a normative "nature." An ethic founded on rules or procedures is thought not to share this difficulty. (I think this argument is shot full of holes, but it is not my focus here.)

The moral considerations are more interesting. They can be captured by three related qualities. The first is freedom, which we are already familiar with. An Aristotelian theory seems to determine my paradigm purposes from the order of nature. To be guided by reason is to be guided by insight into this order. But the modern notion of reason is of a capacity that is procedurally defined. We are rational to the extent that our thinking activity meets certain procedural standards, such as consistency, the analysis of problems into elements, the making of clear and distinct connections, attention to the evidence, conformity to the rules of logic, and the like. To be guided by reason now means to direct one's action according to plans or standards that one has constructed following the canons of rational procedure—for example, to proceed according to clear calculations or to obey a law one has prescribed to oneself according to the demands of reason. Rational direction is therefore seen as synonymous with freedom understood as self-direction, direction according to orders constructed by the subject, as against those which he is supposed to find in nature. From the standpoint of this understanding of freedom and reason, the Aristotelian theory—or any theory based on an antecedent notion of the good as prescribed by nature—is profoundly repugnant. It does not exalt the freedom of the subject as one ought, but rather preempts it. If this is our predicament, then we cannot think of the best human life as defined by the fact that we confer our own order on it. The essence of modern dignity is lost.

To this motive is added the one directed to the other two, closely connected qualities. In its Aristotelian form (though not so much in the Platonic, as we'll see below) a theory of the good can be defined in too close symbiosis with a particular form of life. It will lack critical bite, and thus also universality.

On the other side, a theory that makes rules ultimate satisfies this modern drive to freedom, universality, and critical distance. To translate it (with outrageous presumption) into Aristotelian categories, we might say that the essence of man lies in freedom, which is the imposing of orders on his life meeting the demands of procedural rationality. To set up any substantive goal a priori is to bypass or downgrade this activity of constructing self-imposed order. The norms this activity itself has to meet are those of procedural rationality. Consequently, the only a priori standards that human life can be required to meet and that still respect this freedom are procedural ones. What we do when we carry out this activity in order to direct our lives is determine what we should do, or what is right. Consequently, the proper moral theory should make the right and not the good its fundamental category.

What I seem to have accounted for here is the supersession of theories of the good by theories of the right. But in fact it is evident that I am drawing this distinction differently from the usual way; indeed, scandalously so. These terms were originally introduced by the intuitionists, I believe, in order to distinguish utilitarian from Kantian theories. *Teleological* versus *deontological* were other terms for this distinction. So described, this difference is an intramural squabble within modern philosophy. But the distinction I am drawing pits utilitarianism and Kantianism against Aristotle and Plato.

To draw it my way you have to redefine the criterial difference. It is not just: do you determine the right from the good or the good from the right? Rather, it is something like: do you recognize a hierarchic order in goods? Everybody recognizes that humans must acknowledge de facto, nonmoral goods, the objects of our needs and desires. The moral issue concerns a possible ordering of these, whether some are to be given precedence over others, as allegedly higher or more worthwhile, or truly enjoined on us, whether they are to be sought even at the expense of others, and so forth. The views that issue from modern freedom all shy away from recognizing this kind of good. The task of deciding the hierarchy must fall to the subject's rational construction.

The difference is that for the utilitarians, once the possibility of a higher good is excluded, the only rational procedure must be to sum de facto goods. The right solution, that which enjoys henceforth the aura of the higher or moral way, is that which emerges from the rational procedure. Kant, on the other hand, saw that utilitarianism seemed to reject altogether the hierarchy of motives; there seemed to be no qualitative distinction left between moral and prudential. For the same reason, its notion of freedom was not radical enough. It involved rejecting the spurious hierarchical orders in nature, but it did not establish the will's independence from mere de facto inclination. Kant made up both these inadequacies in one stroke: to act morally is to act from a qualitatively higher motive than the merely prudential; and this motive, being defined procedurally, independently even of de facto ends, offers an even more exalted notion of freedom.

This distinction as I draw it here, between what we could call substantive and procedural notions of ethics, is useful because it makes criterial what were in fact the powerful motives behind these modern doctrines. As a result, it allows us to see the continuities as well as the breaks in modern ethical thought. So defined, procedural theories represent a powerful tradition, from Bentham through Kant to Rawls, Dworkin, and Habermas. Indeed, if we think only of the political dimension, the move to the procedural is anticipated in Grotius's theory of legitimacy, where substantive issues about the form of the state are preempted by the procedural question of how it arose. I do not think it is wrong to see all these theories as affirmations, in rather different forms, of what I have been calling the modern notion of freedom.

This is what I want to identify as the first major metaethical issue, whether ethical theories ought to be procedural or substantive. Having said that, I want to state baldly that procedural theories seem to me to be incoherent, or, better put, that to be made coherent, they require restatement in substantive form. I cannot argue this here, given my basic goal, which is to try to understand what the whole structure of the debate is about and what follows from our metaethical insights. So I am just going to take this as shown. But the weakness of procedural theories is not difficult to find. It comes out when one questions the basis of the hierarchy they do recognize, and that any moral theory must, the sense of what I call strong evaluation. What makes it mandatory to follow the privileged procedures? The answer has to lie in some understanding of human life and reason, in some positive doctrine of man, and hence the good. It is greatly to the credit of Kant that he recognizes this and spells out his view of man, or rather rational agency, and the dignity that attaches to it, that is, what makes it of infinitely higher worth than anything else in the universe. This allows one to see that the logic of "nature," "telos," and "the good" has not been escaped in these theories, but just displaced. For Kant we *are* rational agency. This is different from Aristotle's rational animal, in that its *ergon* has nothing to do with our animal existence, but only with making a certain kind of rational procedure absolutely primary. This primacy, which is equivalent to freedom, is our highest good, although the complete good requires that happiness be added to this, in the proper relation, that is, distributed according to merit.

Any theory that claims to make the right primary really reposes on such a notion of the good, in the sense (a) that one needs to articulate this view of the good in order to make its motivations clear and (b) that an attempt to hold onto the theory of the right while denying any such underpinning in a theory of the good would collapse in incoherence. I hope that my analysis above has made at least (a) more plausible.[2]

2. The first issue concerned the very structure of a moral theory. My second touches on the nature of moral reasoning. On the first, Plato and Aristotle are

together against modern procedural ethics. The second opposes Plato to Aristotle; at least Aristotle thought it did.

Aristotle thought that our moral understanding could never be fully explicit. It could not be stated in a set of rules, however long. The endless variety of the situations of action meant that we could only live well if we had some kind of insightful understanding, not reducible to rules, of the requirements of virtue in each fresh context. This is what Aristotle called phronēsis.

Part of one's grasp of the good lies in knowing how to act in varying circumstances. To explain or communicate this knowledge human beings would often turn to paradigmatic actions, or people, or stories. (MacIntyre points out how vital stories are to our development as children.)

Sometimes our grasp of a good is through our grasp of a practice of which this is the internal good. MacIntyre illustrates this point with his example of portrait painting: we may be inarticulate, virtually unable to talk about it (as he, inevitably, is forced to do in his discussion), but still be excellent and discriminating at the art. But even with practices that have been much more theorized about, say, that of politics as rule through citizen participation, the grasp that an experienced citizen of a modern state has, as shown by his sense of what practices to encourage, what to protest against, and what to treat as indifferent, is far from being exhausted by the explicit theories of democracy or participatory politics. Indeed, one of the catastrophic features of the political action of a Robespierre or Saint-Just seems to be that they made no allowance for such understanding in trying to realize a citizen republic. They expected perfect conformity with a preestablished form.

But our grasp of an existing practice is only one example of this implicit understanding. It by no means signifies that only the goods of the status quo are understood in this way. A revolutionary new value cannot be fully explicit either. We understand it partly through an imaginative grasp on the style of practice it would call for, and often it is communicated to us through model practitioners in reality or fiction. The New Testament is the outstanding example in our culture of a new spirituality that was disseminated largely through story, both those of the Gospels themselves and those related in the Gospels.

Of course, we are frequently called on to articulate this understanding. Disputes arise about what some good means or what the point is of some practice. Rival formulations are proffered. But the fact that we can be convinced in some cases that some of these are more in the spirit of the previously accepted good or practice testifies to the existence of this implicit understanding.

The point made by Wittgenstein, Heidegger, Michael Polanyi, and others is the by now familiar one that this process of articulation never comes to an end; it never exhausts the implicit understanding. Rules, however long and detailed, don't apply themselves. Norms and ideals always need fresh interpretation in new circumstances.

We can readily see how the ethics of modern freedom had a penchant for explicit rules. Free action was that determined by rational procedures, and these strove for exactness and explicitness in order to surmount confusion and error. We have only to think of Descartes. The same spirit that pushed for an ethic of rules over one of the substantive good tended to favor an ethic of explicit rules. What was left to phronēsis seemed to be abandoned to unreason. One had rational control to the extent that one could calculate exactly, or determine one's action according to universal principles alone. All this meant that phronēsis was mistrusted not just because it was not yet fully reduced to reason but also because as a consequence it could be the domain of blind parochial prejudice. An inarticulate moral sense must be a prisoner of the existing practices, and so any concession to it amounted to a strengthening of the status quo. Freedom, universality, and a critical stance all required explicit rules.

This spirit is far from dead in our day. But the sidelining of phronēsis has been tremendously and effectively attacked by the authors I mentioned above and again by MacIntyre in *After Virtue*. This has been part of an attack across the board on the rationalist conception of the mind. But it is not surprising if, in the case of Heidegger and Gadamer at least, as well as in that of MacIntyre, Aristotle's ethical doctrines have been an important reference point.

Once again, I am just going to award victory without argument to the Aristotelian side. The value of raising this point, though, is to distinguish it from the previous issue, pitting proceduralists against substantivists. Aristotle is in both cases lined up against the defenders of modern freedom; and the motives that the latter have in taking sides on both are the same. Nevertheless, the issues are different, as the different position of Plato testifies. The major aim of separating out these issues, however, is to distinguish them both from the third. To this last I now turn.

3. The third issue is the important substantial one. It concerns how closely one's ethical theory is tied to existing practice. Once again, Plato and Aristotle can serve as models. Plato is in a sense the great revisionist. His notion of the good is such that he is ready to propose a radical break with the existing world, at least if one takes the *Republic* seriously.[3] Political life as the search for honor, family life, the accumulation of property as a basis for one's own exercise of liberality and help to one's friends—all these can be sacrificed. What people have believed to be the goods internal to these practices are reinterpreted either as neutral or as potentially dangerous sources of corruption.

Aristotle takes Plato seriously to task for this in his *Politics* (Book II). For Aristotle, it is a fundamental error to write any of the goods out of the good life for man. The good life is constituted by all the goods we seek, in their correct rank and proportion. This means that in some circumstances, lesser goods will almost certainly have to be sacrificed to greater ones. But the idea of ruling some out in principle as unfit to be part of the good life runs against the essence of the *teleion agathon,* which is to include all goods, each in its rightful place. You can't just jump out of the human condition.

This might be understood as a metaethical dispute, because reasons of principle can be found for believing that an ethical view must conform to each of these models. One can take the "Platonic" view, without necessarily being as revolutionary in its application, that no existing practice is to be allowed as legitimate until it has been tested against an independent criterion of the good. Of what use would an ethical theory be, if it did not make possible such an independent check? Recently, for instance, Ronald Dworkin argued in somewhat this spirit against Michael Walzer that a theory of justice has to be defined independently of the particular practices of any society.

But Aristotle too supplies his own reasons of principle, as we saw. We cannot just legislate the goods people are actually seeking and finding as goods out of court. What could the highest good be if it did this? On what basis could we establish a highest good that had this property? A theory of justice must begin with the kinds of goods and the kinds of common practices organized around these goods that people actually have in a given society. Ethical theory has to comprehend given practice; it cannot just abstract from it.

Now, the ethical theories arising from modern freedom have naturally been "Platonic," in the sense of revisionist. The very idea of modern freedom has entailed at least the capacity to stand aside from and put in question all our collective practices and the institutions that carry them on. In the most spectacular case, this emerges in the seventeenth-century doctrine of the social contract. And the drive for universality and the critical stance simply reflects this conception of the task of ethics. But there has been an additional motive for modern revisionism, which is connected with another major strand of modern thought and sensibility different from the one I have been insisting on up to now. Besides this disengaged notion of freedom, there has also been what I might call the promotion of ordinary life.

"Ordinary life" is a term of art that I want to use for the life of production and reproduction, or economic and family life. In Aristotle's famous expression "life and the good life," it is what is covered by the first term. For Aristotle, as his dyad implies, this first term is simply of infrastructural significance. It is a goal of association, because one needs it in order to carry on the good life. The latter is defined in terms of distinct, higher activities. In the tradition, the main candidates were the contemplation of truth and the citizen life. Aristotle integrated both into his ethical view.

A striking feature of modern culture has been a reversal of this hierarchy. One can argue that it started with the Reformers, who had a hierarchy of spiritual vocations to reverse. In denying that any specially dedicated Christians, living a life of poverty, chastity, and obedience, could mediate the salvation of others, they stressed that the fullest possible life of the Christian was one led in marriage and the ordinary calling. The important issue was how one lived—whether in a worshipful spirit, to the glory of God, or not.

This idea had important revolutionary implications in the social and political sense as well, as was evident in the Puritan revolt and the culture of later Puritan societies. But it also becomes secularized. One sees it as an underlying idea of the Baconian revolution, and then it becomes an *idée force* of the Enlightenment. The life of production and reproduction is the center of human concern. The highest life does not reside in some supposedly higher activity, but rather in living ordinary life (in my sense) rationally, that is, under rational control. This in turn spawned radical variants, of which Marx's theory is perhaps the most celebrated and influential. It also helped bring about the cultural revolution that dethroned the ethic of honor and glory in favor of the "bourgeois" ethic of production and rationality.

All sorts of things made the affinity a natural one between the ideal of disengaged reason and the promotion of ordinary life—not least their common hostility for Aristotle and for all the hierarchical conceptions of cosmic order, their common origins in Occamist Christianity, and their convergence on the supreme importance of instrumental reason. Whatever the reasons, this was one of the most important and fateful marriages of our civilization. What I might call Enlightenment humanism and its various heirs, the doctrines of modern naturalism, are the fruits of this synthesis. It goes without saying that the resulting doctrine is firmly in the revisionist camp.

The rejection of the honor ethic is a good example for our discussion, because it involves not only a repudiation of the aristocratic way of life, with its dueling and *disputes de préséance*, but also a rejection of the citizen life and the ethic of civic humanism. The modern bourgeois ethic stands in a long tradition of such repudiations. Plato himself can be considered the first. The competitive struggle for office and honor and fame within the framework of common commitment to the *patria*, through whose laws all citizens enjoy the status of participants or "equals," as they were often called, is surely a paradigm of a practice with internal goods, in MacIntyre's sense. Where certain other aims sought in politics, like protection of life and property, or prosperity, might properly be thought of as external goods, the goods of citizen dignity and fame for one's great deeds are essentially tied to this form of common activity. Citizen dignity attaches to one as a participant in self-rule; the fame relevant here is for the deeds appropriate to one who comes to be asked to rule over equals—leadership in war and counsel.

Plato condemns this competitive striving as *polupragmonein.* It is a kind of disorder, the nonrecognition of limits, and it generates all further disorders. It turns out to be the direct opposite of justice. Here is the classic case of a revisionist doctrine. The internal goods, the citizen dignity and fame, are savagely rein-terpreted as a grasping after mere appearances, simulacra. The fact that fame is essentially involved with recognition, with how one stands in the eyes of others and posterity, facilitates this transvaluation, a connection beautifully reflected in the etymological connections encapsulated in the term *doxa,* meaning both "opinion" and "glory" and derived from the verb "to appear," *dokein.*

Against this, as we saw, Aristotle not only integrates citizen activity into the good life but even makes politics, which he defines in terms of this activity, an essential feature of the human animal. Man is *zōon politikon.* The Stoics return us to the Platonic position, as does Christian Platonism in its Augustinian form. The modern bourgeois rejection of the honor ethic is heir to all this, and it too makes a great deal of the childish attachment to the merely apparent that the honor ethic supposedly involves. Hobbes speaks sneeringly of "vain-glory." Hobbes, of course, is contesting what was merely an aspiration to remake society. But since then, modern Western societies have tried to recreate something like citizen politics. Low as the level of success may have been (and I would not put it as low as MacIntyre does), the repudiation of this ethic today still amounts to a rejection of the internal good of actual social practices. These internal goods are set at naught in the name of external goods like peace, security, and prosperity, which the aspiration to competi-tive, participatory politics allegedly jeopardizes.

I come to the most difficult issue last. I do not propose to decide this one by fiat in favor of Aristotle; there is no one-sided resolution of this conflict. We all must recognize allegiance both to the Platonic and to the Aristotelian sides of this dispute, both to the revisionist and the comprehensive approach. The important issue, about which I shall have all too little to say, is how we reconcile them.

But I also come to this issue last because it must first be distinguished from the other two. They are understandably confused. Because of the historic confrontation of Aristotelianism with the ideal of disengaged freedom, made all the more un-bridgeable when this fuses with the promotion of ordinary life, it is all too easy to believe that the option for revisionism is the same as the option for a procedural ethic, that going for explicit rules against phronēsis is the same as repudiating the status quo, and the like. A historical constellation born out of a certain set of motives is taken for a logical unity. I hope I have shown that this is not so. Certainly Plato shows how one can be a revisionist within a substantive ethic. And what I said above about the spiritual impact of the New Testament was meant to illustrate the obvious fact that revisionism in no way entails the repudiation of phronêsis.

But the confusion still bedevils the debate. Two commonly held positions testify to this. For some, the supposedly intrinsic connection between revisionism and a procedural ethic makes them opt for the latter in the name of the former. I think Habermas exemplifies this. He fears that an ethic of the good must inevitably forfeit universality, and hence a critical standpoint toward any and all cultural forms. From the opposite side, this same alleged connection may cause others to reject revisionism in the name of phronēsis or in the face of the obvious inadequacies of abstract, procedural rationality. Perhaps Oakeshott exemplifies this.[4]

The same confusion has led many people to misunderstand MacIntyre. His talk of the internal good of practices and his criticism of the Enlightenment project lead some to assume that he must be in favor of whatever is, or at least that he gives himself no ground for critique of existing practices. But he clearly says the opposite. First, his concept of a tradition is actually close to the reality, and not the caricature that is bandied about in rationalist thought. Traditions, including those of practices with their internal goods, are the site of ongoing debates, internal revisions, critical turns, and so on. Second, he says very clearly that "any account of the virtues in terms of practices could only be a partial and first account" (p. 187); what we need to complement it is some notion of the good of a whole life. And there follows his profound discussion about the narrative unity of a human life. MacIntyre here gives his own sense to Aristotle's notion of an "architectonic" good, the good that my life as a whole must exhibit and that determines the place and proportions of all partial goods in the totality. This is the end whose name is *eudaimonia,* which Aristotle defines for us.

Here again, I would like to depart somewhat from MacIntyre's way of putting the issue, although I do not think I am far from him in substance. In fact, our moral understanding moves as it were between two poles. On one hand, we do become familiar with certain goods by being brought up in certain practices, to which they are internal, or to which the practices contribute (on the model of Aristotelian virtues) both as cause and proper part. An example of the latter would be the practices of prayer in relation to the good of sanctity. On the other hand, some goods transcend all our practices, such that we are capable of transforming or even repudiating some practices in the name of these goods. So the prophets of Israel could radically downgrade some of the hitherto accepted ritual and tell the people in God's name that their holocausts were an abomination, that they should rather come with a pure heart before God. Examples of other "transcendent" goods, besides sanctity and the fear of God, are Plato's ideal of the ordered hegemony of reason, the Stoic notion of the cosmopolis of which all human beings and gods are citizens, and the modern idea of disengaged freedom. (I must stress that in using the term *transcendent* here, I do not mean to imply that these goods transcend the things of this world—only some of those mentioned above do so—but rather that they transcend our practices in the sense discussed.)

How do we think about or increase our understanding of such goods? Modern philosophy, indeed modern culture, has got into a tremendous muddle about this. It is my claim that our thought inevitably relates in part to these transcendent goods, as well as to the internal goods of practices. In a way, this was implicit in my reconstruction of the motivation for procedural ethics above. I saw them as based on a notion of the good. This comes out clearest in the case of Kant.

But modern philosophy has generated a shyness, to the point of inarticulateness, about these goods. In part, the reasons are already familiar to us: the reluctance implicit in the ideal of disengaged freedom to think in terms of goods as the instance of last appeal, and the skepticism implicit in the associated epistemological doctrines about definitions of the human telos. But we can now see something more about the motives of this latter. The kind of thinking favored by the modern understandings of freedom and reason is disengaged. That is, it strives to draw as little as possible on our implicit understanding of the context of practice in which we act, to offer wherever possible explicit criteria of identification, so that discourse is as far as possible comprehensible independent of particular life experiences and cultural settings. The fact that the goal of total abstraction from the context of practice is a chimera should not blind us to the viability of this ideal of striving in this direction or to the dependence on it of crucial achievements of modern culture, most especially natural science and technology.

But this ideal distorts practical reason beyond all recognition. By its very nature practical reason can only function within the context of some implicit grasp of the good, be it that mediated by a practice to which this good is internal or by practices that contribute to it as cause and constituent, or by contact with paradigmatic models, in life or story, or however. The error of modern rationalism is to believe that such thinking must inevitably be a prisoner of the status quo, that our moral understanding can only be revisionist at the cost of being disengaged. This more than anything else has contributed to that pernicious confusion I am trying to fight here, which has made so many believe that a critical ethic has to be procedural and explicit.

And it has also contributed to skepticism, or at least to that shyness and inarticulateness I denounced above. If the only acceptable form of reason is disengaged and as far as possible context-free, then practical reasoning comes to appear impossible. One cannot prove that man is rational life, or rational agency, or the image of God the way one shows the kinetic theory of heat or the inverse square law. The gains of practical reason are all within a certain grasp of the good, and they involve overcoming earlier distortions and fragmentary understanding. The certainty we gain is not that some conclusion is ultimately valid but that it represents a gain over what we held before. The propositions of which we can be confident are comparative. What we are confident of is that our present formulations articulate better and more fully what we were never entirely without some sense of. Moral knowledge, unlike that gained in natural science, does not deal with the wholly new. This is what Plato was trying to say with his notion of anamnesis.

But once we take the path of disengaged thought, this becomes quite lost to view. In this sense, MacIntyre seems to me entirely right that the Enlightenment project ultimately contributes to the credibility of Nietzsche. An impossible model of reasoning is proposed, and then when one sees that no rational headway can be made in this way in discerning the good, one falls into skepticism and despair. Or at least one has an extra motive for opting for a procedural ethic, on the (false) belief that one thereby can avoid the issue of the good altogether. This of course takes one even further away from any understanding of the viable forms of practical reasoning, and hence it strengthens skepticism and despair, or at least deepens the self-willed inarticulateness about good.

The irony is that this position is powered originally by a vision of the good, that of disengaged, free, rational agency, one of the most important, formative transcendent goods of our civilization.

When one understands practical reason aright, one can see that the goods about which one reasons in a context-related way include transcendent ones and that this reasoning does not by any means have to be comprehensive only, but can be highly revisionist. True, in this latter case, the context will largely be provided not by established practices but by models or stories embodying a higher perfection (like those of the death of Socrates, or the Gospels). But it will be context-related nonetheless, that is, not trying to frame formulas that minimally rely on context but rather trying to articulate better what this context implies.

I should now be in a position to answer the question concerning my third big issue, between Aristotle and Plato, comprehenders and revisionists. But, in fact, I am going to chicken out, in part for the good reason that it should now be evident that no global one-sided answer to this question can be accepted. The idea that it could comes from the confusion of this issue with the other two. On one side, the errors of abstract rationalism are used to cast discredit on all revisionism; on the other, the demands of critical thought are deemed incompatible with allegiance to any internal goods. Freed from this illusion, we see that we are faced with transcendent goods that command our awed consent, with practices whose internal goals seem valuable, and with a distressing amount of prima facie conflict between the two. There is no a priori way to resolve this; we have to work it out case by case.

I want now to connect up the various (possibly too divergent) threads of the discussion. I have examined some motives of those influential and convincing modern metaethical theories that are centered around the conception of a procedural ethics. In a less sharp and less critical form, they shape the foundations of historically influential theories, such as utilitarianism and the theoretical approaches stemming from Kant, which are so often encountered in Anglo-American debates. In a different form, answering to the requirements of a critical theory of society, they shape, no less, the foundations of Apel's and Habermas's discourse ethics.

I have two propositions to offer. First, the claims in regard to the particular form of an ethical theory possess no validity independent of our moral conception—as was asserted, for example, in the context of the fact/value dichotomy, and as Habermas too apparently claims in connection with Weber's differentiation between questions of factual truth and questions of normative rightness. On the contrary, the temptation to adopt this metaethical point of view derives from the antecedent conviction that theories with universalistic claims are justifiable and defensible. The position that I want to emphasize here claims a priority of substantive moral conceptions over metaethical problems of the form of the theory. And this, insofar as it proves correct, would suggest, conversely, that a procedural ethics in the strong sense of the word is a delusion because it itself rests upon a substantive vision of the good.

My second proposition concerns the differentiation of varying constellations of metaethical problems, whose confusion, of which I am convinced, has abetted the attractiveness of procedural ethics and has allowed it the possibility of an apparent grounding of ultimate ends. In particular, the idea that only a procedural ethics can sustain critical claims has misled people into a widespread belief in a false dichotomy; some feel themselves bound to a procedural ethics in order to stand by their critical claims with a peaceful conscience, while others have exploited the nonplausibility of all procedural and calculative moralities in order to call into question any possibility of a critical challenge to the status quo. I am convinced that a thorough examination of these matters shows there is no reason for us to surrender ourselves to the restrictive limits of this alternative.

What follows for the various theories of procedural ethics and in particular for discourse ethics, if my thesis proves itself correct? Can one then regard them as refuted? Not in the least. I come back to what I accomplished in the first section. The issue for me there was to show that the metaethical construction of a strict procedural ethics oriented to formal principles without antecedent commitment to a concept of the good is untenable. The idea of good is, in principle, a basic presupposition. But this means that much of what belongs precisely to the presuppositions of procedural ethics remains intact and increasingly steps more clearly into the light when it is stripped of its distorted metaethical form. As soon as we consider more closely discourse ethics understood as resting upon the concept of good, then in my view it proves itself as especially fruitful and convincing.

This approach may possibly appear somewhat constrained, yet I am convinced that it at least is meaningful in relation to the following significant insights of our moral traditions: (1) the insistence, at bottom Stoic and Christian, put into focus by Kant, that all human beings *qua humanum* be respected; (2) the modern interpretation of this respect for all men and women, which raises the demand for democratic, participatory forms of self-management to all levels of society; and (3) the idea that rational subjects regulate their public affairs according to the perspective of justice. It is precisely in this context that the considerations summed up under the title of "universal pragmatics" have something new to contribute to the understanding of the demands of reason. Moreover, (4) discourse ethics links up with Humboldt's important idea of society, in which members reciprocally complement and enrich themselves, a capacity which is peculiar to man as a linguistic being. At this point, however, I have probably given away my subjective inclinations and, by projecting ahead, exceeded the limits of interpretation.

A discourse ethics reformulated according to the substantive perspective will have disposed of the claim to be seeking to uphold the norms implicitly contained in points 1–4 independently of a theory of the good. This, in my view, constitutes a gain, for I hold this claim to be illusory. On the other hand, it is evident to me that one of the strongest motivations behind this claim—this, I have only begun to go into—is an epistemological one. It appears decidedly problematical, not to say impossible, to ground argumentatively what the good is. This possibility appears as simply the price of relapsing into convictions and theoretical models that have become obsolete, such as Aristotle's "metaphysical biology."

This approach is, in the final analysis, misguided. I must above all concede that the burden of proof for my proposal of a rehabilitation of practical argumentation lies in relation to the good, and that goes as well as for what I have called transcendent goods. I hope I am in a position to realize this claim; for the moment, I reckon myself fortunate to be able to defer this until another occasion.

Notes

1
See Elizabeth Anscombe, "Modern Moral Philosophy," *Philosophy* 33 (1958). All page references in the text are to Alasdair MacIntyre, *After Virtue* (Notre Dame: University of Notre Dame Press, 1981).

2
I have argued against the possibility of a procedural ethic in the particular case of Jürgen Habermas's philosophy, which I think is the most interesting and rich such theory ever produced, in my "Sprache und Gesellschaft," in A. Honneth and H. Joas, eds., *Kommunikatives Handeln: Beiträge zu Jürgen Habermas' Theorie des kommunikativen Handelns* (Frankfurt, 1986).

3
I'm not sure the *Republic* should be taken seriously as a blueprint; indeed, I think it

should not. And this raises questions about how revolutionary Plato really was. But I want to ignore them here. My concern is not the historical Plato, but one way his theory has been taken, which has established one of the master types I want to debate in this section.

4
Michael Oakeshott, *Rationalism in Politics* (London: Methuen, 1962).

Chapter 16

On the Possibility of a
Philosophical Ethics

Hans-Georg Gadamer

Translated by Michael Kelly

It is not self-evident that "philosophical" ethics, a philosophy of morals, is anything other than a "practical" ethics, than the establishment of a table of values consulted by the actor and the knowledge connecting him to that table of values. In the ancient tradition, by contrast, it was evident that practical philosophy, which since Aristotle has been known as "ethics," was itself "practical" knowledge. Aristotle expressed what already lay at the foundation of the Socratic-Platonic doctrine of the knowledge of virtue, namely, that we want not only to know what virtue is but to know it in order to become good. For Aristotle the transition to praxis, which lies in the concept of knowledge, is indeed what is unique about ethical matters, but it also belongs to the ancient concept of knowledge in general: science is not an anonymous totality of truths but a human comportment (*hexis tou aletheuein:* the habit of expressing the truth). Moreover, "theory" does not stand in opposition to praxis but is itself the highest praxis, the highest human way of being. That is true of the highest knowledge—knowledge of the first principle, of philosophy—even though there is, as Aristotle recognized, only a small distance between the knowledge of science (*epistēmē, technē*) and the knowledge gained by experience, which is why the experienced practitioner is often considered the "learned" expert. But this is all the more true in the ethical domain, where such a gap between theory and practice cannot even exist, since there it is not a matter of applying an expertise.

By contrast, the modern concept of rational "theory" is fundamentally determined by reference to its practical application, and that means in opposition to its practical application. The opposition (in its many forms) between the academy and

This essay originally appeared in *Sein und Ethos*, edited by P. Engelhardt, vol. 1 of *Walberberger Studien* (Mainz: Matthias-Grunewald Verlag, 1963), pp. 11–24; reprinted in *Kleine Schriften I: Philosophie. Hermeneutik* (Tübingen: J.C.B. Mohr [Paul Siebeck], 1967), pp. 179–91. This translation follows the revised version in *Gesammelte Werke*, vol. 4, *Neuere Philosophie II: Probleme. Gestalten* (Tübingen: J.C.B. Mohr [Paul Siebeck], 1987), pp. 175–88.

life has always existed. But only with the beginning of modernity did it become fully conscious, particularly in the age of humanism when the Hellenistic ideal of science was revived and linked with the critique of School philosophy, of the doctrines of the academy. Nicholas of Cusa could put his most profound teachings in the mouth of the layman (of an *idiota*) who sees more deeply than the "orator" and "philosopher" with whom he is speaking. With the emergence of modern science, this opposition becomes more permanent, and at the same time the concept of theory gains a new profile. Theory now means the explanation of the many-sidedness of appearances that makes possible their practical mastery. Understood as an instrument, it ceases to be a particular human comportment and thereby also ceases to claim more than relative truth.

As has become quite obvious to us all, the application of such a concept of theory to moral phenomena leads to a confusion that is difficult to resolve. It seems unavoidable that this concept is connected with a certain optimism about progress, since in the course of scientific research, ever new, more adequate theoretical knowledge is achieved. Applied to the moral world, however, that would lead to an absurd belief in moral progress. Here Rousseau's critique of the Enlightenment registered a loud and clear veto. Kant himself acknowledged, "Rousseau set me straight." The *Groundwork of the Metaphysics of Morals* leaves no doubt that moral philosophy can never displace "common moral rational knowledge," that is, the consciousness of duty, of what the simple heart and upright sense say is right. Ever since Kant, moral philosophical reflection may not appear as a mere theory. Rather, Kant's moral renunciation of the Enlightenment's pride in the understanding was so powerful that he insisted on the necessity of the transition to moral philosophy, and, on this basis, moral philosophy could no longer completely deny the demand to be of moral relevance. Max Scheler, the founder of material-value ethics, was taken to task one day by one of his students, because while he so clearly portrayed the order of values and their normative power, he did not live up to them in his own life. His answer to the student—"Does the signpost go in the direction in which it points?"— is obviously unsatisfactory. Nicolai Hartmann, who systematically built on Scheler's ethical conception, could obviously not refuse to grant moral significance to value philosophy. It has a maieutic function for moral value consciousness, that is, it promotes an ever-richer development by revealing forgotten and misunderstood values. Nothing else remains of the old expectation that demanded of the philosopher that, within the moral perplexity and entanglement of public consciousness, he not just follow his theoretical passion but ground ethics anew, that is, build a new binding table of values. Of course, it could be that Heidegger was right, when, in response to the question "when will you write an ethics?," he begins his *Letter on Humanism* with the sentence: "We are still far from pondering the essence of action decisively enough."

Indeed, Kierkegaard's critique of Hegel and of the Christianity of the Church first made known an irresolvable difficulty that seems to lie in the idea of moral philosophy itself. Kierkegaard demonstrated that all "distant knowledge" of the fundamental moral and religious situation of humans is not satisfying. Just as it is the meaning of Christian teaching to be experienced and perceived "at the same time," so the ethical choice is not a matter of theoretical knowledge but rather a matter of the clarity, sharpness, and affliction of conscience. All distant knowledge threatens to disguise or weaken the demand lying in the ethical condition of choice. It is well known that in our century the theological and philosophical critique of neo-Kantian idealism, which was carried out under the influence of Kierkegaard, caused the questionableness of ethics to be fundamentally acknowledged. Insofar as ethics is understood as a knowledge of the universal, it is involved in the moral questionableness that is connected with the concept of the universal law. Consider Paul's Epistle to the Romans. The claim that sin entered through the law was not understood as saying that the prohibited as such is tempting and, as a result, sin increases. Rather, it meant that adherence to the law leads to a peculiar sin that is not just an occasional transgression of the law—in other words, it leads to that supreme sin in which obedience to the law obstructs the commandment to love. It is not the priest and Levite but the Good Samaritan who hears and obeys the commandment to love which arises from the situation. From a philosophical point of view, the concept of the situation brought into sharp focus the very questionable character of the idea of ethics, a challenge set out, for example, by Eberhard Grisebach, the philosophical friend of Gogarten.[1]

Indeed, in the face of such a state of affairs, philosophical ethics seems to be in an irresolvable dilemma. The universality of reflection, within which philosophical ethics necessarily moves, involves it in the questionableness of all law-based ethics. How is it supposed to do justice to the concreteness with which conscience, the sense of fairness, and the forgivingness of love respond to a situation?

I believe that only two ways can possibly lead out of this dilemma within philosophical ethics. One is the way of ethical formalism stemming from Kant; the other is the way of Aristotle. Each may not be adequate by itself, but both together might contribute to the possibility of an ethics.

Kant sought that kind of obligation which, through its unconditioned universality alone, satisfies the concept of the ethical. He saw the mode of ethical obligation, on which alone ethics can be founded, in the unconditionality of duty that, in opposition to interest and inclination, holds to what is commanded. His categorical imperative is to be understood as the principle of everything moral, just because it does nothing other than represent the form of obligation of the ought, that is, the unconditionality of the moral law. If there is a morally good will, then it must satisfy this form. That there can be such an unconditional good will and that therefore the categorical imperative has the power actually to determine our will is, of course, not demonstrated by this knowledge of the general "form" of the moral. It is Kant the metaphysician who first provides an answer, one prepared by the *Critique of Pure Reason:* every factual determination of the will, as belonging to the domain of appearances, is indeed subject to the fundamental laws of experience, under which an unconditioned good action can never be found with certainty. But the self-limitation of pure reason taught that, besides the order of appearances in which there is only the law of cause and effect, another intelligible order exists to which we belong not as sensible beings but as rational beings and within which the standpoint of freedom, of self-legislation through reason, can properly be thought. That we "ought to" is an unconditioned certainty of practical reason that theoretical reason does not contradict. Freedom is not impossible theoretically, and it is practically necessary.

On this basis, an answer emerges for Kant to the question of why moral philosophical reason is necessary, without moral philosophy thereby presuming too much in relation to the upright simplicity of the ordinary consciousness of duty. Kant says, "Innocence is indeed a glorious thing; but, unfortunately, it does not keep very well and is easily led astray."[2] The innocence of the simple heart, which knows its duty unwaveringly, consists not so much in the fact that it is not led astray by the power of inclination; rather, the innocence of the heart shows itself more in the fact that, even in departing from the way of the law, which only a holy will can fully attain, it recognizes without fail its unlawfulness. It does not resist merely the overpowering desires, but the wavering of reason itself. Practical reason develops subject to the effects of a specific dialectic through which it knows how to weaken the obligatory power of commands. It makes use of what I would like to call the "dialectic of exception making," that is, it does not contest the value of the moral law but seeks to insist upon the exceptional character of the situation in which the actor finds himself, in the sense that, under the given circumstances and despite the general validity of the law, an exception would be justified. Moral philosophic reflection comes to the aid of ethical reason threatened by such seductions. Ethical reason requires that help all the more since, in its "common" form, moral philosophic reflection itself indirectly abets this seduction. By thinking of "without exception" as the essence of moral obligation—and that is the meaning of the categorical imperative—Kant's *Groundwork* establishes the purity of rational moral decisions.

The meaning of Kantian formalism, therefore, consists in securing the purity of this rational moral decision, in naive as well as in philosophical consciousness, against all tarnishing by the viewpoints of inclination and interest. To this extent, Kantian rigorism—according to which a will is morally valuable only if it acts purely out of duty and against all inclination—has a clear methodological meaning. What we encounter here is, to speak with Hegel, the form of a law-testing reason.[3]

Yet the question still arises: Considering the empirical dependence of human reason and its ingrained "tendency to evil," how does such a test of the law ever come about? As Gerhard Krüger emphasized before anyone else, Kant's moral philosophical reflection already presupposes a recognition of the moral law.[4] The formulas—for example, those of the law of nature or of the end in itself—that are given in the faculty of judgment as types are so unreal that they do not have any persuasive power in themselves. We are reminded of the example of the person considering suicide, of whom Kant says: if he is still sufficiently in possession of reason that he can test his decision to commit suicide according to the model of such a formula, then he will recognize the untenability of his decision. That is obviously a mere construction. The person with thoughts of suicide does not have that much reason. Even if the moral prohibition against suicide could thereby be understood, it is still the case that the willingness to reflect, and even more the motivation to test conscience, would also have to be presupposed. In what is it supposed to lie? Kant's formula seems to be only of methodical relevance for reflection insofar as it instructs us to eliminate all obfuscation stemming from "inclination."

But obviously Kant's rigorism has a moral meaning other than that of the methodical contrast between duty and inclination. What Kant has in mind are extreme cases in which a person reflects on his *pure duty* as against all inclination, making it possible for him to become aware of the power of his moral reason and thereby to establish a firm foundation for his character. He is made conscious of the fundamental moral principles that guide his life. The exceptional situation in which he passed the test has shaped him (compare the "Methodology of Pure Practical Reason" in the *Critique of Practical Reason*).

On the other hand, it must still be asked: What defines the exceptional situation through which such a contrast of duty and inclination is raised to the sharpness of a decision? One cannot arbitrarily take just any situation and elevate it to the status of a genuine case of ethical decision making or to an instance of the testing of one's conscience. This is Hegel's well-known critique of the nonmorality of the ought—because ought already presupposes the contradiction of the will and, to that extent, also presupposes the bad will. Is Hegel not correct when he sees the essence of ethical life in customs instead of in the self-compulsion of an ethics of imperatives, that is, when he sees the essence of ethics in the substance of the moral order that is embodied in the great objectifications of family, civil society, and the state? The truth of moral consciousness does not reside merely in the scrupulousness with which it constantly becomes conscious, in a tormented way, of the impurity of its drives and inclinations. Certainly there are conflict situations in which such an ethical self-testing takes place. But conscience is not an enduring habitus; it is rather something that strikes one, that awakens one.[5] And by what means? Is there not something like an "elastic" conscience? One cannot deny that the watchfulness of conscience depends on the substance of ethical orders in which one is already embedded. The autonomy of moral reason certainly has the character of intelligible self-determination. But that does not exclude the empirical conditionedness of all human actions and decisions. One can at least not disregard this conditionedness in judging the other, a judgment that also belongs to the moral sphere. What can be demanded from the other (morally, not only legally) is not the same as what one may demand of oneself. The recognition of human conditionedness (in forbearing judgment) is fully compatible with the sublime unconditionality of the moral law. It seems to me characteristic of Kant's reflection that he is not interested in the distinction between judgments of conscience about oneself and ethical judgments about others. For this reason, Kant's response to our question about the moral meaning of moral philosophy is, in the end, unsatisfactory. Indeed, one may concede to him that no human is spared situations of ethical conflict and that, to that extent, the temptation to make an exception for oneself is a general human situation. But from that would it not follow that the transition to a metaphysics of morals is necessary for each and every human? Kant, in fact, draws this conclusion. His foundation of morality seeks only to raise the common metaphysics of everyman to greater clarity and thereby to secure for it a greater moral steadfastness. But is such an inference tenable? Does Kant not thereby transgress once again Rousseau's insight?

Thus, another path of inquiry seems to be called for: a moral philosophical reflection that is oriented not to the exceptional case of conflict but rather to the normal case of the observance of customs. Material-value ethics, developed in our century by Max Scheler and Nicolai Hartmann, objects to the orientation toward the form of reflection of moral consciousness and pure "ought" ethics. It consciously opposed Kantian formalism. If Scheler, in an extravagant and unjustified fashion, completely misunderstood the rational moral character of the Kantian formalism of duty, his ethics nonetheless rendered the undeniably positive service of making the substantive content of ethical life—and not merely the conflict between "I ought" and "I will"—into the object of moral philosophical analysis. The concept of value, which is raised here to a systematic meaning, breaks out of the restricted focus upon the concept of duty, that is, upon the mere goal of striving and the norms of the ought. There is also ethical value in what cannot be an object of striving and cannot be commanded. For example, there is no duty to love. Kant's fatal reinterpretation of the commandment of Christian love as a duty to do practical good deeds is clear in this regard. Is not love, seen from a moral perspective, something higher than a good deed in conformity with duty? In setting out the phenomenological theory of the immediate evidence of the essence of lawfulness and of the a priori in general,

Scheler grounded an a priori value system on the immediacy of the a priori consciousness of value. This not only encompasses the particular goal of ethical will but extends down to the vital sphere and the sphere of utilitarian values and reaches up to the sphere of the holy. Such an ethics truly grasps, therefore, the substantive content of ethical life and not only the reflexive phenomenon of law-testing reason.

Nevertheless, even when such a value ethics explicitly incorporates the concept of ethos and the change of forms of ethos into its reflection, it cannot elude the immanent consequence of its methodic claim to behold a priori value orders. This emerges clearly with Nicolai Hartmann, who does not consider the a priori hierarchy of values as a system closed in itself with its highpoint in the value of the holy, but as an open region of values, an infinite object of human experience, and, at the same time, an infinite domain of research. The progress of research uncovers ever-finer value structures and relations and rectifies the dominant value blindness. In the last analysis, however, that implies that value ethics research brings an advancement and refinement of ethical value consciousness itself. Moral philosophy therefore cannot teach with authority, that is, it cannot establish new values. But it can develop the consciousness of value in such a way that it discovers these values in itself. Moral philosophy has, as Hartmann says, a maieutic function.

Such a theory, however, misses the point that was correctly recognized by Scheler: every morality is a concrete ethical form. Unavoidably, the idea of an infinite refinement of value consciousness, if it represents the principal moral philosophical idea of material-value ethics, must imply and ground its own ethos as one set pitted against other ethical forms. One thinks, for example, of Hartmann's especial emphasis on the importance of ethical fullness, in the sense of a synthesizing of opposing ethical ideals, which is negated by Nietzsche's resolve to "pass by" what is other.[6] Value ethics itself is, necessarily and insurmountably, constrained to determine an ethos that contradicts the methodological claim of this a priori value research. No human—that is, no finite, historically valid—moral system can fulfill this methodological claim. The basic idea of an a priori value system is essentially related to that of an external subject. Although, in contrast to Kantian formalism, material-value ethics grasps the substantive content of ethical life, it does not provide the solution we are seeking. The immediacy of value consciousness and the philosophy of morality are torn asunder.

In place of that approach, let us happily turn to Aristotle, for whom there is no value concept but rather "virtues" and "goods," and who became the founder of philosophical ethics by correcting the one-sidedness of the Socratic-Platonic "intellectualism" without abandoning its essential insights.[7] The concept of ethos, as he established it, expresses precisely the fact that "virtue" does not consist only in knowledge; instead, the possibility of knowledge depends on how one lives. The being of each person is antecedently shaped by education and ways of life. Perhaps

Aristotle's view is focused more on the conditionedness of our ethical being, on the dependency of an individual decision on its present, practical, and social determinations, and less on the unconditionedness that perfects the ethical phenomenon. Kant successfully worked out precisely this unconditionedness in its purity, and it finds its great ancient counterpart in Plato's model of the state set within the abiding question of "justice in itself." But Aristotle succeeded in clarifying the essence of ethical knowledge so that in the concept of "the choice of what is better" he includes both the subjectivity of ethical consciousness, which judges cases of conflict, and the enduring substantiality of law and ethos, which determine its ethical knowledge and present choices. His analysis of *phronēsis* recognizes in ethical knowledge a mode of ethical being itself that is accordingly not detached from the concrete totality that he named ethos. Ethical knowledge recognizes what is appropriate, that which a situation requires, and it recognizes this on the basis of a consideration that relates the concrete situation to that which one holds, in general, to be right and fitting. It therefore has the logical structure of a conclusion, a premise of which is knowledge about what is right expressed in the concepts of ethical virtues. At the same time, however, it is not a matter of a mere subsumption, an act of judgment, for it depends on the human being whether he unwaveringly carries out such reflection. This reflection—that is, the orientation to fundamental principles of ethical deliberation—gets lost in the overflowing of passions. These principles can be eclipsed at any moment (*euthus ou phainetai he archē,* the principle appears incorrectly).[8] Aristotle illustrates this with the example of intoxication: the unaccountability of a drunk is not an ethical unaccountability, for it is within his power to be moderate in drinking.

Thus, the crucial point of Aristotle's philosophical ethics lies in the mediation between logos and ethos, between the subjectivity of knowledge and the substantiality of being. Ethical knowledge does not realize itself in general concepts of courage, justice, and the like but rather in the concrete application that determines what is to be done here and now in light of such knowledge. It is correct to point out that Aristotle's final statement about what is correct consists in the indeterminate formula of "what belongs to it" (*hos dei,* as required). The proper content of Aristotelian ethics is located not in the great leading concepts of a heroic ethical ideal and its "table of values" but rather in the inconspicuousness and unerringness of concrete ethical consciousness (*hos ho logos ho orthos legei,* according to reason, to right reason) that finds its expression in insignificant and all-encompassing concepts, such as what "is proper," what "is decent," what is "good and right." It is a misunderstanding to transform Aristotle's emphasis on the formula of universal concretization into a pseudo-objectivity and see inscribed therein the special "value of the situation" (Hartmann). It is precisely the sense of the doctrine of the "mean," as Aristotle developed it, that every conceptual determination of traditional concepts of virtue possesses only a schematic-typical validity that is created out of "the things spoken" (*legomena*). But then philosophical ethics is in the same situation in which everyone finds himself: that which is considered correct, which we affirm or object to in a judgment about ourselves or others, follows our general representation of what is good and correct. It first receives its own determinancy in the concrete reality of the case, which is not an instance of the application of a general rule but which, on the contrary, concerns the particular in relation to which the typical forms of virtues and the structure of the "mean" that Aristotle analyzes represent only a vague schema. Thus, the virtue through which we achieve this mean and its concretization, and which first shows the appropriate to be the practically good (*prakton agathon*), namely, phronēsis, is in no way a characteristic peculiar to those who philosophize. It seems more often the reverse: that it is the one who thinks about the good and the right in general, referring to practical logos just as everyone else does, who has yet to translate his representations of what is good and right into action. Aristotle recognized explicitly that it was the defect of the people (the *polloi*, the Many) to recur to theorizing (*epi ton logon katapheugontes*) and, instead of doing what is right, to philosophize about it.[9]

It is thus not totally certain, as it often seems to be in Aristotle, that phronēsis has to do only with the right means to pregiven ends. Through the concreteness of ethical reflection, phronēsis first determines the "goal" itself in its concreteness, namely, as the "appropriate" (as the practically good, *prakton agathon*).

Certainly Kant is right when he sees in the ideal of happiness more of an ideal of the faculty of imagination than of reason, and to this extent it is correct that happiness cannot provide a specific content of the determination of our will which would be obligatory in general and which could be claimed as moral law by our reason. One must ask, however, whether it is not the case that the autonomy of practical reason, which guarantees for us the unconditionality of our duty against the urging of our inclinations, represents merely a limiting condition of our *Willkür* and thus does not determine the whole of our ethical being, which, governed by the self-evidence of what is right, behaves practically in each case by choosing what is appropriate. (What is meant by *hexis* is not a possibility of this or that, as with capability and knowledge, but rather a naturelike state of being, a "thus and not otherwise.")[10]

The appropriate is, of course, not only what is right but also what is useful, purposeful, and thus "correct" (proper). The penetration of both senses of "correctness" into the practical behavior of human beings is obvious, and, according to Aristotle, it constitutes the human good. Certainly one does not act in an ethically correct way by having one's actions satisfy a purpose, as does the artisan who knows his craft (*technē*). Ethical action is not correct by virtue of the fact that what is thereby brought about is correct; rather, its correctness lies above all in ourselves, in how we act—precisely as the man who "gets it right" acts (the *spoudaios aner,* the morally serious person). But on the other hand, it is also the case that ethical practice, which depends so much more on our being than on our explicit consciousness (*eidos*), perpetually produces us as we are (and not as we know ourselves). In this respect, however, the whole of our being depends on abilities, possibilities, and circumstances that are not simply at our disposal, and it grasps the *eupraxia* (acting well) at which our actions aim and the *eudaimonia* at which we aim and after which we strive, and indeed that we ourselves are. Our action stands in the horizon of the polis and thereby extends our choice of what is appropriate into the whole of our external, social being.

Ethics shows itself to be a part of politics. For the concretization of ourselves, whose outline is indicated in the forms of virtue and their ordering in the highest and most desirable forms of life, reaches far into the common life which the Greeks called the polis, for the proper form of which we are jointly responsible. This makes it clear for the first time why a central object of Aristotelian practical thought is friendship, not as "loving friendship" but rather as the mediator between virtues and goods that exist only as *met' aretes* (shared virtues). The full life is unthinkable without the (constantly endangered) possession of friendship.[11]

Thus Aristotle does not emphasize the sublime unconditionedness of ethical decisions that Plato and Kant demand. To be sure, Aristotle too knows that ethical action does not simply pursue in a functional manner goods that are arbitrarily chosen, but can choose something for its own sake just because it is "splendid." Yet such choice always stands in the whole of a manifold limiting and conditioning being, where the point is to see and to master. Even the highest ideal of human existence, pure contemplation, in which the whole structure of Aristotelian, as well as Platonic, ethics culminates, is still related to the active life and its proper mastery, on which the contemplative life itself depends.[12]

This brilliant appreciation for manifold conditionality, which constitutes the speculative depth of Aristotle, is precisely what is fruitful for moral philosophy, for it is here and here alone that an answer emerges to the question that has been troubling us, that is, how a philosophical ethics, a human teaching concerning what is human, is possible without its becoming an inhuman conceit.

Moral-philosophical reflection, which resides in the philosophical pragmatics of ethics, is not a theory that must then lead to a practical application. It is not knowledge of universals, knowledge from a distance, which could only conceal the concrete demands of the situation, as for example in the priest's and the Levite's devotion to the law compared with the warmheartedness of the Good Samaritan. The universal or the typical, which can be expressed only in a philosophical investigation that is given over to the universality of the concept, is essentially not much different from that which guides the completely atheoretical, average normative consciousness in its practical-ethical reflection. Above all, it is not distinguished from it inasmuch as it includes the same task of application to given circumstances which is present in all ethical knowledge, that of individuals as well as statesmen. Not only does ethical knowledge that guides concrete action have, in the very form of phronēsis, an ethical being, an *arete* (it is *hexis*—indeed, a *hexis tou aletheuein*, habit of expressing the truth). In addition, the philosophical pragmatics of ethics has moral relevance, and that is not a hybrid claim of the "academy" that is disavowed by "life" but the necessary consequence of the fact that it stands under circumstances that condition it. This is not something that concerns everyone; it concerns only those who would be guided through education in society and state to such a maturation of their proper being that they would be capable, in the concrete state of perplexity in which they find themselves, of recognizing the relevance of universal dicta and of rendering them practically effective. The recipient of Aristotle's lectures on ethics must be immune to the peril of wanting to theorize simply in order to extricate himself from the demands of the situation. It seems to me that the abiding validity of Aristotle consists in his holding this peril constantly in view. As Kant did with his formalism, Aristotle too expelled all false claims from the notion of a philosophical ethics. It was Kant who debunked the moral-philosophical rationality of the Enlightenment and its blind pride in reason by separating the unconditionedness of practical reason from all conditionedness of human nature and by representing it in its transcendental purity. It was Aristotle, however, who placed the conditionedness of the human life situation in the center and identified the concretization of the universal and its application to the present situation as the principal task of philosophical ethics as well as of ethical conduct. Kant performed a great service by uncovering the fatal impurity of ethical reasoning, that "disgusting mishmash" of moral and practical motives that the "practical worldly wisdom" of the age of the Enlightenment took to be a higher form of morality. We were saved from this delusion by Kant. There is another aspect of the matter, however, that makes it necessary to recognize the conditionedness of all human beings and thus also the conditionedness of their use of reason. It is above all the aspect of education in which this essential human conditionedness becomes manifest. Kant also knew that the limit of its truth becomes evident there as well. Kant penetratingly shows the power that the representations of ethical reason, duty, or justice are able to exercise even on a child's mind, and he shows that it would not be right always to work only with the pedagogical means of reward and punishment because they sharpen and perpetuate egotistical inclinations. Certainly there is some truth in that, but still reward and punishment, praise and reproach, model and emulation, and the foundation of solidarity, sympathy, and love on which their effect rests form the ethos of human beings. This is prior to arguments from reason, and indeed it first makes possible a person's receptiveness to such arguments. That is the core of the Aristotelian doctrine of virtue. Kant does not give this its due. The necessary limitation that underlies our insight into what is ethically right does not necessarily lead to the corrupting mixture of motives that Kant exposed. In particular, ancient eudaimonism—in contrast to the worldly wisdom of the Enlightenment—is to be judged neither as an obscuring of the transcendental purity of the ethical nor as heteronomy. The utopian rigorism of Plato's *Republic* (Book II) demonstrates that, but Aristotle as well did not for one moment fail to recognize that one has the right to act on one's own behalf, and that no consideration of hedonistic, utilitarian, or eudaimonic viewpoints can interfere with the ethical unconditionedness of a genuine decision. Yet precisely the conditionedness of our insight—everywhere where it is not a matter of decision in the prevailing sense of the word, but where it concerns the choice of the better (*prohairesis*)—is not a defect or a limitation. Rather, it has the social-political determination of the individual as its positive content. This determination is, however, more than dependence on the changing conditions of social and historical life. Certainly we are all dependent on the preconceptions of our time and our world, but from this follows neither the legitimacy of moral skepticism nor that of technical manipulation of the formation of opinion through the exercise of political power. The changes that gain a hold in the customs and ways of thinking of a period and that habitually give the menacing impression, especially to the old, of a total disintegration of ethics, take place on an unchanging foundation. Family, society, and state determine the essential constitution of human beings by filling their ethos with changing contents. To be sure, nobody can say what may become of humans and their forms of common life—but that does not mean that everything can be arranged and fixed according to fancies and wants as the powerful wish. A "what is right by nature" does exist.[13] Aristotle finds support for the conditionedness of all ethical knowledge pervading the realm of ethical and political being in the conviction, shared by Plato, that the order of being is powerful enough to set a limit on all human disarray. In the face of all deformity, the idea remains indestructible: "How strong is the *polis* on the ground of its own nature!"[14]

Thus, Aristotle can recognize the conditionedness of all human existence in the context of his doctrine of ethos without denying the conditionedness of this doctrine itself. Only a philosophical ethics that not only knows about its own questionableness but has just this questionableness as its essential content seems to me sufficient to satisfy the unconditionedness of the ethical.

Notes

1
[Ed.: Eberhard Grisebach (1880–1945), German existential philosopher; Friedrich Gogarten (1887–1967), German Lutheran theologian.]

2

Kant, *Groundwork of the Metaphysics of Morals,* Academy ed., 4:404f.

3

G. W. F. Hegel, *Phenomenology of Spirit,* trans. A. V. Miller (Oxford: Clarendon Press, 1977), pp. 256ff.

4

Gerhard Krüger, *Philosophie und Moral in der kantischen Kritik* (Tübingen: J. C. B. Mohr [Paul Siebeck], 1931; 2d ed., 1967).

5

As the editor of the *Walberberger Studien* notes, Thomas Aquinas emphasized that "conscience" means an act, and only in an extended sense does it refer to an underlying habitus; *Summa Theologica,* First Part, Q. 79, Art. 13.

6

[Ed.: See Nicolai Hartmann, *Moral Phenomena,* vol. 1 of *Ethics,* trans. Stanton Coit (London: George Allen & Unwin, 1932), pp. 41–44; Nietzsche, *Thus Spoke Zarathustra,* Third Part: "On Passing By." Cf. the discussion of Nietzsche in Hartmann, *Moral Values,* vol. 2 of *Ethics,* trans. Stanton Coit (London: George Allen & Unwin, 1932), pp. 317–20, 462–63.]

7

A basic source here is my essay "Praktisches Wissen" (1930), which has now been published for the first time in my *Gesammelte Werke,* Band 5: *Griechische Philosophie I* (Tübingen: J. C. B. Mohr [Paul Siebeck], 1985), pp. 230–48.

8

Aristotle, *Nicomachean Ethics,* 1140b17 (Book 6, chap. 5).

9

Aristotle, *Nicomachean Ethics,* 1105b12ff. (Book 2, chap. 4).

10

[Ed.: The allusion here is to Aristotle, *Nicomachean Ethics,* 1129a11–13 (Book 5, chap. 1).]

11

Cf. my essay "Freundschaft und Selbsterkenntnis" in the Festschrift for Uvo Hölscher, *Würzburger Abhandlungen zur Altertumswissenschaft,* NF. 1 (1985), pp. 25–33; reprinted in my *Gesammelte Werke,* Band 7: *Griechische Philosophie III* (Tübingen: J. C. B. Mohr [Paul Siebeck], 1991).

12

See my review of *L'Éthique à Nicomaque,* trans. and commentary by Gauthier and Jolif, *Philosophische Rundschau* 10 (1962): 293ff.; reprinted in my *Gesammelte Werke,* Band 6: *Griechische Philosophie II* (Tübingen: J. C. B. Mohr [Paul Siebeck], 1985), pp. 302–06.

13

Cf. a related discussion in *Truth and Method,* ed. Garrett Barden and John Cumming (New York: Seabury Press, 1975), pp. 284ff., 471f.

14

Plato, *Statesman,* 302a.

Contributors

Lewis White Beck is professor of philosophy at the University of Rochester. His publications include *A Commentary on Kant's Critique of Practical Reason* (1960), *Early German Philosophy* (1969), and *Essays on Kant and Hume* (1978).

Ronald Beiner is professor of political science at the University of Toronto. He is the editor of Hannah Arendt's *Lectures on Kant's Political Philosophy* (1982) and the author of *Political Judgment* (1983). His most recent book is *What's the Matter with Liberalism?* (1992).

William James Booth is professor of political science at McGill University. He is the author of *Interpreting the World: Kant's Philosophy of History and Politics* (1986) and *Households: On the Moral Architecture of the Economy* (1993).

Michael W. Doyle is professor of political science at Princeton University. He is the author of *Empires* (1986).

Hans-Georg Gadamer is professor emeritus of philosophy at the University of Heidelberg. He is the author of many books, including *Truth and Method* (1960).

William A. Galston is professor in the School of Public Affairs and senior research scholar in the Institute for Philosophy and Public Policy at the University of Maryland at College Park. He is the author of *Kant and the Problem of History* (1975) and *Justice and the Human Good* (1980). His most recent book is *Liberal Purposes: Goods, Virtues, and Diversity in the Liberal State* (1991).

Mary Gregor is professor of philosophy at San Diego State University. Among her many publications on Kant is her book *Laws of Freedom* (1963) and, most recently, a new edition of Kant's *Metaphysics of Morals* (1991).

Jürgen Habermas is professor of philosophy at the University of Frankfurt. Among his books now translated into English are the two-volume *Theory of Communicative Action* (1984, 1987), *The Philosophical Discourse of Modernity* (1987), *The New*

Conservatism (1989), *Moral Consciousness and Communicative Action* (1990), and *Postmetaphysical Thinking* (1992).

Dieter Henrich is professor of philosophy at the University of Munich. He is author of *Aesthetic Judgment and the Moral Image of the World.*

Joseph M. Knippenberg is assistant professor of political science at Ogelthorpe University in Atlanta, Georgia. He has published articles on Kant's political philosophy in the *Journal of Politics* and the *Political Science Reviewer.*

John Rawls is professor of philosophy at Harvard University. He is the author of *A Theory of Justice* (1971).

Patrick Riley is professor of political science at the University of Wisconsin-Madison. He is the author of *Will and Political Legitimacy* (1982), *Kant's Political Philosophy* (1983), and *The General Will before Rousseau* (1986).

Susan Shell is associate professor of political science at Boston College and the author of *The Rights of Reason: A Study of Kant's Philosophy and Politics* (1980).

Charles Taylor is professor of philosophy at McGill University. His most recent books are *Philosophical Papers* (1985), *Sources of the Self* (1989), and *The Ethics of Authenticity.*

Richard L. Velkley is associate professor of philosophy at Stonehill College in Massachusetts. He is the author of *Freedom and the End of Reason: On the Moral Foundations of Kant's Critical Philosophy* (1989).

Bernard Yack is associate professor of political science at the University of Wisconsin-Madison. He is the author of *The Longing for Total Revolution* (1986) and *The Problems of a Political Animal* (forthcoming).

Index